ESSENTIAL
TAROT
WRITINGS

About the Author

Donald Tyson (Nova Scotia, Canada) is an occult scholar and the author of the popular, critically acclaimed Necronomicon series. He has written more than two dozen books on Western esoteric traditions.

ESSENTIAL
TAROT
WRITINGS

A Collection of Source Texts in
Western Occultism

Llewellyn Publications
Woodbury, Minnesota

FIRST EDITION
First Printing, 2020

Cover art of Hanged Man card from the Minchiate deck, courtesy of Lo Scarabeo
Cover design: Shannon McKuhen
Interior art:
Part One cards are from Court de Gébelin's *Le Monde Primitif*, vol. 8 (1781), with modifications by the author.
Part Two art is by Donald Tyson.
Part Three art is by Donald Tyson.
Part Five art is from *The Secret Teachings of All Ages* by Manly P. Hall.
Part Eight art is from *The Book of Days* by Robert Chambers.

Llewellyn Publications is a registered trademark of Llewellyn Worldwide Ltd.

Library of Congress Cataloging-in-Publication Data
Names: Tyson, Donald, author.
Title: Essential tarot writings : a collection of source texts in Western occultism / by Donald Tyson.
Description: First edition. | Woodbury, Minnesota : Llewellyn Worldwide, [2020] | Includes bibliographical references and index. | Summary: "This book gathers together some of the most important, but most obscure, essays on the esoteric Tarot that were written by prominent occultists of the eighteenth, nineteenth, and twentieth centuries. Edited and annotated by Donald Tyson"—Provided by publisher.
Identifiers: LCCN 2020034204 (print) | LCCN 2020034205 (ebook) | ISBN 9780738765372 (paperback) | ISBN 9780738766348 (ebook)
Subjects: LCSH: Tarot—History—Sources. | Fortune-telling by cards—History—Sources.
Classification: LCC BF1879.T2 T974 2020 (print) | LCC BF1879.T2 (ebook) | DDC 133.3/2424—dc23
LC record available at https://lccn.loc.gov/2020034204
LC ebook record available at https://lccn.loc.gov/2020034205

Llewellyn Worldwide Ltd. does not participate in, endorse, or have any authority or responsibility concerning private business transactions between our authors and the public.
All mail addressed to the author is forwarded but the publisher cannot, unless specifically instructed by the author, give out an address or phone number.
Any internet references contained in this work are current at publication time, but the publisher cannot guarantee that a specific location will continue to be maintained. Please refer to the publisher's website for links to authors' websites and other sources.

Llewellyn Publications
A Division of Llewellyn Worldwide Ltd.
2143 Wooddale Drive
Woodbury, MN 55125-2989
www.llewellyn.com

Printed in the United States of America

Other Books by Donald Tyson

Kinesic Magic (2020)

Tarot Magic (2018)

Serpent of Wisdom (2013)

The Demonology of King James I (2011)

The Dream World of H. P. Lovecraft (2010)

The 13 Gates of the Necronomicon (2010)

The Fourth Book of Occult Philosophy (2009)

Runic Astrology (2009)

Grimoire of the Necronomicon (2008)

Necronomicon Tarot (with Anne Stokes) (2007)

Soul Flight (2007)

Alhazred (2006)

Portable Magic (2006)

Familiar Spirits (2004)

Necronomicon (2004)

1-2-3 Tarot (2004)

The Power of the Word (2004)

Enochian Magic for Beginners (2002)

Tetragrammaton (2002)

The Magician's Workbook (2001)

Sexual Alchemy (2000)

For my wife, Jenny,
my constant companion on
this mystery tour we call life.

Contents

Hermetic, Qabbalistic, and Rosicrucian Symbolical Philosophy. It was privately
published in 1928 in San Francisco. The printer was H. S. Crocker Co.

Part Eight

Introduction to "The Art of Fortune-Telling by Cards"

Chapter 7 of *Breslaw's Last Legacy; or, The Magical Companion*, attributed
to Phillip Breslaw. 2nd corrected edition. Published in 1784 in London
for T. Moore, pp. 102–104.

Introduction to "The Art of Fortune-Telling by Cards"

From Mother Bridget's *The Universal Dream Book, Containing an Interpretation of all Manner of Dreams, Alphabetically Arranged, to Which Is Added,
the Art of Fortune-Telling by Cards, or Tea and Coffee Cups*. Printed and sold
by J. Bailey in London, c. 1816, pp. 49–53.

Introduction to "The Folklore of Playing Cards"

From Robert Chambers's *Book of Days*, volume 1. Printed in London
and Edinburgh by W. & R. Chambers in 1863, pp. 281–284.

Introduction to "Fortune-Telling with Common Playing Cards"

My title. This essay was extracted from the text of *The History of Playing
Cards*, edited by Rev. Ed. S. Taylor and others. Published in London by
John Camden Hotten in 1865, pp. 471–479.

Introduction to "The English Method of Fortune-Telling by Cards"

GENERAL INTRODUCTION

The essays gathered together here span three centuries and two continents. The earliest was published in 1781 in Paris and the latest in 1928 in Los Angeles. What ties them together is their focus on the symbolism of cards, and the use of cards in the Western esoteric tradition for divination and practical magic.

The majority of these essays concern the Tarot, which became so central to Western occultism during the nineteenth century, first in France and then later in England and the United States; but the final part of the work deals with fortune-telling with common playing cards using what was known as the *English Method*. The primary characteristic of this method, popular in England from the seventeenth to the twentieth centuries, is its reliance on the full deck of fifty-two playing cards laid out in rows of nine. This method was included because the divinatory folk meanings for playing cards have many correspondences with the divinatory meanings for the Tarot, particularly with the Tarot folk meanings for the suit cards, and also because the method of divination by nines may be readily applied to the Tarot.

It would not be an exaggeration to say that the occult Tarot owes everything to France, and that it originated from the pen of a single man, Antoine Court de Gébelin, the author of the monumental *Monde Primitif*, a work on philology, linguistics, history, archaeology, philosophy, religion, and occultism in nine volumes that were published from 1773 to 1782. The essay by Court de Gébelin that opens this book appeared in the eighth volume, published in 1781, and it is without question the most important essay ever written on the occult Tarot.

Included by Court de Gébelin directly after his own essay was an essay on the occult Tarot by Louis Raphaël Lucrèce de Fayolle, the Comte de Mellet. Taken together, these two essays establish the place of the Tarot at the center of the modern tradition of Western magic. All that comes after was inspired by the work of these two men.

It was Court de Gébelin who fixed the origin of the Tarot in ancient Egypt. It was he who identified it as a symbolic book of Thoth, the Egyptian god of wisdom and magic. He also associated the Tarot with the Romanies and credited them with carrying it out of Egypt and spreading it throughout Europe. In the word *Tarot* he found the Egyptian root words for "the royal way" (*Ta-Ros*). The Tarot, he believed, was a sacred book of the Egyptian priesthood in which was concealed under a cloak of symbolism all their esoteric wisdom.

The Comte de Mellet supported the Egyptian origin of the Tarot. His essay is noteworthy for its explicit connection of the Tarot trumps with the Hebrew letters, which Court de Gébelin only hinted at, and for his arrangement of the trumps in three groups of seven cards each, coupled with the solitary unnumbered Fool, to which he assigned the zero. Court de Gébelin mentioned this threefold division of the trumps into sevens plus the Fool, but did not examine it at length. Comte de Mellet also compared the Tarot with common playing cards and wrote about the use of the cards for purposes of divination.

These ideas had a profound influence on the French occultists of the nineteenth century. They were adopted enthusiastically and uncritically to various degrees by such luminaries of the Western tradition as Éliphas Lévi, Paul Christian, René Falconnier, Papus, Stanislas de Guaita, and Oswald Wirth. It seemed not to matter that all these ideas were at best unsupported and at worst outright falsehoods. The French occultists embraced them and made the Tarot the centerpiece of their esoteric philosophy.

Christian gave Egyptian names and descriptions to the trumps, and Falconnier brought forth his own set of trumps based on Christian's descriptions. This is known as the Egyptian Tarot today. Papus preferred to focus on the Hebrew connection, and associated the Tarot with the four Hebrew letters of the name of God called by the Greeks *Tetragrammaton*. Lévi, the most influential of the French occultists of the nineteenth century, loaded the Tarot with Egyptian symbolism and also assigned Hebrew letters to the trumps. All of this was inspired by the essays of Court de Gébelin and the Comte de Mellet, but the mythology of the Tarot created by these two men was greatly extended and elaborated on by those who followed them.

It is a curious quirk of occult publishing that these essays have not been readily available in English publication. For this reason, their seminal importance remained largely unknown to many English occultists of the nineteenth and twentieth centuries, who derived these beliefs secondhand through the English translations of the works of Lévi, Papus, and other French occultists. In this way, they absorbed the teachings of Court de Gébelin on the occult Tarot without ever reading the essay that was the source for these beliefs.

Almost two decades ago, while researching the Tarot for a book on its esoteric symbolism, I became aware that I could not obtain an English edition of the Tarot essays in *Monde Primitif*. I resolved to make my own translation of these works to supply this lack, and for many years the initial version of that translation has circulated on the internet, without my support or approval. I would have withdrawn it due to errors it contains, but I can testify to the truth of the saying that once a work is released into the wild on the internet, it cannot be killed.

The main purpose of the present work is to make available in printed form, in English, the seminal essay by Court de Gébelin and the sister essay of the Comte de Mellet. I have made corrections to my earlier translation and have included a comprehensive set of notes that illuminate obscure points in the texts.

All of the essays that follow these two are connected with them, and with each other, by the complex web of esoteric beliefs and symbolism that makes up the common Western occult tradition of France, Great Britain, and the United States. The occult tradition of France crossed the Channel to England in the latter part of the nineteenth century due primarily to the formation of the Rosicrucian society known as the Hermetic Order of the Golden Dawn, and through the teachings of the Golden Dawn it was elaborated on and passed over the Atlantic to the United States and Canada, and around the world to English-speaking countries of the British Empire such as Australia and New Zealand.

The Golden Dawn was founded by three high-level Freemasons who were determined that the magic of the ancient world should not remain merely a historical oddity for academics, but should be brought alive again and practiced by living magicians in modern times. Its formation coincided with a popular revival of interest in occultism, sparked largely by the modern Spiritualism movement, which may be said to have begun in Hydesville, New York, in 1848 with the Fox sisters. The Theosophical Society, created in the US in 1875 by the

Russian mystic and trance medium Helena P. Blavatsky, was in the beginning a Spiritualist society. It was only the most prominent of a number of occult societies created in Europe and the US around the same time as the Golden Dawn, which established its Isis-Urania temple in London in 1888.

What set the Golden Dawn apart from Theosophy and other secret occult orders was its emphasis on practical magic. Theosophy had its spirit teachers, which Blavatsky referred to as Mahatmas, and the Golden Dawn had its spirit teachers, which were known as the Secret Chiefs of the Order; but whereas Theosophy taught an occult philosophy that was a mingling of Western and Eastern lore, with the emphasis on India, the Golden Dawn taught a curriculum of practical ritual magic that was almost wholly Western in its inspiration, deriving as it did from the occult traditions of Egypt, Greece, Rome, and also that of the Jews. The Jewish system of occultism known as the Kabbalah was of central importance in Golden Dawn magic.

This emphasis on Western magic was largely due to the studies of two of the three founders of the Golden Dawn, W. Wynn Westcott and Samuel L. MacGregor Mathers. The third founder, William Woodman, died shortly after the Golden Dawn was established. Westcott, a portion of whose essay on the Isiac Tablet of Cardinal Bembo forms part five of the present work, was knowledgeable in the areas of the Kabbalah and Greek Hermetic wisdom. Mathers studied deeply the ritual magic of Europe as it was preserved in the grimoires.

Both men had a high regard for the writings of Éliphas Lévi and other French occultists, but it was Mathers in particular who was responsible for the central role the Tarot was to play in the Golden Dawn system of magic. Mathers's links with the French occult current were various. He translated *The Book of the Sacred Magic of Abramelin the Mage* from a French grimoire in the Bibliothèque de l'Arsenal in Paris. Although it is based on a faulty and incomplete manuscript, this translation became perhaps the most influential work in the English occult tradition for the past 130 years. It taught a practical ritual method for establishing communication with the spiritual presence known as the holy guardian angel.

Mathers married a French woman who was living in London, Mina Bergson, a talented artist who was the sister of the Nobel Prize–winning French philosopher Henri Bergson. While running the Golden Dawn, Mathers and his wife followed the instructions of the Secret Chiefs and moved their residence from London to Paris, where Mathers lived for a number of years. He was fluent in French and knowledgeable in the writings of all the French occultists. Largely because of Mathers's French connection, English magic became heavily influenced by the French occultists, in particular by their emphasis on the importance of the Tarot.

It was Mathers and his wife, whom he renamed Moïna because it sounded more Celtic to his ears, who created the Golden Dawn Tarot. This was based on hints in the *cipher manuscript*, a document obtained by Wescott that formed the basis for the Golden Dawn, but it was fleshed out by channeled spirit communications that both he and his wife obtained through the use of the pendulum and the planchette and by direct spirit communications. Moïna was a formally trained artist who had studied at the Slade School of Fine Art in London, and it was she who drew and painted the prototype of the Golden Dawn Tarot. This deck was hand-copied by other high-ranking members of the order, who used it for the purpose of divination on important questions by the method known as the *Opening of the Key*, which is fully described in part three of the present work.

Unfortunately, the original Golden Dawn Tarot deck does not appear to have survived, but we have textual descriptions of the designs and of the meanings that Mathers applied to the cards. In part three, I have gathered all the Tarot divination card layouts used by Mathers, along with the set of meanings he assigned to the cards for the purpose of conventional fortune-telling.

The Tarot became the centerpiece of the system of practical magic developed by the Golden Dawn. Mathers drew upon the teachings of French occultists such as Lévi and Papus, and linked the Tarot to the Kabbalah. Each of the 22 trumps was given a Hebrew letter, as they had been given by the Comte de Mellet and Lévi, but in a different order. The four suits of the Tarot, and also the four court cards of each suit, were assigned a Hebrew letter of Tetragrammaton, following the example of Papus. Mathers also assigned the trumps to the pathways or channels on a Kabbalistic design called the *Tree of the Sephiroth*, which illustrates in graphic form the emanation of the universe in ten stages and 22 connecting links. The number cards of the Tarot were assigned these ten stages of emanation, called *Sephiroth*, and the court cards were also placed on this Tree.

It is not an exaggeration to state that the Tarot upon the Tree of the Sephiroth is the very heart of modern Western occultism. By linking the Tarot trumps to the 22 Hebrew letters, and the number cards to the ten emanations, and the four suits and four court cards in each suit to the letters of Tetragrammaton, a complex series of symbolic connections is formed that is mutually reinforcing. The symbolic meaning of a trump augments the symbolism of its Hebrew letter; the significance of a Sephirah adds to the meaning of its associated number card. This magnification of meaning flows in both directions: the meaning of a card adds to the meaning of its letter, but so also does the meaning of the letter add to the meaning of its card.

One of the reasons the Golden Dawn system of magic achieved such widespread acceptance among English-speaking occultists, in addition to its practicality and its rational structure, was the enormous influence of its members, who went on to form their own occult societies and write books on Western magic and the Tarot. In addition to W. Wynn Westcott, whose writing on the Tarot forms part five, there is J. W. Brodie-Innes, whose essay forms part four, and A. E. Waite, whose essay on the symbolism of the trumps forms part six. Waite also contributes an essay on fortune-telling with playing cards in part eight.

The essay by Brodie-Innes is of particular interest due to the references he makes to A. E. Waite. Both Brodie-Innes and Waite had been high-level members of the Golden Dawn at one time, but both were sworn by an oath of secrecy never to reveal the occult teachings of that order. This made their writings on the Tarot awkward, since both were aware of the Golden Dawn Tarot and its uses in divination and practical magic but could not discuss them openly. Brodie-Innes makes several sly asides to Waite in his essay that can only be fully understood when you know the relationship of both men to the Golden Dawn and its Tarot.

Members of the Golden Dawn whose work does not appear in this book, but who had an enormous influence on spreading its system of magic (including its teachings about the Tarot) around the world, include such luminaries as Aleister Crowley, who created his own Tarot based on the designs of Mathers and his wife; Dion Fortune, who wrote a book on the Kabbalah that was based on Golden Dawn teachings; and Paul Foster Case, whose teachings on the Tarot are based directly on the Tarot created by A. E. Waite and on the Golden Dawn Tarot teachings.

From these and other former members of the various branches of the Golden Dawn, the influence of the Order spread. For example, Frater Achad's teachings on the Tarot derive from his association with Aleister Crowley, and Crowley's teachings are elaborations on the teachings of Mathers, who received them from the Secret Chiefs. The writings of Israel Regardie were similarly influenced by Crowley. Gareth Knight, who has written on the Tarot, was associated with Dion Fortune. His teaching are Golden Dawn teachings once removed. The same may be said of William G. Gray, who had brief interactions with Aleister Crowley and Dion Fortune but whose writings are heavily influenced by Golden Dawn teachings. And so for many others. In this way, the influence of the Golden Dawn Tarot extended itself to those unaware that an organization such as the Golden Dawn ever existed.

The works of the French occultists of the nineteenth century went not only to England but also to other nations of Europe. The Russian mystic P. D. Ouspensky, whose essay on the Tarot forms part two of the present work, used the Tarots designed by A. E. Waite and by Oswald Wirth, as well as the traditional Tarot of Marseilles, as his basis. He was heavily influenced by Éliphas Lévi, Paul Christian, Papus, and Wirth. It is unfortunate that he is remembered chiefly as the student of George Ivanovich Gurdjieff, since his was one of the finest occult minds of the early twentieth century. His essay on the Tarot was written before he met Gurdjieff, as was his best work, *Tertium Organum*. In my opinion, his interaction with Gurdjieff, who was more of a showman and a charlatan than a teacher, hindered his progress in esotericism, rather than forwarding it. To his credit, Ouspensky was eventually able to break free from the stifling influence of Gurdjieff.

The essay by Manly P. Hall that forms part seven brings the occult Tarot firmly into the twentieth century. Hall was a well-read and well-studied Freemason. Although he seems to have produced nothing original, in his Tarot essay, which was extracted from his monumental 1928 work, *The Secret Teachings of All Ages*, he epitomizes the understanding of the Tarot trumps that descended from Court de Gébelin, through Lévi, Papus, and Wirth, down to Mathers, Waite, and Ouspensky, and across the Atlantic to Case. His references are copious, although nonspecific. I have tracked them down and given their sources by text and page.

In parallel with the development of the occult Tarot in France and England, a tradition existed of fortune-telling with common playing cards. In England it was known as the English Method and involved the full deck of 52 cards laid out in rows of nine. When and where this method began is lost to history. I have been able to trace it back to around the same time that Court de Gébelin was writing his Tarot essay for *Monde Primitif*, but it is undoubtedly generations older than that, since it was fully formed at that time.

The English Method continued to appear in published works throughout the nineteenth century and into the twentieth century. I have no doubt that this method of card reading is still being used in the twenty-first century. It relies on a set of folk meanings that are surprisingly consistent, in a general way, although variant meanings do occur. These meanings influenced Mathers and A. E. Waite when they wrote about fortune-telling with the Tarot. You will see similarities between the meanings of common playing cards using the English Method and the meanings for the suit cards given by Mathers in his booklet *The Tarot* and by Waite in his book *The Pictorial Key to the Tarot*.

The folk meanings of the Tarot differ from the esoteric meanings both in their purpose and in their derivation. Fortune-telling, both by the Tarot and by common playing cards, is usually done to give guidance to individuals concerning ordinary matters of their daily lives. In past centuries, cartomancy was primarily the interest of women, as the essays in part eight indicate by their references. Fortune-telling was considered beneath the dignity of men. By contrast, divination with the Tarot by serious occultists such as the members of the Golden Dawn was intended to reveal important spiritual matters of life-altering significance. The Tarot was used esoterically to awaken and expand spiritual awareness, to enable psychic vision and astral travel, and as instruments of ritual magic.

It would be impossible to say where the folk meanings for playing cards have their origin. Oftentimes there seems to be no rational basis for them. The occult meanings of the Tarot, on the other hand, are always justified by traditional associations and symbolism. For example, if a card is linked to a sign of the zodiac by a Hebrew letter, then the traditional astrological meaning of that sign influences the interpretation of the card to which it is linked. The interpretation of the number cards of the Tarot may be colored by Pythagorean numerology, by the emanations of the Kabbalah, by the four classical elements associated with the four suits, by the significance of the letters of Tetragrammaton to which they are linked by suit, and so on.

The esoteric meanings of the cards always have some basis that may be explicitly stated, but the folk meanings just are what they are, and must be accepted for what they are. This gives the esoteric meanings a certain stability and rationality, but the folk meanings seem arbitrary. When the folk meanings vary, the variation is often great and no connection to the original meaning can be discerned. In view of the apparent arbitrary nature of the folk interpretations, it is interesting that so much consistency runs through the essays concerning common playing cards that are presented in part eight. Tradition can preserve meaning, even where that meaning is not understood.

Because there are so many prominent individuals referred to in the essays and the notes that follow them, I have included a biographical notes section at the end of the book, which should help clear up any confusion as to who is who. This has allowed me to gather most of the biographical information in one place, rather than scatter it throughout the notes and introductions.

The greatest value of the essays in this book stems from their collective, cumulative instruction. Their authors routinely refer to each other, to the same sources, and to similar esoteric meanings for the cards. Even when they disagree, it is from the common basis of understanding that is the tradition of Western occultism. There is an underlying general unity concerning the origin, interpretation, and importance of the Tarot cards. Although this understanding is, in some cases, historically inaccurate, it is esoterically meaningful. An example is the uniformly expressed belief that the Tarot was of Egyptian origin. This belief, although false and sometimes disputed, shaped the interpretation of the cards and the symbolism that appears on the cards of various Tarot decks. In this sense, the cards actually became Egyptian, even though they never existed in ancient Egypt. Through these essays, the torch of the esoteric Tarot was passed from hand to hand, and from them it has come down to us today, altered but still recognizable.

The most conservative of all human pursuits is magic. We still work essentially the same ritual magic that was worked by the Egyptian priests in the time of the Ptolemies. This makes the appearance of the occult Tarot an uncommonly recent event in Western esotericism. It is only about two and a half centuries old, which in the history of magic is yesterday. Despite its youth, the occult Tarot has achieved a sophisticated form and taken a place at the very heart of the Western tradition. What further evolutions will the Tarot assume? Only time will show. But if history is our guide, we may assume they will be refinements, not radical changes. Magic resists change, and the Tarot is the symbolic embodiment of Western magic.

PART ONE

"The Game of Tarots"
by
ANTOINE COURT DE GÉBELIN
and

"Study on the Tarots"
by the
COMTE DE MELLET

Translated from the French by Donald Tyson

INTRODUCTION
TO PART ONE

The following two essays appear in volume 8, book 1, pages 365–410 of Antoine Court de Gébelin's work *Monde Primitif, Analysé et Comparé avec le Monde Moderne* (*The Primitive World, Analyzed and Compared with the Modern World*). The nine volumes of this mammoth unfinished work were published in Paris over the period of 1773–1782. The first volume was issued in two parts in the years 1773–1774, and the remaining volumes followed at one-year intervals. The eighth volume appeared in 1781.

The first essay, titled "Du Jeu des Tarots"("The Game of Tarots"), was written by Antoine Court de Gébelin (1725–1784). The author of the second essay, titled "Recherches sur les Tarots, et sur la Divination par les Cartes des Tarots, par M. Le C. de M." ("Study on the Tarots, and on Divination with Tarot cards, by M. the C. of M."), has been identified as Louis Raphaël Lucrèce de Fayolle, the Comte de Mellet (1727–1804).[1]

It appears that Court de Gébelin had the essay by the Comte de Mellet in his possession when he wrote his own work on the Tarot, and was influenced by its contents. De Mellet probably composed his work independently, prior to reading Court de Gébelin's essay, although he was aware of some of Court de Gébelin's ideas about the Tarot.

Court de Gébelin's essay is noteworthy for establishing the Tarot as a repository of esoteric wisdom, for placing its origins in ancient Egypt, for linking the dissemination of the Tarot throughout Europe with the Romanies (Gypsies), for alluding to the connection between the 22 trumps and 22 letters of the Hebrew alphabet, and for placing the Fool firmly at the head of the trumps, rather than at the end or second from the end. His views exerted a profound influence on later writers on the Tarot, even though most of his assertions are incorrect. The Tarot was probably not deliberately designed as a book of esoteric wisdom; it did not originate in Egypt; it has no ancient connection with the Romanies; the similarity in number between the trumps and the Hebrew letters may be accidental; and there is no hard evidence to justify shifting the location of the Fool to the head of the trumps.

The Comte de Mellet's essay is significant for his inverted ordering of the trumps that begins with the World and ends with the Fool, for his explicit linking of the trumps with individual Hebrew letters, for his exposition of the method of Tarot divination in use in his day, and for his presentation of the esoteric names and meanings associated with many of the cards.

The present English translation of these seminal treatises in the history of the Tarot arose from my work on the esoteric evolution of these cards. I needed a full knowledge of the material contained in Court de Gébelin's book, and discovered to my surprise that these essays were not freely available in English on the internet. Considering the importance of these works, their age, and their relative brevity, this was quite astonishing. As a consequence, I decided to translate them so that anyone else who might want to read in English what Court de Gébelin and the Comte de Mellet wrote about the Tarot would not be similarly disappointed.

Footnotes that appear in the original text have been placed in square brackets directly following the matter to which they pertain. The footnotes in the essay by the Comte de Mellet appear to have been written by Court de Gébelin. My own notes follow after the two essays at the end of part one. In Court de Gébelin's book, the trump Temperance is incorrectly numbered XIII, when it should be XIIII or XIV. Similarly, the trump the Hermit is incorrectly numbered VIII, when it should be VIIII or IX.[2] I have corrected these errors.

The drawings of the trumps that accompany the text were executed by the artist Mademoiselle Linote, a close friend of Court de Gébelin, who learned how to engrave for the purpose of assisting him in his work. All of them were inverted left to right from the usual Tarot of Marseilles orientation, with the exceptions of the Wheel, Prudence (Hanged Man), Death, and the Sun. This probably occurred during the process of printing the plates, with which Mademoiselle Linote may have been unfamiliar. I have presented them as they appear in *Monde Primitif*, without correcting these inversions. For example, the Fool usually faces to the right in older Tarots, but in the plate he faces to the left; the Juggler (Magician) usually looks to the left, but in the plate he looks to the right; the King (Emperor) usually faces left, yet in the plate he faces right; and so on.

In Court de Gébelin's book, the drawings of the trumps are gathered together in six plates at the end of the volume, which are unlabeled except for the Roman numerals that distinguish the trumps and the Latin letters that distinguish the Aces. Five of these plates each contain four Tarot trump designs in two panels, and the final plate contains two trumps in the top panel and the four Aces in two lower panels. The plates are as follows, from left to right and top to bottom:

Plate III
I. The Juggler, 0. The Fool
IV. The King, III. The Queen

Plate IV
II. The High Priestess, V. The High Priest
VII. Osiris Triumphant, VI. The Marriage

Plate V
XIII. [sic.] Temperance, XI. Fortitude
XII. Prudence, VIII. Justice

Plate VI
VIII. [sic.] The Sage, XIX. The Sun
XVII. The Dog Star, XVIII. The Moon

Plate VII
XV. Typhon, XIII. Death
X. The Wheel of Fortune, XVI. The House of God

Plate VIII
XX. The Last Judgment, XXI. The World
A. Ace of Swords, C. Ace of Cups
B. Ace of Coins, D. Ace of Batons

In the present work, for the sake of convenience, I have included images of the trumps individually near the passages that describe them, captioned with

Court de Gébelin's title and, where necessary, the modern title in parentheses. Some of his titles will be unfamiliar to most readers. For purposes of comparison, I will list the Court de Gébelin's titles beside the traditional titles in the Nicolas Conver Tarot of Marseilles of 1761 and the most common modern titles for the trumps.

	Court de Gébelin title	Marseilles title	Modern title
0	Le Fou (The Fool)	Le Mat (The Fool)	The Fool
I	Le Bateleur (The Juggler)	Le Bateleur (The Juggler)	The Magician
II	La Grande Prêtresse (The High Priestess)	La Papesse (The Popess)	The High Priestess
III	La Reine (The Queen)	L'Imperatrice (The Empress)	The Empress
IV	Le Roi (The King)	L'Empereur (The Emperor)	The Emperor
V	Le Grande Prêtre (The High Priest)	Le Pape (The Pope)	The Hierophant
VI	Le Mariage (Marriage)	L'Amoureux (The Lovers)	The Lovers
VII	Osiris Triomphant (Osiris Triumphant)	Le Chariot (The Chariot)	The Chariot
VIII	La Justice (Justice)	La Justice (Justice)	Justice
IX	Le Sage (The Sage)	L'Hermite (The Hermit)	The Hermit
X	La Roue de Fortune (The Wheel of Fortune)	La Roue de Fortune (The Wheel of Fortune)	The Wheel of Fortune
XI	La Force (Fortitude)	La Force (Strength)	Strength
XII	La Purdence (Prudence)	Le Pendu (The Hanged Man)	The Hanged Man
XIII	La Mort (Death)	(no title)	Death
XIV	La Tempérance (Temperance)	Temperance (Temperance)	Temperance
XV	Typhon (Typhon)	Le Diable (The Devil)	The Devil

	Court de Gébelin title	Marseilles title	Modern title
XVI	Château de Plutus (Castle of Plutus)	La Maison Dieu (The House of God)	The Tower
XVII	La Canicule (The Dog Star)	Le Toille (The Star)	The Star
XVIII	La Lune (The Moon)	La Lune (The Moon)	The Moon
XIX	Le Soleil (The Sun)	Le Soleil (The Sun)	The Sun
XX	Jugement Dernier (The Last Judgment)	Le Jugement (The Judgment)	The Last Judgment
XXI	Le Tems (Time)	Le Monde (The World)	The Universe

Comparison of Trump Titles

It remains only to say a few words about our illustrious author. Antoine Court de Gébelin was born Antoine Court in Nîmes, a town in southern France, or, according to another account, in Geneva, Switzerland. The date of his birth is equally uncertain and is variously given as 1719, 1724, 1725, and 1728. His father, also named Antoine Court (1696–1760), was a prominent leader of the Protestant Huguenots. The father fled France in 1730 to escape religious persecution by the Catholics. The son spent his early life in Lausanne, Switzerland, and was ordained a pastor there in 1754, where he taught philosophy and ethics. His father died in 1760. He appended his paternal grandmother's family name to his own and returned to France in 1762.

In Paris he was initiated into *Les Amis Réunis* lodge of Freemasons in 1771, and later became a member of *Les Neuf Soeurs* lodge, which had among its members Voltaire, whom Court de Gébelin helped to initiate in 1778, and Benjamin Franklin, during his service as American ambassador to France. Court de Gébelin was a strong supporter of American independence. He was also a believer in the therapies of Franz Friedrich Anton Mesmer (1734–1815). On May 10, 1784, he was found dead in a bath while undergoing one of Mesmer's treatments, which involved the application of electricity. The suspicion arose that Mesmer had electrocuted him and induced a fatal heart attack. This gave rise to an anonymous bit of doggerel that served as his unofficial epitaph:[3]

Ci-gît ce pauvre Gébelin,
Qui parloit Grec, Hébreu, Latin;
Admirez tous son héroisme:
Il fut martyr du magnétisme.

[Here lies poor Gébelin,
Who spoke Greek, Hebrew, Latin;
All admire his heroism:
He was a martyr to magnetism.]

In *The Scots Magazine,* June 1785, an obituary notice appears for Court de Gébelin.[4] Notice the misspelling of his name, and that "Court" has become "Comte" in the obituary.

> May 10 1784. At Paris, M. Comte de Gibelin, the celebrated author of the *"Monde Primitif comparé au Monde Moderne"*—He was the son of a Protestant clergyman, and was born in 1725, at Nismes, which place his father quitted on account of his religion, and went when his son was very young to reside at Lausanne. He was seven years old before he began to speak distinctly; but before he was twelve he was considered as a prodigy, as he was master of several languages, was acquainted with geography and history, had a taste for music and drawing, and imitated with great facility and elegance the characters of the most eminent languages. His father, who was become *"pasteur d'un eglise"* [pastor of a church] at Lausanne, intended him for the church, but he chose rather to devote himself wholly to study. Natural history, mathematics, the dead and living languages, mythology, ancient monuments, statues, medals, gems, and inscriptions—his industry and his genius embraced all these. After the death of his father, he went into France, and fixed at Paris, where he soon became known to the literati. At length the plan of his great work, *"Le Monde Primitif,"* made its appearance, after he had employed upwards of ten years in digesting the materials. M d'Alembert was so struck with it, that he asked with enthusiasm, *"Si c'étoit une Societé de 40 hommes qui étoit charges de l'executer?—Non, c'est Gibelin seul—mais Gibelin ne vant-il pas autant qu'une fonte d'ecrivains re uni?"* [If it was a company of 40 men who was responsible for writing

it? No, it is Gébelin alone—but is not Gébelin worth as much as a whole troop of writers?] The French academy were so well satisfied with this undertaking, that they twice decreed to him the prize of 1200 livres, which they give annually to the author of the most valuable work that has appeared in the course of the year. The disease which occasioned his death is attributed to his eagerness to complete this great work. He used to spend whole days over his books, contenting himself with a crust and a draught of water. Among the friendships he contracted, those of two respectable ladies must not be omitted. One of them, Mademoiselle Linote, who died a few years ago, and whose death was a source of great grief to him, learned to engrave, merely that she might be able to assist him, and lessen the expence of his work, many of the plates of which she engraved. The other, Mademoiselle Fleuri, who is still living, advanced 5000 livres towards printing the first volume. As a Protestant, he could not be buried in Catholic ground. His remains were therefore removed to the gardens of his friend and biographer (from whose account these anecdotes are extracted) the Comte d'Albon, at Franconville, where a handsome monument is erected to his memory, with this inscription, *Passant, venerez cette tombe....Gibelin y repose.* [In passing, venerate this tomb....Gébelin rests here.]

"THE GAME OF TAROTS"

Where one deals with the origin, where one explains the allegories,
and where one shows that it is the source of our modern playing cards, etc etc.

by

ANTOINE COURT DE GÉBELIN

I.

The surprise caused by the discovery of an Egyptian book.

If one proceeded to announce that there is still nowadays a work of the former Egyptians, one of their books that escaped the flames that devoured their superb libraries, and which contains their purest doctrines on interesting subjects, everyone who heard, undoubtedly, would hasten to study such an invaluable book, such a marvel. If one also said that this book is very widespread in most of Europe, that for a number of centuries it has been in the hands of everyone, the surprise would be certain to increase. Would it not reach its height, if one gave assurances that no one ever suspected that it was Egyptian; that those who possessed it did not value it, that nobody ever sought to decipher a sheet of it; that the fruit of an exquisite wisdom is regarded as a cluster of extravagant figures which do not mean anything by themselves? Would it not be thought that the speaker wanted to amuse himself, and played on the credulity of his listeners?

2.

This Egyptian book exists.

This fact is certainly very true: this Egyptian book, the only survivor of their superb libraries, exists in our day: it is even so common, that no sage condescends to occupy himself with it; nobody before us has ever suspected its famous origin. This book is composed of 77 layers or tables, even of 78, divided into five classes, each of which offer subjects as varied as they are amusing and instructive. This book is in a word the game of Tarots, the playing of which is admittedly unknown in Paris, but very well known in Italy, in Germany, even in Provence, and also by the bizarre figures which each one of its cards offers, as well as by their multitude.

Even though the regions where it is in use are so extensive, none is more advanced than the others in understanding the value of the strange figures that it presents: and such is the antiquity of its origins, buried in the darkness of time, that no one knows either where or when it was invented, nor the reason why it is made up of so many extraordinary figures, of which so little is known that they offer collectively a single enigma that nobody has ever sought to solve.

This game even appeared so unworthy of attention, that it never came under the consideration of the eyes of those of our savants who dealt with the origins of cards: they only spoke of French cards, which are in use in Paris, whose origin is not very old; and after having proven the modern invention of them, they believed they had exhausted the matter. It is in this way indeed that one constantly confuses the establishment in a country of a certain practice with its primitive invention: it is what we already showed with regard to the compass: the Greeks and the Romans themselves confused only too thoroughly these objects, which deprived us of a multitude of interesting origins.

But the form, the disposition, the arrangement of this game, and the figures which it presents, are so obviously allegorical, and these allegories are so in conformity with the civil, philosophical and religious doctrines of the ancient Egyptians, that one cannot avoid recognizing the work of these sagacious people: they only could be its inventors, who rivaled in this respect the Indians who created the game of chess.

Division.

We will show the allegories which the various cards of this game offer.

The numerical formulas according to which it was made up.

How it was transmitted down to us.

Its relationship with a Chinese monument.

How the Spanish cards were born from it.

And correspondences of these last with the French cards.

This exercise will be followed by an essay where it is established how this game may be applied to the art of the divination; it is the work of a General Officer, the Governor of a province, who honors us with his benevolence, and who found in this game with a very clever sagacity the Egyptian principles on the art of prognosticating by cards, principles which distinguished the earliest bands of Egyptians, incorrectly named Bohemians,[5] who spread themselves throughout Europe; and there still remain some vestiges in our card decks, which lend themselves to divination infinitely less by their monotony and small number of their figures.

The Egyptian game, on the contrary, is suited admirably for this effect, encompassing in a way the whole universe, and all the various conditions of the life of man. Such was the wisdom of this singular people, that they imprinted on the least of their works the seal of immortality, so that others to some extent seem hardly able to walk in their footsteps.

ARTICLE I

Allegories presented by the cards of the game of Tarots.

If this game which always remained obscure to all those which knew of it, stood revealed to our eyes, it was not the effect of some deep meditation, nor of the desire to clear up its chaos: we did not spend an instant thinking about it. Invited as a guest a few years ago to meet with a lady of our acquaintance, Madam la C. d'H.,[6] who had arrived from Germany or Switzerland, we found her occupied playing this game with some other people. We played a game which you surely do not know...That may be; which is it?..the game of Tarots...I had occasion to see it when I was extremely young, but I did not have any knowledge of it...it is a rhapsody of the most bizarre figures, the most extravagant: and here is one, for example; one has care to choose a card filled with figures, bearing no relationship to its name, it is the World: I there cast my eyes, and at once I recognize the allegory: everyone leaves off their game and comes to see this marvelous card in which I apprehend what they have never perceived: each one asks me to expound another of the cards: in one quarter of an hour the cards were comprehended, explained, declared Egyptian: and since it was not the play of our imaginations, but the effect of the deliberate and significant connections of this game with all that is known of Egyptian ideas, we promised ourselves to share the knowledge some day with the public; persuaded that it would take pleasure in the discovery of a gift of this nature, an Egyptian book that had escaped barbarity, the devastations of time, fires accidental and deliberate, and the even greater disaster of ignorance.

A necessary consequence of the frivolous and light form of this book, which made it capable of triumphing over all the ages and of passing down to us with a rare fidelity: the ignorance which until now even we have been in concerning what it represented, was a happy safe conduct that allowed it to cross every century quietly without anyone thinking of doing it harm.

It is time to recover the allegories that it had been intended to preserve, and to show that to the wisest of all peoples, everything including games was founded on allegory, and that these wise savants converted into a recreation the most useful knowledge, and made of it just a game.

We said it, the game of Tarots is composed of 77 cards, even of a 78th,[7] divided into trumps and four suits. So that our readers can follow us, we made engravings of the trumps; and the Ace of each suit, which we call after the Spaniards, *Spadille*, *Baste*, and *Ponte*.

TRUMPS

The trumps number 22, and in general represent the temporal and spiritual leaders of society, the physical leaders of agriculture, the cardinal virtues, marriage, death and resurrection or creation; the various plays of fortune, the sage and the fool, time which consumes all, etc. One understands thus in advance that all these cards are as many allegorical pictures relating to the whole of life, and susceptible to an infinitude of combinations. We will examine them one by one, and will try to decipher the particular allegory or enigma that each one of them contains.

No. 0, Zero.

The Fool.

One cannot fail to recognize the Fool in this card, with his crazed look, and his apparel furnished with shells and bells: he goes very quickly, as mad as he is, bearing behind him his small pack, and thinking to escape thereby from a tiger which bites him on the haunch: as for the pack, it is the emblem of his faults that he wishes not to see; and this tiger, those of his regrets which follow it eagerly, and which jump in to bite behind him.[8]

The Fool

This beautiful idea that Horace framed so well in golden words,[9] would thus never have been invented by him, had it not escaped destruction with the Egyptians: it would have been a vulgar idea, a commonplace; but captured in the eternal truth of Nature, and presented with all the graces of which he was capable, this pleasant and wise poet seemed to have drawn it from his own deep judgement.

As for this trump, we number it zero, though it is placed in the order of cards after the twenty-first, because it does not count when it is alone, and possesses only the value that it gives to the others, precisely like our zero: showing thus that nothing exists without its folly.

No. I.

The Player at Cups, or the Juggler.

The Juggler (Magician)

We start with number I and proceed to XXI, because the current practice is to start with the lowest number and continue on to the highest: it was however that of the Egyptians to begin to count with the higher, continuing down to the lower.[10] Thus they sang the octave while going down, and not while going up like us. In the essay which follows this one, the writer follows the practice of the Egyptians, and makes the best account of it. There are thus here two approaches: ours more convenient when one wants to consider these cards only in themselves: and that other, useful in better conceiving the whole set and their relationships.

The first of all trumps while counting up, or the last while counting down, is a player at cups; this is evident by his table covered with dice, goblets, knives, balls, etc., by his staff of Jacob or rod of the Magi, by the ball which he holds between two fingers and which he will cause to disappear.

It is called the Juggler by card makers: this is the vulgar name for people of this condition: is it necessary to say that the name derives from *baste*, wand?[11]

At the head of all the trumps, it indicates that all of life is only a dream that vanishes away: that it is like a perpetual game of chance or the shock of a thousand circumstances which are never dependant on us, and which inevitably exerts a great influence on any general administration.

But between the Fool and Juggler, which man is better?

No. II, III, IV, V.

Leaders of Society.

Numbers II. and III. represent two women: numbers IV. and V. their husbands:[12] they are the temporal and spiritual leaders of society.

King and Queen.

Number IV. represents the King, and III. the Queen. They have both for symbols the eagle on a shield, and a scepter surmounted by a sphere crowned with a cross, called a Tau,[13] the sign of excellence.

The King (Emperor)

The King is seen in profile, the Queen facing. They are both seated on thrones. The Queen wears a long dress, the back of her throne is high: the King is in a chair shaped like a gondola or shell, his legs crossed. His semicircular crown is surmounted by a pearl with a cross. That of the Queen terminates in a peak. The King carries an order of knighthood.[14]

The Queen (Empress)

High Priest and High Priestess.

Number V. represents the leader of the hierophants or the High Priest: Number II. the High Priestess or his wife: it is known that among Egyptians, the leaders of the priesthood were married. If these cards were of modern invention, one would not see one titled the High Priestess, much less still bearing the name of *Papesse*, as the German card makers ridiculously titled this one.[15]

The High Priestess

The High Priestess sits in an armchair: she wears a long dress with a type of veil behind her head which descends to cross over her breast: she has a double crown with two horns like that of Isis: she holds a book open on her knees; two scarves furnished with crosses cross on her abdomen and form an X there.

The High Priest (Hierophant)

The High Priest wears a long habit with a great coat which serve as his vest-
ments: on his head is the triple crown: one hand holds a scepter with a triple
cross, and the other gives the blessing with two fingers extended toward two
individuals at his knees.

Italian card makers or Germans who brought back this game to their buy-
ers, made these two characters into what the ancients called the Father and
Mother, like our names Abbot and Abbess, Oriental words meaning the same
thing; they called them, I say, Pope and Popess.

As for the scepter with the triple cross, it is a symbol absolutely Egyptian: one
sees it on the Table of Isis,[16] under Letter TT; an invaluable monument which
we have already caused to be engraved in all its details in order to present it some
day to the public. It is related to the triple Phallus that may be observed in the
famous Feast of Pamylies[17] where one rejoices to have found Osiris, and where it
represents the symbol of the regeneration of plants and all of Nature.

No. VII.

Osiris Triumphant.

Osiris Triumphant (Chariot)

Osiris advances; he comes in the form of a king triumphing, his scepter in hand, his crown on his head: he is in the chariot of a warrior, drawn by two white horses. Nobody is unaware that Osiris was the primary god of the Egyptians, the same one as that of all the Sabaean people, or that he is the physical sun symbol of a supreme invisible divinity, but who appears in this masterpiece of Nature. He was lost during the winter: he reappeared in springtime with a new radiance, having triumphed over all against whom he made war.

No. VI.

Marriage.

Marriage (The Lovers)

A young man and a young woman pledge themselves their mutual faith: a priest blesses them, an expression of love on his features.[18] Card makers call this card, the Lovers. They seem also to have added themselves the figure of Love with his bow and its arrows, to make this card more eloquent in their view.

One sees in the *Antiquities* of Boissard [T. III. Pl. XXXVI.],[19] a monument of the same nature, representing the marital union; but it is made up only of three figures.

The lover and his mistress who give themselves their faith: the figure of Love between the two takes the place of the witness and the priest.

This image is entitled *Fidei Simulacrum*, Tableau of Marital Faith: the characters in it are designated by these beautiful names, Truth, Honor and Love. It is unnecessary to say that truth designates the woman here rather than the man, not only because this word is of female gender, but because constant fidelity is more essential in a woman. This invaluable monument was raised by one named T. Fundanius Eromenus or the Pleasant One, with his very dear wife Poppée Demetrie, and with their cherished daughter Manilia Eromenis.

Plate V.
No. VIII, XI, XII, XIV.
The Four Cardinal Virtues.

The figures which we have joined together in this plate, relate to the four cardinal virtues.

Fortitude (Strength)

Number XI. This one represents Fortitude. It is a woman who is the mistress of a lion, and who opens its mouth with the same facility as she would open that of her small spaniel; she has on her head the cap of a shepherdess.[20]

Temperance

Number XIV. Temperance. This shows a woman who pours the water of one vase into another, to temper the liquor which it contains.[21]

Justice

Number VIII. Justice. It is a queen, it is Astraea sitting on her throne, holding with one hand a dagger; with the other, a balance.[22]

Prudence (Hanged Man)

Number XII. Prudence is numbered among the four cardinal virtues: could the Egyptians forget it in this painting of human life? However, one does not find it in this game. One sees in its place under number XII, between Fortitude and Temperance, a man hanging by the feet: but why is he hung like this? It is the work of a bad and presumptuous card maker who, not understanding the beauty of the allegory contained upon this card, took on himself to correct it, and thereby has entirely disfigured it.

Prudence can only be represented in a way sensible to the eyes by a man upright, who having one foot set, advances the other, and holds it suspended while looking for the place where he will be able to safely place it. The title of this card was thus the Man with A Raised Foot, *pede suspenso*: the card maker, not knowing what this signified, made of it a man hung by the feet.[23]

Then one asked, why a hanged man in this game? and another did not fail to say, it is a fit punishment for the inventor of the game, to have represented a female pope.

But placed between Fortitude, Temperance and Justice, who does not see that it is Prudence that is lacking and that must have been originally represented? [24]

Plate VI.
No. VIIII. or IX.

The Sage, or the Seeker of Truth and Justice.

The Sage (Hermit)

Number IX. represents a worthy philosopher in a long coat, a hood on his shoulders: he goes bent on his stick, bearing a lantern in his left hand. It is the Sage who seeks justice and virtue.

One thus imagines, based on this Egyptian painting, the story of Diogenes who with lantern in hand seeks a man in full midday. The witty remarks, know-all epigrams, are of any century: and Diogenes was the man who enacted this scene.[25]

Card makers made of this a wise hermit. It is rather well conceived: philosophers live in voluntary retirement from those who are not cleansed from the frivolity of the times. Heraclitus[26] passed for insane in the eyes of his dear fellow citizens: in the East, moreover, to deliver oneself to speculative or hermetic sciences, is almost the only option. The Egyptian hermits cannot approach in this respect those of the Indians,[27] and in temples of Siam: they all were or are like as many Druids.

No. XIX.

The Sun.

The Sun

We joined together under this plate all the cards relating to the light: thus after the cloaked lantern of the Hermit, we will review the Sun, the Moon and brilliant Sirius or glittering Dog Star, all figures in this game, with various symbols.

The Sun is represented here like the physical father of man and of Nature entire: it illuminates men in society, it regulates their cities: of its rays are distilled gold tears and pearls:[28] thus one marks out the happy influences of this star.

The game of Tarots is perfectly in conformity here with the doctrines of the Egyptians, as we shall examine in more detail in the following article.

No. XVIII.

The Moon.

The Moon

Thus the Moon which goes following the Sun is also accompanied by tears of gold and pearls, to also mark what it contributes in its part to the advantages of the ground.[29]

Pausanias teaches us in his description of Phocide, that according to the Egyptians, it was the tears of Isis which flooded each year the waters of the Nile and which thus rendered fertile the fields of Egypt. The historians of that country also speak about a drop or tear, which falls from the Moon at the time when the water of the Nile must grow bigger.[30]

At the bottom of this card, one sees a crayfish or Cancer, either to mark the retrograde functioning of the Moon, or to indicate that it is at the time when the Sun and the Moon leave the sign of Cancer at which the flood caused by their tears arrives, at the rising of the Dog Star that one sees in the following card.

It may even be that the two reasons are joined together: is it not very common to be persuaded by a crowd of consequences which form a mass one feels too embarrassed to disentangle?

The middle of the card is occupied by two towers, one on each side to indicate the two famous Pillars of Hercules, beyond which these two large luminaries never pass.[31]

Between the two columns are two dogs which seem to bark against the Moon and to guard it: perfectly Egyptian ideas. These people, unique for their allegories, compared the Tropics[32] with two palaces, each one guarded by a dog, which, similar to faithful gatekeepers, held back these stars in the middle region of the skies without allowing them to slip towards one or the other Pole.

These are not fantasies of commentators on customs. Clement, himself Egyptian, since he was of Alexandria, and who consequently knew what he was talking about, assures us in his *Tapestries* [or *Stromates*, Liv. V.] that the Egyptians represented the Tropics under the figure of two dogs, which, similar to gatekeepers or faithful guards, kept the Sun and the Moon from going to the Poles.[33]

No. XVII.

The Dog Star.

The Dog Star (Star)

Here we have under our gaze a card not allegorical, and absolutely Egyptian; it is entitled the Star. One may see there, indeed, a brilliant star, about which are seven different smaller stars. The bottom of the card is occupied by a washer woman on a knee who holds two vases, from which flow two streams. Near this woman is a butterfly on a flower.[34]

It is purely Egyptian.

This Star, pre-eminently, is the Dog Star or Sirius:[35] a star which rises when the Sun leaves the sign of Cancer, in which ends the preceding card, and which this Star immediately follows.

The seven stars that are around it, and seem like courtiers, are the planets:[36] it is to some extent their queen, since it fixes in this moment the beginning of the year; they seem to come to receive its commands in order to regulate their courses on it.

The lady which is below, and extremely attentive at this moment to spread the water of her vases, is the Queen of Heaven, Isis, to the benevolence of whom were attributed the floods of the Nile, which start with the rising of the Dog Star; thus this rising was the signal of the inundation. The reason the Dog Star was consecrated to Isis, is that it was her perfect symbol.

And as the year began simultaneously with the rising of this star, one of its names is Soth-Is, opening of the year; and it is under this name that it was devoted to Isis.

Lastly, the flower and the butterfly which it supports, represent the symbols of regeneration and resurrection: they signify at the same time the blessing of the benefits of Isis, and the rising of the Dog Star, when the lands of Egypt, which were absolutely naked, cover themselves with new crops.

Plate VIII.
No. XIII.
Death.

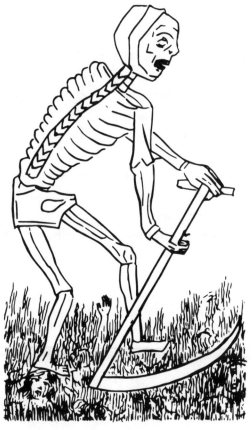

Death

Number XIII. represents Death: it mows down humans, the kings and the queens, the great ones and the small ones; nothing can resist its murderous scythe.

It is not astonishing that it is placed under this number; the number thirteen was always looked upon as unhappy. It is likely that long ago some great misfortune arrived on a similar day, and that it influenced the memories of all the ancient nations. Can it have been by a continuation of this memory that the thirteen Hebrew tribes were never counted other than as twelve?

Let us add that it is not astonishing either that the Egyptians chose to insert Death into a game, which serves to awaken that pleasant idea: this game was a game of war, the dead thus must enter there: thus it is a game of failures finished by a stalemate, or better put, by a checkmate, the death of the king. Besides, we had occasion to recall in the calendar, that in the feasts, this wise and considered people introduced there a skeleton under the name of Maneros,[37] undoubtedly in order to urge the guests not to kill themselves with over-eating. Each one has his manner of seeing, and tastes never should be disputed.

No. XV.

Typhon.

Typhon (Devil)

Number XV. represents a famous Egyptian character, Typhon, brother of Osiris and Isis, the bad principle, the great demon of hell: he has the wings of a bat, the feet and hands of a harpy; on his head, the villainous horns of a stag: he is also ugly, as devilish as one could be. At his feet are two small imps with long ears, with large tails, their lowered hands behind their backs: they themselves are bound by a cord which passes to their necks, and which is attached to the pedestal of Typhon: he never releases those that are with him; he likes those that are his own.[38]

No. XVI.

The House of God, or Castle of Plutus.

The Castle of Plutus (Tower)

Here, we have a lesson against avarice. This card represents a tower, which one calls the House of God, that is, the highest house; it is a tower filled with gold, it is the castle of Plutus: it collapses in ruins, and its adorers fall crushed under its remains.

With this card, one can understand the history of this Egyptian prince about whom Herodotus speaks, and whom he calls Rhampsinitus, who, having made a large tower of stone to contain his treasures, and to which only he had the key, noticed however that they were diminishing under his very gaze, without anyone passing in any manner through the only door which existed in this building. To discover such skillful robbers, this prince proceeded to set traps around the vases which held his riches. The robbers were two sons of the architect who served Rhampsinitus:[39] he had rigged a stone in such a manner, that it was possible to remove it and enter to steal at will without fear of capture. He taught its secret to his children who made use of it marvelously as one sees. They robbed the prince, and then they left the tower at the bottom: thus they are represented here. It is in truth the most beautiful part of the *History*; one will find in Herodotus the remainder of this clever tale: how one of the two brothers was taken in the nets: how he urged his brother to cut his head off: how their mother demanded that her son bring back the body of his brother: how he went with goatskin bottles loaded on an ass to steal the corpse from the guards at the palace: how, after they had taken his goatskin bottles in spite of his cunning tears, and had fallen asleep, he shaved off from all of them the right side of their beards, and he removed the body of his brother: how the king extremely astonished, urged his daughter to compel each of her lovers to reveal to her the cleverest trick which they had ever done: how this devious youth went near the beautiful one, told her all that he had done: how the beautiful one having wanted to detain him, had seized only one false arm: how, to complete this great adventure, and to lead it to a happy end, this king promised in marriage this same daughter to the clever young man who had played him so well, as the person worthiest of her; which was carried out to the great satisfaction of all.

I do not know if Herodotus took this tale for a real history; but people able to invent similar romances or Milesian Fables, could very easily invent any game.

This tale brings back another fact which proves what we said in the history of the calendar, that statues of giants that appear in various festivals, almost always designate the seasons. It says that Rhampsinitus, the same prince of which we came to speak, caused to be raised in the north and the south of the temple of Vulcan two statues of twenty-five cubits, one titled Summer and the other Winter: they adored the one, and sacrificed, on the contrary, to the other: it is thus like the savages who recognize the good principle and admire it, but who sacrifice only to the bad.

No. X.

The Wheel of Fortune.

The Wheel of Fortune

The last number of this plate is the Wheel of Fortune. Here human caricatures, in the form of monkeys, of dogs, of rabbits, etc. rise turn-by-turn on this wheel to which they are attached: it is said that it is a satire against fortune, and those which it elevates quickly, it lets fall down with the same speed.

Plate VIII.
No. XX.

Card badly named the Last Judgment.

The Last Judgment

This card represents an angel sounding a trumpet: one sees immediately rising from the ground an old man, a woman, a naked child. Card makers who forgot the significance of these cards, and more still their numbers, saw here the Last Judgment;[40] and to make it more obvious, they put into it something resembling tombs. Removing these tombs, this card can just as well refer to the Creation, which happened in time, at the beginning of time, which number XXI indicates.

No. XXI.

Time, badly named the World.

Time (World)

This card, which card makers called the World, because they regarded it as the origin of all, represents Time. One cannot be mistaken when all things are considered.[41] In the center is the goddess of Time, with her veil which flies, and which serves her as a belt or *peplum*, as the ancients called it. She is in a posture to run like time, and in a circle which represents the revolutions of time; as well as the egg where all exists in time. At the four corners of the card are the symbols of the four seasons, which form the revolutions of the year, the same which make up the four heads of the Kerubim.[42]

These emblems are, The Eagle, the Lion, the Ox, and the Young Man:

- The Eagle represents spring, when the birds return.
- The Lion, the summer or burning of the Sun.
- The Ox, the autumn when one plows and when one sows.
- The Young Man, the winter, when one meets in company.

ARTICLE II

The Suits.

In addition to the trumps, this game is composed of four suits distinguished by their symbols: they are called Sword, Cup, Baton and Coin. One can see the Aces of these four suits in Plate VIII.

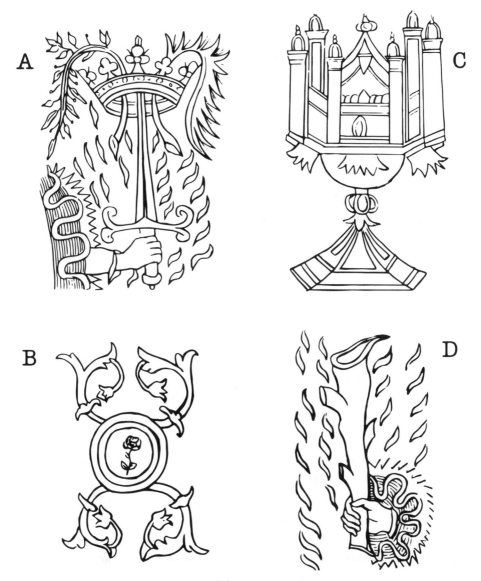

1.23 The Four Aces

A represents the Ace of Swords, surmounted by a crown surrounded with palms.

C, the Ace of Cups: it has the appearance of a castle; it is how one made in former times large money cups.

D, the Ace of Batons; it is truly a bludgeon.

B, the Ace of Coins, surrounded by garlands.

Each one of these suits is made up of fourteen cards, that is, of ten cards numbered I to X, and of four illustrated cards, which one calls the King, the Queen, the Knight or Horseman, and his Page or Servant. These four suits relate to the four classes between which the Egyptians were divided. The Sword designates the sovereign and the military or nobility. The Cup, the clergy or priesthood. The Baton, or bludgeon of Hercules, agriculture. The Coin, trade of which money is the sign.

This game is based on the number seven.

This game is absolutely founded on the sacred number of seven. Each suit is of twice seven cards. Trumps are three times seven; the total number of the cards is seventy-seven; the Fool being like 0. However, nobody is unaware of the role that this number played among the Egyptians, and that it became in their nation a formula with which they reconciled the elements of all sciences.[43]

The sinister idea attached in this game to the number thirteen, recollects also extremely well this same beginning.

This game can thus have been invented only by the Egyptians, that has as a base the number seven; that is related to the division of the inhabitants of Egypt into four classes; that has the majority of its trumps related absolutely to Egypt, such as the two heads of hierophants, man and woman, Isis or the Dog Star, Typhon, Osiris, the House of God, the World, the dogs which indicate the Tropics, etc; that this game, entirely allegorical, could only be the work of the Egyptians.

Invented by a man of genius, before or after the game of chess, and joining together utility with delight, it has passed down to us through all the centuries; it has endured the utter ruin of Egypt and of the wise men which distinguished that nation; and while one may have no idea of the wisdom of the lessons only they could teach, one nevertheless enjoys playing with what they have invented.

It is easy besides to trace the road which it followed to arrive in our regions. In the first centuries of the Church, the Egyptians were very widespread in Rome; they carried there their ceremonies and the worship of Isis; consequently the game in question.

This game, interesting by itself, was limited to Italy until relations between the Germans with the Italians made it known to this second nation; and until the counts from Italy living in Provence, during the stay in Avignon of all the Court from Rome, naturalized it in Provence and in Avignon.

That it did not come to Paris, should be attributed to the strangeness of its figures and the number of its cards, which were not likely to appeal to the vivacity of the ladies of France. Also one was obliged, as it will soon be seen, to excessively reduce this game in their favor.

However that same Egypt does not enjoy the fruit of its invention: reduced to the most deplorable servitude, and the most profound ignorance, deprived of all arts, its inhabitants are scarcely in a position to manufacture a card game.

If our French cards, infinitely less complicated, require the constant work of a multitude of hands and the mingling of several arts, how were these unfortunate people to preserve their own? Such are the evils which befall a subjugated nation, even to the loss of the objects of its amusements: not having been able to preserve its most invaluable advantages, of what right pretends it to that which was only a pleasant recreation?

Eastern names preserved in this game.

This game preserved some names which also would declare it to be an Oriental game if one had no other evidence.

These names are those of Taro, Mat and Pagad.

1. Tarots.

The name of this game is pure Egyptian: it is composed of the word *Tar*, which means way, path; and of the word *Ro, Ros, Rog*, which means king, royal. It is, literally, the Royal Path of Life.

It indeed refers to the entire life of citizens, since it is formed of the various classes between which they are divided, and follows them from their birth to death, showing all the virtues and all physical and moral guides to which they must abide, such as the king, the queen, heads of religion, the Sun, the Moon, etc.

It teaches them at the same time by the Player at Cups and the Wheel of Fortune, that nothing is more inconstant in this world than various states of man: that his only refuge is in virtue, which never fails when needed.

2. Mat.

The Mat, which is vulgarly named the Fool, and which remains in its Italian form, come from the Eastern word *mat*, struck, bruised, cracked. Fools were always represented as having a cracked brain.

3. Pagad.

The Player at Cups is called Pagad in the modern version of the game.[44] This name which resembles nothing in our Western languages, is pure Oriental and very well chosen: *pag* means in the East chief, master, lord: and *gad*, fortune. Indeed, it is represented as showing Fate with its rod of Jacob or its rod of the Magi.

Article III

The way in which one plays Tarots.

1st. Manner of dealing the cards.

One of our friends, Mr. A. R., agreed to explain to us the way in which one plays it: it is he who will speak, if we have understood well.

This game is played by two, but one deals the cards as if there were three players:[45] each player thus has only one-third of the cards: thus during the combat there is always a third of the troops which rest; one calls this the body in reserve.

For this game is a game of war, and not a peaceful game as it has incorrectly been described: however in all armies there is a body in reserve. Moreover, this reserve makes the game more difficult, since one has much more trouble guessing the cards which his adversary may have.

One deals the cards by five, or by five and five.

Of the 78 cards, there thus remain three at the end of the deal; instead of sharing them between the players and the reserve or discarding them, the dealer keeps them; what gives him the advantage of three cards.

2nd. The manner of counting points during play.

The trumps do not all have the same value.

Those numbered 21, 20, 19, 18 and 17 are termed the five large trumps.

Those numbered 1, 2, 3, 4, 5 are called the five small ones.

If there are three of the large or three of the small, five points are counted: ten points, if there are four of them; and fifteen, if there are five of them.

This is also an Egyptian manner of counting: the *dinaire* or denier of Pythagoras being equal to the quaternary, since one, two, three and four added together make ten.

If there are ten trumps in this game, they are spread out, and they are worth ten more points; if there are thirteen of them, one also spreads them out, and they are worth fifteen points, independently of the other combinations.

Seven cards bear the name of Tarots especially: they are the privileged cards; and here again, the number seven. These cards are:

The World or trump 21.
The Fool or Madman 0.
The Juggler or trump 1.
(Trumps-Tarots)
And the four Kings.

If there are two of these trumps-Tarots, one asks the other whether or not he has it. If the other cannot answer by showing the third, he who asked the question marks 5 points: the other marks 15 of them if he has all three of them. Sequences or the four court figures of the same suit are worth 5 points.

3rd. Manner of playing the cards.

The Fool takes anything, but nothing takes it: it forms a trump, and it is of any suit also.

If one plays a King, but does not have the Queen, one plays the Fool, which is called the Excuse.

The Fool with two Kings, counts 5 points: with three, 15.

A King cut, or killed, 5 points for that which delivers the blow.

If one takes the Juggler from his adversary, one marks 5 points.

Thus the game is to take from one's adversary the figures which count the most points, and to make all efforts to form sequences: the adversary must do all he can to save his great figures: in consequence of seeing it coming, by sacrificing petty trumps, or petty cards of his suits.

He must always be willing to sacrifice, in order to save his strong cards while cutting those of his adversary.

4th. Variation for the one who deals.

The dealer can neither put aside trumps nor Kings; it would be too nice a game for him, because he could save himself without risk. All that can be permitted to him in light of his primacy is to discard a sequence: because it counts, and it can allow him to make a refusal, which is a double advantage.

5th. Manner of counting the hands.

The division is into a hundred, as with Piquet, with this difference, that it is not the one who arrives the first at a hundred when the counting is started who gains, but he who then makes the most points; because it is necessary that all counting started continue until the end: it offers thus more resources than Piquet.

To count the points which one has in his hands, each of the seven cards called Tarots, with a card of a suit, is worth 5 points.

A Queen with a card, 4.
A Knight with a card, 3.
A Page with a card, 2.
Two simple number cards, 1.

The surplus of the points is counted that one of the adversaries has over the others, and he marks them down: one continues the evening of play until one arrives at a hundred.[46]

Article IV

The Game of Tarots regarded as a game of political geography.

Someone showed to us in a catalogue of Italian books, the title of a work where the geography is interlaced with the Tarots: but we could not obtain this book containing its lessons of geography engraved on each card of this game: this is an application of this game to geography: the field of conjecture is without end, and perhaps by multiplying the combinations, we may steal away some of the images from this work. Without us being hindered by what may actually be written there, let us conjecture ourselves how the Egyptians would have been able to apply this game to political geography, such as it was known in their times, three thousand years ago.

Time or the World, represents the moment when the earth left chaos, where matter took a form, being divided into lands and into seas, and where man was created to become its master, the king of this beautiful property.

The four cardinal virtues correspond to the four coasts of the world, east, west, north and south, these four points relating to man, by whom he is in the center of all; that one can call his right, his left, his front and his back, and from where his awareness extends in rays until the end of all, according to the extent of his physical eyes firstly, and then of his intellectual eyes by a different perception.

The four suits will be the four areas or parts of the world corresponding to the four cardinal points, Asia, Africa, Europe and Celto-Scythia or the frozen countries of North: a division which was increased by America since its discovery, when the polar grounds of the North and the South were substituted for the ancient region of Celto-Scythia.

The Sword represents Asia, nations of great monarchies, great conquests, great revolutions.

The Baton, Egypt, nourisher of humanity, and symbol of the South, the black peoples.

The Cup, the North, from which humanity descended, and from which came teaching and science.

The Coin, Europe or the West, rich in gold mines in the beginnings of the world that we so badly term the olden times or ancient times.

Each ten numbered cards of these four suits, will be one of the great regions of these four areas of the world.

The ten cards of Swords will represent: Arabia; Idumea, which rules over the seas of the South; Palestine populated by Egyptians; Phoenicia, mistress of the Mediterranean; Syria or Aramée; Mesopotamia or Chaldea; Media; Susiana; Persia; and India.

The ten numbered cards of Batons will represent the three great divisions of Egypt, the Thebaid or Upper Egypt, the Delta or Lower Egypt, Heptanome or Middle Egypt divided into seven governments. Then Ethiopia; Cyrenaica, or in its place the land of Jupiter Ammon; Libya or Carthage; the peaceful Telamones; the vagabond Numides; Moors pressed on the Atlantic Ocean; Gétules, which is placed in the south by the atlas, and spreads over those vast regions which we call today Nigeria and Guinea.

The ten cards of Coins will represent the Isle of Crete, monarchy of the famous Minos; Greece and its isles; Italy; Sicily and its volcanoes; the Balearic Islands famous for the dress of their troops of the line; Baetica rich in herds; Celtiberia abundant in gold mines; Gades or Cadiz, isle most closely associated with Hercules, most commercial of the universe; Lusitania; and the Fortunate Isles, or the Canaries.

The ten cards of Cups, Armenia and its Mount Ararat; Iberia; Scythes of Imaus; Scythes of the Caucasus; Cimmerians of Palus-Maeotis; Getae or Goths; the Dacians; Hyperboreans so celebrated in high antiquity; the Celts wandering in their frozen forests; the Isle of Thule at the ends of the world.

The four illustrated cards of each suit will stand for certain geographical details relative to each area.

The Kings, the state of the governments of each one, forces of the empires which compose them, and how they are more or less considerable according to whether agriculture is of use and in honor; this source of inexhaustible riches always reappearing.

The Queens, the development of their religions, their manners, their customs, especially of their opinions, opinion having always been regarded as Queen of the World. Happy he who is able to direct it; he will always be king of the universe, master of the same; he is an eloquent Hercules who leads men with a golden bridle.

The Knights, the exploits of the people, the history of their heroes or warriors; of their tournaments, of their games, their battles.

The Pages, the history of arts, their origin, their nature; all that looks at the industrious portion of each nation, that which produces machines, manufacturers, commerce which varies in one hundred ways the form of wealth without adding anything to the base, which causes to circulate in the universe these riches and the products of industry; which puts them at the use of farmers to create new riches while providing an efficient outlet for those to which they have already given birth, and how all are strangled as soon as this circulation does not play freely, since the goods are hoarded, and those who provide them discouraged.

The whole of the 21 or 22 trumps, the 22 letters of the Egyptian alphabet common to the Hebrews and to the East, and which were also used as numbers, are necessary to keep an account of so many regions.

Each one of these trumps will have had at the same time a particular use. Several will have related to the principal objects of celestial geography, if one can use such an expression. Hence:

The Sun, the Moon, Cancer, the Pillars of Hercules, the Tropics or their Dogs.[47]

The Dog Star, this beautiful and brilliant portal of the heavens.[48]

The Celestial Bear, on which all the stars lean by carrying out their revolutions around it, admirable constellation represented by the seven Tarots,[49] and which seems to publish in characters of fire imprinted on our heads and in the firmament, that our solar system was founded like our sciences on the formula of seven, as was even the entire structure of the universe.

All the others can be considered relative to the political and moral geography, the true government of the states: and even with the government of each man in particular. The four trumps relating to civil and religious authority,[50] make known the importance for a state of a united government, and of respect for the ancients.

The four cardinal virtues[51] show that the social classes can be supported only by the kindness of government, by the excellence of instruction, by the practice of the virtues in those who control and who are controlled: Prudence to correct abuses, Fortitude to maintain peace and union, Temperance in the means, Justice towards all. How ignorance, pride, greed, stupidity in the one, generates in others a disastrous contempt: from which disorders result which shake even to their foundations the empires where justice is violated, where force is the only means, where one misuses his power, and where one lives without security. Disorders which destroyed so many families whose names had resounded so long a time across all the earth, and who ruled with such an amount of glory on the astonished nations.

These virtues are no less necessary to each individual. Temperance regulates one's duties towards himself, especially towards his own body which he treats too often only like an unhappy slave, martyr of his disordered affections.

Justice which regulates one's duties towards those nearest and the Divinity itself to which he owes all.

Fortitude with which he is supported in the midst of the ruins of the universe, in spite of the vain and foolish efforts of passions which unceasingly besiege him with their impetuous floods.

Lastly, Prudence with which he patiently awaits the success of his plans, equal to any event and similar to a fine player who never risks his game and can benefit from all circumstances.

The triumphing King[52] then becomes the emblem of that man who by means of these virtues was wise towards himself, right towards others, extreme against passions, foresighted enough to pile up resources against the times of adversity.

Time who uses up all with an inconceivable speed; Fortune who is played of all; the Juggler who conjures away all; the Fool who is of all; the Miser who loses all; the Devil who is inside all; Death who absorbs all:[53] seven singular numbers who are of all countries, can give place to observations not less significant and not less varied.

Lastly, he who has very much to gain and nothing to lose, the true King triumphing, is the true Sage[54] who lantern in hand is unceasingly careful where he steps, does not adopt any school, knows all that is good to enjoy, and recognizes all that is evil and to be avoided.

Such is sufficient concerning the geographical-political-moral explanation of this antique game: and such must be the end of all mankind, which would be happy, if all its games ended thus![55]

Article V

Relationship of this game with a Chinese monument.

Mr. Bertin who returned so great a benefit to literature and the sciences, by the excellent *Memoirs* that he wrote and published concerning China,[56] told us about a unique monument which was sent to him from this vast region, and which we assume dates from the first ages of this empire, since the Chinese on it looks like an inscription by Yao relating to the receding waters of the Flood.

It is composed of characters which form large compartments in quarter-length, all equal, and precisely the same size as the cards of the game of Tarots. These compartments are distributed in six perpendicular columns, of which the first five contain fourteen compartments each, while the sixth which is not completely filled contains only seven of them.

This monument is thus composed in this way of seventy-seven figures like the set of Tarots: and it is formed according to the same combination of the number seven, since each column is of fourteen figures, and the one which is not is that with half, containing seven of them.

Without that, one would have been able to arrange these seventy-seven compartments in a manner so as to make unnecessary this sixth column: one would have had only to make each column of thirteen compartments; and the sixth would have had twelve.

This monument is thus perfectly similar, numerically, with the set of Tarots, if one withholds from them only one card: the four suits filling the first four columns with fourteen cards each: and the trumps that number twenty-one, filling the fifth column, and precisely half of the sixth.

It seems quite strange that so similar a relationship was the result of simple chance: it is thus very apparent that both of these monuments were formed according to the same theory, and on the connection with the sacred number seven; they both seem thus to be only different applications of a single formula, perhaps anterior to the existence of the Chinese and the Egyptians: perhaps one will even find something similar among the Indians or the people of Tibet who are located between these two ancient nations.

We were extremely tempted to also make an engraving of this Chinese monument; but feared it would appear badly when reduced to a size smaller than the original, and also the impossibility, given the means available to us to do all that was required for the perfecting of our work, prevented us.

Let us not omit that the Chinese figures are in white on a jet black background; which makes them very prominent.

Article VI

Relationship of this game with squares or tournaments.

During a great number of centuries, the nobility mounted on horseback, and divided into colors or factions, exercised between them pretended combats or tournaments perfectly similar to that carried out in the games of cards, and especially in that of Tarots, which was a military game just as that of chess, up until the time that it came to be considered a civil game, an aspect it has taken on presently.

In the beginning, the knights of the tournaments were divided into four, even into five bands relating to the four suits of the Tarots and with the set of trumps. The last entertainment of this kind which was seen in France, was given in 1662 by Louis XIV, between the Tuileries and the Louvre, in that great place where is preserved the name Carousel. It was composed of five squares. The King was the leader of the Romans: his brother, head of the House of Orleans, with the leader of the Persians: the Prince of Condé commanded the Turks: the Duke of Enguien his son, the Indians: the Duke de Guise, the Americans. Three queens were seated there on a platform: the Queen Mother, the reigning Queen, the widowed Queen of England of Charles II. The Count de Sault, son of the Duke of Lesdiguieres, placed the prizes for the matches into the hands of the Queen Mother.

The squares were usually made up of 8 or 12 knights for each color: which, to 4 colors by 8 squares, gives the number 32, which forms that of the cards for the game of Piquet: and to 5 colors, the number 40, which is that of the cards for the game of Quadrille.

Article VII

Spanish card decks.

When one examines the card decks in use among Spaniards, one cannot avoid noticing that they are a diminutive form of the Tarots.[57]

Their most distinctive games are that of Hombre which is played by three: and Quadrille which is played by four and which is only a modification of the game of Hombre.

This name signifies the game of man, or human life; it thus has a name which corresponds perfectly to that name Tarot. It is divided into four suits which bear the same titles as in the Tarots, such as *Spadille* or Swords, *Baste* or Batons, which are the two black suits; *Copa* or Cups, and *Dinero* or Coins,[58] which are both red suits.

Several of these names were carried into France with this game: thus the Ace of Spades is called *Spadille* or Swords; the Ace of Clubs, *Baste*, that is, Batons. The Ace of Hearts is named *Ponte*, from the Spanish *punto*, having a point.

Those trumps, which are the strongest, are called *Matadors*, or the Slaughtermen, the triumphant who destroyed their enemies.

This game is entirely formed on the tournaments; the proof is striking, since the suits collectively are called *Palos* or Pales, the lances, the pikes of the knights.

The cards themselves are called *Naypes*, from the Oriental word *nap*, which means to take, to hold: literally, the Keepers.

There are thus four or five squares of knights who fight in tournaments.

They are forty, called *Naypes* or Keepers.

Four suits called *Palos* or rows of pikes.

The trumps are called *Matadors* or Slaughtermen, those who came in the end to demolish their enemies.

Finally the names of the four suits, that even of the game, show that it was formed entirely on the game of Tarots; that the Spanish cards are only an imitation in miniature of the Egyptian game.

Article VIII

French cards.

According to this information, no one will have difficulty perceiving that the French cards are themselves an imitation of the Spanish cards, and that they are thus the imitation of an imitation, and in consequence a well-degenerated institution, far from being an original invention and first, as is incorrectly expressed in remarks our savants, who do not focus on points of comparison, but only seek to discover the causes and relationships of all.

It is usually supposed that the French cards were invented during the reign of Charles VI, in order to amuse this feeble and infirm prince: but what we believe ourselves is right to assert, is that they were not an imitation of the southernmost games.

Perhaps we may even be right to suppose that the French cards are older than Charles VI, since it is attributed in the dictionary of Ducange[59] [with the word *Charta*] to St. Bernard of Sienne, contemporary of Charles V, to have condemned to fire, not only masks and the game of dice, but even the triumphal cards, or cards of the game called Triumph.[60]

One finds in this same Ducange the criminal statutes of a city called Saona, which defend the legality of card games.

It is necessary that these statutes are very old, since in this work one could not indicate the time of it: this city must be that of Savone.

No doubt it happens that these games are much older than St. Bernard of Sienne: why else would he confuse dice and masks[61] with a game lately invented to amuse a great king?

Besides, our French cards present no vision, no ingenuity, no cohesion. If they were invented according to the tournament, why was the Knight removed, while his Page was retained? why allow at the time only thirteen cards instead of fourteen per suit?

The names of the suits have degenerated at this point and offer no consistency. If one can recognize the Swords in the Spades, how did the Batons become the Clubs? How do the Hearts and the Diamonds correspond with Cups and Coins; and what ideas are revealed by these suits?

Whose idea was it to introduce the names given to the four Kings? David, Alexander, Caesar, Charlemagne, do not correspond either to four famous monarchs of antiquity, nor with those of modern times. They are a monstrous composition.[62]

It is the same for the names of the Queens: they are called Rachael, Judith, Pallas and Argine: it is true that one believed that they were allegorical names relating to the four ways in which a lady attracts to herself the attentions of men: that Rachael indicates beauty, Judith strength, Pallas wisdom, and Argine, where one only sees the anagram Regina, queen, birth.[63]

But what relationships have these names with Charles VI or with France? What are these forced allegories?

It is true that among the names of Pages one finds that of Hire, which may refer to one of the French Generals of Charles VI; but is this solitary correspondence sufficient to scramble all the periods of history?[64]

We were here when one spoke to us about a work of the Abbot Rive, which discusses the same subject: afterwards having sought it in vain at the greater number of our booksellers, M. de S. Paterne lent it to us.

This work is entitled:

Historical and critical notes of two Manuscripts of the Library of the Duke of Valliere, of which one has for its title Le Roman d'Artus, Comte de Bretaigne, and the other, Le Romant de Pertenay or de Lusignen, by The Abbot Rive, etc. at Paris, 1779, in 4o. 36 pages.

On page 7, where the author starts to discuss the origin of the French cards; we saw with pleasure that it supports, (1) that these cards are older than Charles VI; (2) that they are an imitation of Spanish cards: now let us give a brief summary of his evidence.

"Cards, he states, date from at least the year 1330; and it is neither in France, nor in Italy, nor in Germany that they appeared for the first time. One sees them in Spain around this year, and it is a long time before one finds the least trace in any other nation.

"They were invented there, according to the Castillan Dictionary of 1734, by one named Nicolao Pepin...

"One finds them in Italy towards the end of this same century, under the name of *Naibi*, in the Chronicle of Giovan Morelli, which is of the year 1393."

From this learned abbot we discover at the same time that the first Spanish work which attests the existence of cards is from approximately the year 1332.

"They are the Statutes of an order of knighthood established around this period in Spain, and founded by Alphonse XI, King of Castille. Those who were admitted swore an oath not to play cards.

"One then sees them in France under the reign of Charles V. Little Jean of Saintré was not honored with the favors of Charles V because he played neither with dice nor with cards, and this king proscribed them along with several others games, in his Edict of 1369. One sees them in various provinces of France; one gave to some of the figures on the cards names made to inspire horror. In Provence, one of the Knaves is named the *Tuchim*.[65] The name signifies a race of robbers who, in 1361, caused in this country and that of Venaissin, a devastation so horrible, that the popes were obliged to preach a crusade to exterminate them. Cards were not introduced into the Court of France because under the successor of Charles V one feared even by their introduction, to wound the standard of morality, and consequently a pretext was conceived: it was said to be done to calm the melancholy of Charles VI. Under Charles VII the game of Piquet was invented. This game was the reason that cards spread, from France, into several other parts of Europe."

These details are very interesting; their consequences are still more so. These cards that were condemned in the XIVth century, and proscribed by the orders of knighthood, are necessarily very old: they have been regarded as only shameful remainders of paganism: they thus must have been the cards of the Tarot; their strange figures, their odd names, such as House of God, the Devil, Popess, etc., their high antiquity which is lost in the night of time, their use in fortune-telling, etc. all serve to make them look like a diabolic recreation, a work of the blackest magic, of a sorcery condemnable.

However the agony of not gaming! Thus were invented more human games, more purified, free from figures that were only good to frighten: the result, Spanish cards and French cards which were never prohibited like these bad cards that came out of Egypt, but which however lent themselves perfectly to these clever games.

Especially the game of Piquet, where two opponents play, where one draws aside, where one has sequences, where one goes in a hundred: where one counts the cards in hand, and the pickups, and where one finds a number of other correspondences too striking.

Conclusion

We thus dare to flatter ourselves that our readers will receive with pleasure these various opinions on so common a subject as cards, and that they will find them to perfectly rectify the vague and poorly reconciled ideas that have been available until now on this subject:

That no one can bring forth proof in support of these proposals.

That the cards have existed only since Charles VI.

That the Italians are the last people who adopted them.

That the figures of the game of Tarots are extravagant.

That it is ridiculous to seek the origin of the cards in the various states of civil life.

That this game of cards is patterned on peaceful life, while that of chess is patterned on war.

That the game of chess is older than that of cards.

Thus the absence of truth, in some manner or other, generates a crowd of errors of all kinds, which becomes more or less harmful, according to whether they unite with other truths, contrast with them or oppose them.

Application of this game to divination.

To finish this examination and these considerations on the Egyptian game, we will put under the eyes of the public the essay that we announced above, where it is proven how the Egyptians applied this game to the art of divination, and how this same use was transmitted down to our gaming cards, made in imitation of these former.

One will see there in particular what we already said in this volume, wherein is explained the relationship between the prophetic dreams in ancient times with the hieroglyphic and philosophical science of the sages, who sought to reduce by their science into a set of images the visions which the Divinity permitted them to receive; and that all this science declined over the course of time, but was wisely preserved, because it was reduced to vain and futile practices, which in the not very enlightened centuries that followed have managed to survive as the preoccupation of fools and the superstitious.

This judicious observer will provide us new evidence that the Spanish cards are an imitation of Egypt, since he teaches us that it is only with the game of Piquet that the fates are consulted, and that several names of these cards relate absolutely to Egyptian ideas.

The Three of Coins is called the Lord, or Osiris.

The Three of Cups, the Sovereigness, or Isis.

The Two of Cups, the Cow, or Apis.

The Nine of Coins, Mercury.

The Ace of Batons, the Snake, symbol of agriculture among Egyptians.

The Ace of Coins, the One-eyed, or Apollo.

This name of One-eyed, given to Apollo or the Sun as having only one eye, is an epithet taken from Nature that provides us a proof, along with several others, that the famous character of the *Edda* who lost one of his eyes in a famous allegorical fountain, is no other than the Sun, the One-eyed One or the preeminent single Eye.[66]

This essay is so filled besides with matter, and so apt to give healthy ideas on the way in which the sages of Egypt consulted the book of destiny, that we do not doubt it will be well received by the public, until now deprived of similar research, because until now nobody has had the courage to deal with subjects which appeared lost forever in the deep night of time.

"STUDY ON THE TAROTS"

and on the Divination by the Cards of the Tarots

by

M. LE C. DE M.***

I

The Book of Thoth.

The desire to teach developed in the heart of man as his spirit acquired new knowledge: the need to preserve it, and eagerness to transmit it, made him imagine characters of which Thoth or Mercury was looked upon as the inventor.[67] These characters were not, in the beginning, conventional signs, and did not express, like our current letters, the sound of the words; they were the same true images that make up the pictures on the cards, which presented to the eyes the things about which one wanted to speak.

It is natural that the inventor of these images was the first historian: indeed, Thoth is regarded as having painted the gods [the gods, in the writing and the hieroglyphic expression, are the eternal and the virtues, represented with one body], that is to say, acts of absolute power, or creation, to which he joined precepts or morals. This book was to be named *A-Rosh*; from *A*, doctrines, science; and from *Rosch* [Rosh is the Egyptian name of Mercury and of its festival which is celebrated the first day of the new year], Mercury, which, joined to the article *T*, means pictures of the doctrines of Mercury; but as *Rosh* also means commencement, this word *Ta-Rosh* was particularly devoted to his cosmogony; just as *Ethotia*, the *History of Time*, was the title of his astronomy; and perhaps that Athothes, which one took for King, son of Thoth, is only the child of his genius, and the history of the kings of Egypt.

This ancient cosmogony, this book of *Ta-Rosh*, except for some minor corruptions, has come down to us in the cards which still bear this name [twenty-two pictures form a book not very bulky; but if, as is quite probable, the first traditions were preserved in poems, a simple image which fixed the attention of the people, by which one illustrated the event, served to help them to retain them, as well as the verse which described them.], that is to say, greed has preserved for an idle amusement, or superstition has preserved from the injury of time, mysterious symbols which serve them, as formerly they served the Magi, to mislead credulity.

The Arabs communicated this book [We still say booklet of the *Lansquenet*,[68] or *Lands-Knecht*, for the series of cards that one gives with the deal.] or game to the Spaniards, and the soldiers of Charles V carried it into Germany. It is composed of three higher series, representing the first three ages, of gold, silver and bronze: each series is made up of seven cards [Three times seven, a mystical, famous number for Kabbalists, Pythagoreans, etc.].

But like the Egyptian writing which reads to the left or the right, the twenty-first card, which was not numbered with an Arabic numeral, is nonetheless also the first, and must be read in the same way in order to understand the history; as it is the first in the game of Tarots, and in the species of divination that one performs with these images.

Lastly, there is a twenty-second card without number as without power, but which increases the value of that which it precedes; it is the zero of magic calculations: it is called the Fool.

First Series.

Age of Gold.

The twenty-first, or first card, represents the Universe[69] by the goddess Isis in an oval, or an egg, with the four seasons in the four corners: the Man or the Angel, the Eagle, the Ox, and the Lion.

Twentieth, this one is titled the Judgment: indeed, an angel sounding a trumpet, and the men leaving the ground, had to induce a painter, not very well versed in mythology, to see in this picture only the image of the Resurrection; but the ancients looked upon the men as children of the Earth [The teeth sown by Cadmus, etc.]; Thoth wanted to express the Creation of Man by painting Osiris, a generating god, with the speaking pipe or verb which orders matter, and by tongues of fire which escape from the cloud, the Spirit [Painted even in our sacred histories.] of God reviving this same matter; finally, by men leaving the ground in order to adore and admire the Absolute Power: the posture of these men does not announce culprits who go to appear in front of their Judge.[70]

Nineteenth, the creation of the Sun which brightens the union of man and woman, expressed by a man and a woman who give to each other their hands: this sign became, after that of Gemini, androgynous: *Duo in carne una.*[71]

Eighteenth, the creation of the Moon and the terrestrial animals, expressed by a wolf and a dog,[72] to stand for domestic animals and wild: this emblem is well chosen, in as much as the dog and the wolf are the only beasts which howl at the appearance of this star, as though regretting the loss of the day. This card would make me believe that its picture once announced very great misfortunes to those who chose to consult the Fates, if it were not for its depiction of the line of the Tropic, that is to say, of the departure and return of the Sun, which leaves the comforting hope of a beautiful day and of a better fortune. However, two fortresses which defend a path traced in blood, and a marsh which terminates the image, still suggest difficulties without number that must be surmounted in order to banish so sinister a presage.

Seventeenth, the Creation of Stars and Fishes, represented by stars and Aquarius.

Sixteenth, the House of God overthrown, or the terrestrial Paradise from which man and woman are precipitated by the blazing tail of a comet or star, joined with a fall of hailstones.

Fifteenth, the Devil or Typhon, final card of the first series, come to disturb the innocence of man and to abolish the golden age. His tail, his horns and his long ears announce that he is a degraded being: his raised left arm and folded wing, forming N, symbol of produced beings, makes us think it signifies having been created; but the torch of Prometheus which he holds with his right hand, serves to complete the letter M, which expresses generation:[73] indeed, the history of Typhon naturally persuades us to this explanation; because it shows that, by depriving Osiris of his virility, Typhon desired to encroach on the rights of the producing Power; also he was the father of evils which were spread on the ground.

The two beings bound at his feet mark degraded and subjected human nature, as well as a new and perverse generation, whose hooked nails express cruelty; they miss only the wings (spiritual or angelic nature), to be very similar to the devil: one of these beings touches with its claw the thigh of Typhon; a symbol which in mythological writing was always that of carnal generation[74] [the birth of Bacchus and of Minerva[75] are the mythological images of two such generations.]: he touches it with his left claw to signify illegitimacy.

Typhon finally is often taken for Winter, and this picture finishing the golden age announces the bad weather of the seasons, which will torment man driven out of Paradise thereafter.

Second Series.

Age of Silver.

Fourteenth, the Angel of Temperance comes to inform man, to make him avoid the death to which he is lately condemned: it is painted pouring water into wine [Perhaps its attitude is marked with the culture of the vine.], to show man the need for diluting this liquor, or for moderating his emotions.

Thirteenth; this number, always unhappy, is devoted to Death, who is represented mowing crowned heads and vulgar heads.

Twelfth, the accidents which afflict human life, represented by a man hanged by the foot; which wants also to say that, to avoid them, it is necessary in this world to go with prudence: *Suspenso pede.*[76]

Eleventh, Strength that is assisted by Prudence, and overcomes the lion, which was always the symbol of uncultivated and wild ground.

Tenth, the Wheel of Fortune, at the top of which is a crowned monkey, teaches us that after the fall of man, it was no longer virtue which gave dignities: the rabbit that goes up and the man who is precipitated,[77] express the injustices of the inconstant goddess: this wheel at the same time is an emblem of the wheel of Pythagoras,[78] a way of drawing lots by numbers: this form of divination is called arithomancy.

Ninth, the Hermit or the Sage, lantern in hand, seeking justice on the earth.

Eighth, Justice.

Third Series.

Age of Iron.

Seventh, the Chariot of War in which is an armored king, armed with a javelin, expresses the dissensions, the murders, the combats of the age of bronze, and announces the crimes of the age of iron.[79]

Sixth, the man depicted wavering between vice and virtue, is not led any more by reason: Love or Desire [concupiscence], with bandaged eyes, ready to release a dart, will make him lean to the right or to the left, whichever way he is guided by chance.[80]

Fifth, Jupiter or the Eternal together with his eagle, lightning in hand, threatens the earth, and will visit its kings with his anger.[81]

Fourth, the King armed with a bludgeon, which ignorance thereafter made an imperial globe [Osiris is often represented with a whip in his hand, with a sphere and a T: all these things united, have produced in the head of a German card maker an imperial globe]: his helmet is furnished behind with saw-like teeth, to make known that nothing serves to appease his insatiability [Or his revenge, if it has irritated Osiris.].

Third, the Queen, bludgeon in hand; her crown has the same ornaments as the helmet of the King.

Second, the pride of power, represented by the peacock, on which Juno pointing to the sky on the right side, and to the earth of the left, announces a terrestrial religion or idolatry.

First, the Juggler holding the rod of the Magi, making miracles and misleading the credulity of the people.

It is followed by a single card representing the Fool who carries his bag or his errors behind him, while a tiger or his regrets, devouring his haunch, delays his march towards crime [This card does not have a row: it completes the sacred alphabet, and answers to the *Tau* which expresses completion, perfection: perhaps it was intended to represent by this image the natural result of the actions of men.].

These twenty-two first cards are not only hieroglyphics, which when placed in their natural order recall the history of the earliest times, but they are also as many letters [the Hebrew alphabet is composed of 22 letters.] which when differently combined, can form as many sentences; also their name (*A-tout*) is only a literal translation of their general employment and property.[82]

II

This game applied to divination.

When the Egyptians had forgotten the first interpretation of these images, and that they had been used as simple letters for their sacred writing,[83] it was natural that such a superstitious people attached occult virtues to the characters, respected for their antiquity [Also the science of numbers and the value of letters was extremely renowned formerly.], and that the priests, who possessed the only knowledge of them, employed them solely for religious matters.

New characters were even invented, and we see in the holy writings that the Magi along with those who were initiated into their Mysteries, used a divination by cup [Cup of Joseph.].[84]

That they worked wonders with their wand [The rod of Moses and of the magicians of Pharaoh.].[85]

That they consulted talismans [The gods of Laban and the teraphim, Urim and Thummim.] or engraved stones.[86]

That they divined future things by swords [They did more: they fixed the fate of battles; and if King Joas had struck the ground seven times, instead of three, it would have destroyed Syria, II Kings, XIII, 19], by arrows, by axes, finally by weapons in general.[87] These four signs were introduced among the religious images when the establishment of kings had brought different social classes into society.

The Sword marked royalty and power of the earth.

The priests made use of vessels for sacrifices, and the Cup designated sacred.

The Coin, commerce.

The Baton, the Hoe, the Needle represent agriculture.

These four already mysterious characters, once joined together in the sacred pictures, gave hope of greater illuminations; and the fortuitous combination that one obtains by mixing these images forms the sentences that the Magi read or interpreted like statements of Destiny; which was to them all the easier since what is revealed by a pattern due to chance, naturally produces an obscurity sacred to the style of oracles.

Each social class thus had its symbol which characterized it; and among the different cards bearing this symbol, some were happy, others unhappy, and according to their position, the number of the symbols and their ornaments, they each served to announce happiness or misfortune.

III

Names of various cards, preserved by the Spaniards.[88]

The names of several of these cards preserved by the Spaniards, we think very appropriate. These names are seven.

The Three of Coins, a mysterious number, called the Lord, the Master, devoted to supreme God, with Great Jove.

Three of Cups, called the Lady, devoted to the Queen of Heaven.

The One-eyed or the Ace of Coins, *Phoebeoe lampadis instar.*,[89] devoted to Apollo.

The Cow or Two of Cups, devoted to Apis[90] or Isis.

The Grand Nine, the Nine of Cups; devoted to Destiny.

The Little Nine of Coins, devoted to Mercury.

The Serpent or the Ace of Batons (Ophion)[91] a famous and sacred symbol among the Egyptians.

IV

Mythological attributes of several others.

Several other pictures are accompanied by mythological attributes which were intended to impart to them a particular and secret virtue.

Such as the Two of Coins surrounded by the mystical Belt of Isis.[92]

The Four of Coins, devoted to good Fortune, painted in the midst of the card, on the ball of her foot and her veil deployed.

The Queen of Batons devoted to Ceres; this Lady is crowned with spikes, and carries the skin of a lion in the same way as Hercules, the quintessential farmer.

The Page of Cups carrying his hat in his hand, and respectfully bearing a mysterious cup, covered with a veil; he seems by extending his arm, to push away from himself this cup, to teach us that one has to approach sacred things with fear, and not to seek to know those things which are hidden by discretion.

The Ace of Swords devoted to Mars. The sword is decorated with a crown, a palm and a branch of the olive tree with its berries, to signify victory and its fruits: it is not possible to have a happier card in this suit than this one. It is single, because there is only one way of making war well; that is to prevail in order to achieve peace. This sword is supported by a left arm extended from a cloud.

The card of Batons of the Serpent, about which we spoke above, is decorated with flowers and fruits just as is that of the victorious Sword; this mysterious wand is supported by a right arm extending from a cloud, but bright with rays. These two images seem to say that agriculture and the sword are the two arms of empire and the support of society.

The Cups in general announce happiness, and the Coins wealth.

The Batons are devoted to agriculture and prognosticate more or less abundant harvests, the things which are seen in the countryside or which pertain to it.

They stand for a mixture of good and evil: the four court figures have a green wand, similar to the wand of Fortune, but the other cards express, by compensating symbols, an indication neither good nor bad: two only, whose wands are the color of blood, seems devoted to misfortune.

All the Swords predict only misfortunes, especially those marked with an odd number, that carry still a bloody sword. The only sign of victory, the crowned sword, is in this suit the one sign of a happy event.

V

Comparison between these attributes and the values
that one assigns to the modern cards for divination.

Our fortune tellers, not knowing how to read hieroglyphics, withdrew all the trumps from them and changed the names of Cups, Batons, Coins and Swords, of which they knew neither the etymology, nor the expression; they substituted those of Hearts, Diamonds, Clubs and Spades.[93]

But they retained certain turnings and several expressions the use of which lets us perceive the origin of their divination. According to them,

The Hearts, (Cups), announce happiness.

The Clubs, (Coins), fortune.

Spades, (Swords), misfortune.

Diamonds, (Batons), indifference and the countryside [It is to be noticed that in their symbolic writing system the Egyptians employed squares to express the countryside.].

The Nine of Spades is a disastrous card.

That of Hearts, the card of the Sun; it is easy to recognize the Greater Nine, that of the Cups: just as it is the Lesser Nine in the Nine of Clubs, which they also regard as a happy card.

The Aces announce letters, news: indeed who is more capable to bring news than the One-eyed, (Sun) which traverses, sees and lights all the universe?

The Ace of Spades and the Eight of Hearts predict victory; the Ace Crowned prognosticates in the same way, and all the more happily when it is accompanied by the Cups or the fortunate signs.

The Hearts and more particularly the Ten, reveal the news that must arrive at the city. Cup, symbol of the priesthood, seems intended to express Memphis and the stay of the Pontiffs.

The Ace of Hearts and the Queen of Diamonds announce a happy and faithful tenderness. The Ace of Cups expresses a single happiness, that one possesses alone; the Queen of Diamonds indicates a woman who lives in the countryside, or partly in the countryside: and in which places can one aspire to more truth, of innocence, than in the villages?

The Nine of Clubs and the Queen of Hearts, mark jealousy. However, the Nine of Coins is a fortunate card, a great passion, even happiness; for a lady living in the great world, does not always leave her lover without concern, etc. etc. One finds an infinity of similar things into which it is futile to search, and here already are too many.

VI

Way in which one proceeds to consult the Fates.

Now let us suppose that two men who want to consult the Fates, have, one the twenty-two letter cards, the other the four suits, and that after having shuffled the cards, and each having cut the cards of the other, they start to count together up to the number fourteen, holding the trumps and the lesser cards in their hands face down so that only their backs are visible; then if a suit card turns up in its natural place, that is, which bears the number named, it must be put aside with the number of the accompanying letter card at the same time, which will be placed above: the one who holds the trumps places this same letter there, so that the book of Destiny is always in its entirety, and there is, in no case, an incomplete sentence; then the cards are mixed again and again receive a cut. Finally the cards are run through to the end a third time with the same attentions; and when this operation is completed, it is a question of reading the numbers which express the accompanying letters. Whatever happiness or misfortune is predicted by each one of them, must be combined with what the card announces that corresponds to them, in the same way that their greater or lesser power is determined by the number of this same card, multiplied by that which characterizes the letter. And for this reason the Fool which does not produce anything, is without number; it is, as we have said, the zero of this calculation.[94]

VII

It made up a great portion of ancient wisdom.

But if the sages of Egypt made use of sacred pictures to predict the future, at the same time they spared no indication which could apprise them of future events, with the hope of encouraging their understanding when their search was preceded by dreams which served to help to develop the sentence produced by the images of the fates!

The priests of this ancient people formed in a good hour a learned society, charged to preserve and to extend human knowledge. The priesthood had its leaders, whose names were Jannes and Jambres,[95] that Saint Paul preserved to us in his Second Epistle to Timothy, titles which characterize the august functions of the pontiffs. Jannes [Just as Pharaoh means the Sovereign without being the particular name of any prince who controlled Egypt.] means Explicator, and Jambres Permutater, he who makes wonders.

Jannes and Jambres wrote their interpretations, their discoveries, their miracles. The unbroken continuation of these memoirs [Pope Gelase I[96] put the 491 books of Jannes and Jambres among the number of apocryphal books.] formed a body of science and doctrines, that showed their deep understanding of physics and morals: they observed, under the inspection of their leaders, the course of the stars, the floods of the Nile, the phenomena of meteorology, etc. The kings brought them together sometimes to make use of their consultings.

We see that in the time of the Patriarch Joseph they were called by Pharaoh to interpret a dream; and if Joseph alone had glory to discover the sense of it, none the less it proves that one of the functions of the Magi was to explain dreams.

The Egyptians could not avoid falling into the errors of idolatry [Long still after this time the Magi recognized the finger of God in the Miracles of Moses.]; but back in those times God often moved men with an expression of his will, and if someone boldly questioned him on his eternal decrees, it was at least due to a forgivable desire to seek to penetrate them, when the Divinity seemed, not only to approve, but to even cause, by dreams, this curiosity: also their interpretation was a sublime art, a sacred science of which one made a particular study, reserved for the ministers of the altars: and when the officers of Pharaoh, prisoners with Joseph, grieved themselves not to have anybody to explain their dreams, it is not that they did not have companions in their misfortune; but it was that, locked up in prison by the leader of the militia, there remained nobody among the soldiers who could conduct the religious rituals associated with the sacred tables,[97] let alone anyone having the knowledge to interpret them. The answer that the Patriarch spoke explains their thoughts: the interpretation, he said to them, does it not depend on the Lord? Tell me what you saw.

But to return to the functions of the priests, they began by writing in vulgar letters the dream of which they inquired, as in all divination where they make a positive request of which they proceed to seek the answer in the book of the Fates, and after having mixed the sacred letters they drew the cards, with the attention of scrupulously placing under the one the words of the explanation for which they searched; the sentence formed by these cards was deciphered by Jannes.

Let us suppose, for example, that a Magus had wanted to interpret the dream of Pharaoh about which we will speak presently, as they tried to imitate the miracles of Moses, and that he had drawn the Fortunate Baton, preeminent symbol of agriculture, followed by the Knight and the King [the Page is worth 1, Knight 2, Queen 3, the King 4]; that he drew out at the same time from the book of destiny the cards the Sun, Fortune and the Fool, this will be the first member of the sentence which he seeks. If he draws the Two and the Five of Batons, whose symbol is marked with blood, and of the sacred trumps he draws Typhon and Death, he has obtained a kind of interpretation of the dream of the king,[98] which may be written thus in ordinary letters:

Seven fat cows and seven thin which devour them.

Ace of Batons	The King	The Knight	2 of Batons	5 of Batons
1	4	2	–	–
The Sun	Fortune	The Fool	Typhon	Death

Natural calculation which results from this arrangement.

The Ace of Batons is worth 1. The Sun announces happiness.

The King, 4. Fortune [Preceded by a happy card.] in the same way.

The Knight, 2. The Fool or zero puts the Sun to the hundreds.[99]

Total 7.

The sign of agriculture[100] gives seven.

One will thus read, seven years of a fortunate agriculture will give an abundance a hundred times larger than one will ever have experienced.

The second member of this sentence, closed by the Two and the Five of Batons, gives also the number of seven which, combined with Typhon and Death, announces seven years of food shortage, famine and the evils that it involves.

This explanation will prove even more natural if one pays attention to the direction and the value of the letters that these trumps represent.

The Sun answering to *Gimel*,[101] signifies, in this context, remuneration, happiness.

Fortune or *Lamed* means rule, law, science.

The Fool does not express anything by itself, it corresponds with the *Tau*, it is simply a sign, a mark.

Typhon or *Zain* announces inconstancy, error, faith violated, crime.

Death or *Teth* indicates the action to reap: indeed, Death is a terrible reaper.

Teleuté, which in Greek means the end, seems to be, in this way, a derivative of *Teth*.

It is not difficult to find in Egyptian manners the origin of the greater part of our superstitions: for example, the practice of turning the sieve in order to discover a thief, owes its birth to the habit that these people had to mark robbers with a hot iron, of one ת T, and of one ס *Samech* [*Tau*, sign: *Samech*, adhesion], by putting these two characters, one on the other, to make a figure of it, *signum adherens* [joined sign], which was used to announce that one should be wary of the person who bore it, by which one produces a figure which resembles a pair of scissors cutting a circular screen, which must fall off when the name of the robber is pronounced, and make him known.[102]

Divination by the Bible, the Gospel and our Canonical Books, which is called the oracle of the saints, of which it is spoken in the 109th letter of Saint Augustine and in several Councils, among others that of Orleans; the fates of Saint Martin de Tours which were so famous, deserve to be considered an antidote to Egyptian divination by the book of destiny. It is these same presages that one drew from the Gospel, *ad apperturam libri* [by the open book], when after the election of a bishop one sought to know which position he would control in the Episcopate.[103]

But such is the fate of human things: of such a sublime science, which occupied powerful men, wise philosophers, the greatest saints, it remains among us only the practice of children to draw the beautiful letter.

VIII

Cards to which fortune tellers attach predictions.

It is like a game of Piquet where one shuffles and cuts for the interested person.

One draws a card which is named Ace, the second Seven, and thus while going up to the King: one puts aside all the cards which arrive in the order of calculation that one has just established: that is to say, if by naming Ace, Seven, or such, there is dealt an Ace, a Seven, or that which was named, it is that which it is necessary to put aside. One starts again, always until one has exhausted the cards; and if at the end there do not remain enough cards to reach the King inclusively, one takes up the cards again, without mixing them or cutting them, to complete the calculation to the King.

This operation of the whole deck is made three times in the same way. It is necessary to have the greatest care to arrange the cards which are pulled from the deck, in the order which they arrive, and on the same line, which produces a hieroglyphic sentence;[104] and here is the means of reading it.

All the picture or court cards represent the persons who may be involved in the question; the first which arrives is always the one who it is all about.

The Kings represent sovereigns, parents, generals, magistrates, old men.

The Queens have the same character in their nature relative to the circumstances, that is to say in political matters, serious or merry: sometimes they are powerful, skilful, intriguing, faithful or fickle, are impassioned or indifferent, sometimes rivals, obliging, confidants, perfidious, etc. If there arrive two cards of the same kind, it is the second which plays the supporting role.

The Pages are young people, warriors, those in love, dandies, rivals, etc.

The Sevens and the Eights are young ladies of all kinds. The Nine of Hearts is named, pre-eminently, Card of the Sun, because it always announces brilliant things, pleasures, successes, especially if it is joined together with the Nine of Clubs, which is also a card of marvelous forecasts. The Nines of Diamonds indicates a delay in good or in evil.

The Nine of Spades is the worst card: it predicts only ruin, diseases, death.

The Ten of Hearts indicates the town; that of Diamonds, the countryside; Ten of Clubs, fortune, money; that of Spades, pains and sorrows.

The Aces announce letters, news.

If the four Queens arrive together, that means prattle, quarrels.

Several Pages together announce competition, argument and combats.

The Clubs in general, especially if they are drawn together, announce success, favors, fortune, money.

Diamonds, the countryside, indifference.

Hearts, satisfaction, happiness.

Spades, shortages, concern, sorrows, death.

It is necessary to have a care to arrange the cards in the same order that they are drawn, and on the same line, in order not to disturb the sentence, and to make interpretation easier.

The predicted events, in good or evil, can be more or less advantageous or unhappy, according to how the principal card which announces them is accompanied: Spades, for example, accompanied by Clubs, especially if they arrive between two Clubs, are less dangerous; similarly a Club between two Spades or coupled with a Spade, is less fortunate.

Sometimes the beginning announces disastrous accidents; but the end of the cards is favorable, if there are many Clubs; one regards the risks as reduced, more or less, according to the quantity: if they are followed by the Nine, by the

Ace or the Ten, that proves that one ran great dangers, but that they passed, and that Fortune has had a change of face.

The Aces:

1 of Diamonds, 8 of Hearts, good news.
1 of Hearts, Queen of Spades, visit of a woman.
1 of Hearts, Knave of Hearts, a victory.
1, 9 and Page of Hearts, the happy lover.
1, 10 and 8 of Spades, misfortune.
1 of Spades, 8 of Hearts, a victory.
1 of Clubs, Page of Spades, friendship.

The 7s:

7 and 10 of Hearts, friendship of a young lady.
7 of Hearts, Queen of Diamonds, friendship of a woman.
7 of Diamonds, King of Hearts, delay.

The 9s:

Three Nines or three Tens, success.

The 10s:

10 of Clubs, King of Spades, a present.
10 of Clubs and Page of Clubs, a lover.
10 of Spades, Page of Diamonds, somebody anxious.
10 of Hearts, King of Clubs, sincere friendship.

Notes to Part One

1. Ronald Decker, Thierry Depaulis, and Michael Dummett, *A Wicked Pack of Cards* (New York: St. Martin's Press, 1996), p. 66.

2. Antoine Court de Gébelin, *Monde Primitif, Analysé et Comparé avec le Monde Moderne*, vol. 8 (Paris: privately published, 1781), pp. 371–372. Temperance is also incorrectly labeled "XIII." in Plate V. The Hermit is correctly numbered "VIIII. or IX." in the heading and "IX." in the text on p. 372, but is incorrectly numbered "VIII." where it appears on Plate VI. Stuart Kaplan makes note of these errors in numbering on the plates—see *The Encyclopedia of Tarot*, vol. 1 (Stamford, CT: U.S. Games Systems, 1978), p. 139. In some older Tarots, the Roman numeral IV is printed as

IIII. This is the practice, for example, in the 1761 Tarot of Nicolas Conver, where the Emperor is numbered IIII, the Hermit is numbered VIIII, Temperance is numbered XIIII, and the Moon is numbered XVIIII.

3. Decker, Depaulis, and Dummett, *A Wicked Pack of Cards*, p. 64 and notes 51 and 52 on p. 271.

4. *The Scots Magazine*, MDCCLXXXV, Volume XLVII (Edinburgh: Printed by Murray and Cochrane, 1785), pp. 310–311.

5. The references to the Egyptians and the Bohemians is, of course, to the Romanies, formerly known as Gypsies, who for a long time were presumed to have originated from Egypt. Their actual land of origin is India.

6. Madame la C. d'Helvétius (1719–1800). See Decker, Depaulis, and Dummett, *A Wicked Pack of Cards*, p. 58.

7. The Fool, which is unnumbered in traditional Tarot packs, is the "78th" card referred to by Court de Gébelin.

8. Even in the rather crude redrawing of this trump by Mademoiselle Linote, it is quite obvious that the beast is a dog, not a tiger, and that it is digging with its forepaws at the anus of the Fool. Why? Because the Fool, being mentally unsound, has soiled his hose with excrement after failing to clean himself properly, and the dog smells it and is attracted to it. When he came to design his own Tarot, the Swiss occultist Oswald Wirth took Court de Gébelin literally and made the beast on his Fool a diminutive tiger. Perhaps he would not have done so had he reflected that there are no tigers in Egypt, nor indeed in all of Africa.

   A variation of the traditional figure of the Fool occurs on the Five of Cups in the Sola Busca Tarot, where the Fool is shown with a sheaf of grain slung over his shoulder, the hose on his right leg sagging around his ankle as an extremely diminutive dog bites and pulls at it Again, we must assume that something has attracted the dog to the hose of the Fool, or why would it be tugging at it so obsessively?

9. The reference would seem to be to Book 2, Satire 3, of Horace, which concerns madness; specifically to the following section: "These arms Stertinius, the eighth of the wise men, gave to me, as to a friend, that for the future I might not be roughly accosted without avenging myself. Whosoever shall call me madman, shall hear as much from me [in return]; and shall learn to look back upon the bag that hangs behind him." C. Smart, trans., *The Works of Horace, Translated Literally into English Prose* (New York: Harper & Brothers, 1863), p. 205. An explanatory footnote is attached to this passage which reads, "This passage may be explained by the fifty-third line, *caudam trahat*, or by the fable, which says that Jupiter threw over the shoulder of every mortal two bags; that the faults of his neighbor were put into the bag before him, and his own into that behind him."

10. It is difficult to imagine how the Egyptians could have begun by counting backward, unless they already knew the total, in which case they would have had to first count forward, in the usual way, to attain it.

11. The French term for the Magician that is used in traditional French Tarot decks is *Le Bateleur*, which is usually translated as *Juggler*, in the old sense of a street performer or street magician. He stands before a table of magic tricks such as the cup and balls, and holds in his hand a small baton, or wand. Court de Gébelin is making a comparison here between the French term *Bateleur* and the French word for wand, *baton*.

12. The traditional French names for trumps II and V are *La Papesse* (the Popess, or Female Pope) and *Le Pape* (the Pope). It seems unlikely that these two would be married. However, Court de Gébelin chose to consider them to be an Egyptian priest and priestess, and priests in ancient Egypt could indeed get married.

13. The Tau cross is T-shaped, based on the form of the Greek letter Tau, whereas the cross that surmounts the scepter in the hand of the Empress is the more familiar Christian shape.

14. On the Emperor trump in the traditional French Tarot of Marseilles, the bearded male ruler wears a medallion around his neck on a thick gold chain or braid. This may be the order of knighthood referred to in the text. Mademoiselle Linote, who did the engravings of the plates that accompany Court de Gébelin's Tarot essay, omitted this medallion from her version of this trump, although she included the heavy braided chain around the figure's neck. Some early French Tarots have the medallion, while others do not. For example, the 1760 Tarot of N. Conver shows a medallion around the neck of the Emperor; the Jean Payen Tarot of 1743 does not show a medallion. See Kaplan, *The Encyclopedia of Tarot*, vol. 1 (Stamford, CT: U.S. Games Systems, 1978), pp. 148–149.

15. The most common name in the eighteenth century in France, Italy, and Switzerland for the trump that Court de Gébelin calls the High Priestess was *La Papesse* or *La Papessa*, which means "the Female Pope." The card is an obvious allusion to the medieval legend of Pope Joan. German card makers of this century sometimes named this trump Ivnon, or Juno, after the Roman goddess, but also used the traditional French title *La Papesse*.

16. The reference is to the Bembine Tablet of Isis, a first-century Roman enameled tablet of bronze and silver, some thirty by fifty inches in size, depicting Egyptian figures, which in reproductions of the tablet are labeled with Greek letters. For centuries it has fascinated occultists, from Athanasius Kircher to Éliphas Lévi, from Thomas Taylor to Manly P. Hall. W. Wynn Westcott wrote about it in an 1887 essay titled *The Isiac Tablet of Cardinal Bembo: Its History and Occult Significance* (Bath: M. H. Fryar, 1887); see part five of the present work. I have examined the tablet

and can find no triple cross similar to the one held by the figure of the High Priest, or Pope, in the Tarot.

17. The feast of Pamylia was an Egyptian festival at the spring equinox celebrating the re-creation by Isis of the viral member of Osiris, after it had been cut off and cast away by Set (Greek: Typhon). Pamyles was a priapic god. During the festival, an image of Osiris was carried through the streets along with a triple phallus. "There are others that affirm that one Pamyles, as he was fetching water at Thebes, heard a voice out of the temple of Jupiter, bidding him to publish with a loud voice that Osiris, the great and good king, was now born; and that he thereupon got to be foster-father to Osiris, Saturn entrusting him with the charge of him, and that the feast called Pamylia (resembling the Priapeian procession which the Greeks call Phallephoria) was instituted in honor of him." Plutarch, "Of Isis and Osiris," para. 12 in *Plutarch's Morals*, vol. 4 (Boston, MA: Little, Brown and Company, 1874), pp. 74–75.

18. Court de Gébelin has completely missed the meaning of this trump. It shows a young man between two women who vie for his affections. One woman is a pure and virtuous virgin, the other an ugly, bent-nosed harlot. The moral message is the war between virtue and vice that takes place in the heart of every man. The bow of Cupid points its arrow between the virtuous woman and the man, indicating that the power of love will join them in marriage, overcoming the power of lust. Note that the virtuous woman has her hand resting over the heart of the young man. This detail occurs in a number of older French decks, such as the Jean Payen Tarot of 1743 and the N. Conver Tarot of 1760, which have already been mentioned above.

19. The plate to which Court de Gébelin makes mention, plate 36 in book 3 of *Romanae urbis topographia et antiquitates* by Jean Jacques Boissard (published in Paris: 1597–1602), shows three figures from the waist up. A man and woman gaze into each other's eyes as the man holds the woman's right hand in his right hand. Between and behind them is a young man who looks meaningfully outward at the viewer. He may be intended to represent Cupid. Above his head is the word *Amor* (Love), and above that the words *Fidei Simulacrum* (Image of Fidelity). Beside the woman is the word *Veritas* (Truth), and beside the man the word *Honor* (Honor). See the biographical note on Jean Jacques Boissard.

20. By another interpretation, the female figure representing Strength, or Fortitude, is closing the jaws of the lion, rather than opening them. This seems more appropriate, symbolically. It is difficult to imagine why she would be opening the mouth of the lion, unless she is trying to rip its jaws apart and kill it—but there is nothing in the posture of the figure to indicate a struggle. On the other hand, gently closing the jaws of the maned lion demonstrates her feminine superiority over its brute male force, and adds a mystical level of meaning. In the fifteenth-century Gringonneur Tarot, the female figure is depicted effortlessly snapping a phallic-shaped stone pillar, an obvious

expression of the power of the divine feminine over brute masculinity. See Kaplan, *The Encyclopedia of Tarot*, vol. 1, p. 114.

21. In past centuries, water was often mixed with wine and other alcoholic drinks to increase its volume, and also to lessen its intoxicating effects. For example, it was the practice of the British Navy in the eighteenth century to serve its seamen a daily measure of rum mixed with an equal measure of water. The alcohol to some extent neutralized the bacteria in the impure water, rendering it safer to drink. Water impurities were a constant threat before the innovations of enclosed sewers and proper well construction.

22. In Greek mythology, Astraea (from the Greek for "star maiden") is a virgin goddess of justice who ascended into the stars to escape the evils of humanity. She is associated with the constellation Virgo. The weapon she holds in one of her hands is obviously a sword, not a dagger. This is confirmed by comparing this trump with the same trump in other French Tarots. Court de Gébelin may have been confused by the absence of a cross guard on the sword in his illustration, which might have led him to assume that the weapon was a Scottish dirk or some similar long knife. The dirk is the length of a short sword and lacks a cross guard. In most traditional Tarots, the sword does have a cross guard. The set of scales in her other hand is a traditional symbol of justice.

23. The meaning of our author seems to be that the card should be titled not the Hanged Man but the Hung Foot.

24. Court de Gébelin has again completely misinterpreted one of the trumps. The key to understanding the Hanged Man is the very fact that he is suspended between heaven and earth. In the literal sense, he is obviously a criminal who is being tortured or punished, but in the symbolic sense, he is caught in a timeless transition between one state of being and another, between life and death, between the physical realm and the spiritual realm. It appears that Court de Gébelin may not have been the first to commit this error. In a French pack conjecturally dated circa 1720, this trump is labeled *La prudence* and shows a young courtier dancing on one foot, with his hands at his hips (see Kaplan, *The Encyclopedia of Tarot*, vol. 1, p. 146). If the conjectured date is anywhere near accurate, it puts this card decades prior to the interpretation of Court de Gébelin. A few later Tarot designers followed Court de Gébelin's lead and also called this trump Prudence. Etteilla changed the figure of Prudence into a woman who hesitates with her foot raised to step over a serpent. In some Tarots, the male figure of the Hanged Man is shown in the ridiculous posture Court de Gébelin placed him in, standing upright on one foot, which is tied and staked to the ground—see the eighteenth-century Vandenborre Belgian Tarot in Kaplan's *The Encyclopedia of Tarot*, vol. 1, p. 145. It was more usual for nineteenth-century occultists to identify the virtue of prudence with the Hermit, or Sage.

25. See the biographical note on Diogenes of Sinope.

26. See the biographical note on Heraclitus of Ephesus.

27. A comparison is being made here between the Christian hermits who lived in Egypt and surrounding lands during the early centuries of the first millennium and the gymnosophists of India, who were written about in Greek works such at the biography of the mage Apollonius of Tyana by Philostratus (born c. 170). The Christian hermits were noted for their extreme austerities. The most famous among them was Simeon Stylites (c. 390–459), who is reputed to have lived on top of a tall stone pillar for thirty-seven years without ever descending to the ground. Court de Gébelin is making the point that the gymnosophists of India, a class of philosophers who lived naked out in the open, were even more severe in their self-denial.

28. The droplets that fall from the Sun are generally known as *yods*, after the tenth letter in the Hebrew alphabet, which has a similar shape. They are sometimes characterized as the sweat of the Sun. Their sperm-like shape suggests impregnation of the Earth by the Sun. They are twelve in number, which is a significant number, being the same as the signs in the zodiac and the hours in a day. (It was the practice in Renaissance magic to divide the day into twelve equal hours and the night into twelve equal hours.) However, this number may merely be accidental on this design of Mademoiselle Linote. It is curious that Court de Gébelin made no mention at all of the two figures, young boys who appear to be twins, who stand together in front of a low stone wall. Perhaps they did not appear on the Tarot card he used as his reference. One boy has his hand on the shoulder of the other and may be comforting him. A possible interpretation is that they represent the brothers Romulus and Remus, and the low wall is the foundation for the wall around the city of Rome.

29. What Court de Gébelin refers to as the tears of the Moon, the yods that fall from her orb, is often called the sweat of the Moon, and is identified with the falling dew. Their number, 20, does not appear to me to be occultly significant. It was the practice of Greek witches during classical times to ritually torture the Moon, so that her sweat would fall to the grass, where it could be gathered up by soaking it into sheets of cloth and wringing them out. Dew gathered in this way was believed to hold great potency and to be a powerful poison. It was also a fable that the sweat of the Moon, falling on the tongues of dogs while they were howling at her orb, would drive them mad.

30. "They say, that the Egyptians celebrate the festival of Isis in that part of the year in which she bewails Osiris; that then the Nile begins to ascend; and that the vulgar of the natives say, that the tears of Isis cause the Nile to increase and irrigate the fields." Pausanias, bk. 10, chap. 32; Thomas Taylor, trans, *Description of Greece, by Pausanias*, vol. 3 (London: R. Priestly, 1824), p. 174.

31. The Pillars of Hercules were said by the ancient Greek poet Pindar to mark the extreme bounds of the world beyond which it was not possible to travel either by sea or by land. Their conjectured location varied from writer to writer. Pindar placed them in Hyperborea.

32. The Tropic of Capricorn and the Tropic of Cancer, which mark the limits of the travel of the Sun northward and southward in the sky during the course of the year.

33. "And in what is called among them the Komasiæ of the gods, they carry about golden images — two dogs, one hawk, and one ibis; and the four figures of the images they call four letters. For the dogs are symbols of the two hemispheres, which, as it were, go round and keep watch; the hawk, of the sun, for it is fiery and destructive (so they attribute pestilential diseases to the sun); the ibis, of the moon, likening the shady parts to that which is dark in plumage, and the luminous to the light. And some will have it that by the dogs are meant the tropics, which guard and watch the sun's passage to the south and north. The hawk signifies the equinoctial line, which is high and parched with heat, as the ibis the ecliptic." Saint Clement of Alexandria, *Stromata*, bk. 5, chap. 7, trans. William Wilson, from *Ante-Nicene Christian Library*, vol. 2 (Edinburgh: T. & T. Clark, 1869), p. 246.

34. There is no butterfly on a flower in the depiction of the Star that occurs in *Monde Primitif*. A bird, not a butterfly, on a bush, not a flower, does occur on traditional French Tarot decks of Court de Gébelin's period, such as on the Jean Payen deck of 1743 and the N. Conver deck of 1760, to which I have previously referred. On the Lando Tarot of 1760, a bird is very clearly drawn on a stump from which sprouts a sprig of leaves, which bear a vague resemblance to a butterfly—see Kaplan, *The Encyclopedia of Tarot*, vol. 1, p. 150. On the Tarot of Marseilles by B. P. Grimaud, which bears the date 1748 on the Two of Coins, it is a bird on a bush. Some Tarots of the period show only the bush, not the bird. The butterfly appears to be a figment of Court de Gébelin's imagination.

35. It is not unreasonable to assume that the star referred to in the title of this trump is Sirius, the Dog Star. Sirius is the brightest true star of the heavens. However, in past times it was common in astrology and occultism to refer to the planets as "stars," and the planet Venus is the brightest thing in the sky after the Sun and the Moon, so it is very possible that the trump the Star refers to is Venus.

36. It seems plausible upon initial consideration that the seven stars around the largest star represent the seven planets. However, in old woodcuts, the Sun and Moon are usually depicted as disks, or as a disk and a crescent, not as stars. Only the number of these surrounding stars, seven, inclines one to the view that they are the planets, and in the Lando Tarot of 1760 their number is five, not seven. If the seven surrounding stars do represent the seven visible planets, it becomes more likely that the large star is Sirius rather than Venus.

37. Maneros is referred to by Plutarch in his essay "Of Isis and Osiris" (sec. 17) and by Herodotus in his *History* (bk. 2, chap. 79). The following quotation is from Louis C. Elson's *Curiosities of Music: A Collection of Facts Not Generally Known, Regarding the Music of Ancient and Savage Nations* (Boston, MA: Oliver Ditson, 1880), pp. 16–17.

   "Among the mythical musical personages of the earliest Egyptian music, may be mentioned Maneros, who was son of the first king of Egypt, who succeeded the second dynasty of demi gods. He seems to be analogous to the Linus, (son of Apollo), of the Greeks; he died young, and the first song of the Egyptian music was in his honor; it was a lament over his untimely end, the swift passing away of Youth, Spring, etc. The song was sung under various guises, for Maneros, Linus, Adonis, etc., among various ancient nations, and Herodotus was surprised at hearing it in Egypt. But in course of time the song itself, and not the king's son, was called Maneros, and gradually diffused its influence, (the warning of the passing away of Joy) through Egyptian social life; at their banquets a perfectly painted statue of a corpse was borne round and shown to each guest, and there was sung the following warning:

   'Cast your eyes upon this corpse
   You will be like this after Death.
   Therefore drink and be merry now.'"

38. It is interesting to note that the figure of the Devil, which Court de Gébelin calls *Typhon*, the Greek name for the Egyptian god of evil, *Set* (or *Seth*), is wearing a collar and a belt. Since the figure is otherwise naked, this seems odd, unless the collar is intended to support the bat wings on its back, and the belt supports the male genitalia. It may be that this is a depiction of a human figure wearing a costume to represent Satan, or some other evil god or demon. That the horns are the horns of a stag rather than those of a goat suggests that it may be a pagan deity. The figure is hermaphroditic, having female breasts and a penis.

39. The story of Rhampsinitus related by Court de Gébelin occurs in Herodotus, *The History*, bk. 2, chap. 121–122, trans. George Rawlinson, vol. 2 (London: John Murray, 1858), pp. 191–197.

40. When you have an angel sounding a trumpet and human figures rising up out of the ground, it's difficult to imagine what other interpretation you could put on this card except the resurrection of the dead. Court de Gébelin's description of it as creation seems completely unfounded. In Genesis, God created Adam, then Eve— he didn't create a child.

41. Court de Gébelin had it fixed in his head that the Egyptians began counting at the end rather than at the beginning. This is why he was so certain trump XXI represents time rather than the world. In support of his interpretation, the changing of the seasons was said by the ancient Greeks to be the dance of the Horae, goddesses who represented the orderly progress of time. Usually they were said

to be three in number and were associated with the three seasons of the Greeks: Thallo (spring), Auxo (summer), and Carpo (autumn). Later, when four seasons were recognized, their number was increased to four. The short batons, or wands, held in the hands of the dancer are a curious feature of this trump—there does not appear to be a correspondence for these wands in classic mythology. Her posture is an obvious counterpoint to that of the Hanged Man.

42. It is more usual to associate the four Kerubic symbols with the four fixed signs of the zodiac: Lion-Leo, Bull-Taurus, Man-Aquarius, and Eagle-Scorpio. In the sense that the zodiac represents the revolution of the year, Court de Gébelin is not wrong to link the Kerubim, at the corners of the zodiac, with the seasons.

43. The pyramid is a structure with a square base and four sides, each of which is in the shape of a triangle: $3 + 4 = 7$. Symbolically, the Egyptian pyramid represents the coming forth of spirit (3) from the dimensionless point at the apex (1), and its expansion downward into manifestation, where it is materialized (4). In this sense, the pyramid is a physical model of the emanation of the universe.

44. The "Player at Cups" is the Magician, or Juggler, who entertained crowds in the marketplace with the illusion of the cups and balls, which stage magicians still use to this day. Three of the trumps, called *oudlers* (honors), have a special higher value in the French game of Tarot: the Fool (*excuse*), the Magician (*paguet*), and the World, which does not seem to have a special title attached to it in the game of Tarot. These three trumps are also sometimes known as *bouts* (ends).

45. French Tarot can be played by two, three, four, five, or six players. During the nineteenth century, the least common number of players was two. The anonymous author of the pamphlet *Règles du Jeu de Tarots* (*Rules of the Game of Tarot*), published in Besançon in 1862, wrote on page 4, "Le jeu à 2 ou *nemo* est trop peu usagé pour qu'on s'occupe de ses règles, qui sont, du reste, peu déterminées." ("The game of 2 or *nemo* is too little used to provide its rules, which are, moreover, little known.")

46. For a complete and lucid description of the French game of Tarot as it is presently played, see Michael Dummett, *Twelve Tarot Games* (London: Duckworth, 1980), pp. 30–52.

47. XIX. Sun and XVIII. Moon.

48. XVII. Dog Star (Star).

49. The "seven Tarots" referred to by Court de Gébelin appear to be the same as the "seven Tarots" enumerated in the previous section on counting the points in the game of Tarot. They are 0. Fool, I. Juggler, XXI. Time (World), and the four Kings. Here, de Gébelin links these cards with the seven stars in the constellation *Ursa Major*, the Great Bear, more commonly known as the Big Dipper.

50. II. High Priestess, V. High Priest (Pope), III. Queen (Empress), IV. King (Emperor).

51. VIII. Justice, XI. Fortitude (Strength), XII. Prudence (Hanged Man), XIV. Temperance.

52. VII. Osiris Triumphant (Chariot).

53. XXI. Time (World), X. Wheel of Fortune, I. Juggler, 0. Fool, XVI. Castle of Plutus (Tower), XV. Typhon (Devil), XIII. Death.

54. IX. Sage (Hermit).

55. The trumps VI. Marriage (Lovers) and XX. Last Judgment appear to have been omitted from this listing.

56. *Mémoires Concernant les Chinois* (*Memoirs Concerning the Chinese*), an encyclopedia of Chinese history and biography published in fifteen volumes over the years 1776–1791 under the general editorship of Henri-Léonard Jean-Baptiste Bertin (1720–1792), who was a minister of state for the French kings Louis XV (reigned 1715–1774) and Louis XVI (reigned 1774–1792).

57. Spanish playing card decks have either 48 cards, with pip cards 1–9, plus King (*rey*), Knight (*caballo*), and Knave (*sota*) in each suit, or 40 cards, with pip cards 1–7, plus King, Knight, and Knave in each suit.

58. The suit of Coins in Spanish card decks is known as *oros*, or golds—that is, gold coins.

59. Charles du Fresne, Sieur du Cange (1610–1688). About him Voltaire observed in the fifth volume of his work *Siècles de Louis XIV et Louis XV* (Paris: 1817, p. 209), "One is appalled at the immensity of his learning and his labours."

60. This burning of dice and cards took place in Bologna in 1424 in front of the church of San Petronio. "A pulpit had to be erected in the open, and so great was the force and pathos of the preacher's eloquence that he ended by so far uprooting this vice that, during the last days of Lent, the gamblers came one by one to deposit their gaming implements with the saint, who, after amassing a huge quantity of these objects, caused them to be made into a great bonfire, which he himself kindled amid the applause of the assembled multitude. There was one class of persons, however, to whom this spectacle afforded no kind of satisfaction, and those were the card manufacturers and sellers, one of whom came to Bernardine with the complaint that he was depriving him of his living." Paul Thureau-Dangin, *Saint Bernardine of Siena* (London: J. M. Dent and Co., 1906), p. 72.

61. It was the custom in Italy for the nobility to wear masks while gambling in the gaming houses, or *ridotti*, as they were called, to conceal their identities. Indeed, it was a requirement—only the croupiers (*barnabotti*) were permitted to go unmasked.

62. David (K. of Spades), Charlemagne (K. of Hearts), Caesar (K. of Diamonds), Alexander (K. of Clubs).

63. Pallas (Q. of Spades), Judith (Q. of Hearts), Rachael (Q. of Diamonds), Argine (Q. of Clubs). Argine is an anagram for Regina.

64. Ogier (P. of Spades), La Hire (P. of Hearts), Hector (P. of Diamonds), Lancelot (P. of Clubs).

65. Some nineteenth-century authorities on cards believed that the word *Tuchim* derived from the Arabic word *tu'chan*, which signifies obscurity or darkness. See William Hughes Willshire, *A Descriptive Catalogue of Playing and Other Cards in the British Museum* (London: Chiswick Press, 1876), p. 9.

66. The reference here is to the *Poetic Edda*, where Odin, the father of the gods, sacrifices one of his eyes to Mimir in order to drink the magic waters of Mimir's well and learn his future fate.

67. Thoth and Mercury are not the same god, although they were often equated by the Romans, who made a habit of projecting their own gods onto the pantheons of foreign cultures. They did this most often and most completely with the Greek pantheon of gods, but also with that of the Egyptians.

    Thoth shares some qualities with the Greek god Hermes, whom the Romans equated with their own Mercury. Both Thoth and Hermes are gods of wisdom. Thoth most often is depicted in human form with the head of an ibis, a large Egyptian waterfowl with a long, curved beak. He was particularly associated with writing, and with the invention of various studies such as astronomy, medicine, geometry, and magic. He gave advice to Isis regarding the resurrection of her husband and brother, Osiris, after Osiris was murdered by Set. In Egyptian scrolls and tomb art, Thoth is shown interrogating the newly dead and writing down their responses. The baboon is his sacred animal.

    By contrast, Hermes takes the form of a young man who carries a winged staff on which two serpents entwine, called a caduceus. He has a pair of magic sandals that enable him to fly through the air, but sometimes he is depicted with wings on his heels. He is a god of commerce, merchants, money, gambling, and deception. Able to travel easily between the worlds of gods and mortals, he carried messages for the gods and was associated with prophetic dreams. The most important of his functions was that of psychopomp, the escort for the souls of the newly dead into the Underworld. He is a doorkeeper or guardian of gateways.

    Herodotus was the first Greek writer to identify Hermes with Thoth. Plato found the two gods to be dissimilar. Their qualities are sometimes merged under the compound name Hermes-Thoth, or more particularly concerning magic and alchemy, under the name Hermes Trismegistus (Thrice-great).

68. The Landsknecht (plural: Landsknechte) were a force of German mercenary pikemen who fought in European wars during the late fifteenth and sixteenth centuries. The term literally translates as "servant of the land." It first appeared in the German language around 1470. The cards of the deal are thus being described as pikemen.

69. The use by the Comte de Mellet of the term *universe* for the trump the World is interesting because this is the term by which this card is more commonly known today by occultists. S. L. MacGregor Mathers used it in his 1888 essay *The Tarot*

(New York: Samuel Weiser, n.d., p. 16), and his infamous student Aleister Crowley followed suit in his Book of Thoth Tarot deck—see Aleister Crowley, *The Book of Thoth* (1944; repr., New York: Samuel Weiser, 1974), pp. 116–119.

70. This interpretation of the Last Judgment is ridiculous, but it is necessary if one is going to begin the sequence of the trumps at its end, as Court de Gébelin and the Comte de Mellet were determined to do. You can hardly begin the story of creation with the last trump (although, of course, this is exactly what they did).

71. *Duo in carne una* is Latin for "the two become one."

72. It is not at all clear that the two beasts on the trump of the Moon in the older French Tarots are a wolf and a dog. They look more like two dogs to me. In the version of the card in Court de Gébelin's book, they are virtually identical. In the Joannes Pelagius Mayer deck, circa 1750, both beasts have drooping dog ears (see Kaplan, *The Encyclopedia of Tarot*, vol. 1, p. 136). This is also true in the F. Gumppenberg Tarot of the late eighteenth century (Kaplan, p. 154). Many nineteenth-century Tarots show floppy ears for both beasts, such as the Edoardo Dotti Milan Tarot of 1862 and the Giuseppe Versino Piedmontese Tarot of the same year (Kaplan, pp. 160–161). In the Jean Payen deck of 1743, one dog is light and the other shadowed, presumably to express the light and dark phases of the Moon, but this may have suggested to some interpreters that the beasts are two different species (Kaplan, p. 148).

73. It is possible that *N* stands for *naissance* (birth) and *M* stands for *mort* (death). The sexual climax was known in French as *la petite mort* (the little death). The Comte de Mellet appears to be contrasting sexual creation of children with sterile sexuality or masturbation, the spilling of the seed onto the ground. Note the reference a little further down to the theft of the penis of Osiris by Typhon, and to Typhon as "the father of evils which were spread on the ground." In attempting to steal the creative power of Osiris, Typhon perverts and wastes it.

74. In chapter 19 of the *Life of Pythagoras* by Iamblichus (c. 245–c. 325), the Greek philosopher Pythagoras (570–495 BCE) has a habit of showing his "golden thigh" to men he meets on his travels, such as Abaris the Hyperborean. This is a euphemism for displaying his erect penis, or perhaps even for homosexual union. See *Iamblichus' Life of Pythagoras*, trans. Thomas Taylor (London: printed by A. J. Valpy, 1818), p. 67. When men swore an oath in Old Testament times, they would sometimes place their hand "under the thigh" of the man to whom they made the oath—that is, they would cup the other man's testicles with their hand. See Genesis 24:2–9.

75. Bacchus, the Dionysus of the Greeks, was said to have been born from the thigh of Zeus; however, Minerva, the Athena of the Greeks, was said to have been born from the forehead of Zeus. To be "born from the thigh"—that is, from the penis—is to be born in the usual way by sexual coupling. To be "born from the head"—by the word, or logos—is an intellectual birth.

76. *Suspenso pede* is Latin for "with halting steps."

77. The monstrous figures on the Wheel of Fortune, which the Comte de Mellet took to be a rabbit, a monkey, and a man, are too badly drawn to be identified with any certainty. They all have tails in the design of Mademoiselle Linote, which would lead one to doubt that one of the figures is human, unless the tails are presumed to be part of costumes. All three figures have tails on other French Tarots of the eighteenth century, such as that of Jean Payen (1743) and N. Conver (1760), but not all Tarot decks of the period show all three tails.

78. The fortune-telling device called the Wheel of Pythagoras is illustrated on page 62 of *The Familiar Astrologer* by Raphael [Robert Cross Smith] (London: Printed for John Bennett, 1831). The Latin alphabet of 24 letters (the I and J are combined, as are the U and V) is written clockwise in a circle, beginning at the nine o'clock position. A number is assigned to each letter: A (1), B (3), C (22), D (24), E (22), F (3), G (7), H (6), I/J (20), K (1), L (10), M (23), N (12), O (17), P (14), Q (27), R (13), S (9), T (8), U/V (2), W (4), X (5), Y (11), and Z (16). The open middle of this wheel is divided into four quadrants by a cross through its center. The two upper quadrants are labeled "fortunate" and the two lower quadrants "evil." The two quadrants on the left are labeled "short time" and the two on the right "long time." This produces the four combinations: fortunate—short time; fortunate—long time; evil—short time; and evil—long time. Each quadrant has numbers written in it: 1, 2, 3, 4, 7, 9, 11, 13, 14 in the upper-left; 5, 6, 8, 12, 15, 18, 21 in the lower-left; 16, 17, 19, 20, 22, 23, 10, 26, 27 in the upper-right; and 24, 25, 28, 29, 30 in the lower-right.

    George Oliver had the following to say about the Wheel of Pythagoras: "Some authors have ascribed to Pythagoras the invention of an onomantic kind of arithmetic, in which particular numbers are assigned to the letters of the alphabet, the planets, the signs of the zodiac, and the days of the week; thereby resolving questions concerning nativities, victory, journeys, thefts, prosperity or adversity, life or death. Dr Fludd, in his 'Microcosm,' affirms, that future events may be prognosticated by virtue of a wheel invented by Pythagoras, whereby everything connected with the life of man may be truly foretold. There are great doubts, however, whether this wheel was not an invention of the cabalists of an age long subsequent to the time of Pythagoras, because it is not mentioned by any ancient writer." George Oliver, *The Pythagorean Triangle; or, The Science of Numbers* (London: John Hogg & Co., 1875), pp. 202–203.

    On this topic, see also Thomas Stanley, *The History of Philosophy*, vol. 3, sec. 1, chap. 15 (London: Printed for Humphrey Moseley and Thomas Dring, 1660), pp. 65–66. Stanley wrote that Trithemius and others acknowledge the Wheel to be "an invention of later times." Rosa Baughan states that the Wheel of Pythagoras and the way of working it appear in "a work in old French on Chiromancy and Geomancy, compiled by the Sieur de Peruchio, and published at Paris, 1657." The method given by Baughan appears to be the same as that given by Raphael, which is not surprising since Raphael quotes from the work of Peruchio on another topic. See Baughan, *The Influence of the Stars: A Book of Old World Lore* (London: Kegan Paul, Trench, Trübner & Co., 1891), pp. 191–194. The Wheel of Pythagoras forms the frontispiece of this work, where it is labeled "from an old woodcut, date 1657."

79. The Greek poet Hesiod (c. 700 BCE) in his *Works and Days* divided human history into five periods, or ages. The earliest is the Golden Age, a time of harmony when men and gods lived together in peace under the rule of Cronos; the Silver Age, dominated by immaturity and strife in which men refused to worship the gods and were destroyed for their impiety by Zeus; the Bronze Age, during which mankind devoted itself to warfare; the Heroic Age, an age of heroes; and the Iron Age, characterized by lies, crime, and dishonor in which the gods turn their backs on mankind due to its evils. We are still living in the Iron Age. The Roman poet Ovid (43 BCE–18 CE) reduced the number of ages to four in his *Metamorphoses* by excluding the Heroic Age. It seems that the Comte de Mellet had Ovid's four ages in mind when he wrote his essay, since he made no mention of the Heroic Age but did notice the ages of Gold, Silver, Bronze, and Iron, although the Bronze Age is merely alluded to in passing.

80. The Comte de Mellet's interpretation of the trump the Lovers as a choice between vice and virtue differs from that of Court de Gébelin, who saw this card only as a card of marriage.

81. The fifth trump is usually depicted in older Tarot decks as the Pope, but in some decks he is shown as the figure of Jupiter, father of the gods. For example, in the Tarot of L. Carey (Strasbourg, 1791), Jupiter is depicted standing naked on the wings of a golden eagle, with thunderbolts clutched in both his hands (see Kaplan, *The Encyclopedia of Tarot*, vol. 1, p. 155). Jupiter appears on this trump in some modern decks that are reproductions of older designs, such as the Tarot d'Epinal, which is based on a nineteenth-century deck, and the 1JJ Swiss Tarot, where a tired and somewhat morose-looking Jupiter sits leaning with his head on his hand. In these decks where Jupiter takes the place of the Pope, Juno with her peacocks fills the role of the Popess, or High Priestess.

82. The French term *à-tout* means an "asset."

83. The hieroglyphic writing of the ancient Egyptians, much like that of the modern Chinese, did not employ an alphabet of letters representing simple sounds that were combined to make words, but rather pictographs, many of which stood for whole words or ideas. As a consequence, it could not express meaning with only 22 symbols, but required over two thousand symbols. The Egyptians also used an Hieratic script, which was a simplified form of the hieroglyphic characters—however, the structure of Hieratic writing was the same as hieroglyphic, so the same limitation applied.

84. Joseph used his silver drinking cup for purposes of divination. See Genesis 44:5.

85. The rod of Moses, also known as the rod of God, was used by Moses to call down plagues on Egypt (Exodus 9:22–23, 10:12–13), to part the Red Sea (Exodus 14:16), and to bring water out of a rock (Exodus 17:5–7). God transformed the rod into a serpent, and back to a rod, when Moses was alone (Exodus 4:2–4), but it was the Rod of Aaron that was transformed into a serpent before the magicians of Pharaoh, who did the same trick with their own rods (Exodus 7:10–12). Aaron also used his rod to call down plagues on Egypt (Exodus 7:19–21, 8:5–7, 8:16–17). It has been speculated that the rod of Moses and the rod of Aaron were a single rod used by both men at different times.

86. Urim and Thummim were two objects kept in the breastplate of the High Priest of Israel (Exodus 28:30) that were used for divination, when seeking a divine judgment on a question. They gave either a positive or a negative response. The teraphim were small carved figures used as household gods. Rachel stole the teraphim from her father, Laban (Genesis 31).

87. Divination by arrows was called *belomancy*. Divination by swords was known as *macharomancy*. Divination by axes was called *axinomancy*. A variety of methods were used, but they usually involved interpreting the way the weapon pointed when cast or spun.

88. These names refer to Spanish playing cards.

89. *Phoebeae lampadis instar* (the light of the sun). From Virgil's *Aeneid*, bk. 3, line 637.

90. The Apis bull of Egyptian mythology, son of the goddess Hathor, and worshipped at Memphis.

91. Orpheon (Greek: serpent) was the ruler of the world in the most ancient times. He was cast down from Olympus into the sea by Cronus, who replaced him as ruler. A serpentine ribbon or banner sometimes coils around the staff on the Ace of Batons —see this card in the Trappola Tarot, designed in 1782 (Kaplan, *The Encyclopedia of Tarot*, vol. 1, p. 57).

92. On traditional Spanish and French Two of Coins, a banner surrounds the two foliate disks that is in the shape of an inverted *S*. Flowering plants terminate each end of this banner, which is not a lemniscate, but open and unjoined. The name of the card maker usually appears on this banner.

93. The Comte de Mellet associated the Tarot suit of Coins with the common suit of Clubs, and the Tarot suit of Batons with the common suit of Diamonds. It is more usual to assign the Tarot suits to the suits of common playing cards in this way: Swords—Spades; Batons—Clubs; Cups—Hearts; and Coins—Diamonds (see Kaplan, *The Encyclopedia of Tarot*, vol. 1, p. 5). However, the Hermetic Order of the Golden Dawn followed the Comte de Mellet's assignment—see Israel Regardie,

"Second Knowledge Lecture," *The Golden Dawn* (St. Paul, MN: Llewellyn Publications), p. 128 of the 4th edition of 1971, or p. 66 of the 6th edition of 1989.

94. This description is not entirely clear, but it is based on the similar method of card selection that the Comte de Mellet later describes for divination with common playing cards—see note 104. By comparing the two methods, it is possible to determine the author's intention.

The divination is done by two people together. The Tarot is divided into two packs, one containing the 22 trumps and the other the 56 suit cards. Both are shuffled, and each person cuts the pack of the other person. Holding the packs face down, they simultaneously turn up cards one by one as they count up to 14, which is the number of cards in each suit. They continue counting until a suit card is turned up that is the same number as the number of the count. For example, if the count is at 13, and the Queen of Cups is turned up, that is the 13th card in the suit of Cups. That card is put aside face up, and above it is placed face up the corresponding trump that was dealt at the same time, whatever it happens to be. De Mellet calls the trumps the "letter cards" because he associated them with the Hebrew letters.

When the count of 14 reaches its end or a card has been selected, a new count of 14 begins on the next card, and the card selection continues in this way to the end of the suit pack. The final count always ends on the King, the 14th card, so if the end of the pack is reached before the number 14 is named, the discarded cards are picked up and turned face down, and the count is continued to 14 without shuffling them. Similarly, when the person counting out the trumps reaches the end of his pack, he picks up the discarded cards without shuffling, turns them face down, and continues until the suit pack has been exhausted.

The packs are then shuffled, cut, and run through two more times in this same manner. The number of pairs selected by this method depends on chance and will vary. It is possible that no suit card will fall on its own number when running through the suit pack. It is even possible, though unlikely, that no suit card will be selected after running through the pack three times, in which case the divination would have to be abandoned or repeated.

95. These are the usual names attached to the Egyptian magicians who contested against Moses and Aaron in feats of magic before Pharaoh. See Exodus 7:10–12.

96. Pope Gelasius I (d. 496 CE). In a work attributed to him titled *Decretum Gelasianum*, the apocryphical text *Pœnitentia Jannis et Mambre* (*Book of Jannes and Jambres*) is prohibited and condemned. It detailed the doings of the famed Egyptian magicians Jannes and Jambres. The Comte de Mellet may have confused this work with the Hermetic books when he wrote of 491 books.

97. That is, the Tarot cards.

98. The dreams of Pharaoh interpreted by Joseph are described in Genesis 41:1–7.

99. The Sun is two places to the left from the Fool, just as the 1 in 100 is two places to the left from the final zero.

100. The "sign of agriculture" is the staff in the suit of Batons, or Wands.

101. De Mellet applied the trumps to the Hebrew letters in reverse order. Consequently, the third Hebrew letter, *Gimel*, is placed by de Mellet on the third-from-last Tarot trump, which is XIX. The Sun. The seventh Hebrew letter, *Zain*, falls on the seventh trump from the end, XV. Typhon (the Devil). He placed 0. The Fool at the beginning of the trumps, which for de Mellet was their end, so it receives the final Hebrew letter, *Tau*.

102. The symbol described by de Mellet is an X (cross tipped at an angle) above an O. Divination by the sieve was a form of divination to discover a thief that was used in rural Europe during the Middle Ages and Renaissance, in which a round sieve for sifting flour was held vertically between the downturned blades of a large pair of shears. Because the sieve was so large, the shears could just barely be opened wide enough to grip it. The handles of the shears were in turn supported only by the tips of the index fingers of two people standing on either side, so that the grip of the vertical shears on the round sides of the sieve was precarious, allowing the sieve to slip out and fall at the slightest faltering of the finger pressure on the shears. One by one, the names of those suspected of the theft were spoken aloud. When the name of the thief was uttered, the sieve dropped out from between the blades of the shears and fell to the floor.

103. This was a form of book divination, or bibliomancy, by which the Bible or some other holy book was opened at random and a verse selected with the eyes closed. Reading the verse provided an oracle concerning the question being asked, and this verse was interpreted both explicitly and symbolically.

104. This is very similar to the method of selecting the Tarot cards that was described in section 7 of de Mellet's essay, but instead of two people, only a single person selects the cards for the divination layout, which forms a single line of cards. The cards described are ordinary playing cards, a Piquet pack from which the cards Deuce to Six have been removed from each suit, resulting in a pack of only 32 cards. This is why de Mellet jumps from the Ace to the Seven in his description of the count. A Piquet pack was commonly used by French fortune-tellers, in contrast to the English card readers of the eighteenth century, who used a full deck of 52 cards—see part eight of the present work for the English Method.

De Mellet is not perfectly clear in his description, but I will give my interpretation based on a comparison of his method for selecting playing cards with his method for selecting Tarot cards. The Piquet pack is shuffled and cut. Then the cards are dealt out face up one by one, and as each is turned, the dealer counts from Ace to King in the following manner: "Ace, Seven, Eight, Nine, Ten, Knave, Queen, King." When the card turned up happens to correspond with the card named in the count, the count is stopped and the card put aside. No notice is taken of the suits during this selection process, only the numbers.

The count from Ace to King is begun again on the next card without shuffling the deck, and repeated until the end of the deck is reached. The count must end on the King, so if the deck is exhausted before the final count reaches the King, the count is paused and the discarded cards taken up in their order, then the count is resumed and continued to the King. The deck is shuffled and cut, and the same procedure is done two more times. The number of cards selected by this method will vary, since the selection process is dependent on chance. Each time a card falls on its own number in the count, it is put aside. The cards selected form a line from left to right and are read based on their interrelationship.

It is my belief that de Mellet's method for selecting cards from the Piquet pack is a folk method in use during his own period—I do not believe he invented it. However, he was probably the first to apply it to the Tarot cards. It seems obvious to me that the method of card selection for divination with the Tarot is based on an existing method used to select common playing cards from the Piquet pack.

PART TWO

The Symbolism of the Tarot
by
P. D. OUSPENSKY

Translated from the Russian by A. L. Pogossky

INTRODUCTION
TO PART TWO

*T*he Symbolism of the Tarot: Philosophy of Occultism in Pictures and Numbers was one of the earlier works of Pyotr Demianovich Ouspenskii (1878–1947), whose name appears most often in English publications as P. D. Ouspensky. Published in St. Petersburg in Russian under the title *Symboly Taro* in 1912, it was translated into English by Madame Aleksandra Loginova Pogosskaia (1848–1921), better known to English readers as Madame A. L. Pogossky (or Pogosky). This English edition was published in St. Petersburg, Russia, in 1913 by the Trood Printing and Publishing Company. In 1931 Ouspensky incorporated the essay in a slightly modified form into his book *A New Model of the Universe* (see chapter 5 of that work). The present text is drawn from the Dover edition of 1976, which is a reprint of the 1913 English edition.

Ouspensky's analysis of the Tarot is based on the notion put forward by the French occultist Jean-Baptiste Pitois (1811–1877), who wrote under the name Paul Christian, that the Tarot originated in Egypt, where the trumps were preserved in a pillared gallery beneath the Sphinx in two parallel rows of eleven trumps.[1] By trying to force his interpretation of the trumps to accommodate this fanciful parallel structure, Ouspensky strains the meanings of the cards. His interpretations are interesting and insightful, but should not be accepted as the only possible analysis of the trumps, nor even as the best analysis.

A typically Russian pessimism about life is evident at the end of Ouspensky's sequence of the trumps, where the soul, having attained the highest level of wisdom, finds only suffering. It cannot reconcile what is small with what is great in its own nature. This bleak view of transcendence is not to be taken too seriously. While it is true that every pilgrim on the road of self-awareness must face a period of trial, most mystics assert that this trial can be overcome, and that on the other side lies pure bliss.

The description of the trump the Fool, given by Ouspensky in his essay, indicates pretty clearly that he had the Tarot of Joseph Paul Oswald Wirth (1860–1943) in front of him while he wrote his impressions of the Major Arcana. Wirth's Tarot, which consisted only of the trumps (suit cards have recently been added to some modern versions), was suggested by the French occultist Stanislas de Guaita (1861–1897) as a way of realizing the dream that Éliphas Lévi (real name Alphonse Louis Constant, 1810–1875) had of creating a truly esoteric Tarot. Wirth's trump designs were published in 1889 by E. Poirel in a limited edition Tarot of 350 sets under the title *Les 22 Arcanes du Tarot Kabbalistique.*

Ouspensky's essay was published as a book by Dover Publications of New York in 1976, accompanied by color illustrations of the trumps of the Rider Tarot, so-called because it was first published by Rider and Company. It is also known as the Rider-Waite Tarot because it was designed by Arthur Edward Waite (1857–1942), or the Smith-Waite Tarot because it was drawn by the artist Pamela Colman Smith (1878–1951). A note that accompanies the Dover edition reads in part: "Ouspensky does not identify the set of tarot cards on which he based his meditations, but the set prepared by Pamela C. Smith under the supervision of A. E. Waite, a noted British student of the occult, fits Ouspensky's descriptions almost perfectly. There are only a few minor deviations."[2]

It is obvious upon reading the card descriptions that Ouspensky combined details from the Wirth trumps (such as the "lynx" that attacks the Fool) with details from the Waite trumps (such as the pomegranates on the veil between the two pillars behind the High Priestess). Ouspensky himself confirmed this in a footnote to his revised Tarot essay, included as part of *A New Model of the Universe.* He wrote that when he was composing the essay in 1911, he had "the modern English pack of the Tarot, which had been re-designed and in many cases altered according to theosophical interpretation."[3] This "modern English pack" was the Rider pack. The influence upon it was more Golden Dawn than Theosophy, but Ouspensky did not know this. He did not care for some of Waite's interpretations of the trumps, and wrote in the same footnote, "I used the Tarot of Oswald Wirth as it appears in Papus' book *Le Tarot des Bohémiens.*" At a still later date (presumably when he was preparing the essay for *A New Model of the Universe*), he changed some of his "pen-pictures" of the trumps

based both on the designs by Wirth and on what he called "the old cards"—
that is, the Tarot of Marseilles.

To more fully understand Ouspensky's descriptions, they should be considered in relation to both the Waite and Wirth Tarots, and also compared with the descriptions of the trumps in Éliphas Lévi's *Transcendental Magic*, A. E. Waite's 1896 English translation of Lévi's *Dogme et Ritual de la Haute Magie*. These prose poems express the cogitations of a brilliant mind untrammeled by conventional views of reality, coupled with the emotional impressions of a poetic soul. No one was better equipped than Ouspensky to represent the uniquely Russian response to the occult Tarot.

THE SYMBOLISM OF THE TAROT

by

P. D. OUSPENSKY

WHAT IS THE TAROT?

No study of occult philosophy is possible without an acquaintance with symbolism, for if the words occultism and symbolism are correctly used, they mean almost one and the same thing. Symbolism cannot be learned as one learns to build bridges or speak a foreign language, and for the interpretation of symbols a special cast of mind is necessary; in addition to knowledge, special faculties, the power of creative thought and a developed imagination are required. One who understands the use of symbolism in the arts, knows, in a general way, what is meant by occult symbolism. But even then a special training of the mind is necessary, in order to comprehend the "language of the initiates," and to express in this language the intuitions as they arise.

There are many methods for developing the "sense of symbols" in those who are striving to understand the hidden forces of Nature and Man, and for teaching the fundamental principles as well as the elements of the esoteric language. The most synthetic, and one of the most interesting of these methods, is the Tarot.[4]

In its exterior form the Tarot is a pack of cards used in the south of Europe for games and fortune-telling. These cards were first known in Europe at the end of the fourteenth century, when they were in use among the Spanish gypsies.[5]

A pack of Tarot contains the fifty-two ordinary playing cards with the addition of one "picture card" to every suit, namely, the Knight, placed between the Queen and the Knave. These fifty-six cards are divided into four suits, two black and two red, and have the following designation: sceptres (clubs), cups (hearts), swords (spades), and pentacles or disks (diamonds). In addition to the fifty-six cards the pack of Tarot has twenty-two numbered cards with special names:[6]

1 —The Magician.	**12** —The Hanged Man.
2 —The High Priestess.	**13** —Death.
3 —The Empress.	**14** —Temperance.
4 —The Emperor.	**15** —The Devil.
5 —The Chariot. (7).	**16** —The Tower.
6 —The Lovers.	**17** —The Star.
7 —The Hierophant. (5).	**18** —The Moon.
8 —Strength.	**19** —The Sun.
9 —The Hermit.	**20** —Judgment.
10 —The Wheel of Fortune.	**21** —The World.
11 —Justice.	**0** —The Fool.

This pack of cards, in the opinion of many investigators, represents the Egyptian hieroglyphic book of seventy-eight tablets, which came to us almost miraculously.[7]

The history of the Tarot is a great puzzle. During the Middle Ages, when it first appeared historically,[8] there existed a tendency to build up synthetic symbolical or logical systems of the same sort as *Ars Magna* by Raymond Lully.[9] But productions similar to the Tarot exist in India and China, so that we cannot possibly think it one of those systems created during the Middle Ages in Europe; it is also evidently connected with the Ancient Mysteries and the Egyptian Initiations. Although its origin is in oblivion and the aim of its author or authors quite unknown, there is no doubt whatever that it is the most complete code of Hermetic symbolism we possess.[10]

Although represented as a pack of cards, the Tarot really is something quite different. It can be "read" in a variety of ways. As one instance, I shall give a metaphysical interpretation of the general meaning or of the general content of the book of Tarot, that is to say, its metaphysical title, which will plainly show that this work could not have been invented by illiterate gypsies of the fourteenth century.

The Tarot falls into three divisions: The first part has twenty-one numbered cards; the second part has one card 0; the third part has fifty-six cards, i.e., the four suits of fourteen cards. Moreover, the second part appears to be a link between the first and third parts, since all the fifty-six cards of the third part together are equal to the card 0.[11]

Now, if we imagine twenty-one cards disposed in the shape of a triangle, seven cards on each side, a point in the centre of the triangle represented by the zero card, and a square round the triangle (the square consisting of fifty-six cards, fourteen on each side), we shall have a representation of the relation between God, Man and the Universe, or the relation between the world of ideas, the consciousness of man and the physical world.[12]

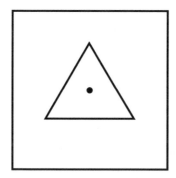

God, Man, and the Universe

The triangle is God (the Trinity) or the world of ideas, or the noumenal world. The point is man's soul. The square is the visible, physical or phenomenal world. Potentially, the point is equal to the square, which means that all the visible world is contained in man's consciousness, is created in man's soul.[13] And the soul itself is a point having no dimension in the world of the spirit, symbolized by the triangle. It is clear that such an idea could not have originated with ignorant people and clear also that the Tarot is something more than a pack of playing or fortune-telling cards.

H. P. Blavatsky mentions the Tarot in her works, and we have some reason for believing that she studied the Tarot. It is known that she loved to "play patience." We do not know what she read in the cards as she played this game, but the author was told that Madame Blavatsky searched persistently and for a long time for a MSS. on the Tarot.[14]

In order to become acquainted with the Tarot, it is necessary to understand the basic ideas of the Kabala and of Alchemy. For it represents, as, indeed, many commentators of the Tarot think, a summary of the Hermetic Sciences—the Kabala, Alchemy, Astrology, Magic, with their different divisions. All these sciences, attributed to Hermes Trismegistus, really represent one system of a very broad and deep psychological investigation of the nature of man in his relation to the world of noumena (God, the world of Spirit) and to the world of phenomena (the visible, physical world). The letters of the Hebrew alphabet and the various allegories of the Kabala, the names of metals, acids and salts in alchemy; of planets and constellations in astrology; of good and evil spirits in magic—all these were only means to veil truth from the uninitiated.[15]

But when the true alchemist spoke of seeking for gold, he spoke of gold in the soul of man.[16] And he called gold that which in the New Testament is called the Kingdom of Heaven, and in Buddhism, Nirvana. And when the true astrologer spoke of constellations and planets he spoke of constellations and planets in the soul of man, i.e., of the qualities of the human soul and its relations to God and to the world. And when the true Kabalist spoke of the Name of God, he sought this Name in the soul of man and in Nature, not in dead books, nor in biblical texts, as did the Kabalist-Scholastics. The Kabala, Alchemy, Astrology, Magic are parallel symbolical systems of psychology and metaphysics. Any alchemical sentence may be read in a Kabalistic or astrological way, but the meaning will always be psychological and metaphysical.

We are surrounded by a wall built of our conceptions of the world, and are unable to look over this wall at the real world. The Kabala presents an effort to break this "enchanted circle." It investigates the world as it is, the world in itself.

The world in itself, as the Kabalists hold, consists of four elements, or the four principles forming one. These four principles are represented by the four letters of the name of Jehovah. The basic idea of the Kabala consists in the study of the Name of God in its manifestation. Jehovah in Hebrew is spelt by four letters, Yod, He, Vau and He—I. H. V. H. To these four letters is given the deepest symbolical meaning. The first letter expresses the active principle, the beginning or first cause, motion, energy, "I"; the second letter expresses the passive element, inertia, quietude, "not I;" the third, the balance of opposites, "form"; and the fourth, the result or latent energy.[17]

The Kabalists affirm that every phenomenon and every object consists of these four principles, i.e., that every object and every phenomenon consists of the Name of God (The Word)—Logos.

The study of this Name (or the four-lettered word, tetragrammaton, in Greek) and the finding of it in everything constitutes the main problem of Kabalistic philosophy. To state it in another way the Kabalists hold that these four principles penetrate and create everything. Therefore, when the man finds these four principles in things and phenomena of quite different categories (where before he had not seen similarity), he begins to see analogy between these phenomena. And, gradually, he becomes convinced that the whole world is built according to one and the same law, on one and the same plan. The richness and growth of his intellect consists in the widening of his faculty for finding analogies. Therefore the study of the law of the four letters, or the name of Jehovah, presents a powerful means for widening consciousness.

This idea is perfectly clear, for if the Name of God be really in all (if God be present in all), all should be analogous to each other—the smallest particle analogous to the whole, the speck of dust analogous to the universe, and all analogous to God. The Name of God, the Word or Logos is the origin of the world. Logos also means Reason; the Word is the Logos, the Reason of everything.[18]

There is a complete correspondence between the Kabala and Alchemy and Magic. In Alchemy the four elements which constitute the real world are called fire, water, air and earth; these fully correspond in significance with the four kabalistic letters. In Magic they are expressed as the four classes of spirits: elves (or salamanders), undines, sylphs and gnomes.[19]

The Tarot in its turn is quite analogous to the Kabala, Alchemy and Magic, and, as it were, includes them. Corresponding to the four first principles or four letters of the Name of God, or the four alchemistic elements, or the four classes of spirits, the Tarot has four suits—sceptres, cups, swords and pentacles. Thus every suit, every side of the square, equal to the point, represents one of the elements, controls one class of spirits. The sceptres are fire or elves (or salamanders); the cups are water or undines; the swords are air or sylphs; and pentacles, earth or gnomes. Moreover, in every suit the King means the first principle or fire; the Queen—the second principle or water; the Knight—the third principle or air; and the Page (Knave)—the fourth principle or earth.

Then again, the ace means fire; the deuce water; the three-spot, air; the four-spot earth. Then again the four-spot is the first principle, the five spot, the second etc.[20]

In regard to the suits, one may add that the black suits (sceptres and swords) express activity and energy, will, initiative and the subjective side of consciousness; and the red (cups and pentacles) express passivity, inertia and the objective side of consciousness. Then the first two suits (sceptres and cups) signify "good" and the other two (swords and pentacles) mean "evil."[21] Thus every card of the fifty-six indicates (independently of its number) the presence of the principle of activity or passivity, of "good" or "evil," arising either in man's will or from without. And the significance of each card is further deciphered through its various combinations with the suits and numbers in their symbolical meaning. The fifty-six cards as a whole represent, as it were, a complete picture of all the possibilities of man's consciousness. And this makes the Tarot adaptable for fortune-telling. Thus, including the Kabala, Astrology, Alchemy and Magic, the Tarot makes it possible to "seek gold," "to evoke spirits," and "to draw horoscopes,"[22] simply by means of this pack of cards without the complicated paraphernalia and ceremonies of an alchemist, astrologer or magician.

But the main interest of Tarot is in the twenty-two numbered cards. These cards have numerical meaning and also a very involved symbolical significance. The literature relating to the Tarot has in view mainly the reading of the symbolical designs of the twenty-two cards. Very many writers on occultism have arranged their works on the plan of the Tarot. But this is not often suspected because the Tarot is rarely mentioned. Oswald Wirth speaks of origin of the Tarot in his Essay upon the Astronomical Tarot.

> According to Christian [*Histoire de la Magie*], the twenty-two major arcana of the Tarot represent the hieroglyphic paintings which were found in the spaces between the columns of a gallery which the neophyte was obliged to cross in the Egyptian initiations. There were twelve columns to the north and the same number to the south, that is, eleven symbolical pictures on each side. These pictures were explained to the candidate for initiation in regular order, and they contained the rules and principles for the Initiate....This opinion is confirmed by the correspondence which exists between arcana when they are thus arranged.[23]

In the gallery of the Temple the pictures were arranged in pairs, one opposite another, so that the last picture was opposite the first, the last but one opposite the second, etc. When the cards are so placed we find a highly interesting and deep suggestion. In this way the mind finds the one in the two, and is led from dualism to monism, which is what we might call the unification of the duad. One card explains the other and each pair shows moreover that they can be only mutually explanatory and mean nothing when taken separately.[24]

Thus, for instance, the cards 10 and 13 ("Life" and "Death")[25] signify together a certain whole or complementary condition which we cannot conceive by the ordinary, imperfect mental processes. We think of life and death as two "opposites," antagonistic one to the other, but, if we thought further, we should see that each depends on the other for existence and neither could come into existence separately.

A symbol may serve to transfer our intuitions and to suggest new ones only so long as its meaning is not defined. Real symbols are perpetually in process of creation; but when they receive a definite significance they become hieroglyphs and finally a mere alphabet. As this they express simply ordinary concepts, cease to be a language of the Gods or of initiates and become a language of men which everyone may learn.

Properly speaking, a symbol in occultism means the same as in art. If an artist uses ready-made symbols his work will not be true art, but only pseudo-art. If an occultist begins to use ready-made symbols, his work will not be truly occult, for it will contain no esotericism, no mysticism, but only pseudo-occultism, pseudo-esotericism, pseudo-mysticism. Symbolism in which the symbols have definite meanings is pseudo-symbolism.[26]

Having made this idea clear in his mind, the author found that the key to the Tarot must lie in imagination and he decided to make an effort to re-design the cards, giving descriptive pictures of the Tarot, and to interpret the symbols, not by means of analysis, but by synthesis. The reader will find in the following little "pen pictures" reflections of many authors who wrote on the Tarot as St. Martin,[27] Éliphas Lévi,[28] Dr. Papus[29] etc. and of other authors who certainly never thought of the Tarot as, for example, Plotinus,[30] Gichtel[31] (XVII century), Friedrich Nietzsche,[32] M. Collins[33] etc., who came nevertheless to the same fundamental principles as the unknown authors of the Tarot.

Descriptions of the arcanas in these "pen pictures" often represent a conception which is almost entirely subjective, for instance, that of card 18. And the author likes to think that another might conceive of the same symbols differently, in any case he considers this quite possible.

Any one interested in this philosophical puzzle might well ask, What then is the Tarot? Is it a doctrine or merely a method? Is it a definite system or merely an alphabet by means of which any system may be constructed? In short, is it a book containing specific teachings, or is it merely an apparatus, a machine which we may use to build anything, even a new universe.

The author believes that the Tarot may be used for both purposes, though, of course, the contents of a book that may be read either forward or backward cannot be said to be, in the ordinary sense, strictly definite. But perhaps we find in this very indefiniteness of the Tarot and in the complexity of its philosophy, the element which constitutes its definiteness. The fact that we question the Tarot as to whether it be a method or a doctrine shows the limitation of our "three dimensional mind," which is unable to rise above the world of form and contra-positions or to free itself from thesis and antithesis! Yes, the Tarot contains and expresses any doctrine to be found in our consciousness, and in this sense it has definiteness. It represents Nature in all the richness of its infinite possibilities, and there is in it as in Nature, not one but all potential meanings. And these meanings are fluent and ever-changing, so the Tarot cannot be specifically this or that, for it ever moves and yet is ever the same.

In the following "pen-pictures" cards are taken in pairs:—I and 0; II and XXI; III and XX etc.—in each pair one card completing the sense of another and two making one.

Card I.—"The Magician."
"Man" Superman.[34] The Initiate. The Occultist. Higher consciousness. Human Logos. The Kabalistic "Adam Kadmon."[35] Humanity. "Homo Sapiens."

Card II.—"The High Priestess."
Occultism. Esoterism. Mysticism. Theosophy. Initiation. Isis. Mystery.

Card III.—"The Empress."
Nature in its phenomenal aspect. The ever re-newing and re-creating force of Nature. The objective reality.

Card IV.—"The Emperor."
Tetragrammaton. The law of four.[36] Latent energy of Nature. Logos in the full aspect with all possibilities of the new Logos. Hermetic philosophy.

Card V.—"The Chariot."
"Man." The Imagination. Magic. Self-suggestion. Self deceit. Artificial means of attainment. Pseudo-occultism. Pseudotheosophy.

Card VI.—"The Lovers."
"Man." Another aspect of the "Adam Kadmon," the "Perfect Man," "The divine androgyne." Love as the efforts of "Adam Kadmon" to find himself. The equilibrium of contraries. The unification of the duad, as the means of attaining the Light.

Card VII.—"The Hierophant."
Mysticism. Theosophy. Esoteric side of all religions.

Card VIII.—"Strength."
The Real Power. Strength of love. Strength of Union (Magic chain).[37] Strength of the Infinite. Occultism. Esoterism. Theosophy.

Card IX.—"The Hermit."
"Man." The Path to the Initiation. Seeking for truth in the right way. Inner Knowledge. Inner Light. Inner Force. Theosophy. Occultism.

Card X.—"The Wheel of Chance."
The Wheel of Life. The life ever changing and ever remaining the same. The Circle of Time and the four elements. The idea of the circle.

Card XI.—"Justice."
Truth. Real Knowledge. Inner Truth. Occultism. Esoterism. Theosophy.

Card XII.—"The Hanged Man."
"Man." The Pain of the higher consciousness bound by the limitations of the body and mind. Superman in the separate man.

Card XIII.—"Death."
Another aspect of Life. Going away in order to come back at the same time. Completion of the circle.

Card XIV.—"Temperance." (Time).

The first attainment. The "Arcanum Magnum" [Great Secret] of the occultists.[38] The Fourth Dimension. Higher space. "Eternal Now."

Card XV.—"The Devil."

"Man." Weakness. Falsehood. The Fall of man into separateness, into hatred and into finiteness.

Card XVI.—"The Tower."

Sectarianism. Tower of Babel. Exoterism. Confusion of tongues. Fall of exoterism. The force of Nature re-establishing the truth distorted by men.

Card XVII.—"The Star."

The real aspect of the Astral World. That which may be seen in ecstasy. The imagination of Nature. Real Knowledge. Occultism.

Card XVIII.—"The Moon."

The Astral World as it is seen by the artificial means of magic. "Psychic," "spiritistic" world. Dreads of the night. The real light from above and the false representation of that light from below. Pseudo-mysticism.

Card XIX.—"The Sun."

The Symbol and manifestation of the tetragrammaton. Creative power. Fire of life.

Card XX.—"Judgment."

The resurrection. Constant victory of life over death. Creative activity of nature in the death.

Card XXI.—"World."

Nature. The World as it is. Nature in its noumenal aspect. Esoteric side of nature. That which is made known in esoterism. Inner reality of things. Human consciousness in the circle of time between the four elements.

Card 0.—"The Fool."

"Man." An ordinary man.[39] A separate man. The uninitiate Lower consciousness. The end of a ray not knowing its relation to the centre.

The twenty-two cards may be divided into three divisions including each seven cards[40] of similar meaning, the 22-nd card (No 21) as a duplicate (of the No 10) standing outside the triangle or forming a point in its centre.

The three sets of sevens belong: the first one to the *Man*, the second to the Nature and the third to the higher knowledge or to the Theosophy in the large sense of the word.

The First set of 7 Cards: I—Magician; 0—The Fool; V—The Chariot; IX—The Hermit; VI—Lovers; XV—The Devil; XII—The Hanged Man.

The contents of these seven cards if taken *in time* picture seven degrees of the path of Man in his way to the Superman, or if taken in the Eternal Now picture seven faces of Man or seven I-s of man co-existing in him. This last meaning represents the inner sense of the secret doctrine of the Tarot in its relations to *Man*.

The second set of 7 (Nature) includes cards: III—The Empress; X—Life; XIII—Death; XIV—Time; XVI—The Tower; XIX—The Sun; XX—Judgement.

The third set of 7 (Theosophy) includes cards: II—The High Priestess; IV—The Emperor; VIII—Strength; VII—The Hierophant; XI—Justice; XVII—The Star; XVIII—The Moon.

THE SYMBOLS

CARD I.
THE MAGICIAN.
I Saw the Man.

His figure reached from earth to heaven and was clad in a purple mantle. He stood deep in foliage and flowers and his head, on which was the head-band of an initiate, seemed to disappear mysteriously in infinity.

Before him on a cube-shaped altar were four symbols of magic—the sceptre, the cup, the sword and the pentacle.

His right hand pointed to heaven, his left to earth. Under his mantle he wore a white tunic girded with a serpent swallowing its tail.

His face was luminous and serene, and, when his eyes met mine, I felt that he saw the most intimate recesses of my soul. I saw myself reflected in him as in a mirror and in his eyes I seemed to look upon myself.

And I heard a voice saying—

"Look, this is the Great Magician!

"With his hands he unites heaven and earth, and the four elements that form the world are controlled by him.

"The four symbols before him are the four letters of the name of God, the signs of the four elements, fire, water, air, earth."

I trembled before the depth of the mysteries I touched... The words I heard seemed to be uttered by the Great Magician himself, and it was as though he spoke in me.

I was in deep trepidation and at moments I felt there was nothing before me except the blue sky; but within me a window opened through which I could see unearthly things and hear unearthly words.

CARD 0.

THE FOOL.

And I saw another man.

Tired and lame he dragged himself along the dusty road, across the deserted plain under the scorching rays of the sun. He glanced sidelong with foolish, staring eyes, a half smile, half leer on his face; he knew not where he went, but was absorbed in his chimerical dreams which ran constantly in the same circle. His fool's cap was put on wrong side front, his garments were torn in the back; a wild lynx[41] with glowing eyes sprang upon him from behind a rock and buried her teeth in his flesh. He stumbled, nearly fell, but continued to drag himself along, all the time holding on his shoulder a bag containing useless things, which he, in his stupidity, carried wherever he went.

Before him a crevice crossed the road and a deep precipice awaited the foolish wanderer. Then a huge crocodile[42] with open mouth crawled out of the precipice. And I heard the voice say:—

"Look! This is the same man."

I felt my head whirl.

"What has he in the bag?" I inquired, not knowing why I asked. And after a long silence the voice replied: "The four magic symbols, the sceptre, the cup, the sword and the pentacle. The fool always carries them, although he has long since forgotten what they mean. Nevertheless they belong to him, even though he does not know their use. The symbols have not lost their power, they retain it in themselves."

CARD II.

THE HIGH PRIESTESS.

When I lifted the first veil and entered the outer court of the Temple of Initiation, I saw in half darkness the figure of a woman sitting on a high throne between two pillars of the temple, one white, and one black. Mystery emanated from her and was about her. Sacred symbols shone on her green dress; on her head was a golden tiara surmounted by a two-horned moon; on her knees she held two crossed keys and an open book. Between the two pillars behind the woman hung another veil all embroidered with green leaves and fruit of pomegranate.

And a voice said:

"To enter the Temple one must lift the second veil and pass between the two pillars. And to pass thus, one must obtain possession of the keys, read the book and understand the symbols. Are you able to do this?"

"I would like to be able," I said.

Then the woman turned her face to me and looked into my eyes without speaking. And through me passed a thrill, mysterious and penetrating like a golden wave; tones vibrated in my brain, a flame was in my heart, and I understood that she spoke to me, saying without words:

"This is the Hall of Wisdom. No one can reveal it, no one can hide it. Like a flower it must grow and bloom in thy soul. If thou wouldst plant the seed of this flower in thy soul—*learn to discern the real from the false. Listen only to the Voice that is soundless…Look only on that which is invisible,* and remember that in thee thyself, is the Temple and the gate to it, and the mystery, and the initiation."

CARD XXI

THE WORLD.

An unexpected vision appeared to me. A circle not unlike a wreath woven from rainbow and lightnings, whirled from heaven to earth with a stupendous velocity, blinding me by its brilliance. And amidst this light and fire I heard music and soft singing, thunderclaps and the roar of a tempest, the rumble of falling mountains and earthquakes.

The circle whirled with a terrifying noise, touching the sun and the earth, and, in the centre of it I saw the naked, dancing figure of a beautiful young woman, enveloped by a light, transparent scarf, in her hand she held a magic wand.

Presently the four apocalyptical beasts began to appear on the edges of the circle; one with the face of a lion, another with the face of a man, the third, of an eagle and the fourth, of a bull.

The vision disappeared as suddenly as it appeared. A weird silence fell on me. "What does it mean?" I asked in wonder.

"It is the image of the world," the voice said, "but it can be understood only after the Temple has been entered. This is a vision of the world in the circle of Time, amidst the four principles. But thou seest differently because thou seest the world outside thyself. Learn to see it in thyself and thou wilt understand the infinite essence, hidden in all illusory forms. Understand that the world which thou knowest is only one of the aspects of the infinite world, and things and phenomena are merely hieroglyphics of deeper ideas."

CARD III.

THE EMPRESS.

I felt the breath of the spring, and accompanying the fragrance of violets and lilies-of-the-valley I heard the tender singing of elves. Rivulets murmured, the treetops rustled, the grasses whispered, innumerable birds sang in choruses and bees hummed; everywhere I felt the breathing of joyful, living Nature.

The sun shone tenderly and softly and a little white cloud hung over the woods.

In the midst of a green meadow where primroses bloomed, I saw the Empress seated on a throne covered with ivy and lilacs. A green wreath adorned her golden hair and, above her head, shone twelve stars.[43] Behind her rose two snowy wings and in her hands she held a sceptre. All around, beneath the sweet smile of the Empress, flowers and buds opened their dewy, green leaves. Her whole dress was covered with them as though each newly opened flower were reflected in it or had engraved itself thereon and thus become part of her garment.

The sign of Venus, the goddess of love, was chiselled on her marble throne.

"Queen of life," I said, "why is it so bright and joyful all about you? Do you not know of the grey, weary autumn, of the cold, white winter? Do you not know of death and graveyards with black graves, damp and cold? How can you smile so joyfully on the opening flowers, when everything is destined to death, even that which has not yet been born?"

For answer the Empress looked on me still smiling and, under the influence of that smile, I suddenly felt a flower of some clear understanding open in my heart.

CARD XX.

JUDGMENT.

I saw an ice plain, and on the horizon, a chain of snowy mountains. A cloud appeared and began to grow until it covered a quarter of the sky. Two fiery wings suddenly expanded in the cloud, and I knew that I beheld the messenger of the Empress.

He raised a trumpet and blew through it vibrant, powerful tones. The plain quivered in response to him and the mountains loudly rolled their echoes. One after another, graves opened in the plain and out of them came men and women, old and young, and children. They stretched out their arms toward the Messenger of the Empress and to catch the sounds of his trumpet.

And in its tones I felt the smile of the Empress and in the opening graves I saw the opening flowers whose fragrance seemed to be wafted by the out-stretched arms.

Then I understood the mystery of birth in death.

CARD IV.

THE EMPEROR.

After I learned the first three numbers I was given to understand the Great Law of Four—the alpha and omega of all.

I saw the Emperor on a lofty stone throne, ornamented by four rams' heads. On his forehead shone a golden helmet. His white beard fell over a purple mantle. In one hand he held a sphere, the symbol of his possession, and in the other, a sceptre in the form of an Egyptian cross[44]—the sign of his power over birth.

"I am The Great Law," the Emperor said. "I am the name of God. The four letters of his name are in me and I am in all.

"I am in the four principles. I am in the four elements. I am in the four seasons. I am in the four cardinal points. I am in the four signs of the Tarot.

"I am the beginning; I am action; I am completion; I am the result.

"For him who knows how to see me there are no mysteries on earth.

"I am the great Pentacle.

"As the earth encloses in itself fire, water and air; as the fourth letter of the Name encloses in itself the first three and becomes itself the first, so my sceptre encloses the complete triangle and bears in itself the seed of a new triangle.[45]

"I am the Logos in the full aspect and the beginning of a new Logos."

And while the Emperor spoke, his helmet shone brighter and brighter, and his golden armour gleamed beneath his mantle. I could not bear his glory and I lowered my eyes.

When I tried to lift them again a vivid light of radiant fire was before me, and I prostrated myself and made obeisance to the Fiery Word.

CARD XIX.

THE SUN.

As soon as I perceived the Sun, I understood that It, Itself, is the expression of the Fiery Word and the sign of the Emperor.

The great luminary shone with an intense heat upon the large golden heads of sun-flowers.

And I saw a naked boy, whose head was wreathed with roses, galloping on a white horse and waving a bright-red banner.[46]

I shut my eyes for a moment and when I opened them again I saw that each ray of the Sun is the sceptre of the Emperor and bears life. And I saw how under the concentration of these rays the mystic flowers of the waters open and receive the rays into themselves and how all Nature is constantly born from the union of two principles.

CARD V.

THE CHARIOT.

I saw a chariot drawn by two sphinxes, one white, the other black.[47] Four pillars supported a blue canopy, on which were scattered five-pointed stars. The Conqueror, clad in steel armour, stood under this canopy guiding the sphinxes. He held a sceptre, on the end of which were a globe, a triangle and a square. A golden pentagram sparkled in his crown. On the front of the chariot there was represented a winged sphere and beneath that the symbol of the mystical lingam, signifying the union of two principles.

"Everything in this picture has a significance. Look and try to understand," said the voice.

"This is Will armed with Knowledge. We see here, however, the wish to achieve, rather than achievement itself. The man in the chariot thought himself a conqueror before he had really conquered, and he believes that victory must come to the conqueror. There are true possibilities in this beautiful conception, but also many false ones. Illusory fires and numerous dangers are hidden here.

"He controls the sphinxes by the power of a magic word, but the tension of his Will may fail and then the magic word will lose its power and he may be devoured by the sphinxes.

"This is indeed the Conqueror, but only for the moment; he has not yet conquered Time, and the succeeding moment is unknown to him.

"This is the Conqueror, not by love, but by fire and the sword,—a conqueror against whom the conquered may arise. Do you see behind him the towers of the conquered city? Perhaps the flame of uprising burns already there.

"And he is unaware that the city vanquished by means of fire and the sword is the city within his own consciousness, that the magic chariot is in himself and that the blood-thirsty sphinxes, also a state of consciousness within, watch his every movement. He has externalized all these phases of his mind and sees them only outside himself. This is his fundamental error. He entered the outer court of the Temple of knowledge, but thinks he has been in the Temple itself. He regarded the rituals of the first tests as initiation, and he mistook for the goddess, the priestess who guarded the threshold. Because of this misconception great perils await him.

"Nevertheless it may be that even in his errors and perils the Great Conception lies concealed. He seeks to know and, perhaps, in order to attain, mistakes, dangers and even failures are necessary.

"Understand that this is the same man whom you saw uniting Heaven and Earth, and again walking across a hot desert to a precipice."

CARD XVIII.

THE MOON.

A desolate plain stretched before me. A full moon looked down as if in contemplative hesitation. Under her wavering light the shadows lived their own peculiar life. On the horizon I saw blue hills, and over them wound a path which stretched between two grey towers far away into the distance. On either side of the path a wolf and dog sat and howled at the moon.[48] I remembered that dogs believe in thieves and ghosts. A large black crab crawled out of the rivulet into the sands. A heavy, cold dew was falling.

Dread fell upon me. I sensed the presence of a mysterious world, a world of hostile spirits, of corpses rising from graves, of wailing ghosts. In this pale moonlight I seemed to feel the presence of apparitions; someone watched me from behind the towers,—and I knew it was dangerous to look back.

CARD VI.

THE LOVERS.

I saw a blooming garden in a green valley, surrounded by soft blue hills.

In the garden I saw a Man and a Woman naked and beautiful. They loved each other and their Love was their service to the Great Conception, a prayer and a sacrifice; through It they communed with God, through It they received the highest revelations; in Its light the deepest truths came to them; the magic world opened its gate; elves, undines, sylphs and gnomes came openly to them; the three kingdoms of nature, the mineral, plant and animal, and the four elements—fire, water, air and earth—served them.

Through their Love they saw the mystery of the world's equilibrium, and that they themselves were a symbol and expression of this balance. Two triangles united in them into a six-pointed star. Two magnets melted into an ellipsis. They were two. The third was the Unknown Future. The three made One.

I saw the woman looking out upon the world as though enraptured with its beauty. And from the tree on which ripened golden fruit I saw a serpent creep.[49] It whispered in the woman's ear, and I saw her listening, smiling at first suspiciously, then with curiosity which merged into joy. Then I saw her speak to the man. I noticed that he seemed to admire only her and smiled with an expression of joy and sympathy at all she told him.

"This picture you see, is a picture of temptation and falls," said the voice. "What constitutes the Fall? Do you understand its nature?"

"Life is so good," I said, "and the world so beautiful, and this man and woman wanted to believe in the reality of the world and of themselves. They wanted to forget service and take from the world what it can give. So they made a distinction between themselves and the world. They said, 'We are here, the world is there.' And the world separated from them and became hostile."

"Yes," said the Voice, "this is true. The everlasting mistake with men is that they see the fall in love. But Love is not a fall, it is a soaring above an abyss. And the higher the flight, the more beautiful and alluring appears the earth. But that wisdom, which crawls on earth, advises belief in the earth and in the present. This is the Temptation. And the man and woman yielded to it. They dropped from the eternal realms and submitted to time and death. The balance was disturbed. The fairyland was closed upon them. The elves, undines, sylphs and gnomes became invisible. The Face of God ceased to reveal itself to them, and all things appeared upside down.

"This Fall, this first 'sin of man,' repeats itself perpetually, because man continues to believe in his separateness and in the Present. And only by means of great suffering can he liberate himself from the control of time and return to Eternity—leave darkness and return to Light."

CARD XVII.

THE STAR.

A strange emotion seized me. A fiery trembling ran in waves through all my body. My heart quickened its beating, tumult agitated my mind.

I felt that I was surrounded by portentous mysteries. And presently shafts of Light penetrated my being and illuminated many things before in darkness, whose existence even I had never suspected. Veils vanished of which I had been before unaware. Voices spoke to me. And suddenly all my former knowledge took a new and different meaning.

I discovered unexpected correlations in things which hitherto I had thought foreign to each other. Objects distant and different from one another appeared near and similar. The facts of the world arranged themselves before my eyes according to a new pattern.

In the sky there appeared an enormous star surrounded by seven smaller stars. Their rays intermingled, filling space with immeasurable radiance and splendour. Then I knew I saw that Heaven of which Plotinus speaks:[50]

"Where...all things are diaphanous; and nothing is dark and resisting, but everything is apparent to every one internally and throughout. For light everywhere meets with light, since everything contains all things in itself, and again sees all things in another. So that all things are everywhere, and all is all. Each thing likewise is everything. And the splendour there is infinite. For everything there is great, since even that which is small is great.

"The sun too, which is there, is all the stars; and again each star is the sun and all the stars. In each however, a different property predominates, but at the same time all things are visible in each. Motion likewise there is pure; for motion is not confounded by a mover different from it. Permanency also suffers no change of its nature, because it is not mingled with the unstable. And the beautiful there is beautiful, because it does not subsist in beauty. Each thing, too, is there established, not as in a foreign land, but the seat of each thing is that which each thing is....Nor is the thing itself different from the place in which it subsists. For the subject of it is intellect, and it is itself intellect....In this sensible region, therefore, one part is not produced by another, but each part is alone a part. But there each part always proceeds from the whole, and is at the same each time part and the whole. For it appears indeed as a part; but by him whose sight is acute, it will be seen as a whole.

"Where...is likewise no weariness of the vision which is there, not any plenitude of perception which can bring intuition to an end.

"For neither was there any vacuity which when filled might cause the visible energy to cease; nor is this one thing, but that another, so as to occasion a part of one thing not to be amicable with that of another.

"Where...the life is wisdom; a wisdom not obtained by a reasoning process, because the whole of it always was, and is not in any respect deficient, so as to be in want of investigation. But it is the first wisdom, and is not derived from another."

I understood that all the radiance here is thought; and the changing colours are emotions. And each ray, if we look into it, turns into images, symbols, voices and moods. And I saw that there is nothing inanimate, but all is soul, all is life, all is emotion and imagination.

And beneath the radiant stars beside the blue river I saw a naked maiden, young and beautiful. She stooped on one knee and poured water from two vessels, one of gold and one of silver. A little bird in a near by bush lifted its wings and was poised ready to fly away.

For a moment I understood that I beheld the Soul of Nature.

"This is Nature's Imagination," said the voice gently. "Nature dreams, improvises, creates worlds. Learn to unite your imagination with Her Imagination and nothing will ever be impossible for you. Lose the external world and seek it in yourself. Then you will find Light. But remember, unless you have lost the Earth, you will not find Heaven. It is impossible to see both wrongly and rightly at the same time."

CARD VII.

THE HIEROPHANT.

I saw the great Master in the Temple. He was sitting on a golden throne set upon a purple platform, and he wore the robe of a high priest with a golden tiara. He held a golden eight-pointed cross,[51] and lying at his feet were two crossed keys. Two initiates bowed before him and to them he spoke:—

"Seek the Path, do not seek attainment, Seek for the Path within yourself.

"Do not expect to hear the truth from others, nor to see it, or read it in books.[52] Look for the truth in yourself, not without yourself.

"Aspire only after the impossible and inaccessible. *Expect only that which shall not be.*

"Do not hope for Me,—do not look for Me,—do not believe—that I am outside yourself.

"Within your soul build a lofty tower by which you may ascend to Heaven. Do not believe in external miracles, expect miracles only within you. Beware of believing in a mystery of the earth, in a mystery guarded by men; for treasuries which must be guarded are empty. Do not search for a mystery that can be hidden by men. Seek the Mystery within yourself.

"Above all, avoid those towers built in order to preserve the mysteries and to make an ascent to Heaven by stone stairways. And remember that as soon as men build such a tower they begin to dispute about the summit.

"The Path is in yourself, and Truth is in yourself and Mystery is in yourself."

CARD XVI.

THE TOWER.

I saw a lofty tower extending from earth to heaven; its golden crowned summit[53] reached beyond the clouds. All round it black night reigned and thunder rumbled. Suddenly the heavens opened, a thunder-clap shook the whole earth, and lightning struck the summit of the tower and felled the golden crown. A tongue of fire shot from heaven and the whole tower became filled with fire and smoke. Then I beheld the builders of the tower[54] fall headlong to the ground.

And the voice said:

"The building of the tower was begun by the disciples of the great Master in order to have a constant reminder of the Master's teaching that the true tower must be built in one's own soul, that in the tower built by hands there can be no mysteries, that no one can ascend to Heaven by treading stone steps.

"The tower should warn the people *not to believe in it*. It should serve as a reminder of the inner Temple and as a protection against the outer; it should be as a lighthouse, in a dangerous place where men have often been wrecked and where ships should not go.

"But by and by the disciples forgot the true covenant of the Master and what the tower symbolized, and began *to believe in the tower* of stone, they had built, and to teach others to so believe. They began to say that in this tower there is power, mystery and the spirit of the Master, that the tower itself is holy and that it is built for the coming Master according to His covenant and His will. And so they waited in the tower for the Master. Others did not believe this, or interpreted it differently. Then began disputes about the rights of the summit. Quarrels started, 'Our Master, your Master,' was said; 'our tower, your tower.' And the disciples ceased to understand each other. Their tongues had become confused.

"You understand the meaning here? They had begun to think that this is the tower of the Master, that He builds it through them, and that it must and, indeed, can be built right up to Heaven.

"And you see how Heaven responded?"

CARD VIII.

POWER.

In the midst of a green plain, surrounded by blue hills, I saw a woman with a lion. Girdled with wreaths of roses, a symbol of infinity over her head, the woman calmly and confidently covered the lion's mouth and the lion obediently licked her hand.

"This is a picture of power," said the voice. "It has different meanings. First it shows the power of love. Love alone can conquer wrath. Hatred feeds hatred. Remember what Zarathustra said: 'Let man be freed from vengeance; this is a bridge for me which leads to higher hope and a rainbow in heaven after long storms.'[55]

"Then it shows power of unity. These wreaths of roses suggest a magic chain. Unity of desires, unity of aspirations creates such power that every wild, uncontrolled, unconscious force is subdued. Even two desires, if united, are able to conquer almost the whole world.

"The picture also shows the power of infinity, that sphere of mysteries. For a consciousness that perceives the symbol of infinity above it, knows no obstacles and cannot be withstood."

CARD XV.
THE DEVIL.

Black, awful night enveloped the earth. An ominous, red flame burned in the distance. I was approaching a fantastic figure which outlined itself before me as I came nearer to it. High above the earth appeared the repulsive red face of the Devil, with large, hairy ears, pointed beard and curved goats' horns. A pentagram, pointing downwards, shone in phosphoric light between the horns on his forehead. Two large, grey, bat-like wings were spread behind him. He held up one arm, spreading out his bare, fat hand. In the palm I saw the sign of black magic.[56] A burning torch held down-end in his other hand emitted black, stifling smoke. He sat on a large, black cube, gripping it with the claws of his beast-like, shaggy legs.

A man and woman were chained to the cube—the same Man and Woman I saw in the garden, but now they had horns and tails tipped with flame. And they were evidently dissatisfied in spirit, and were filled with protest and repulsion.

"This is a picture of weakness," said the voice, "a picture of falsehood and evil. They are the same man and woman you saw in the garden, but their love ceasing to be a sacrifice, became an illusion. This man and woman forgot that their love is a link in the chain that unites them with eternity, that their love is a symbol of equilibrium and a road to Infinity.

"They forgot that It is a key to the gate of the magic world, *the torch which Lights the higher Path*. They forgot that Love is real and immortal and they subjugated it to the unreal and temporary. And they each made love a tool for submitting the other to himself.

"Then love became dissension and fettered them with iron chains to the black cube of matter, on which sits deceit."

And I heard the voice of the Devil: "I am Evil," he said, "at least so far as Evil can exist in this best of worlds. In order to see me, one must be able to see unfairly, incorrectly and narrowly. I close the triangle, the other two sides of which are Death and Time.[57] In order to quit this triangle it is necessary to see that it does not exist.

"But how to do this is not for me to tell. For I am the Evil which men say is the cause of all evil and which they invented as an excuse for all the evil that they do.

"They call me the Prince of Falsehood, and truly I am the prince of lies, because I am the most monstrous production of human lies."

CARD IX.

THE HERMIT.

After long wanderings over a sandy, waterless desert where only serpents lived, I met the Hermit.

He was wrapped in a long cloak, a hood thrown over his head. He held a long staff in one hand and in the other a lighted lantern, though it was broad daylight and the sun was shining.

"The lantern of Hermes Trismegistus," said the voice, "this is higher knowledge, that inner knowledge which illuminates in a new way even what appears to be already clearly known. This lantern lights up the past, the present and the future for the Hermit, and opens the souls of people and the most intimate recesses of their hearts.

"The cloak of Apollonius[58] is the faculty of the wise man by which he isolates himself, even amidst a noisy crowd; it is his skill in hiding his mysteries, even while expressing them, his capacity for silence and his power to act in stillness.

"The staff of the patriarchs[59] is his inner authority, his power, his self-confidence.

"The lantern, the cloak and the staff are the three symbols of initiation.[60] They are needed to guide souls past the temptation of illusory fires by the roadside, so that they may go straight to the higher goal. He who receives these three symbols or aspires to obtain them, strives to enrich himself with all he can acquire, not for himself, but, like God, to delight in the joy of giving.

"The giving virtue is the basis of an initiate's life.

"His soul is transformed into 'a spoiler of all treasures' so said Zarathustra.[61]

"Initiation unites the human mind with the higher mind by a chain of analogies. This chain is the ladder leading to heaven, dreamed of by the patriarch."[62]

CARD XIV.

TIME (TEMPERANCE).

An angel in a white robe, touching earth and heaven, appeared. His wings were flame and a radiance of gold was about his head. On his breast he wore the sacred sign of the book of the Tarot—a triangle within a square, a point within the triangle;[63] on his forehead the symbol of life and eternity, the circle.[64]

In one hand was a cup of silver, in the other a cup of gold and there flowed between these cups a constant, glistening stream of every colour of the rainbow. But I could not tell from which cup nor into which cup the stream flowed.

In great awe I understood that I was near the ultimate mysteries from which there is no return. I looked upon the angel, upon his symbols, his cups, the rainbow stream between the cups,—and my human heart trembled with fear and my human mind shrank with anguish and lack of understanding.

"Yes," said the voice, "this is a mystery that is revealed at Initiation. 'Initiation' is simply the revealing of this mystery in the soul. The Hermit receives the lantern, the cloak and the staff so that he can bear the light of this mystery.

"But you probably came here unprepared. Look then and listen and try to understand, for now understanding is your only salvation. He who approaches the mystery without complete comprehension will be lost.

"The name of the angel is Time. The circle on his forehead is the symbol of eternity and life. Each life is a circle which returns to the same point where it began. Death is the return to birth. And from one point to another on the circumference of a circle the distance is always the same, and the further it is from one point, the nearer it will be to the other.

"Eternity is a serpent, pursuing its tail, never catching it.[65]

"One of the cups the angel holds is the past the other is the future. The rainbow stream between the cups is the present. You see that it flows both ways.

"This is Time in its most incomprehensible aspect.

"Men think that all flows constantly in one direction. They do not see that everything perpetually meets and that Time is a multitude of turning circles. Understand this mystery and learn to discern the contrary currents in the rainbow stream of the present.

"The symbol of the sacred book of the Tarot on the angel's breast is the symbol of the correlation of God, Man and the Universe.

"The triangle is God, the world of spirit, the world of ideas. The point within the triangle is the soul of man. The square is the visible world.

"The consciousness of man is the spark of divinity, a point within the triangle of spirit. Therefore the whole square of the visible universe is equal to the point within the triangle.

"The world of spirit is the triangle of the twenty-one signs of the Tarot. The square represents fire, air, water and earth, and thus symbolises the world.

"All this, in the form of the four symbols, is in the bag of the Fool, who himself is a point in a triangle. Therefore a point without dimension contains an infinite square."

CARD X.

THE WHEEL OF CHANCE.

I walked along, absorbed in deep thought, trying to understand the vision of the Angel. And suddenly, as I lifted my head, I saw midway in the sky a huge, revolving circle covered with Kabalistic letters and symbols. The circle turned with terrible velocity, and around it, falling down and flying up, symbolic figures of the serpent and the dog revolved; above it sat an immovable sphinx.

In clouds, on the four quarters of heaven, I saw the four apocalyptical beings, one with the face of a lion, another with the face of a bull, the third with a face of an eagle, and the fourth with the face of a man.[66] And each of them read an open book.

And I heard the voices of Zarathustra's beasts:[67]

"All go, all return—the wheel of life ever turns. All die, all flourish again—the year of existence runs eternally.

"All perish, all live again, the same house of existence is ever building. All separate, all meet again, the ring of existence is ever true to itself.

"Existence begins at every moment. Round each 'here' rolls 'there.' The middle is everywhere. The way of eternity is a curve."

CARD XIII.

DEATH.

Fatigued by the flashing of the Wheel of Life, I sank to earth and shut my eyes. But it seemed to me that the Wheel kept turning before me and that the four creatures continued sitting in the clouds and reading their books.

Suddenly, on opening my eyes, I saw a gigantic rider on a white horse, dressed in black armour, with a black helmet and black plume. A skeleton's face looked out from under the helmet. One bony hand held a large, black, slowly-waving banner, and the other held a black bridle ornamented with skulls and bones.

And, wherever the white horse passed, night and death followed; flowers withered, leaves drooped, the earth covered itself with a white shroud; grave-yards appeared; towers, castles and cities were destroyed.

Kings in the full splendour of their fame and their power; beautiful women loved and loving; high priests invested by power from God; innocent children— when they saw the white horse all fell on their knees before him, stretched out their hands in terror and despair, and fell down to rise no more.

Afar, behind two towers, the sun sank.[68]

A deadly cold enveloped me. The heavy hoofs of the horse seemed to step on my breast, and I felt the world sink into an abyss.

But all at once something familiar, but faintly seen and heard, seemed to come from the measured step of the horse. A moment more and I heard in his steps the movement of the Wheel of Life!

An illumination entered me, and, looking at the receding rider and the de-scending sun, I understood that the Path of Life consists of the steps of the horse of Death.

The sun sinks at one point and rises at another. Each moment of its motion is a descent at one point and an ascent at another. I understood that it rises while sinking and sinks while rising, and that life, in coming to birth, dies, and in dying, comes to birth.

"Yes," said the voice. "The sun does not think of its going down and com-ing up. What does it know of earth, of the going and coming observed by men? It goes its own way, over its own orbit, round an unknown Centre. Life, death, rising and falling—do you not know that all these things are thoughts and dreams and fears of the Fool?"

CARD XI.
JUSTICE.
When I possessed the keys, read the book and understood the symbols, I was permitted to lift the curtain of the Temple and enter its inner sanctum. And there I beheld a Woman with a crown of gold and a purple mantle. She held a

sword in one hand and scales in the other. I trembled with awe at her appearance, which was deep and mysterious, and drew me like an abyss.

"You see Truth," said the voice. "On these scales everything is weighed. This sword is always raised to guard justice, and nothing can escape it.

"But why do you avert your eyes from the scales and the sword? They will remove the last illusions. How could you live on earth without these illusions?

"You wished to see Truth and now you behold it! But remember what happens to the mortal who beholds a Goddess!"

CARD XII.

THE HANGED MAN.

And then I saw a man in terrible suffering, hung by one leg, head downward, to a high tree. And I heard the voice:

"Look! This is a man who saw Truth. Suffering awaits the man on earth, who finds the way to eternity and to the understanding of the Endless.

"He is still a man, but he already knows much of what is inaccessible even to Gods. And the incommensurableness of the small and the great in his soul constitutes his pain and his golgotha.

"In his own soul appears the gallows on which he hangs in suffering, feeling that he is indeed inverted.

"He chose this way himself.

"For this he went over a long road from trial to trial, from initiation to initiation, through failures and falls.

"And now he has found Truth and knows himself.

"He knows that it is he who stands before an altar with magic symbols, and reaches from earth to heaven; that he also walks on a dusty road under a scorching sun to a precipice where a crocodile awaits him; that he dwells with his mate in paradise under the shadow of a blessing genius; that he is chained to a black cube under the shadow of deceit; that he stands as a victor for a moment in an illusionary chariot drawn by sphinxes; and that with a lantern in bright sunshine, he seeks for Truth in a desert.

"Now he has found Her."

Notes to Part Two

1. The hall of Tarot images beneath the Sphinx is described in vol. 1, bk. 2, chap. 2 of Paul Christian's *Histoire de la Magie* (Paris: 1870). See the abridged English edition of Christian's work, *The History and Practice of Magic* (New York: Citadel Press, 1963), pp. 93–94.

2. P. D. Ouspensky, *The Symbolism of the Tarot* (1913; repr., New York: Dover, 1976, p. 20.

3. P. D. Ouspensky, *A New Model of the Universe* (1931; repr., New York: Vintage Books, 1971), footnote on p. 199.

4. Ouspensky makes an important point here. The only way to understand occult symbols is to experience them as symbols. Reading about what they are supposed to mean won't give this understanding. When I was around twenty years old, I began to play with a deck of Tarot cards. I had no interest in the occult at this time, and no knowledge about the origin or meaning of the Tarot—I merely began to arrange the cards in groups and sequences that seemed meaningful, based on their symbolism. Much to my surprise, the cards began to "talk" to me in a language that was more basic than words. I continued in this way for a period of several weeks before deciding that I should probably do some study on the Tarot and learn about its history and uses. I credit those weeks with convincing me to devote my life to the study of Western magic. Quite by accident I had stumbled on the very best way to experience occult symbolism—with a receptive intuition unswayed by preexisting dogmatic definitions.

5. It is highly unlikely that Romanies in Spain used Tarot cards in the fourteenth century, since regular cards were only introduced into Europe at this time and the Tarot did not appear until about a century after the recorded use of playing cards. See Decker, Depaulis, and Dummett, *A Wicked Pack of Cards*, p. ix. Stuart Kaplan wrote that the arrival of cards into Europe predated the coming of the Romanies—see *The Encyclopedia of Tarot*, vol. 1, p. 21.

6. It is odd that Ouspensky offers no explanation or justification for his inversion of the places of the trumps the Chariot and the Hierophant. It is not supported by any major authority of whom I am aware. Evidently it was a quirk of the Russians—see Decker and Dummett, *A History of the Occult Tarot*, chap. 13, p. 256, note 4. When he came to revise his essay for inclusion in his book *A New Model of the Universe* in 1931, Ouspensky evidently repented of this inversion, since he returned these two trumps to their usual places—see *A New Model of the Universe*, p. 198. He also followed the example of A. E. Waite and inverted the traditional places of Justice and Strength, without, however, indicating this in his table of the trumps.

7. The fanciful notion that the Tarot is Egyptian in origin comes entirely from the imaginative speculations of Court de Gébelin. The idea was embraced with enthusiasm by French occultists of the nineteenth century such as Etteilla, Éliphas Lévi, and Paul Christian, even though it is without historical basis.

8. Tarot cards can be traced back to the end of the fourteenth century. I would be inclined to place the Tarot in the Renaissance period (1350–1600) rather than the Middle Ages. The innovative nature of the cards is more in keeping with the spirit of the Renaissance. However, some historians date the close of the Middle Ages to 1500, so Ouspensky is not necessarily wrong in his statement that the Tarot first appeared in the Middle Ages. The Tarot was invented just about the time when the social current of the Middle Ages in Europe transitioned into the dynamic quest for enlightenment that we call the Renaissance.

9. Raymond Lully published his work *Ars Magna*, or *Ars Generalis Ultima* (*Great Art*, or *Ultimate General Art*), in 1305. See his biographical note.

10. Something similar to ordinary playing cards existed in China and India prior to the appearance of playing cards in Europe; however, the Tarot trumps did not appear in Eastern countries before they were known in Europe. The symbolism of the trumps is completely European, apart from a few faux-Persian trappings.

11. It is more usual to divide the Tarot into two parts: the 56 suit cards and the 22 trumps or picture cards. Ouspensky's assertion that one of the trumps, the Fool, is somehow a second part of the Tarot, and equal to a third part, the suit cards, is his own insight, and is not widely supported in the literature of the Tarot.

12. Ouspensky's division of the trumps into three sets of seven follows the teaching of both Court de Gébelin and the Comte de Mellet. He associates 0. The Fool at the central point in his diagram with the human soul, and the triangle around it, formed from the other 21 trumps, with the Holy Trinity. At first consideration, it might seem more reasonable to place God at the center, on the monad (that is, the single card, the Fool). However, in an occult sense, each person is the center of his own universe. Each person looks out from this center point, and considers all other things to be separate and beyond it, including the manifest qualities of God, those aspects of divinity we can conceive and define in words. In this sense, God is outside of the human soul—not of outside it spiritually, because the separation is an illusion, but seemingly outside of it due to the limitations in the way human consciousness functions.

13. It is in this sense that the Fool (point) may be said to be equal to the 56 suit cards (square). The soul encompasses and reflects the world, because the phenomenal world, as we perceive it, is a creation of the human mind. This is the meaning of the Hermetic axiom "That which is below is like to that which is above, and that

which is above is like to that which is below." The microcosm mirrors the macrocosm because both are products of mind.

14. H. P. Blavatsky wrote very little concerning the Tarot. The game of patience or solitaire is played with an ordinary deck of 52 cards and has nothing to do with the Tarot. Ordinary cards were often used to divine the future in the eighteenth and nineteenth centuries—see part eight of the present work. Blavatsky did make passing reference to the Tarot:

"Again the Alphabet of Thoth can be dimly traced in the modern Tarot which can be had at almost every bookseller's in Paris. As for its being understood or utilized, the many fortune-tellers in Paris, who make a professional living by it, are sad specimens of failures of attempts at reading, let alone correctly interpreting, the symbolism of the Tarot without a preliminary philosophical study of the Science. The real Tarot, in its complete symbology, can be found only in the Babylonian cylinders, that anyone can inspect and study in the British Museum and elsewhere. Anyone can see these Chaldaean, antediluvian rhombs, or revolving cylinders, covered with sacred signs; but the secrets of these divining 'wheels,' or, as de Mirville calls them, 'the rotating globes of Hecate,' have to be left untold for some time to come." (Helena Blavatsky, "The Hexagon with the Central Point, or the Seventh Key," in *Collected Writings*, vol. 14, compiled by Boris de Zirkoff (Wheaton, IL: Theosophical Publishing House, 2009), p. 106.

It is perhaps needless to add that the Babylonian cylinders have no connection with the Tarot, or with Hecate for that matter.

15. Neither the Kabbalah nor astrology have any strong association with Hermes Trismegistus. This semi-divine figure, the purported author of the Hermetic books, is linked primarily with alchemy and ritual magic in ancient writings. Of course, magic makes extensive use of astrology, and the numerological methods of the Kabbalah are somewhat similar in their general procedures to the numerology of Pythagoras, which can be associated obliquely with Hermes Trismegistus.

16. Many intelligent, serious alchemists of the Middle Ages and the Renaissance devoted all their time to the manufacture of gold from base metals. They were interested in spiritual perfection only as a means to attain this material purpose. One such was Edward Kelley, the seer of Dr. John Dee. He sought gold the metal, not the gold of the spirit.

17. The French occultist Papus made an extensive analysis of the occult meaning of Tetragrammaton, the supreme name of God with four Hebrew letters (Yod-Heh-Vau-Heh), and its application to the Tarot in his 1889 book *Le Tarot des Bohémiens (The Tarot of the Bohemians)*. He related the initial letter, *Yod*, to the active principle and the ego; the second letter, *Heh*, to the passive principle and the non-ego; the third letter, *Vau*, to the link that unites the active to the passive; and the final letter,

Heh, to transition, the passage from one world to another. See the 1910 English translation of *The Tarot of the Bohemians*, p. 23.

18. Logos is a complex concept. Most Christians are familiar with the term from the first verse in the Gospel of John, which in the King James version of the Bible reads, "In the beginning was the Word, and the Word was with God, and the Word was God." *Word* is a translation for the Greek *logos*. In this biblical passage, it stands for Christ, and indicates that Christ existed from the beginning, both with God, and God himself. But the term is also used to express the faculty of human reason, the ability to engage in self-awareness and introspection, in analysis and deduction. Logos is self-knowledge. But it is more than just reason in itself; it is reason as an extension of the divine spirit within humanity. It is the human ability to recognize truth, and to divide truth from falsehood. It is the quality of the divine that was represented by gray-eyed Athene, the goddess of Athens in ancient Greece who stood for reason and discernment. Athene is logos personified, as is Christ. On a lower and more formal level in rhetoric, logos is an appeal to reason by the speaker, an attempt to persuade by what makes logical sense. It is contrasted with *ethos*, an appeal to ethics, or what seems right; and *pathos*, an appeal to the emotions of the audience to arouse their pity or outrage. Logos may be contrasted with the Greek term *gnosis*—whereas logos is the divine gift of reasoning, gnosis is the divine gift of transcendent knowledge. Through logos we achieve gnosis.

19. Elves are usually not considered to be synonymous with Salamanders, the elemental spirits of Fire. Elves are traditionally thought to be household spirits or woodland spirits. The names of the four classes of elemental spirits—Salamanders (Fire), Undines (Water), Sylphs (Air), and Gnomes (Earth)—derive from the writings of Paracelsus, a German alchemist of the fifteenth century whose real name was Theophrastus Bombastus von Hohenheim (1493–1541). He wrote about the elementals in his work *Liber de nymphis, sylphis, pygmaeis et salamandris et de caeteris spiritibus* (*The Book of Nymphs, Sylphs, Pygmies and Salamanders and Other Spirits*), which was published posthumously in 1566. Paracelsus usually referred to the Gnomes as Pygmies, but he wrote, "The name of the water people is also undina, and of the air people sylvestres, and of the mountain people gnomi, and of the fire people vulcani rather than salamandri." See C. Lilian Temkin, George Rosen, Gregory Zilboorg, and Henry E. Sigerist, *Four Treatises of Theophrastus Von Hohenheim, Called Paracelsus* (Baltimore, MD: Johns Hopkins University Press, 1941), p. 231.

20. This overlapping of the elemental sets in the number cards of each Tarot suit is derived from Papus, who wrote, "The second *He* of the preceding series becoming the *Yod* of the following series: thus 4, the fourth term of the first series, becomes the first term of the second series; 7, the fourth term of the second, becomes the first term of the third." Papus, *The Tarot of the Bohemians*, pp. 38–39.

21. Very few modern commentators on the Tarot would make the sweeping statement that the suits of Wands and Cups signify good and the suits of Swords and Disks signify evil. Each suit exerts its own active force and has its own unique nature. Whether this force and nature express themselves in a good way or an evil way depends on the circumstances surrounding the card in question.

22. It is not really possible to "draw a horoscope" using only the Tarot, although the cards of the Tarot have been associated with astrological factors by modern occultists, and some Tarot divination spreads rely upon astrological symbolism. See Papus, *The Tarot of the Bohemians*, pp. 233–251, and the unpaginated diagram of the zodiac that follows them.

23. Oswald Wirth's "Essay Upon the Astronomical Tarot" occupies pages 242–251 of Papus's book *The Tarot of the Bohemians*.

24. It is necessary to emphasize to those who might be inclined to accept Ouspensky's statements on face value that no evidence for the ancient Egyptian gallery of Tarot Trumps under the Sphinx has ever been found, and there is not even so much as a hint or suggestion that such a gallery ever existed. Either Paul Christian invented this Tarot trump gallery out of whole cloth for his 1870 book *Histoire de la Magie*, or he borrowed the idea from an existing literary source without giving credit to its creator. Christian pretends to be referring to Iamblichus when he writes of this gallery, but I find no mention of it in Iamblichus.

25. There is no Tarot trump called "Life"—Ouspensky is referring to the Wheel of Fortune, which is numbered with the Roman numeral X in most Tarot decks. He associates the vagaries of Fortune, the ups and downs of life, with the cycle of human existence.

26. This is a very subtle and important point. Occult symbols must be living to possess power. To be alive, they must be unfixed—when a symbol is fixed into place, it is like a butterfly pinned to a corkboard: it is dead. Being alive means constantly shifting and being elusive in meaning. You can never really know a living symbol; you can only grasp aspects of its meaning, and even as you hold that meaning in your mind, it shifts and changes. This is the power of the barbarous words of evocation, words that have no explicit meaning but were used to evoke spirits. Their power lies in their potential, their possibilities of meaning. Living symbols dance in our minds, sometimes revealing parts of themselves, sometimes withholding meaning from us. They must be experienced repeatedly over spans of time, and under various circumstances, before a sense of what they signify can be built up in the mind. The trumps of the Tarot are complex living occult symbols.

27. See biographical note on Louis Claude de Saint-Martin.

28. See biographical note on Alphonse Louis Constant.

29. See biographical note on Gérard Anaclet Vincent Encausse.

30. See biographical note on Plotinus.

31. See biographical note on Johann Georg Gichtel.

32. See biographical note on Friedrich Nietzsche.

33. See biographical note on Mabel Collins.

34. This is a reference to the *Übermensch* of Nietzsche.

35. Adam Kadmon, the primordial or higher Adam, is a concept in the Jewish system of mystical-religious thought known as the Kabbalah. The universe, emanating from God in ten successive states known as Sephiroth, took the pattern of the heavenly first man, which was replicated in a smaller scale in the actual physical mind and body of Adam, on the universal occult principle that what is above is like that which is below. This concept stems from the fact that in Genesis, the creation of man is described twice (Genesis 1:27 and 2:7). Why should Adam be created twice, the rabbis reasoned, unless it was two different levels or kinds of Adam? The concept of a "heavenly man" first appeared in the writings of Philo Judaicus (c. 20 BCE–c. 50 CE). "The races of men are twofold; for one is the heavenly man, and the other is the earthly man. Now the heavenly man, as being born in the image of God, has no participation in any corruptible or earth-like essence." Philo Judaeus, *Legum Allegoriae*, bk. 1, chap. 12, in *The Works of Philo: Complete and Unabridged,* trans. C. D. Yonge (1854–1855; repr., Peabody, MA: Hendrickson, 1993), p. 28.

36. The "law of four" is a reference to Papus, who in his book *The Tarot of the Bohemians* makes frequent reference to the law of Tetragrammaton, or Yod-Heh-Vau-Heh—see pages 37 and 39 in this work for examples.

    On pages 22–23 of *The Tarot of the Bohemians*, Papus wrote:

    "The Trinity is the synthetic and absolute formula to which all the sciences converge; and this formula, forgotten with regard to its scientific value, has been transmitted to us integrally by all the religions of the world, those unconscious depositaries of the science-wisdom of primitive civilizations.

    Thus, the Great Sacred name is formed of three letters only. The fourth term of the Name is produced by the repetition of the second letter, *He.*

    This repetition indicates the passage of the Trinitarian law into a new application—that is, to speak correctly, a transition from the metaphysical to the physical world, or generally, of any world whatsoever to the world that immediately follows it.

    The knowledge of the property of the second *He* is the key to the whole Divine Name, in every application of which it is susceptible."

37. The "magic chain" is a reference to Éliphas Lévi's *Dogme et Rituel*, specifically to chapter 11 of the second part of this work. This chapter is titled "The Triple Chain." Lévi wrote, "The Great work in Practical Magic, after the education of the will and the personal creation of the Magus, is the formation of the magnetic

chain, and this secret is truly that of priesthood and royalty. To form a magnetic chain is to originate a current of ideas which produces faith and draws a large number of wills in a given circle of active manifestation" (Lévi, *Transcendental Magic*, p. 277). Lévi went on to explain that this "magic chain" may be created by signs or gestures, by speech, and by physical contact.

38. Éliphas Lévi completed a work titled *Le Grand Arcane; ou, l'Occultisme Dévoilé (The Great Secret; or, Occultism Unveiled)* in 1868. It was not published in French until after his death in 1898, and was first published in English in 1925 in successive issues of the periodical *The Montana Mason*. The translation was made by J. R. Lenmert, the editor of the periodical. In this book, which Lévi regarded as "the last word on occultism," he wrote, "The great arcanum, the inexpressible arcanum, the dangerous arcanum, the incomprehensible arcanum may be definitively formulated thus: The divinity of man." Éliphas Lévi, *The Great Secret* (Wellingborough, Northamptonshire: Thorsons, 1975), p. 175.

39. This characterization of the Fool as "an ordinary man" is quite different from that of most occultists, who see the Fool as a spiritualized version of man. A. E. Waite wrote, "He is a prince of the other world on his travels through this one...He is the spirit in search of experience." He added somewhat contemptuously a little further on, "The conventional explanations say that the Fool signifies the flesh, the sensitive life." A. E. Waite, *The Pictorial Key to the Tarot* (1910; repr., New York: Samuel Weiser, 1980), pp. 152, 155.

40. The division of the trumps into three sets of seven cards is similar to that used by the Comte de Mellet, and it was suggested by Court de Gébelin; but whereas de Mellet takes the trumps of each set in their sequence, but in reverse order, starting with the final numbered trump, to form his ages of gold, silver, and iron, Ouspensky selects his cards for each set out of sequence and out of order based on his interpretation of their meaning.

41. The animal behind the figure on trump 0. The Fool is called a "lynx" due to the influence of Court de Gébelin and the Comte de Mellet, who both called it a "tiger" in their Tarot essays. Éliphas Lévi also referred to the beast as a "tiger" in his *Dogma et Rituel (Transcendental Magic)*, p. 392. Oswald Wirth made it into a wildcat of some sort on his Tarot of 1889, based on these authorities. We must presume that Ouspensky recognized the absurdity of calling such a diminutive animal a "tiger" and decided to downsize it to a "lynx." In the image of the Fool in the traditional French Tarot that is placed alongside the image of Wirth's Fool in *The Tarot of the Bohemians* of Papus (p. 184 of that work), the beast behind the Fool is so poorly drawn that it could be interpreted to be almost anything. However, in other Tarots of the eighteenth and nineteenth centuries, it is quite obviously a small dog, and it is also obvious to me that it is smelling the buttocks and pawing

at the deranged hose of the Fool, not biting him. My interpretation is that the Fool has soiled himself while defecating, and this has attracted the dog's interest.

42. The rather odd image of the crocodile makes its way into Ouspensky's description of this trump from Paul Christian's *The History and Practice of Magic*, where this trump is titled the Crocodile. Christian described the Fool as a blind man about to trip over a fallen obelisk "on which a crocodile is waiting with open jaws" (*The History and Practice of Magic*, p. 110). Christian's description of the trump was illustrated in the Egyptian Tarot that appears in *Practical Astrology* by Comte C. de Saint-Germain (real name Edgar de Valcourt-Vermont, 1846–1909). Saint-Germain's book was published in 1901, but the designs for the cards in it were lifted from René Falconnier's *Les XXII Lames Hermétiques du Tarot Divinatoire*, published in Paris in 1896. The Falconnier designs were based directly on Christian's descriptions.

43. The twelve stars are described by Waite as on her diadem, gathered in a cluster—*The Pictorial Key to the Tarot*, p. 80. The twelve stars also appear in Paul Christian's description of this trump. He wrote, "She is crowned by twelve stars and her feet rest on the moon" (*History and Practice of Magic*, p. 97). In Oswald Wirth's design, there are only nine stars visible in a crescent around the head of the Empress (but three may be hidden behind her head), and one foot rests on the crescent moon. Papus in his description wrote, "She wears a crown of twelve points, or twelve stars" (*The Tarot of the Bohemians*, pp. 115–116). Papus made no mention of the moon, even though Wirth's card illustrates his description of this trump. Éliphas Lévi also gave her twelve stars, and made the important explicit link with Revelation 12:1, calling this figure the "Queen of Heaven," which is only implied by Christian's description (*Transcendental Magic*, p. 387). Lévi also put the moon beneath her feet, but Waite did not in his Tarot design, writing, "She is not *Regina coeli* [Queen of Heaven] but she is still *refugium peccatorum* [refuge of sinners]"—*Pictorial Key*, p. 80. The lack of a moon in Ouspensky's description suggests that he agreed with Waite on this point—instead, he called her "Queen of life."

44. The ankh, an ancient Egyptian symbol representing life, has the shape of an oval or circle above a Greek letter *Tau*. The Coptic Orthodox Church of Egypt adopted the ankh as their Christian cross, in which function it became known as the *crux ansata* (handle-shaped cross). In ancient Egyptian art, figures are often shown holding the ankh by its loop and pointing with it. It is worth noting that the symbol of Venus, described by Ouspensky as present on the Empress trump, is very close in shape to the ankh.

45. This paragraph is based directly on Papus and his law of Tetragrammaton—that the first three letters in the name are complete unto themselves and the fourth letter becomes the first letter of the next trine. The *Yod* is the positive principle; the *first He* the reactive negative principle; the *Vau* the reconciling principle expressed by the union of Yod and the first He; and the *second He* the principle of transition

to the next interlinked cycle. That is to say, if the letters of the name are regarded as numbers, 4 of the first cycle becomes the 1 of the next cycle, and this is repeated up and down like the links of a chain.

It may help to think of the first three letters as forming the points of a two-dimensional triangle, and the fourth letter as defining the third-dimensional apex of a tetrahedron. Then this fourth point becomes the first point of another two-dimensional triangle, and the fourth point from it the apex of another tetrahedron, and so on.

A similar concept exists in the Kabbalah, where the universe is emanated in ten stages, called Sephiroth, but there are various higher and lower worlds in which these emanations express themselves, so that the worlds are linked in such a way that the tenth, or lowest, emanation of one world is the first, or highest, emanation of the world immediately below. These worlds are usually said to be four in number.

46. Ouspensky's description of the trump the Sun comes from Waite's Tarot. Lévi described both the more conventional design of two children standing before a wall and also a child riding on a horse. Wirth chose the symbol of the two children, Waite that of the child on a horse. But the sunflowers appear to be Waite's inspiration, although Paul Christian does describe a circle of flowers in which two small children stand (*The History and Practice of Magic*, p. 109).

47. Lévi described the chariot as drawn by two sphinxes, one white and the other black. This was a departure from Court de Gébelin and the traditional image. Paul Christian followed Lévi's lead, as did Oswald Wirth and Papus. So did A. E. Waite, who wrote, "I have accepted the variation of Éliphas Lévi" (*The Pictorial Key to the Tarot*, p. 96).

48. Court de Gébelin describes the beasts on the trump the Moon as two dogs, but the Comte de Mellet understood them to be a dog and a wolf. Éliphas Lévi adopted de Mellet's choice, as did Papus, but the beasts on Wirth's design in Papus's book look like two dogs. Indeed, in Wirth's 1927 book *The Tarot of the Magicians*, he stated, "Two dogs guard the route" (p. 139); this, in spite of the fact that the later version of Wirth's trump depicted in this work makes one dog resemble a large black wolf. A. E. Waite followed Lévi on this point and made them wolf and dog. This change from dog and dog to dog and wolf was popular because it increased the meaning of this symbolism and lent it depth. Dogs and wolves are closely related; they are both beasts of the Moon, but they are very different in nature. One is tame, the other wild. The dog represents the restraint of reason, and the wolf the feral ferocity of instinct.

49. The concept of the Lovers as Adam and Eve in the Garden of Eden was strongly stressed by A. E. Waite on this trump in his Tarot, but not by other authorities.

50. Plotinus, "On the Intellectual Beauty," ennead 5, tractate 8, section 4. See *Plotinus: The Six Enneads* (Chicago: Encyclopaedia Britannica, 1980), p. 241.

51. By "eight-pointed cross," Ouspensky means a cross with three beams. The ends of the beams make up six points, the top of the column the seventh, and the bottom of the column the eighth.

52. This interpretation of the Hierophant, or Pope, usually numbered *V* in Tarot decks, not *VII*, is directly contrary to the meaning of this trump, which represents the outward pomp and show of religion, the ceremony, the instruments and robes, the rituals and laws. It is in contrast to the Popess, or High Priestess, which expresses the secret and hidden aspect of spirituality, its mystery. Presumably, Ouspensky was aware that his interpretation was the opposite of the actual symbolism of the card. The Pope is the guardian of the Holy Word, in the form of a book, the Bible—yet Ouspensky explicitly says not to expect to read the truth in books. He is warning the reader not to place faith in material or external things, foreshadowing in this way trump XVI. The Tower, which he pairs with the Hierophant.

53. In the Gringonneur trump titled the House of God, the top of the falling tower is a serrated battlement that vaguely resembles a crown—see Kaplan, *The Encyclopedia of Tarot*, vol. 1, p. 115. Similarly, on the trump in the Joannes Pelagius Mayer pack, circa 1750, the crown-like battlements of the tower have been snapped off by a thunderbolt from the Sun, which the Comte de Mellet rightly assumes is probably intended to represent a comet—comets are harbingers of the overthrow of kingdoms and monarchs. A. E. Waite made the suggestive shape of the top of the tower explicit by turning it into an enormous gold crown. Waite wrote, "It is the ruin of the House of Life, when evil has prevailed therein, and above all that it is the rending of a House of Doctrine"—*The Pictorial Key to the Tarot*, p. 132. This statement by Waite appears to be the inspiration for Ouspensky's interpretation of the trump as the overthrow and ruin of the outward religious pomp and ceremony depicted on the trump the Hierophant.

54. Éliphas Lévi wrote, "Two persons, doubtless Nimrod and his false prophet or minister, are precipitated from the summit of the ruins" (*Transcendental Magic*, p. 391). In Jewish and Christian tradition, Nimrod was said to be the king of Babylon who built the Tower of Babel. See Flavius Josephus, *The Antiquities of the Jews*, bk. 1, chap. 4, para. 3, in *The Complete Works of Flavius Josephus*, p. 35.

55. Frederick Nietzsche, pt. 2, sec. 7, "Of Tarantulae," in *Thus Spake Zarathustra*, p. 136.

56. An inverted cross. Oddly enough, a cross on the palm of the Devil appears only on the Waite trump, and is not mentioned by A. E. Waite in his description of the card. There is no cross on the palm in the Marseilles Tarot or other traditional Tarots I have examined, and it does not appear in the Oswald Wirth trump, the description by Papus, the description by Paul Christian, or the description by Éliphas Lévi—Ouspensky's primary sources.

57. Ouspensky's alternative name for the trump Temperance was *Time*. The triangle of XIII. Death, XIV. Temperance, and XV. The Devil is illustrated by Papus in his *The Tarot of the Bohemians*, p. 156.

58. The cloak is an important symbol to Martinists, particularly the cloak of Apollonius. Julie Scott, Grand Master of the Traditional Martinist Order for the English Grand Lodge for the Americas, mentioned the cloak of Apollonius in her essay "The Cloak," which was published in *Rosicrucian Digest* vol. 92, no. 1 (2014): pp. 44–48. She wrote, "As we learn in our earliest Martinist initiation, the cloak renders us invulnerable to attacks of ignorance and it symbolizes the hermetic seal, which creates a place for inner transformation to take place" (p. 46).

59. According to legend, the staff of Moses, with which miracles were worked, was passed down from Adam. It is sometimes known as the "rod of God."

60. "The initiate is he who possesses the lamp of Trismegistus, the mantle of Apollonius, and the staff of the patriarchs. The lamp of Trismegistus is reason illuminated by science; the mantle of Apollonius is full and complete self-possession, which isolates the sage from blind tendencies; and the staff of the patriarchs is the help of the secret and everlasting forces of nature. The lamp of Trismegistus enlightens present, past, and future, lays bare the conscience of men, and manifests the inmost recesses of the female heart. The lamp burns with a triple flame, the mantle is thrice-folded, and the staff is divided into three parts." Éliphas Lévi, *Transcendental Magic*, pt. 1, chap. 9, p. 92.

61. "Unsatisfied your soul seeketh after treasures and trinkets because your virtue is ever unsatisfied in willing to give away." Nietzsche, "Of Giving Virtue," in *Thus Spake Zarathustra*, p. 103.

62. Jacob's ladder. See Genesis 28:10–19.

63. The angel on A. E. Waite's version of this trump does have a triangle within a square on his chest, but there is no point within the triangle, nor does Waite mention a point in his textual description of the card. See *The Pictorial Key to the Tarot*, p. 125.

64. On Waite's trump there is a point within the circle on the angel's forehead, making it a symbol of the Sun. Waite wrote, "A winged angel, with the sign of the sun upon his forehead, and on his breast the square and triangle of the septenary" (*The Pictorial Key to the Tarot*, p. 124). The septenary relates to Tetragrammaton. Seven is 3 + 4. There are both three letters, yet at the same time four letters, in IHVH. This is why the Hebrew letters in the name of God are written above the square and triangle on Waite's trump.

65. Eternity is a circle; infinity is a lemniscate, or figure eight, on its side.

66. The 1913 English text has "face of a bull" repeated here—I have corrected it to read "face of a man."

67. "And lo! an eagle swept through the air in wide circles, a serpent hanging from it not like a prey, but like a friend: coiling round its neck. 'They are mine animals,' said Zarathustra, and rejoiced heartily." Nietzsche, sec. 10 of introductory speech, in *Thus Spake Zarathustra*, p. 21.

68. These twin towers with the sun between them appear on the Waite design for the trump Death. It is an obvious reference to the trump the Moon in the Waite Tarot. Waite remarked that it is "the sun of immortality" (*The Pictorial Key to the Tarot*, p. 120).

PART THREE

Tarot Divination Methods
of S. L. MacGregor Mathers
by
DONALD TYSON

INTRODUCTION
TO PART THREE

The most significant magical society of the past two centuries was the Hermetic Order of the Golden Dawn. Its influence on modern magic has been immense and continues to this day. It may be argued that the Theosophical Society of Madame Helena Blavatsky was larger and more enduring, and in a general sense perhaps more influential on esoteric thought; but the Theosophical Society was not devoted to the teaching and practice of ritual magic, and it is this that distinguished the Golden Dawn from most of the other esoteric orders and fraternities of its period.

The Golden Dawn was a self-declared Rosicrucian society founded in 1887 by three high-level Freemasons, all of them keen students of Hermetic philosophy and Western magic. Whereas Theosophy was focused mainly on the esoteric teachings of India, the Golden Dawn concerned itself with the occult practices of Egypt, Greece, Rome, and Renaissance Europe, including alchemy, astrology, Enochian magic, and the Kabbalah.

The leader of the Golden Dawn was Samuel Liddell MacGregor Mathers, a visionary Freemason devoted not only to the study of traditional Western magic but also to its restoration and rehabilitation as a path to spiritual enlightenment. His fanatical devotion to the practice of magic is to a large degree what gave the Golden Dawn its unique focus. He was a gifted psychic and spirit medium who, in conjunction with his wife, Moïna, who was also a psychic, received from spirits many of the teachings that formed the Golden Dawn system of magic.

This point is often glossed over but needs to be stressed. Mathers did not compose or create the magic of the Golden Dawn; he received it from spiritual beings. He was in regular communication with the spirits who presided over the Golden Dawn occult current, known as the Secret Chiefs. It is these spiritual beings who are the ultimate architects of Golden Dawn magic, which is firmly rooted in the Western esoteric tradition.

The basic framework of Golden Dawn teachings was contained in a coded Masonic manuscript that was either obtained or created by William Wynn Westcott, one of the founding members of the Order, prior to the establishment of the Golden Dawn. The origin of this cipher document remains a mystery. We don't know if Westcott wrote it or if he merely found it, but it was undoubtedly written by a Freemason. It lays out the structure of the Golden Dawn, but it is a skeleton without a body. It was Mathers and his wife who filled in this outline with flesh and blood and transformed it into a living system of practical ritual magic. Neither of them claimed to have invented the material they added—it was dictated by the spirits who presided over the occult current of the Golden Dawn through the planchette, the pendulum, and table rapping and by direct spirit communication.

Those who are not directly involved in practical occultism will be inclined to scoff at this assertion and dismiss it. However, the leading members of the Golden Dawn believed implicitly in Mathers's psychic link with the Secret Chiefs. They believed that they were being instructed by the Secret Chiefs, through Mathers, both in higher spiritual truths and in the secret techniques of ritual magic. Let me only add that all occult societies have as their basis the shared conviction that they are guided and instructed by spiritual teachers who exist above and beyond the level of our everyday physical reality.

Central to the system of magic that was taught to members of the Order was the Tarot. Members learned to use the cards not only for purposes of divination, but also for meditation, scrying, astral projection, the transformation and elevation of states of consciousness, the creation of composite spirits known as telesmatic images, and for making talismans and charms. The esoteric structure of the Tarot connected and integrated all the diverse aspects of the curriculum of magic taught by the Order. It might be said that the Tarot is the beating heart of Golden Dawn magic.

There is some obscurity over who was specifically responsible for the Golden Dawn teachings on the Tarot. Without question, it was Mathers and his wife, a talented artist, who played the key roles in channeling and setting down the unique titles and descriptions of the symbolism, and in designing the images on the cards; but W. Wynn Westcott was also deeply involved with the Kabbalistic aspect of the Golden Dawn esoteric Tarot, and other members of the Order, such as the actress Florence Farr, did extensive scrying work with it on the pathways of the Tree of Life. Perhaps it is best to say that the Golden Dawn Tarot was a group effort, the result of the spirit instructions received by Mathers, the artwork done by Moïna, the Kabbalistic knowledge of W. Wynn Westcott, the experimentation in scrying by Florence Farr, and the work of other unsung members of the Order who will probably never receive due credit for their contributions.

The original Order of the Golden Dawn did not have a lengthy existence. It effectively came to an end in 1903, although various offshoots continued for decades longer and some still exist to this day. Its immense influence stems from the esoteric work of its former members, some of whom continued to practice and teach magic, established magical societies of their own, and wrote books about magic. The most prominent of these graduates of the Golden Dawn were A. E. Waite, Dion Fortune, Paul Foster Case, and Aleister Crowley. All of them went on to create their own occult societies, and all but Dion Fortune brought forth their own esoteric Tarots that were based in part on the Tarot of the Golden Dawn.

This part of the present work was extracted from an exhaustive examination of esoteric Tarot symbolism that I wrote two decades ago. It is as yet unpublished due to a number of factors, one being its immense length (it was over 2,500 pages in manuscript), another being the large number of quotations I used from sources, some of which may still be under copyright, thanks to our constantly changing and lengthening copyright laws.

I have included this extract because the method of divination used by the Hermetic Order of the Golden Dawn has great historical and practical interest to students of the Western occult tradition. The long and convoluted Golden Dawn method known as the *Opening of the Key* appears in Israel Regardie's great work, *The Golden Dawn*,[1] where the teaching documents of the Order have been collected together. However, it is not as clearly described there as might be wished, and in fact it contains errors that make an accurate comprehension of the method quite difficult. I have corrected these errors and have, I hope, in the following commentary made the method clearer for readers who may wish to experiment with it.

There is one peculiarity of the Golden Dawn Tarot that must be mentioned, if only to avoid suspicions that it has been overlooked. That is the arrangement of the court cards. In the Golden Dawn Tarot, the Knights are elevated to the role of the Kings and receives the alternative title of *King*, and the Kings are demoted to the position of the Knights and are renamed with the alternative title of *Prince*. The Pages or Knaves are termed the *Princesses*. The result is a royal family of court cards in each suit: King (Knight), Queen, Prince, and Princess.

This change was the result of the dynamic interplay of forces that was understood to take place when the four cards representing the four elements and the four letters of Tetragrammaton interacted with each other. The Knight was understood to be elevated by this interaction to the throne of the King, whom he displaced, and to unite with the Queen to engender a new generation through the Prince and Princess. Crowley described this incestuous family interaction as "extraordinarily complex, quite beyond the limits of any ordinary treatise to discuss."[2]

This elevation of the Knight to the position of the King was dynamic, and was not always observed in the Golden Dawn documents. In the description of the Opening of the Key that is analyzed here, the Princes are identified with the Knights and occupy the rank of the Knights, just beneath the Queens, and the Princesses are identified with the Knaves or Pages. The working arrangement of the court cards in this essay is Kings, Queens, Princes (Knights), Princesses (Knaves).

The other three methods of divination with the Tarot that make up the remainder of this part of the present work are described in Mathers's pamphlet *The Tarot*, published in London in 1888. It is in every respect an inferior writing on the subject of Tarot. Although it was published the same year the Isis-Urania Temple of the Golden Dawn was established in London, Mathers made no attempt to probe into the esoteric aspects of the symbolism of the trumps, but merely provided a quick reference to the traditional Tarot for those wishing to use it for fortune-telling. The interest in these three methods, apart from their inherent value as forms of divination, lies in their association with Mathers and the influence they may have exerted on other members of the Golden Dawn.

In *The Tarot*, Mathers did assign a zero to the Fool, an assignment that played a key role in the esoteric Tarot teachings of the Golden Dawn, but he placed the card in its traditional location, second to last in the sequence of the trumps (between XX. The Last Judgment and XXI. The World or Universe). Note that some of his brief definitions of the trumps were influenced by the essay of Court de Gébelin, from which he quoted in his pamphlet.[3]

Mathers stated in his pamphlet that the Tarot he used for his descriptions was an Italian Tarot. "There are Italian, Spanish, and German Tarot packs, and since the time of Etteilla French also, but these latter are not so well adapted for occult study owing to Etteilla's attempted 'corrections' of the symbolism. The Italian are decidedly the best for divination and practical occult purposes, and I shall, therefore, use them as the basis of the present treatise."[4]

Following Mathers's three divination methods, I have included his divinatory meanings for the cards, as given in his pamphlet. The result is a compact and relatively complete reference to the types of Tarot divinations used by the founder and leader of the Golden Dawn. It will be of interest to the reader to compare the card meanings given by Mathers for the suit cards to those in part eight of the present work, where divination with common playing cards is described.

TAROT DIVINATION METHODS OF
S. L. MACGREGOR MATHERS

by

DONALD TYSON

I.
The Opening of the Key

MacGregor Mathers and the other leaders of the Golden Dawn considered the Tarot an important instrument of magic, not an amusement. The Opening of the Key, the method of Tarot divination taught in the magical system of the Golden Dawn, is protracted and at first consideration appears to be bewilderingly complex. It is designed to allow occult influences to affect the fall of the cards as completely as possible. Its involved procedure ensures that it will only be used for inquiring into serious questions of major life significance.

This form of divination is described in an essay that was among the Golden Dawn documents collected and published by Israel Regardie. It follows directly after the primary Golden Dawn document on the Tarot, *Book T*. Mathers was probably the original author of the essay, although it does not bear his signature.[5] In any case, he edited it and expanded it at a later time with a detailed sample reading that shows both the technique of divination and the method of interpreting the cards used by the Golden Dawn.

The author of the essay stated in its introductory remarks, "This form is especially applicable to Divination concerning the ordinary material events of daily life."[6] This statement is somewhat optimistic. By the time the diviner makes his way through the convoluted procedure of the Opening of the Key, half the day will have elapsed. Yet despite the procedure's complexity and length, an understanding of the Golden Dawn method of divination is essential for a complete comprehension of the Golden Dawn Tarot symbolism and esoteric attributions.

The Opening of the Key is presented in full in Regardie's *The Golden Dawn*, but I have reexamined it in this work with the intention of making the method a little easier for the beginner to grasp, and to clarify several ambiguous details that might easily provoke mistakes in procedure. Be aware that I am not quoting the text of the Golden Dawn procedure below, but rather providing a commentary on it.

Choosing the Significator

Before a divination can commence, it is necessary for the diviner to select a card that will represent the querent—the person inquiring information from the Tarot. This representative card is termed the *significator*. If the diviner performs a reading for himself, he picks a card that signifies his own identity. In some forms of Tarot divination, the significator plays no active part, but in the Golden Dawn method it is essential. Every detail of the subsequent reading is keyed to the significator card.

The significator is drawn from among the sixteen court cards. Its selection is based upon a similarity between the physical qualities of the querent and the qualities of age, sex, hair color, eye color, and complexion associated with the court cards in the Golden Dawn system.

In general, it may be stated that Kings represent men, Queens women, Princes (Knights) young men, and Princesses (Pages) young women. Occasionally Kings and Princes may stand for masculine, assertive women, and by the same token, Queens and Princesses may represent feminine or submissive men. The court cards in the suit of Wands signify blond or red-headed individuals with fair complexions, those in the suit of Cups slightly darker persons with sandy or light brown hair, those in the suit of Swords stand for persons with brown hair and dark complexions, and those in the suit of Disks for individuals with very dark or black hair and swarthy skin. The ideal hair and eye colors assigned to each court figure are given in a table[7] in *Book T* and are as follows:

Court Card	Hair Color	Eye Color
King of Wands	Red-gold	Gray or Hazel
Queen of Wands	Red-gold	Blue or Brown
Prince of Wands	Yellow	Blue-gray
Princess of Wands	Red-gold	Blue
King of Cups	Fair	Blue
Queen of Cups	Gold-brown	Blue
Prince of Cups	Brown	Gray or Brown
Princess of Cups	Brown	Blue or Brown
King of Swords	Dark-brown	Dark
Queen of Swords	Light-brown	Gray
Prince of Swords	Dark	Dark
Princess of Swords	Light-brown	Blue
King of Pentacles	Dark	Dark
Queen of Pentacles	Dark	Dark
Prince of Pentacles	Dark-brown	Dark
Princess of Pentacles	Rich-brown	Dark

In the original Golden Dawn Tarot deck painted by Moïna Mathers, which has either perished or is in the hands of some private collector, all of the figures in the court cards very likely faced either to the left or to the right. We may advance this conjecture, without having seen the deck, because the direction in which the figure on the significator card faces or gazes plays a vital role in the divination technique known as the Opening of the Key. This necessity to face the court figures either left or right was not understood by Chic and Tabatha Cicero, who in their re-creation of the Golden Dawn Tarot (Llewellyn, 1991) show all court figures staring straight out from the cards they occupy. The Robert Wang re-creation (U.S. Games, 1978), which was designed with the assistance of Israel Regardie, does depict the court figures gazing either to the left or to the right. The Thoth deck of Aleister Crowley, painted by Lady Frieda Harris (1942), shows some court figures gazing to the side but others looking straight ahead. The Rider-Waite Tarot (1909) shows the King of Swords gazing straight ahead, but all the other court figures in the pack look either to the left or to the right.

As a result, the Cicero version of the Golden Dawn Tarot and the Thoth Tarot of Crowley are both unsuited to divination using the Opening of the Key. The Wang version of the Golden Dawn Tarot may be employed, and the Marseilles Tarot may also be used, since all court figures in the Wang and Marseilles decks face either right or left. In my opinion, the figures on the court cards in the original Golden Dawn Tarot of Moïna Mathers probably faced the same directions they face in the Tarot of Marseilles. This is not true of the Wang re-creation of the Golden Dawn Tarot. The Rider-Waite pack can only be used for Golden Dawn divination if a decision is made to presume, for the purpose of divination, that the King of Swords faces left, from the viewer's perspective, since his sword does lean toward the left side of the design.

In some modern Tarot decks, the direction in which the figures on the court cards face may be quite subtle. The important consideration is whether the eyes of the figure are directed to the left side or the right side of the card, not which way the countenance of the figure may be turned—however, almost invariably the eyes and the countenance will be directed the same way. In the Marseilles deck there is no doubt. All the court figures face strongly to one side or the other.

The General Procedure

The Opening of the Key contains five distinct operations, each of which is really a separate divination. The first stage relates to the beginning of the matter under question, stages two, three, and four concern its progression, and stage five relates to its conclusion. In the dimension of time, the first stage concerns the present situation, and each subsequent stage reveals matters further into the future, with the fifth stage showing the final fulfillment of the subject under question.

Each of these five operations employs the same basic technique for selecting the cards that are to be considered during that operation, and the order in which they are to be read. For every operation, the querent shuffles the cards. The complete Tarot pack is divided into smaller packets of cards—each operation uses a different method for making this division into packets. The packet containing the significator is located by examining all the cards without disturbing their relative order. Only this packet is used. The other packets of cards are set aside.

Mathers laid down some basic rules for the proper way of shuffling, cutting, and handling the cards, which I will quote here:

> In shuffling, the mind of the Enquirer should be earnestly fixed on the matter concerning which he desires information. If any cards fall in the process, they should be taken up without being noticed and the shuffling resumed. The shuffling being concluded, and the pack placed upon the table, if any cards fall to the ground, or become turned in a different direction, the shuffling should be done again.
>
> A cut should be clean and decided. If any cards fall from the hand in the performance, the operation of shuffling should be repeated before they are again cut. In dealing, care should be taken not to invert the cards, and their relative order should be rigidly maintained, as without care in this respect, one may be easily pushed under or over another, which would of course have the effect of completely altering the counting in the Reading.[8]

What Mathers did not mention in his description of the shuffle is that it is necessary, either before or during the shuffle, to invert some of the cards randomly so that their relative positions will be reversed top to bottom. This is vital so that at each shuffling, all of the court cards, and especially the card chosen as significator, have the opportunity to become either upright or inverted, because this changes the direction in which their figures face. The easiest way to accomplish this is to cut the deck into two packets and rotate one packet top-to-bottom before shuffling to thoroughly mix the cards. In this way, half the cards are inverted randomly at each shuffling operation.

The random inversion top-to-bottom of some of the cards is absolutely essential before the cards are dealt out in the spreads. Do not be confused by the language Mathers uses. When he writes "if any cards fall to the ground, or become turned in a different direction, the shuffling should be done again," he is talking about after the shuffle has been concluded. He means that if any card gets flipped over or falls off the table when the pack is being set down, the shuffle must be redone.

On this topic, elsewhere he writes, "In the laying out of the Cards, if any are inverted, they must remain so and must not be turned round, as that would alter the direction in which they would be looking. A card has the same meaning and forces whether right or inverted, so that no particular attention need be paid to the circumstances."[9] He means that if any of the court cards are upside down when dealt into the layout, they must remain so to preserve the direction of the gaze of the figure, either left or right. They could only be dealt out inverted if some of them were inverted before or during the shuffle. In Golden Dawn divination, upright and inverted cards are interpreted the same way, but the direction their eyes look is of prime importance, and the court cards must be given the opportunity to face either left or right.

The significator packet is spread out by the diviner faceup in a crescent or horseshoe, the horns of which point toward the diviner, so that all its cards are clearly visible. The individual cards that will actually be read in a particular operation are selected by counting around the arc of the horseshoe in the direction in which the royal figure on the significator card gazes. Since any card may be either upright or inverted after the shuffle, each royal card may look either to the right or to the left along the horseshoe. The horseshoe is treated as if it were a complete circle of cards—when one end of the crescent is reached during counting, the count continues up the opposite end of the crescent just as though the two ends touched.

Mathers was unclear in his description of the Opening of the Key as to how the horseshoe of cards is to be laid out. In his essay he gave only the following hint: "The packet containing the significator is now spread out face upwards in the form of a horseshoe (count in the way the Significator looks) and its meaning is read in the manner previously described."[10] The method of laying out the horseshoe is important, since different ways of laying out or spreading the cards of the packet result in different cards being selected for the reading.

Fortunately, it is possible to infer the method by studying Mathers's examples. The packet containing the significator is laid on the table with the cards facing up, and fanned out in a crescent in whichever direction the royal figure on the significator card gazes. This is done without disturbing the order of the cards. If the significator looks left, the top card is slid to the left, drawing each successive card after it, like the opening of a fan; but if the significator is noted to look to the right, the top card on the packet is slid to the right, drawing the lower cards successively after it. This establishes the correct relative order.

The same system of counting out the cards to be considered is used for each stage or operation in the divination. It may seem a bit complex at first but is really very simple. Counting always begins at the significator and proceeds around the imaginary circle of the horseshoe of cards in whichever direction the significator gazes. Each card of the Tarot receives its own number value for the purpose of counting. The numbers are based upon the basic occult divisions of the Tarot. The procedure in the fourth operation of the Opening of the Key is slightly different, but the basic method of counting is the same.

The count for each card always begins from the card itself, not from the card next to it. Subsequent cards are selected by noting which card each count terminates upon. The process of counting then continues from the selected card, using its particular number, until the next card is located. Then its number is used to continue the counting process, and so on until the final number of a card's count falls upon a card that has already been selected.

The number values employed for counting around the horseshoe may be tabulated in this manner:

From the Kings, Queens, Princes—count four cards (letters of Tetragrammaton).

From the Princesses—count seven cards (seven palaces of Malkuth).

From the Aces—count five cards (Spirit and four elements).

From the number cards Two to Ten—count each card's own number (a Sephirah).

From trumps linked to the mother letters of Hebrew (the Fool, Hanged Man, and Judgement)—count three (the number of the mother letters).

From trumps linked to the double letters of Hebrew (the Magus, Priestess, Empress, Wheel of Fortune, Tower, Sun, and Universe)—count nine (the number of double letters or traditional astrological planets, plus the two nodes of the moon).

From trumps linked to the single or simple letters of Hebrew (the Emperor, Hierophant, Lovers, Chariot, Justice, Hermit, Strength, Death, Temperance, Devil, Star, and Moon)—count twelve (the number of zodiac signs).

The number of cards to be read during any of the five operations of the divination will vary from operation to operation and from divination to divination. It depends upon when the final count of a card falls upon a card that has already been selected, at which point the counting process terminates. Also, the number of cards in the horseshoe of fanned cards will vary, since the packets are selected in different ways, some of which use chance to determine the number of cards in a packet. The direction of counting to select the cards to be read in a packet will be either left or right around the horseshoe of fanned cards, depending on which way the figure of the significator gazes.

The cards selected by the counting process are read successively as each is determined. The meaning of each card depends upon its own essential meaning, and upon the cards on either side, which determine its dignity. Good cards on either side of the card under consideration give it a good dignity, whereas unfavorable cards on either side give it an evil dignity. In the divination of the Golden Dawn, whether a card is upright or inverted has no bearing on its interpretation.

Importance is placed on which way other court cards apart from the significator face in the horseshoe. In general, court cards bearing figures that gaze or face in a direction opposite to the direction of the significator's gaze hinder or oppose the querent, while those that gaze or face in the same direction as the significator facilitate or act in harmony with the querent.

Mathers mentions that Princes and Queens almost always represent actual men and women who are connected with the matter under consideration. Kings sometimes stand for men, but often indicate the arrival of a person or the coming on of an event if they face in a direction opposite that of the significator card; however, they show the departure of a person or the going off or decline of an event if they face in the same direction as the significator.[11] Princesses generally indicate thoughts, opinions, or ideas that are either in harmony with the purposes of the querent or the progress of the matter under question (if they face the same direction as the significator) or opposed to the querent's purposes or progress of the matter (if they face a direction opposite the significator's gaze).[12]

After all the cards selected by the counting process are read successively one by one, and their dignities considered, the cards of the horseshoe are read in pairs of opposite cards, beginning with the two cards on the ends of the horseshoe. Next, the two cards in the second places on the ends of the horseshoe are considered together, then the two cards in the third places, and so on until all the cards of the packet have been considered in pairs. If the packet contains an odd number of cards, the final card read will not have an opposite, and must be read by itself.

Concerning the significance of the opposite pairs, Mathers wrote:

> On pairing the cards each is to be taken as of equal force with the other. If of opposite elements they mutually weaken each other. If at the end of the pairing of the cards in a packet, one card remains over, it signifies the partial result of that particular part of the Divination only. If an evil card and the others good, it would modify the good.
>
> If it be the Significator of the Enquirer, or of another person, it would show that matters would much depend on the line of action taken by the person represented. The reason of this importance of the single card is, that it is alone, and not modified. If two cards are at the end instead of a single one, they are not of so much importance.[13]

Example of the Method of Counting

This process of selecting the cards to be read for each stage or operation in the divination is difficult to comprehend in the abstract. I will present the first example provided by Mathers in his description of Golden Dawn Tarot reading,[14] and you will see that it is both elegant and straightforward.

We will suppose that whichever operation of the divination we are conducting has resulted in a packet of twelve cards that contains among them the significator. The other packets divided by the operation are discarded by the diviner, who fans the significator packet faceup in a horseshoe or crescent over the surface of the table. In the example, the significator looks to the left, so the packet is fanned to the left to expose the following cards:

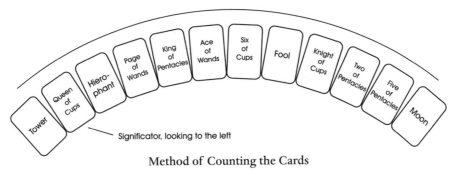

Method of Counting the Cards

Since the divination is being conducted for a fair woman with light brown hair and blue eyes, the Queen of Cups was selected at the outset to be the significator. It has fallen in the second place from the left end of the horseshoe. The card is upright from the perspective of the diviner, which causes the figure of the queen to face to the left (in the Marseilles Tarot and, presumably, in the original Golden Dawn Tarot). The counting process that will select the cards to be read in this operation, and the order of their reading, will proceed to the left around the loop of the horseshoe.

Beginning with the significator, the Queen of Cups, we count four places to the left. The count starts on the Queen of Cups itself. Since the Queen is so near the left end of the horseshoe, the count must jump from the left end of the crescent of cards to its right end. By counting four from the Queen, we arrive at the Five of Pentacles. Since this is a number card, we count its face number, still moving to the left, and beginning at the Five itself. This carries us to the Six of Cups. From the Six we count six places left to arrive at the Queen of Cups. Since this is one of the cards we have already selected, the process of counting terminates. Note that the significator is considered to be a selected card.

The cards that will be read in this particular operation of the divination are, in their order of reading, the Queen of Cups (significator), Five of Pentacles, and Six of Cups. Mathers's example implies that the cards selected are to be read one after the other in the process of counting, as they are arrived at. He made no mention about recording the cards selected. However, this is necessary to ensure that the order of selection and the cards selected in each operation are not forgotten or confused. Sometimes more than three cards are indicated, and the result of a counting gets increasingly complex the longer it continues.

First Operation

The method used to divide the Tarot deck into smaller packets of cards is unique for each of the five operations of the divination, even though the examination of the packet containing the significator during each operation always follows the same procedure, outlined above. In the first operation, which relates to the beginning of the matter under question, the structure of Tetragrammaton is used to make the division of the deck into packets.

At the outset of the reading, the significator card is mentally selected by the diviner to represent the querent. The entire Tarot deck is thoroughly shuffled by the querent, who at the same time concentrates strongly on the question the reading is intended to answer. If the querent were absent at the time of the reading, the diviner would shuffle the deck in the querent's place and concentrate on the question. After shuffling, the querent places the deck of cards facedown on the table. At this stage, it represents the four letters of *IHVH* combined.

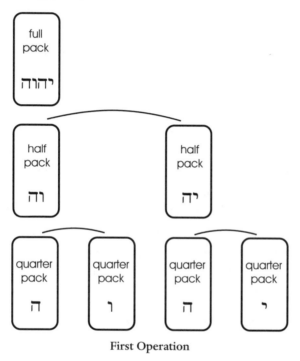

First Operation

The querent cuts the deck once, making the cut as nearly as possible in the middle of the cards, and sets the upper packet facedown about six inches to the right side of the lower packet. Since Hebrew is read from right to left, the packet of cards on the right side represents the *I-H* (י-ה) of Tetragrammaton, and the packet on the left represents the *V-H* (ו-ה) of this holy name.

In the same manner, the querent cuts both of these two stacks of cards as nearly as possible in the middle, and sets the upper packet of each to the immediate right of its lower packet. This forms a row of four packets of cards. The packet on the far right relates to the *I* of the Name, the packet on its left to the *first H*, the packet on its left to the *V*, and the packet on its left to the *second H*.

If you imagine these four more or less equal packets of cards still stacked one above the other in the original deck, you will see that the letters of *IHVH* were to be read in order moving from the top to the bottom of the deck. The two cutting operations merely separated these four groups of cards, and their related letters, in a row across the tabletop.

The diviner turns over the four packets without changing their positions in relation to one another. This is best done by turning each packet over from right to left about its long axis. This maintains the orientation of the cards. Strictly speaking, it does not matter whether the packets are turned right to left or top to bottom. If they are flipped over top to bottom about their short axis, all of the cards in each packet will be inverted, but since Golden Dawn divination does not place a special interpretation on inverted cards, this is immaterial insofar as the process of reading the cards is concerned. What is vital is that the relative order of the packets, and the relative order and orientation of the cards within each packet to one another, does not change.

The four packets relate to the letters of Tetragrammaton, and by extension to the four Princesses who rule the four quarters of the celestial heavens, and the four Aces that embody the four elemental energies, which Mathers termed the "radical forces." From right to left, from the perspective of the querent who has cut the deck and laid out the four packets, the packets represent:

Yod: Princess of Wands, Ace of Wands (Fire)

Heh (first): Princess of Cups, Ace of Cups (Water)

Vau: Princess of Swords, Ace of Swords (Air)

Heh (second): Princess of Disks, Ace of Disks (Earth)

Mathers wrote that at this stage, the four cards that appear faceup on the tops of the upturned packets may be considered "as an indication of the matter." Presumably he meant as an indication of the foundation or present circumstances of the matter under question, since this is the focus of the first operation. However, this reading of the four cards uppermost is optional.

The diviner examines each of the packets in turn to discover which contains the significator card. Care is taken not to change the order or orientation of the cards within the packets. Notice should be taken of which letter of Tetragrammaton is related to the packet with the significator. If this packet occupies the place of the *Yod*, the meaning is energy and strife; if the place of the *first Heh*, pleasure; if the place of the *Vau*, sickness and trouble; if the place of the *second Heh*, business and money.

When the packet with the significator has been located, the other packets are set aside and the packet with the significator is fanned out, with its cards facing up, across the table in a crescent or horseshoe in the direction in which the figure on the significator card gazes. General indicators should be noted. If there is a predominance of Wands, they signify energy, quarreling, and opposition. A predominance of Cups means pleasure and merriment. A predominance of Swords means trouble and sadness, and sometimes sickness and death (if other factors support this interpretation). A predominance of Pentacles relates to business, money matters, and material possessions. A majority of Tarot trumps in the horseshoe suggests that the matter under question is at the mercy of forces that are beyond the querent's control. Three or four Minor Arcana cards of any one type, such as three Kings, four Aces, four Fives, and so on, have a special meaning that I have tabulated below.

After these general indicators are noted, the cards that will form the subject of the first operation are selected by counting from the significator in the direction in which the figure on the significator card gazes. Counting continues from card to card until one of the counts terminates on a card that has already been selected or on the significator. Remember, each step in the counting begins with the card itself, which is counted as one. Thus, if the significator was the King of Disks, and by its orientation faced to the right, we would count, beginning from the King of Disks itself as one, four places to the right on the horseshoe. Whatever card occupied the fourth place (which would actually be the third card to the right of the King of Disks) would be selected, and its number would form the basis for the continuation of the count, which would begin with the card itself and continue to the right around the horseshoe.

The selected cards are read in the order of their selection from the significator, and their meaning is modified by the cards on either side. If the card under consideration occupies one of the ends of the horseshoe, it is influenced by the card next to it and the card on the opposite end of the horseshoe (as though the two ends touched). When the cards on either side of the individual card under consideration are of contrary elements, they weaken its power. However, if only one of these adjacent cards is contrary, and the other is harmonious, their influence is slight.

Air (Swords) and Earth (Pentacles) are contrary elements, as are Fire (Wands) and Water (Cups). Air is friendly with Water and Fire. Fire is friendly with Air and Earth.[15]

For example, if we were considering the Three of Swords, and it lay between the Seven of Wands and the Prince of Cups, the action of the Three of Swords would be strengthened on an elemental level. On the other hand, if the Three of Swords lay between the King of Pentacles and the Tarot trump the Universe (related to Earth through Saturn), its elemental action would be weakened.[16]

Each card selected in an operation by the process of counting is influenced by the selected card that came before it, and in turn influences the selected card that comes after it, so that a chain of causality is formed beginning with the significator and ending with the final selected card. On rare occasion, counting from the significator around the horseshoe of a packet will immediately select the significator itself. For example, if the significator is the Princess of Wands, whose number is seven, and the packet of fanned cards contains only six cards, then counting seven places from the significator will end on the significator itself.

Mathers noted this rare event, and commented, "This would show that the Enquirer would act according to his own ideas in this point of the question, and would not let his line of action be influenced by the opinion of others."[17] Only the cards on either side of the significator would have a direct bearing on its interpretation. However, the opposite pairs of cards on either side of the horseshoe would be considered successively in the usual way, moving in from the horns of the horseshoe to its middle, and these pairs would give an indication of this stage in the matter under question.

Second Operation

The division of the deck into packets during the second operation is based on the twelve houses of the zodiac and their related signs. The querent shuffles the cards and sets them down on the table without cutting them. The diviner takes them up and deals one card at a time in the circle of the zodiac counterclockwise, beginning in the place of the first house, the Ascendant, which is the house of Aries. Care must be taken by the diviner to preserve the orientation of the cards as it exists after the querent has shuffled the deck. The cards are dealt facedown on the zodiac with their long axes radiating from the center like the spokes of a wheel. The diviner must deal the cards as though standing at the center of the zodiac.

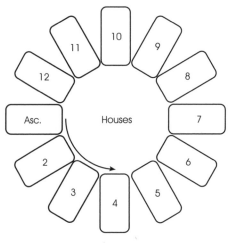

Second Operation

The result will be twelve packets of cards. Since twelve divides into 78 six times, with six left over, the packets from Aries to Virgo (1–6) will each contain seven cards, and the packets from Libra to Pisces (7–12) only six cards each.

The diviner turns each packet and sorts through it to find the significator. The astrological house and sign upon which the significator has been dealt are noted. These have a bearing on the early development of the matter under question, which is the time frame of the second operation. Also noted is the suit that predominates, and whether three or four Minor Arcana cards of the same type occur (Mathers remarked in his essay that this is unlikely in such a small packet of cards).

The packet of six or seven cards that contains the significator is fanned out faceup in the direction in which the figure on the significator gazes, and the other eleven packets are set aside. The selection of cards to be read in this operation proceeds as already described, by counting from the significator in the direction of the significator's gaze. The selected cards are interpreted in sequence as before, their dignities noted, then the cards of the horseshoe are read in opposite pairs beginning with the pair of cards on the ends of the horseshoe. If the packet contains seven cards, a single card will be left at the end, and should be given added weight in the reading.

Third Operation

The procedure for this stage in the divination is the same as that of the second stage. The querent shuffles the deck while thinking intently about the matter under question, but does not cut the cards. The diviner deals them one by one onto the circle of the zodiac into twelve packets, beginning at Aries and proceeding counterclockwise until all the cards are dealt. However, instead of relating the cards to the twelve houses of the zodiac, the packets are related to the twelve Tarot trumps that are linked in the Golden Dawn system to the twelve zodiac signs as follows:

Emperor—Aries

Hierophant—Taurus

Lovers—Gemini

Chariot—Cancer

Strength—Leo

Hermit—Virgo

Justice—Libra

Death—Scorpio

Temperance—Sagittarius

Devil—Capricorn

Star—Aquarius

Moon—Pisces

The diviner sorts through the packets of cards without disturbing their order to locate the packet containing the significator. Note is taken of which Tarot trump is linked to the zodiacal house where the significator packet resides. The other packets of cards are set aside, and the significator packet is fanned faceup into a horseshoe in the direction in which the significator gazes. As always, the direction of the gaze will depend upon whether the significator card is upright or inverted.

The cards to be read in the third operation are selected by counting from the significator in the direction of the significator's gaze, as has previously been described. After interpreting the cards sequentially, the opposite pairs of cards on the horseshoe are read in the manner outlined above.

The Fourth Operation

This operation concerns the more distant evolution of the matter under inquiry. The querent shuffles the deck while thinking of the question, and places the deck on the table facedown, but does not cut it. The diviner sorts through the deck to find the significator, then cuts the deck just above (when the deck is facedown) the significator card and places the packet of cards above the significator under the packet of cards below the significator. This causes the significator to become the top card of the deck, and the card that was formerly just above the significator to become the bottom card of the deck. The deck is returned to the table facedown.

Although this is a simple procedure, it was described so poorly by Mathers that it is difficult to grasp from his essay. Wynn Westcott (Golden Dawn motto: *Sapere Aude*) added a note in parentheses cautioning that care be taken with this step. Presumably many Golden Dawn members failed to comprehend it based on Mathers's description. Someone else, probably Israel Regardie, inserted a second note in parentheses that gives an incorrect direction, demonstrating that he did not understand Mathers:

> The Diviner takes the Pack, turns it face upwards, and goes through it, being careful not to disarrange the order of the cards, till he finds the Significator; at this point he cuts the Pack, that is to say, he takes the Significator and the cards which had been beneath it and places them on the top of the remainder, turning the whole face downwards again, ready for dealing out. (Very careful here: S.A.)
>
> The consequence of this Operation is that the Significator becomes the top card in the pack (bottom really: face on table.)[18]

Whoever inserted the second note in parentheses mistakenly assumed that the deck was to be cut with the cards faceup, with the cards above the significator in this face-up attitude being placed below the faceup cards beneath the significator. If this were done, the significator would end up as the bottom card, facedown on the table, when the deck was turned facedown. But this was not Mathers's intention. The facedown deck is to be cut into two packets between the significator card and the cards above it, and the upper packet of this facedown deck is to be moved under the lower packet. In this way, when the deck is facedown, the significator is the top card and the card that was originally just above the significator is the bottom card.

Regardie's little note in parentheses—if it is Regardie's note—has undoubtedly caused confusion over the years. Fortunately, Mathers makes his meaning clear in his subsequent example of the fourth operation, although the illustration that accompanies this description is so obscure, it would be easy to fail to understand him.

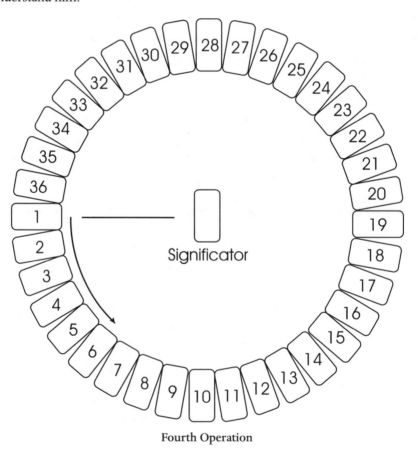

Fourth Operation

The top card of the facedown deck is dealt faceup on the table. The next thirty-six cards are dealt faceup in a circle counterclockwise around the decans of the zodiac, beginning with the first decan of Aries, on the left side of the circle from the diviner's perspective. The remainder of the deck is set aside. Observe the overall division of the cards into trumps and suits, and take note of which predominates. A greater number of cards of the same suit indicates the forceful action of the suit's element. A greater number of trumps indicates influences of a cosmic or fateful nature that are beyond the control of the querent.

Counting to select the cards that will constitute the primary reading of this operation proceeds from the significator to the card on the first decan of Aries, and from there counterclockwise, in the natural order of the signs. Thus, for practical purposes, in the fourth operation, the significator, no matter which court card it may be, has a value of two, since its count terminates on the card of the first decan of Aries. As always, the counting continues until the count of any card ends on a card that has already been counted. The meanings of the cards selected by the counting are interpreted one by one in their sequence.

When the cards are read in opposite pairs, the significator at the center of the circle is read first in combination with the first (1) and last (36) cards on the decans. Then the card on the middle decan of Aries (2) is paired with the card on the middle decan of Pisces (35), and the two are considered together; the card on the third decan of Aries (3) is paired and read with the card on the first decan of Pisces (34); and so on to the final pair, which occupy the last decan of Virgo (18) and the first decan of Libra (19).

Fifth Operation

The final operation of the Opening of the Key reveals the conclusion of the matter under question. The division and arrangement of the packets of cards is based on the structure of the Tree of the Sephiroth in the Kabbalah, which in the Golden Dawn was invariably referred to as the *Tree of Life*. (Strictly speaking, the Tree of the Sephiroth contains in symbolic form both the Tree of Life and the Tree of the Knowledge of Good and Evil.)

The querent shuffles the Tarot deck while concentrating on the question, but does not cut the cards. The diviner picks up the deck, taking care as usual to orient it to himself in the same way it was oriented to the querent, and deals out the cards in rotation into packets on the ten Sephiroth of an imaginary

Tree in the natural order of the Sephiroth (1-Kether, 2-Chokmah, 3-Binah, 4-Chesed, 5-Geburah, 6-Tiphareth, 7-Netzach, 8-Hod, 9-Yesod, 10-Malkuth). In this way, all the Sephiroth receive at least seven cards, and those from Kether to Hod receive eight.

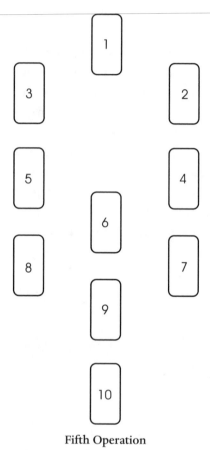

Fifth Operation

The packets are sorted through until the significator is located. The Sephirah that the packet occupies is noted, and the other packets are set aside. The packet is fanned faceup into a horseshoe in the direction in which the figure on the significator gazes. Notice is taken of which suit predominates, and whether or not there is a predominance of trumps. Cards to be read in this horseshoe of either seven or eight cards are selected, as before, by counting from the significator in the direction in which the significator gazes. The selected cards are interpreted in sequence, then the pairs on the horseshoe are read. This concludes the Golden Dawn method of Tarot divination known as the Opening of the Key.

Tabulation of Divinatory Meanings

Mathers attached a list of brief meanings for the Tarot cards, or sets of cards, to be used when divining by the Opening of the Key.[19] I have reproduced it below in a slightly modified form that eliminates the repetition of information already provided and clarifies Mathers's meaning where it is difficult to grasp in the original essay. Also, I have made a few additions that seemed necessary, such as providing brief divinatory meanings for the individual Aces.

Majorities of Card Types in a Reading

Wands—energy, quarreling, opposition
Cups—pleasure and merriment
Swords—trouble and sadness, sometimes sickness or death
Pentacles—business, money, possessions
Trumps—forces of considerable strength beyond the querent's control
Court Cards—society, meeting with many persons
Aces—strength generally

Fours and Threes

Four Aces—great power and force
Three Aces—riches and success

Four Twos—conference and conversations
Three Twos—reorganization and recommencement

Four Threes—resolution and determination
Three Threes—deceit

Four Fours—rest and peace
Three Fours—industry

Four Fives—order, regularity
Three Fives—quarrels, fights

Four Sixes—pleasure
Three Sixes—gain and success

Four Sevens—disappointments
Three Sevens—treaties and compacts

Four Eights—much news
Three Eights—much journeying

Four Nines—added responsibility
Three Nines—much correspondence

Four Tens—anxiety and responsibility
Three Tens—buying, selling, commercial transactions

Four Princesses—new ideas and plans
Three Princesses—society of the young

Four Princes—meetings with the great
Three Princes—rank and honor

Four Queens—authority and influence
Three Queens—powerful and influential friends

Four Kings—great swiftness and rapidity
Three Kings—unexpected meetings

Wands

Ace—forceful will
Two—influence over another; dominion
Three—pride and arrogance; sometimes power
Four—settlement; arrangement completed
Five—quarreling, fighting
Six—gain and success
Seven—opposition; sometimes courage when opposed
Eight—a hasty communication, letter or message; swiftness
Nine—strength; power; health; energy
Ten—cruelty and malice toward others; overbearing strength; revenge; injustice

Cups

Ace—powerful feelings, impulsiveness

Two—marriage, love, pleasure; warm friendship

Three—plenty; eating, drinking; hospitality; pleasure, dancing, merriment; new clothes

Four—receiving pleasures or kindness from others, yet with some discomfort

Five—disappointment in love, marriage broken off, etc.; unkindness from friends (whether deserved or not is revealed by its dignifiers); loss of friendship

Six—wish; happiness; success; enjoyment

Seven—lying, deceit; promises unfulfilled, illusion, deception; error, slight success but not enough energy to retain it

Eight—success abandoned, decline of interest in a thing; ennui

Nine—complete success; pleasure and happiness; wishes fulfilled

Ten—matters definitely arranged and settled in accordance with one's wishes; complete good fortune

Swords

Ace—evil thoughts; malicious intentions and plans

Two—quarrel made up; peace restored, yet some tension in relations remains

Three—unhappiness, sorrow, tears

Four—convalescence, recovery from sickness; change for the better

Five—defeat, loss; malice, slander, evil-speaking

Six—labor, work in progress; journey, probably by water (if indicated by dignifiers)

Seven—untrustworthy character; vacillation; journey, probably by land (if indicated by dignifiers)

Eight—narrow or restricted opinions or circumstances; pettiness; a prison

Nine—illness, suffering, pain; malice, cruelty

Ten—ruin, failure, disaster; possibly death (if indicated by dignifiers)

Disks

Ace—investment; start of a business; financial scheme

Two—pleasant change; visit to friends

Three—business, paid employment, commercial transactions

Four—gain of money and influence; a present

Five—loss of profession; loss of money; anxiety about money

Six—success in material things; prosperity in business

Seven—unprofitable speculations or employments; voluntary work done for the love of it rather than a reward

Eight—skill, prudence; sometimes artfulness and cunning (if indicated by dignifiers)

Nine—inheritance, much increase of money

Ten—riches and wealth

Major Arcana

0. Fool—Idea, thought, spirituality, efforts to rise above materialism, when the question concerns spiritual matters. However in material questions of ordinary life this card signifies folly, stupidity, eccentricity, sometimes mental weakness or illness if badly dignified. This trump is too ideal and unstable to be good in material things.

1. Magician—Skill, wisdom, adaptation; alternatively craft or cunning (depending on its dignifiers). Sometimes occult or esoteric wisdom.

2. High Priestess—Change, alteration, increase and decrease. The fluctuation may be good or bad, depending on the dignifying cards. Compare it with Death and the Moon.

3. Empress—Beauty, happiness, pleasure, success; luxury. Sometimes dissipation, if this trump is ill-dignified.

4. Emperor—War, conquest, victory; strife; ambition.

5. Hierophant—Divine wisdom; manifestation; explanation; teachings. Occult wisdom. Compare this trump with the Magician, the Hermit, and the Lovers.

6. Lovers—Passive or mediumistic inspiration (in contrast to that of the Magician, Hierophant, and Hermit, which is active). Motivation, power, and action that arises from inspiration and unconscious impulse.

7. Chariot—Triumph, victory; robust physical health. Success which sometimes is not stable or enduring.

8. *Justice*—Cosmic justice and the balance of the universe. The final resolution of strength or force, as occurs in acts of judgement—compare this trump with Strength. Depending on its dignifiers, this trump may indicate legal proceedings, a court of law, a civil or criminal trial.

9. Hermit—Also called the Prophet in the Golden Dawn. Wisdom sought for and obtained from above. Active divine inspiration (in contrast to the passive inspiration of the Lovers). Together with the Magician and Hierophant, this trump makes up what was termed in the Golden Dawn the Three Magi.

10. Wheel of Fortune—Generally good fortune and measured happiness. If dignifiers indicate it, this trump sometimes means a dizziness or intoxication with success.

11. *Strength*—Courage, strength, fortitude. Power that is not arrested in an act of judgment (compare with Justice), but that passes on to further action. Sometimes obstinacy or willfulness are indicted, depending on the dignifiers.

12. *Hanged Man*—Also called the Drowned Man by the Golden Dawn. Enforced or involuntary sacrifice. Punishment, loss. Generally suffering, which may (depending on dignifiers) prove fatal.

13. *Death*—Time, the ages or aeons, transformation. Involuntary change (compare with the trump the Moon). Sometimes death if the trump is ill-dignified, but very rarely destruction. Also compare this card with the High Priestess.

14. *Temperance*—Combination or coalescing of forces. Realization. Physical actions with material results. Effect either for good or evil.

15. *Devil*—Materialism and material force. Physical temptation. Sometimes an obsessing desire, especially if this trump is associated in a spread with the Lovers.

16. *Tower*—Ambition, fighting, warfare, courage—compare this trump with the Emperor. If ill-dignified, destruction, danger, fall, ruin.

17. *Star*—Hope, faith, unexpected help in time of need; if ill-dignified, dreaminess, wishful thinking, hope deceived.

18. *Moon*—Dissatisfaction with present circumstances, voluntary change (compare with the trump Death). When ill-dignified, it may mean error, lying, falseness, deception.

19. *Sun*—Glory, gain, riches; sometimes arrogance. When very badly dignified, this trump can signify vanity and vain display, but this card is almost always favorable.

20. *Judgment*—A final decision or judgment. Sentence. Determination of a matter that cannot be appealed unless there is a transcendent change.

21. *Universe*—The matter of the reading itself. For this reason, the meaning of this trump depends entirely on the cards that dignify it. It also stands for synthesis; the world; a kingdom or domain.

Dignifications

Card between cards of same suit—strengthen the middle card, either for good or evil depending on their natures.

   Example: 9 Swords—10 Swords—5 Swords

   The Ten of Swords is made very potent in its action by this dignification, and also very evil.

Card between cards of contrary suit—weaken the middle card, either for good or evil depending on their natures; Swords and Disks are contrary, as are Wands and Cups.

   Example: 10 Cups—2 Wands—6 Cups

   The dominating nature of the Two of Wands in the middle is weakened and perverted to excess and vice by the Ten of Cups and Six of Cups, which in themselves are good cards, but are contrary in their watery elemental nature to the fiery nature of Wands. Mathers interpreted this arrangement as "victory which is perverted by debauchery and evil living."[20]

Card between two cards contrary to each other—not much affected, since the contrary cards on either side cancel each other out.

   Example: 10 Swords—6 Cups—9 Pentacles

Mathers commented that the Six of Cups is "fairly strong and good" in this arrangement, because the Ten of Swords and Nine of Pentacles "being opposite elements counteract each other. Therefore is it as if they were not there."[21]

Card between two cards not contrary to each other, one of which is contrary to it— fairly strong, since the card not contrary to the middle card acts as a moderating and connecting influence on the antagonism of the two contrary cards.

Example: 10 Swords—6 Cups—10 Wands

Mathers commented, "Fairly good. Some trouble, but trouble which is overcome. If 6 C. were a bad card the evil would carry the day."[22]

II.
Three Other Methods
of Divination

The main method of Tarot divination used by Mathers has already been presented in detail. It is the Opening of the Key, which formed the primary type of divination for members of the Hermetic Order of the Golden Dawn. In his booklet *The Tarot*, first published in 1888, the same year the Isis-Urania Temple of the Golden Dawn was established in London, Mathers presented three other methods of divining by Tarot cards.

These are interesting for several reasons. One of the methods employs a variation on the *Grand Jeu* pattern of Etteilla. All of them use the same basic technique of reading the cards of a spread individually from right to left, then in opposite pairs, which figures so prominently in the Opening of the Key. Mathers even described the laying out of the cards in the form of a horseshoe, a definite echo of the Golden Dawn divination. He also presented the Golden Dawn method for selecting the significator in his booklet, but made no reference to the innovations of the esoteric Golden Dawn Tarot, which he considered to be Order secrets not to be revealed in a public document. It is quite possible that at this period the Golden Dawn Tarot was still in its formative stages.

Equally interesting is the list of brief divinatory meanings Mathers supplied for all the Tarot cards. These meanings should be compared with the divinatory meanings that accompany the Opening of the Key. The evolution of Mathers's understanding of the Tarot can be perceived in this comparison.

Before giving his three methods of divination, Mathers described the way to select the significator card that will represent the querent in the readings.

Since this is identical to the technique for selecting the significator used by the Golden Dawn, I will not repeat it here. Mathers also emphasizes strongly the need to invert some of the cards during the shuffle so that they are upside down in the spread. It is worth quoting him on this matter, since it is important but was not treated in his Golden Dawn essay on Tarot divination.

> Whatever mode of laying out be adopted, it is necessary that the person inquiring should carefully shuffle the cards, with two objects in view; firstly, that of turning some of the cards upside down; secondly, that of *thoroughly* altering their position and sequence in the pack. They should then be cut. During the shuffling and cutting the inquirer should *think earnestly* of the matter concerning which he is anxious for information; for unless he does this the cards will rarely be read correctly. This shuffling and cutting should be thrice repeated. The back of the cards should be towards the person shuffling.[23]

By his last remark, Mathers meant that during shuffling, the person shuffling should not see the faces on the cards. They must be mixed randomly.

First Method

The first divination described by Mathers uses essentially the same laying out of the cards as was used in the initial operation of the method of Etteilla that was included by Papus in *The Tarot of the Bohemians*.[24] However, the manner of dealing the cards into packets is different. Mathers probably did not derive it from Papus, but from the writings of Etteilla, or from some secondary source that presents this method used by Etteilla or some variation on it. It is more elegant and simple than the technique given by Papus. Mathers wrote, "This is a very ancient mode of reading the Tarot, and will be found reliable."[25]

The querent shuffles the cards and cuts them once while thinking strongly about the question of the reading. The diviner then picks up the deck, taking care to preserve the same orientation of the cards to himself as they had with the querent, and deals two cards facedown on the table side by side, the first on the right and the second on the left. These form the basis for two packets. On top of the card on the right, two more cards are dealt, and on top of the card on the left, a single card, then two more on the right packet, one on the left, two on the right, one on the left, and so on until the entire deck has been dealt into two packets. The packet on the right will contain fifty-two cards, and the packet on the left twenty-six cards. The smaller packet is set aside to the diviner's right.

Taking up the packet of fifty-two cards, the diviner deals two cards face-down side by side to form the basis of two packets, the first on the right and the second on the left. On top of the card on the right, he deals two more cards, and on top of the card on the left, one card, then two more on the right, one on the left, two on the right, and so on until all the cards have been dealt. This results in thirty-five cards in the packet on the right, and seventeen in the packet on the left. The smaller packet of seventeen cards is set aside on the diviner's right just below the packet of twenty-six cards that was set aside after the first deal.

Taking up the packet of thirty-five cards, the diviner deals two cards face-down side by side on the table to form the basis for two packets, the first on the right and the second on the left. Two cards are dealt on the right card, one on the left, two on the right, one on the left, and so on until all the cards are dealt. The result is twenty-four cards in the right packet and eleven in the left packet. The smaller packet is placed to the diviner's right under the packets of twenty-six and seventeen already set aside. The remaining packet of twenty-four cards is discarded, since it will not be used in the reading and has no bearing on the question.

The packet of twenty-six cards is turned faceup and spread by the diviner into a horseshoe by fanning the cards from right to left in a crescent, the horns of which point toward the diviner. Alternatively, the same result can be achieved by dealing the cards individually into a horseshoe beginning at the right end, and turning each faceup as it is dealt by flipping it over from side to side. Both techniques result in the top card of the packet occupying the lower-right end of the horseshoe. Do not flip the cards from top to bottom, as this will invert them.

The cards of the horseshoe are read sequentially from right to left as a connected narrative. Then they are read in opposite pairs, moving inward from the horns to the middle of the horseshoe, the first pair being cards one and twenty-six, the second pair cards two and twenty-five, and so on. In his description, Mathers failed to mention dignities. Dignification of the cards does not appear to have played a part in his early methods, or he may simply have omitted reference to dignification to make his divinations easier for the average reader to understand. Mathers also made no allusion to the significator. It does not appear to play a part in the first method, and is probably not intended by Mathers to be selected.

After the packet of twenty-six cards is read, the packet of seventeen is turned faceup and fanned from right to left in the shape of a horseshoe, so that the card that was topmost when the original packet was held face downward now occupies the lower-right end of the horseshoe. The exposed cards are read in sequence from right to left, then read in opposite pairs from the ends inward, as before, the first pair being cards one and seventeen, the second pair cards two and sixteen, and so on.

Mathers gives the direction that the horseshoe of twenty-six cards be removed from the table before the second horseshoe of seventeen cards is spread out, but I would advise that the diviner leave the first horseshoe where it is and spread the second horseshoe of cards just below it.

After the reading of the seventeen cards is concluded, the final packet of eleven cards is turned faceup and fanned into a horseshoe from right to left so that the card that was formerly the top card when the packet lay facedown now occupies the right end of the horseshoe. As before, the cards are read individually from right to left, then read in opposite pairs. Since the second and third packets contain odd numbers of cards, one card will remain after the reading of the second and third horseshoes in opposite pairs. These cards should be given added importance in the reading.

I advise that the third horseshoe of cards be fanned out below the other two, so that at the end of the reading, three nesting crescents of cards remain. Mathers intended that the second horseshoe be removed from the table before the third horseshoe was spread out, so that only a single crescent of cards be displayed at any one time. This is really a matter of individual preference.

If the three horseshoes of cards are laid out together one above the other, it becomes possible to achieve an added level of meaning by reading opposite pairs on the combined three crescents. The cards are treated as though the three horseshoes were a single large horseshoe, with the crescent of twenty-six on the right, the crescent of seventeen in the middle, and the crescent of eleven on the left of this imaginary larger horseshoe. The first pair would be card one of the top crescent and card eleven of the bottom crescent, the second pair would be card two of the top crescent and card ten of the bottom crescent, and so on to the final pair, which would be cards one and two of the middle crescent.

Mathers did not assign the three horseshoes to the three levels of the microcosm, as they are assigned in the description by Papus of Etteilla's related operation.[26] However, there is no reason why this assignment should not be made. By Etteilla's method, the upper crescent would be linked to soul, the middle crescent to mind, and the lower crescent to body.

Another useful assignment is to relate the top packet of twenty-six to the phase of the waxing moon, the middle packet of seventeen to the full moon, and the bottom packet of eleven to the phase of the waning moon. In magic, the waxing moon represents expansion, growth, vitality, youth, an increase of strength, the acquisition of knowledge, and works of good. The full moon stands for attainment, fulfillment, the perfection of strength and power, maturity, knowledge revealed, and good works. The waning moon signifies decay, decline, weakening of strength and loss of virility, old age, senility, concealment, and works of evil or destruction.

Second Method

In this method, the significator that will represent the querent is selected by the diviner from among the court cards according to Mathers's practice of linking the card to the querent by the elemental hair color, eye color, and complexion of the querent, as has already been described. The significator card is withdrawn from the deck and placed faceup on the table to the right of the diviner. The querent shuffles the cards, inverting some end to end in the process, and cuts the deck once, all the while concentrating earnestly on the question.

The diviner takes up the deck, being careful to maintain the same orientation of the cards to himself as they had to the querent, and deals out the top card and every seventh card thereafter from right to left in three rows of seven cards each, beginning with the top row. The deck is held facedown during this deal. Each card is turned faceup by flipping it edge to edge as it is dealt. The first card in laid at the right end of the upper row, then the seventh card in the deck below it is laid to its left, and the seventh card further down from it to its left, and so on until the three rows, each of seven cards, are complete.

Mathers was not absolutely clear about the manner in which the successive seventh cards are to be selected:

Now go carefully through the pack, taking the top card first, then the seventh card from it; and so on through the pack, recommencing if necessary, until you have drawn 21 cards by taking every seventh. Arrange these 21 cards in three rows of seven each, from *right to left*, on the left-hand side of the Significator, thus:–

7,	6,	5,	4,	3,	2,	1	Significator
14,	13,	12,	11,	10,	9,	8	"
21,	20	19,	18,	17,	16,	15	"

Read the meaning of each row from *right to left*, beginning with the Significator; then combine the 1st and 21st, the 2nd and 20th, and so on, as in the previous method.[27]

It is not certain from these instructions whether Mathers meant each count of seven to begin from the card previously selected or from the card following the card selected. In my opinion, he intended the second way of counting. You will recall that it was the practice in the Opening of the Key to begin a count from the previously selected card. However, Mathers used the words "by taking every seventh," which suggests to me that the cards dealt should be the first, eighth, fifteenth, twenty-second, and so on, counting through the deck from top to bottom. When the end of the deck is reached, this count carries on at the beginning once again, until all twenty-one cards have been selected.

There is a simple procedure for achieving this result. It may have been used by Mathers, even though he failed to describe it. Hold the deck facedown and deal the top card faceup on the first place of the top row, without inverting the card. Then count down through the facedown cards of the deck seven cards by fanning them slightly. Separate this packet of seven cards from the deck and lay them faceup on the table. Transfer the top card of this faceup packet (which was the seventh card when the packet was facedown) onto the second place of the top row of the spread. Count seven more cards from the top of the facedown deck, turn this packet faceup, and place it on top of the first packet of seven. Transfer the top card of the faceup packet onto the third place of the top row of the spread.

Keep going in this way until you can no longer count seven cards from the original deck, which has less than seven remaining. When you reach this point, pick up the faceup packet, turn it facedown, and place it under the remaining cards of the deck in your hand. Then count seven as before, turn this packet of cards faceup, and lay the packet on the table. Transfer the top card of this new packet to its place in the spread. Continue until all twenty-one cards of the spread have been dealt. You will find that you need to invert the faceup packet and replace it beneath the facedown cards in your hand twice to complete this procedure.

In this method, each of the three rows is read sequentially card by card from right to left, beginning from the significator court card, which is to be applied to the beginning of each row in turn. Mathers did not explicitly state it, but almost certainly the top row is read first, then the middle, then the bottom. Because each row is read beginning with the significator card, the narrative meaning of each row will commence with the querent and go on from him or her to illuminate the circumstances of the question.

Take note that the rows are not read individually by opposite pairs. Mathers indicated that opposite pairs are to be read only for the entire spread, beginning with cards one and twenty-one. However, there is no reason why opposite pairs should not also be read for each individual row, beginning with the significator and the last card of the row. If the rows are read individually by opposite pairs, the pairs of a row should be read immediately after reading its individual cards.

As in the previous method, Mathers assigned no general meanings to the rows. If desired, the top row (which is read first) can be linked to the origin of the matter under question, the middle row to its evolution, and the bottom row to its resolution. This provides a useful framework upon which the cards of the spread may be interpreted.

Third Method
The third method of divination given by Mathers in his booklet *The Tarot* is a variation on the *Grand Jeu* layout of Etteilla. The illustration provided by Papus

in his book *The Tarot of the Bohemians* shows six lines of cards, three of which are curved into a circle that surrounds the significator.[28] Mathers also indicated six lines of cards, but all the lines are straight, and the three lines around the significator form a downward-pointing triangle rather than a circle.[29] Also, Mathers gave a different order for laying out these lines of cards.

The significator is located and removed from the deck to be placed faceup in the middle of the table. The querent shuffles and cuts the cards while concentrating on the question. Then the diviner takes up the deck and deals out sixty-six cards around the significator, turning each card faceup as it is laid upon the spread. The numbers in the accompanying illustration show the correct sequence for laying out the spread.

```
        33 32 31 30 29 28 27 26 25 24 23
         66 65 64 63 62 61 60 59 58 57 56
   22        55                    44        11
   21        54                    43        10
   20        53                    42         9
   19          52  Significator  41           8
   18            51              40            7
   17            50            39              6
   16            49          38                5
   15            48        37                  4
   14              47    36                    3
   13                46    35                  2
   12                  45 34                   1
```

Mathers's Version of the *Grand Jeu* Layout

Mathers described this spread as "a triangle within a species of arch."[30] The remaining eleven cards not used in the laying out of the spread are set aside and not consulted during the reading.

Since this mode of reading the cards is complex, I will describe each stage of the reading separately.

Step One: The two lines of cards on the right side of the spread, which contain the cards dealt on the numbered positions 1–11 and 34–44, pertain to the past of the question. First, read these cards individually in sequence from positions 1 to 44. Second, combine each parallel pair of cards with the significator and read these groups in order from bottom to top (S-34-1, S-35-2, S-36-3, etc.). Third, combine each opposite pair of cards with the significator and read these groups one after the other (S-44-1, S-43-2, S-42-3, etc.).

Step Two: The two lines of cards across the top of the spread, which contain the cards dealt on the numbered positions 23–33 and 56–66, pertain to the present of the question. First, read the cards individually from positions 23 to 66. Second, combine each parallel pair of cards with the significator and read these groups in order from right to left (S-56-23, S-57-24, S-58-25, etc.). Third, combine each opposite pair of cards with the significator and read these groups one after the other (S-66-23, S-65-24, S-64-25, etc.).

Step Three: The two lines of cards on the left side of the spread, which contain the cards dealt on the numbered positions 12–22 and 45–55, pertain to the future of the question. First, read the cards individually from positions 12 to 55. Second, combine each parallel pair of cards with the significator and read these groups in order from bottom to top (S-45-12, S-46-13, S-47-14, etc.). Third, combine each opposite pair of cards with the significator and read these groups one after the other (S-55-12, S-54-13, S-53-14, etc.).

Step Four: Combine the cards of the entire spread into opposite pairs and read each pair one after the other for a general understanding of the question (66-1, 65-2, 64-3, etc.). As each pair is read, remove the cards from the spread and place them in the order of their reading faceup in a single pile. The bottom card of this pile is the card on position 66, because it is the first card read. The card in position 1 goes on top of 66 faceup. Then the second opposite pair, 65-2, is read, and the cards on positions 65 and 2 are placed onto the pile faceup. This process of reading continues until the last opposite pair of the spread, 34-33, has been place on the top of the pile. Finally, place the significator faceup on the pile.

Circle Layout of Pairs of Opposites

Step Five: Deal out the sixty-seven cards in the pile faceup on a circle clockwise. Place the first card in the pile, which is the significator, at the top of the circle. To its right, put the second card, which formerly occupied position 33 in the spread. To the right of the card that was on position 33, place the card that formerly occupied position 34. Continue to deal the cards one at a time from the top of the packet around the circle clockwise until the card that occupied position 66 in the spread (the final card of the packet) is placed on the left side of the significator. The circle of cards is read in pairs of cards on opposite sides of the circle, beginning with the pair made up of the significator and the card to its left, and moving down both sides of the circle to its bottom (S-66, 33-1, 34-65, 32-2, 35-64, etc., to the final card, which occupied position 17 in the original spread). As each pair is read, its cards are taken away from the circle and set aside.

Mathers appears to have made a mistake in his example of this step. He directed in *The Tarot,* "Deal the whole 66 cards in one large circle, placing the Significator as a starting-point, when 33 will be the first card and 66 the last card on either side of the Significator. Now gather them up thus in pairs for the last reading, S. 66; 33 1; 34 2; and so on up to the last card, which will be a single one."[31] If I have understood Mathers's instructions, the third pair of cards in his example should be those that were on positions 34-65.

Step Six: Since the circle originally contained an odd number of cards, the last remaining card, which occupied position 17 in the original spread, has no pair. Fan out facedown on the table the packet of eleven cards that were not used to form the spread of the first deal. Draw out from this packet two cards at random, and place the first card drawn faceup on the right side of the last remaining card in the circle, and the second card drawn faceup on the left side of the last card in the circle. Be sure to deal these cards faceup by flipping them from side to side rather than top to bottom. Mathers stated that these three cards "form a surprise." They are read individually from right to left, the meaning of one card leading into the next so as to form a connected meaning. The reading derived from these three surprise cards reveals the conclusion to the whole matter under question.

Divinatory Meanings of Mathers

In his booklet *The Tarot,* Mathers provided a numbered list of brief meanings for the cards, to be applied when reading them during divinations (pp. 14–22). He added a scattering of meanings "chiefly taken from Etteilla" which he obviously found helpful in his own readings (pp. 22–24). In the following section, I have quoted these divinatory meanings verbatim, and have joined the additional meanings from Etteilla with the cards to which they are related.

The curious numbering of the cards in Mathers's list applies to the comments Mathers reproduced from Etteilla, where individual cards are indicated only by their numbers in the Etteilla sequence. Mathers's numbering system totals 77 rather than 78 because the Fool is given a zero and, though included in its traditional place between the trumps Judgment and the Universe, does not interrupt the numbered sequence of the other cards.

Mathers's sequence preserves the traditional numbering of the trumps in the Marseilles deck with one highly significant exception: in the traditional Marseilles arrangement, the Fool has no number of any kind, not even zero, assigned to it.

Etteilla numbered the Fool 0 and placed it between the end of the trumps and the beginning of the small cards. Since the Fool was regarded as possessing no numbered position in the deck, the last of the trumps in Etteilla's Tarot was numbered 21 and the first of the suit cards 22. Note that modern versions of Etteilla's Tarot usually number the Fool 78, but this was not Etteilla's original practice. Etteilla's trumps do not correspond with the Marseilles arrangement of trumps, but his numbering for the Lesser Arcana is the same as that used by Mathers for the suit cards, so Etteilla's references to the suit cards by their numbers in the excerpts used by Mathers also apply to Mathers's numbers for these cards.

Meanings of the Cards

1. The Juggler—*Upright:* will, will-power, dexterity; *Reversed:* will applied to evil ends, weakness of will, cunning, knavishness.

2. The High Priestess—*Upright:* science, wisdom, knowledge, education; *Reversed:* conceit, ignorance, unskillfulness, superficial knowledge.

3. The Empress—*Upright:* action, plan, understanding, movement in a matter, initiative; *Reversed:* inaction, frittering away of power, want of concentration, vacillation.

4. The Emperor—*Upright:* realization, effect, development; *Reversed:* stoppage, check, immature, unripe.

5. The Hierophant—*Upright:* mercy, beneficence, kindness, goodness; *Reversed:* over-kindness, weakness, foolish exercise of generosity.

6. The Lovers—*Upright:* wise dispositions, proof, trials surmounted; *Reversed:* unwise plans, failure when put to the test.

7. The Chariot—*Upright:* triumph, victory, overcoming obstacles; *Reversed:* overthrown, conquered by obstacles at the last moment.

8. Themis, or Justice—*Upright:* equilibrium, balance, justice; *Reversed:* bigotry, want of balance, abuse of justice, over-severity, inequality, bias.

9. The Hermit—*Upright:* prudence, caution, deliberation; *Reversed:* over-prudence, timorousness, fear.

10. The Wheel of Fortune—*Upright:* good fortune, success, unexpected luck; *Reversed:* ill-fortune, failure, unexpected ill-luck.

11. Strength, or Fortitude—*Upright:* power, might, force, strength, fortitude; *Reversed:* abuse of power, overbearingness, want of fortitude.

12. The Hanged Man—*Upright:* self-sacrifice, sacrifice, devotion, bound; *Reversed:* selfishness, unbound, partial sacrifice.

13. Death—*Upright:* death, change, transformation, alteration for the worse; *Reversed:* death just escaped, partial change, alteration for the better.

14. Temperance—*Upright:* combination, conformation, uniting; *Reversed:* ill-advised combinations, disunion, clashing interests, etc.

15. The Devil—*Upright:* fatality for good; *Reversed:* fatality for evil.

16. The Lightning-struck Tower—*Upright:* ruin, disruption, overthrow, loss, bankruptcy; *Reversed:* these in a more or less partial degree.

17. The Star—*Upright:* hope, expectation, bright promises; *Reversed:* hopes not fulfilled, expectations disappointed or fulfilled in a minor degree.

18. The Moon—*Upright:* twilight, deception, error; *Reversed:* fluctuation, slight deceptions, trifling mistakes.

19. The Sun—*Upright:* happiness, content, joy; *Reversed:* these in a minor degree.

20. The Last Judgment—*Upright:* renewal, result, determination of a matter; *Reversed:* postponement of result, delay, matter re-opened later.

0. The Foolish Man—*Upright:* folly, expiation, wavering; *Reversed:* hesitation, instability, trouble arising herefrom.

21. The Universe—*Upright:* completion, good reward; *Reversed:* evil reward, or recompense.

22. King of Sceptres—*Upright:* man living in the country, country gentleman, knowledge, education; *Reversed:* a naturally good but severe man, counsel, advice, deliberation.

23. Queen of Sceptres—*Upright:* woman living in the country, lady of the manor, love of money, avarice, usury; *Reversed:* a good and virtuous woman who is strict and economical, obstacles, resistance, opposition.

24. Knight of Sceptres—*Upright:* departure, separation, disunion;
Reversed: rupture, discord, quarrel.

From Etteilla—*Upright:* This card is not to be read singly; it means the departure of the card which follows it. *Reversed:* Again, notice the card which follows it: if a woman, quarrel with a woman; if money, then loss of money; etc.

25. Knave of Sceptres—*Upright:* a good stranger, good news, pleasure, satisfaction; *Reversed:* ill news, displeasure, chagrin, worry.

From Etteilla—*Reversed:* Notice between what cards the news falls, which will show whence it comes, and of what nature it is.

26. Ten of Sceptres—*Upright:* confidence, security, honor, good faith;
Reversed: treachery, subterfuge, duplicity, barrier.

27. Nine of Sceptres—*Upright:* order, discipline, good arrangement, disposition;
Reversed: obstacles, crosses, delay, displeasure.

28. Eight of Sceptres—*Upright:* understanding, observation, direction;
Reversed: quarrels, intestine disputes, discord.

29. Seven of Sceptres—*Upright:* success, gain, advantage, profit, victory;
Reversed: indecision, doubt, hesitation, embarrassment, anxiety.

30. Six of Sceptres—*Upright:* attempt, hope, desire, wish, expectation;
Reversed: infidelity, treachery, disloyalty, perfidy.

31. Five of Sceptres—*Upright:* gold, opulence, gain, heritage, riches, fortune, money; *Reversed:* legal proceedings, judgments, law, lawyer, tribunal.

32. Four of Sceptres—*Upright:* society, union, association, concord, harmony;
Reversed: prosperity, success, happiness, advantage.

33. Three of Sceptres—*Upright:* enterprise, undertaking, commerce, trade, negotiation; *Reversed:* hope, desire, attempt, wish.

34. Deuce of Sceptres—*Upright:* riches, fortune, opulence, magnificence, grandeur; *Reversed:* surprise, astonishment, event, extraordinary occurrence.

 From Etteilla—*Reversed:* If the cards fall 49 (reversed), 34 (reversed), you will be surprised by a change. If 47, 49 (reversed), 34 (reversed), it will be happy; but the reverse if they fall 54, 49 (reversed), 34 (reversed).

35. Ace of Sceptres—*Upright:* birth, commencement, beginning, origin, source; *Reversed:* persecution, pursuit, violence, vexation, cruelty, tyranny.

36. King of Cups—*Upright:* a fair man, goodness, kindness, liberality, generosity; *Reversed:* a man of good position but shifty in his dealings, distrust, doubt, suspicion.

37. Queen of Cups—*Upright:* a fair woman, success, happiness, advantage, pleasure; *Reversed:* a woman in good position but intermeddling and to be distrusted, success but with some attendant trouble.

38. Knight of Cups—*Upright:* arrival, approach, advance; *Reversed:* duplicity, abuse of confidence, fraud, cunning.

 From Etteilla—*Upright:* This shows the arrival of the card which follows it, as 38, 54, the arrival of affliction or grief; 38, 39, the visit of a fair young man, etc.

39. Knave of Cups—*Upright:* a fair youth, confidence, probity, discretion, integrity; *Reversed:* a flatterer, deception, artifice.

40. Ten of Cups—*Upright:* the town wherein one resides, honor, consideration, esteem, virtue, glory, reputation; *Reversed:* combat, strife, opposition, differences, dispute.

41. Nine of Cups—*Upright:* victory, advantage, success, triumph, difficulties surmounted; *Reversed:* faults, errors, mistakes, imperfections.

42. Eight of Cups—*Upright:* a fair-haired girl, friendship, attachment, tenderness; *Reversed:* gaiety, feasting, joy, pleasure.

43. Seven of Cups—*Upright:* idea, sentiment, reflection, project; *Reversed:* plan, design, resolution, decision.

From Etteilla—Upright: Explains the card which follows; thus, 43, 30, 33, the idea of attempting some undertaking. This will again be modified by the following cards.

44. Six of Cups—*Upright:* the past, passed by, faded, vanished, disappeared; *Reversed:* the future, that which is to come, shortly, soon.

From Etteilla—Upright: Shows either that what precedes it is past, has occurred already; or if reversed, what is going to happen.

45. Five of Cups—*Upright:* union, junction, marriage, inheritance; *Reversed:* arrival, return, news surprise, false projects.

46. Four of Cups—*Upright:* ennui, displeasure, discontent, dissatisfaction; *Reversed:* new acquaintance, conjecture, sign, presentiment.

From Etteilla—Upright: The following cards might show what the displeasure or anxiety was about, the preceding cards, whence it originated.

47. Three of Cups—*Upright:* success, triumph, victory, favorable issue; *Reversed:* expedition of business, quickness, celerity, vigilance.

48. Deuce of Cups—*Upright:* love, attachment, friendship, sincerity, affection; *Reversed:* crossed desires, obstacles, opposition, hindrance.

49. Ace of Cups—*Upright:* Feasting, banquet, good cheer; *Reversed:* change, novelty, metamorphosis, inconstancy.

50. King of Swords—*Upright:* a lawyer, a man of law, power, command, superiority, authority; *Reversed:* a wicked man, chagrin, worry, grief, fear, disturbance.

51. Queen of Swords—*Upright:* widowhood, loss, privation, absence, separation; *Reversed:* a bad woman, ill-tempered and bigoted, riches and discord, abundance together with worry, joy with grief.

From Etteilla—Upright: This is not necessarily to be taken by itself; it may signify that the person symbolized by the cards near it has just lost, or is likely soon to lose, wife or husband. In some instances it may merely signify that if two people are married, the one will die some time before the other, but not necessarily that the event will occur immediately.

52. Knight of Swords—*Upright:* a soldier, a man whose profession is arms, skillfulness, capacity, address, promptitude; *Reversed:* a conceited fool, ingenuousness, simplicity.

53. Knave of Swords—*Upright:* a spy, overseeing, authority; *Reversed:* that which is unforeseen, vigilance, support.

From Etteilla—*Reversed:* If 72, 53 (reversed) an unexpected present. If 53 (reversed), 54, unexpected grief, etc.

54. Ten of Swords—*Upright:* tears, affliction, grief, sorrow; *Reversed:* passing success, momentary advantage.

55. Nine of Swords—*Upright:* an ecclesiastic, a priest, conscience, probity, good faith, integrity; *Reversed:* wise distrust, suspicion, fear, doubt, shady character.

From Etteilla—*Reversed:* The card following will show whom or what to distrust, etc.

56. Eight of Swords—*Upright:* sickness, calumny, criticism, blame; *Reversed:* treachery in the past, event, accident, remarkable incident.

From Etteilla—*Reversed:* Shows treachery or deceit in the past, and will be explained by the neighboring cards.

57. Seven of Swords—*Upright:* hope, confidence, desire, attempt, wish; *Reversed:* wise advice, good counsel, wisdom, prudence, circumspection.

From Etteilla—*Reversed:* The cards which come next will show whether it will be good to follow the advice given or not. Also, the preceding cards will show from whom, and why, the advice comes.

58. Six of Swords—*Upright:* envoy, messenger, voyage, travel; *Reversed:* declaration, love proposed, revelation, surprise.

59. Five of Swords—*Upright:* mourning, sadness, affliction; *Reversed:* losses trouble (same signification, whether reversed or not).

60. Four of Swords—*Upright:* solitude, retreat, abandonment, solitary, hermit; *Reversed:* economy, precaution, regulation of expenditure.

From Etteilla—*Reversed:* The cards near will show whether it is health or money that requires care.

61. Three of Swords—*Upright:* a nun, separation, removal, rupture, quarrel; *Reversed:* error, confusion, misrule, disorder.

From Etteilla—*Reversed:* May show simply that something is lost, or mislaid for a time.

62. Deuce of Swords—*Upright:* friendship, valor, firmness, courage; *Reversed:* false friends, treachery, lies.

From Etteilla—*Reversed:* If confirmed by the other cards may simply mean that the friends are not of much use to the inquirer in the matter under consideration.

63. Ace of Swords—*Upright:* triumph, fecundity, fertility, prosperity; *Reversed:* embarrassment, foolish and hopeless love, obstacle, hindrance.

64. King of Pentacles—*Upright:* a dark man, victory, bravery, courage, success; *Reversed:* an old and vicious man, a dangerous man, doubt, fear, peril, danger.

65. Queen of Pentacles—*Upright:* a dark woman, a generous woman, liberality, greatness of soul, generosity; *Reversed:* certain evil, a suspicious woman, a woman justly regarded with suspicion, doubt, mistrust.

From Etteilla—*Reversed:* (If this card does not signify any particular person). If 65 (reversed), 31 (reversed), it is not said that there will be a lawsuit. If 31 (reversed), 65 (reversed), if you gain your case you won't be much the better for it.

66. Knight of Pentacles—*Upright:* a useful man, trustworthy, wisdom, economy, order, regulation; *Reversed:* a brave man who is out of employment, idle, unemployed, negligent.

67. Knave of Pentacles—*Upright:* a dark youth, economy, order, rule, management; *Reversed:* prodigality, profusion, waste, dissipation.

From Etteilla—*Reversed:* Consult the following cards to see in what the person is prodigal. If 67 (reversed), 57 (reversed), it may simply mean that the person is too fond of giving advice, intermeddles too much with other people's business.

68. Ten of Pentacles—*Upright:* house, dwelling, habitation, family; *Reversed:* gambling, dissipation, robbery, loss.

69. Nine of Pentacles—*Upright:* discretion, circumspection, prudence, discernment; *Reversed:* deceit, bad faith, artifices, deception.

70. Eight of Pentacles—*Upright:* a dark girl, beauty, candor, chastity, innocence, modesty; *Reversed:* flattery, usury, hypocrisy, shifty.

71. Seven of Pentacles—*Upright:* money, finance, treasure, gain, profit; *Reversed:* disturbance, worry, anxiety, melancholy.

From Etteilla—*Reversed:* The next card will show the reason of the anxiety, and so on.

72. Six of Pentacles—*Upright:* presents, gifts, gratification; *Reversed:* ambition, desire, passion, aim, longing.

73. Five of Pentacles—*Upright:* lover or mistress, love, sweetness, affection, pure and chaste love; *Reversed:* disgraceful love, imprudence, license, profligacy.

From Etteilla—*Upright:* Shows simply that there is some one whom the person loves.

74. Four of Pentacles—*Upright:* pleasure, gaiety, enjoyment, satisfaction; *Reversed:* obstacles, hindrances.

75. Three of Pentacles—*Upright:* nobility, elevation, dignity, rank, power; *Reversed:* children, sons, daughters, youths, commencement.

76. Deuce of Pentacles—*Upright:* embarrassment, worry, difficulties; *Reversed:* letter, missive, epistle, message.

77. Ace of Pentacles—*Upright:* perfect contentment, felicity, prosperity, triumph; *Reversed:* purse of gold, money, gain, help, profit, riches.

Notes to Part Three

1. Israel Regardie, *The Golden Dawn*, 6th ed. (St. Paul, MN: Llewellyn Publications, 1989), pp. 566–589.

2. Aleister Crowley, *The Book of Thoth* (1944; repr., New York: Samuel Weiser, 1974), pp. 150–151.

3. S. L. MacGregor Mathers, *The Tarot: Its Occult Signification, Use In Fortune-Telling, and Method of Play, Etc.* (1888; repr., New York: Samuel Weiser, n.d.), pp. 5–6.

4. Ibid., p. 6.

5. There is some debate over who had more influence over the Golden Dawn Tarot, S. L. MacGregor Mathers or his wife, Moïna. There seems little doubt that Moïna drew and painted the first deck of the Golden Dawn Tarot, but Mathers's interest in and involvement with the symbolism of the Tarot was intense. Both Mathers and his wife were psychic, and both received communications from spirits regarding the system of magic developed within the Hermetic Order of the Golden Dawn.

   It seems probable to me that Mathers directed the designs of the cards painted by Moïna, just as A. E. Waite dictated the designs of the Tarot drawn by Pamela Colman Smith, and Aleister Crowley determined the designs painted by Lady Frieda Harris. By the way, I do not regard this pattern as a coincidence. In all three cases, occult agencies were at work that seemed to require both the critical, analytical faculties of the men and the intuitive, artistic talents of the women.

   A note at the end of the primary Tarot document of the Golden Dawn, known as *Book T*, emphasizes Mathers's intense focus on the Tarot: "In all of this I have not only transcribed the symbolism, but have tested, studied, compared, and examined it both clairvoyantly and in other ways. The result of these has been to show me how *absolutely* correct the symbolism of the Book T is, and how exactly it represents the occult Forces of the Universe." Israel Regardie, *The Golden Dawn*, 6th ed., p. 565.

6. Regardie, *The Golden Dawn*, 6th ed., p. 566.

7. Ibid., p. 551.

8. Ibid., p. 581.

9. Ibid., p. 568.

10. Ibid., p. 570.

11. In the Golden Dawn Tarot, the Kings are elevated Knights and are depicted mounted on horseback. The horse is an ancient symbol of travel or rapid change of place.

12. In traditional fortune-telling with common playing cards, the Knave or Page represents either the thoughts of the King of its suit (see part eight, section I) or the thoughts of the King and Queen of its suit (see part eight, section III).

13. Regardie, *The Golden Dawn*, 6th ed., p. 586.

14. Ibid., p. 568.

15. Ibid., p. 585.

16. It is possible to link each trump to an element, so that its elemental association may be considered in assessing its dignities. This is done through the mediation of the Hebrew letters, which are connected with the trumps and are themselves linked to the elements Fire, Water, and Air, the seven planets of traditional astrology, and the twelve signs of the zodiac. Each zodiac sign has an elemental association. Among the planets, the Sun and Mars are fiery, the Moon is watery, Mercury and Jupiter are airy, and Saturn and Venus are earthy.

For convenience, the elements linked through the Hebrew letters to the trumps are tabulated here:

0. Fool—(*Aleph*: Air) Air

I. Magician—(*Beth*: Mercury) Air

II. High Priestess—(*Gimel*: Moon) Water

III. Empress—(*Daleth*: Venus) Earth

IV. Emperor—(*Heh*: Aries) Fire

V. Hierophant—(*Vau*: Taurus) Earth

VI. Lovers—(*Zayin*: Gemini) Air

VII. Chariot—(*Cheth*: Cancer) Water

VIII. Strength—(*Teth*: Leo) Fire

IX. Hermit—(*Yod*: Virgo) Earth

X. Fortune—(*Kaph*: Jupiter) Air

XI. Justice—(*Lamed*: Libra) Air

XII. Hanged Man—(*Mem*: Water) Water

XIII. Death—(*Nun*: Scorpio) Water

XIV. Temperance—(*Samekh*: Sagittarius) Fire

XV. Devil—(*Ayin*: Capricorn) Earth

XVI. Tower—(*Pe*: Mars) Fire

XVII. Star—(*Tzaddi*: Aquarius) Air

XVIII. Moon—(*Qoph*: Pisces) Water

XIX. Sun—(*Resh*: Sun) Fire

XX. Judgment—(*Shin*: Fire) Fire

XXI. Universe—(*Tau*: Saturn) Earth

17. Regardie, *The Golden Dawn*, 6th ed., p. 576.

18. Ibid.

19. Ibid., p. 581–587.

20. Ibid., p. 586.

21. Ibid.

22. Ibid.

23. Mathers, *The Tarot*, p. 25.

24. Papus, *The Tarot of the Bohemians* (1889; repr., New York: U.S. Games Systems, 1978), pp. 327–332.

25. Mathers, *The Tarot*, p. 26.

26. Papus, *The Tarot of the Bohemians*, p. 329.

27. Mathers, *The Tarot*, p. 27.

28. Papus, *The Tarot of the Bohemians*, p. 331.

29. Mathers, *The Tarot*, p. 27.

30. Ibid., p. 28.

31. Ibid.

PART FOUR

"The Tarot Cards"
by
J. W. BRODIE-INNES

INTRODUCTION
TO PART FOUR

This essay is a general overview of the Tarot from the perspective of a high-ranking member of the Golden Dawn, John William Brodie-Innes (1848–1923). It was published in the English periodical *The Occult Review* in its February 1919 issue. In it, Brodie-Innes makes a strong appeal to tradition in the interpretation and use of Tarot symbolism, and expresses dismay at modern Tarot designers who boldly throw out the old symbols and replace them with their own innovations.

He had knowledge of the Golden Dawn Tarot deck designed by Mathers and painted by Mathers's wife, Moïna. It was common for members of the Order to hand-copy her Tarot to make their own deck of cards. He was certainly familiar with *Book T*, the Golden Dawn teaching document on the Tarot that describes her cards. However, he was bound by his oath of secrecy to the Order not to discuss its occult teachings.

It may be that Brodie-Innes placed little value in Moïna Mathers's Tarot card designs, if we may judge by remarks in his essay: "No good end can be served by redrawing the cards, however skilfully or artistically it is done. They will remain nothing but an evidence of the taste, and skill, and opinions of the artist, or his inspirer."[1] He found worth in the symbolism of the older traditional designs, and in his essay expressed a wish to preserve it.

In the traditional designs of the Tarot of Marseilles, Brodie-Innes thought he was able to detect traces of Egyptian symbolism, but he was not bold enough to assert an Egyptian descent for the cards. The primary message of his essay is the necessity for keeping an open mind regarding the origins of the Tarot and the meaning of its symbolism.

Brodie-Innes made a connection in his essay between the suit cards and Pythagorean numerology, stating that it was suggested to him by Florence Farr Emery (1860–1917), a prominent member of the Golden Dawn, but he was not explicit concerning this connection. Nowhere did he speak a word about the Kabbalah, which was a primary source of meaning for the Golden Dawn Tarot.

He berated A. E. Waite, another leading member of the Golden Dawn, for his error in *The Pictorial Key to the Tarot* of associating the Tarot suit of Swords with the suit of Clubs, then went on to give the Golden Dawn correspondence between the suits of the Tarot and common playing cards. Both men knew full well this esoteric correspondence, which is contained in the cipher manuscript that was the inspiration for the Hermetic Order of the Golden Dawn,[2] so I can only suspect that Waite's error was a deliberate blind intended to mislead the uninitiated. This seems even more likely given that in the fourth edition of his book *A Manual of Cartomancy*, published under the pseudonym the Grand Orient in 1909, Waite gave the Golden Dawn set of associations for the suits, as one might expect.

Waite was sufficiently annoyed by these and other comments Brodie-Innes directed toward him to dash off a rebuttal essay, which was published in the March 1919 issue of *The Occult Review* under the title "The Tarot and Secret Tradition." On the matter of his association of the Tarot suits with the suits of common playing cards, Waite wrote in this essay:

Mr. Brodie-Innes speculates as to the authority for my allocation of Tarot suits to those of ordinary playing-cards. Its source is similar to that from which Florence Emery—one of my old friends and of whom I am glad to be reminded—derived her divinatory meanings mentioned by Mr. Brodie-Innes. The source to which I refer knew well of the alternative attribution and had come to the conclusion that it was wrong. In adopting it I was careful that no allocation should be of consequence to "the outer method of the oracles" and the meanings of the Lesser Cards. Nothing follows therefore from the attribution of Swords to Clubs and Pentacles to Spades. In my book on the Graal I had already taken the other allocation of Swords to Spades and Pentacles to Clubs. I cannot say that I am especially satisfied by either mode of comparison. There is no connexion in symbolism between a sword and spade, at least until the League of Nations turns all our weapons of offence into ploughshares and reaping-hooks. As little correspondence appears between so-called pentacles and clubs, but it is Hobson's choice.[3]

These remarks suggest that Waite had no firm conviction regarding the relationship between the suits of the Tarot and those of common playing cards, and that his inclination on this matter changed over time but without ever causing him to commit himself. The book Waite referred to is his work *The Hidden Church of the Holy Graal*, published in 1909.[4]

As a quick reference, I will tabulate the correspondences between the Tarot suits and common playing cards that were asserted by various occult writers on the Tarot. For the sake of unity, a single terminology has been used for the names of the Tarot suits, which differ from one authority to another. As you can see, the suit of Cups is the only suit about which there was universal agreement in associating it with Hearts. In my opinion, Court de Gébelin got it right, and most modern authorities agree with him. Papus, Ouspensky, Crowley, Case, even Zain followed his lead. Oddly enough, Frater Achad departed from his teacher, Crowley, which seems very strange, but the association I have given in the table appears in his sequential listings of the suits in *Q.B.L.*, p. 41.

Playing Cards	Clubs	Hearts	Spades	Diamonds
Court de Gébelin (*Monde Primitif*, vol. 8)	Wands	Cups	Swords	Pentacles
Comte de Mellet (*Monde Primitif*, vol. 8)	Pentacles	Cups	Swords	Wands
Gérard Encausse, as Papus (*Tarot of the Bohemians*)	Wands	Cups	Swords	Pentacles
S. L. MacGregor Mathers (*The Tarot*)	Pentacles	Cups	Swords	Wands
Golden Dawn (Cipher Manuscript)	Pentacles	Cups	Swords	Wands
Israel Regardie (*The Golden Dawn*)	Pentacles	Cups	Swords	Wands
A. E. Waite (*Pictorial Key to the Tarot*)	Swords	Cups	Pentacles	Wands
A. E. Waite (*Holy Graal*)	Pentacles	Cups	Swords	Wands

Playing Cards	Clubs	Hearts	Spades	Diamonds
A. E. Waite, as the Grand Orient (*Manual of Cartomancy*)	Pentacles	Cups	Swords	Wands
J. W. Brodie-Innes (*Occult Review*, Feb. 1919)	Pentacles	Cups	Swords	Wands
W. Wynn Westcott (*Isiac Tablet of Cardinal Bembo*)	Wands	Cups	Swords	Pentacles
P. D. Ouspensky (*Symbolism of the Tarot*)	Wands	Cups	Swords	Pentacles
Aleister Crowley (*Book of Thoth*)	Wands	Cups	Swords	Pentacles
C. S. Jones, as Frater Achad (*Q.B.L.*)	Wands	Cups	Pentacles	Swords
Paul Foster Case (*The Tarot*)	Wands	Cups	Swords	Pentacles
C. C. Zain (*Sacred Tarot*)	Wands	Cups	Swords	Pentacles
P. R. S. Foli (*Fortune-Telling by Cards*)	Pentacles	Cups	Swords	Wands

"THE TAROT CARDS"

by

J. W. BRODIE-INNES

(*The Occult Review*, February 1919, pp. 90–98)

The strange, weird-looking cards known as the Tarot, with their bizarre designs, have interested and puzzled archaeologists, mystics and occultists for over a century; and many books have been written, from ponderous and learned tomes to popular manuals, from M. Court de Gebelin's *Monde Primitif* in 1781 to Mr. A. E. Waite's *Key to the Tarot* in 1910. Yet the mystery remains unsolved. What was their origin? What do they mean? Are they primarily an occult treatise told in hieroglyphics, or merely the implements of a game of chance or skill, used as an afterthought for purposes of divination? Was their origin Egyptian, or Indian, or Chinese, or some as yet unguessed source? There is no reliable evidence, though there is plenty of bold assertion. The fact remains that we know they existed in the fourteenth century, and prior to that they are wrapt in impenetrable obscurity. Having read all the books I could get access to on the subject, and studied many theories and speculations, I finally arrived at the Scottish verdict of "not proven."[5] Under these circumstances I should hesitate to intrude into the distinguished circle of writers on the Tarot, even to the extent of an article, but that it so chances that I have one or two slight contributions to the study, which may be of interest to inquirers.

Many years ago it was my privilege to examine at leisure the magnificent collection of playing cards made by my friend, Mr. George Clulow,[6] one of the greatest living experts on the subject. That collection is now in America, where I am told it is the model for all such collections. The item that chiefly interested me was a splendid series of Tarot packs of all ages and all countries. And the point that struck me most was the continuance of the designs throughout, often it is true corrupted, where an ignorant engraver, copying from a copyist, and obviously unable to understand a symbol, had expressed it by an unmeaning flourish, or substituted a flower, or some object he was acquainted with, for an uncomprehended symbol. Thus the Bateleur[7] who in the oldest examples had magical implements before him, came to have a shoemaker's tools. But by comparison of one pack with another these could easily be rectified. Occasionally some local or political cause had produced variations, but these also were detected without trouble. One such occurs in a modern French pack in my possession, where a strong antipapal bias has occasioned the substitution of the figures of Juno and Jupiter for the original La Papesse[8] and Le Pape.[9] Now and then some enterprising innovator has redrawn the entire pack to suit his own ideas of the symbology, as did the fantastic peruquier[10] Alliette, who under the pseudonym Etteilla (being his own name spelt backwards) posed as an illuminated adept. But these have attained no vogue, and are now merely of interest to collectors, for they embody, not the ideals, whatever they may be, of the old Tarot, but only Etteilla's notion of what they ought to be. Discounting however these variants, the persistence of the designs through some five centuries, and many countries, is, to say the least of it, remarkable. And whether or no those designs are comprehensible, one feels thankful that the redrawers have not succeeded in displacing the old traditional patterns.

That the cards have long been used in Italy, and perhaps elsewhere, for a game is certain, and that before ever they were written about as occult emblems or implements of divination. Lord Mahon, in his *History of the Forty-Five*,[11] quotes an English lady who met Prince Charles Edward in Rome in 1770 at the Princess Palestrini's, when he asked her if she knew the game of Tarrochi, and she spoke of his handling the Tarot cards and explaining them. But one may conclude from the designs that they were originally intended for more than this. As played in Italy to-day the 22 Atus or Trumps are often omitted, and many packs are sold without these. But taking the ordinary pip cards, if they were simply used for a game, the ancient designs, which have persisted through so many years and in divers countries, would seem meaningless. The numbers of pips as in the common English packs would be sufficient. Why, for example, should the two of pentacles have a serpent coiled round the two pips in the form of the algebraic symbol of infinity. And here we may say that those well-meaning writers who have redrawn the cards have gone on the wrong tack. Admitting that we have no evidence of the original meaning (there may or may not be a secret tradition, I wish to make no assertion as to this) it is surely the part of wisdom to preserve the ancient symbol as clearly as we can, and await enlightenment, rather than to assume a meaning, and form a new symbol consonant thereto, which may be miles away from the primitive intention.

This at all events was the thought that came to me on examining Mr. Clu-low's wonderful collection, and noting the persistence of the designs, and the variants of which I have spoken.

With regard to the 22 Atus or Trumps the case is different. It would be impossible in the compass of a single article to go into all the various interpretations that have been put upon them, nor am I sure that it would serve any good purpose to do so. In the absence of evidence as to the intention of the original designer they must remain as merely the speculations of individual writers. But there is much to be said for the idea of Eliphaz Levi that they were to be referred to the Hebrew alphabet.[12] Students of the Qabala, who are familiar with the symbology of the Hebrew letters, have often been struck with the correspondence of some of the Atus with some of the letters.[13] There can be no doubt that these cards are hieroglyphics of some kind, though the meaning seems to be in dispute; but whether they represent a series, such as the history of the soul, or cosmical evolution, or the grades of training of an initiate, or a synthesis of all of these and possibly others, there seems no positive evidence, but a great wealth of speculation. The connection with the Hebrew alphabet would largely depend on the attribution, and as twenty-one out of the twenty-two cards are numbered, the position assigned to the card marked zero called le Mat, or the Fool, must be the crucial point; and as to this there is wide divergence among commentators.[14] The wise student will maintain an open mind, and wait for further evidence; Eliphaz Levi appears to take one a certain distance, and then slams the door in one's face, but whether because he did not know, or whether, knowing the secret tradition, he was unable to tell more, who shall say? In any case all are agreed as to the fascinating quality of his work, and undoubtedly no one can read it without having his interest profoundly stirred in these ancient cards.

It is generally supposed that they were unknown in France, or at all events in Paris, prior to M. Court de Gébelin, who it is said, found and introduced them to the French occultists. This, however, may be doubted. I have in my possession a French Tarot of the early eighteenth century, a very interesting feature of which is that some of the cards have MS. inscriptions of their meaning, and apparently the records of an experiment in divination, which from internal evidence would seem to be pre-Revolution.[15] This, so far as it goes, would support the theory that they were known in France before M. de Gébelin wrote about them. I would not, however, press this further than as a warning against too confident dogmatism concerning the date of the Tarot, and the history of its introduction into Europe.

The cards have been called the "Tarot of the Bohemians,"[16] and have often been popularly spoken of as the gipsy fortune-telling cards. As a fact, however, when gipsies lay the cards for the fortune of an inquirer it is the ordinary pack that is used, and it seems certain, as Mr. Waite points out, that the Tarot cards were known in Europe before the arrival of the gipsies.[17] Moreover gipsy folklorists, with the exception of Vaillant,[18] have very little to say about the Tarot.

The only evidence on this head that has come under my own observation was from a woman of pure Romani blood, whom I knew many years ago, a Mrs. Lee, but of what tribe I cannot say; she was reputed to be an Epping Forest gipsy, but she said herself that her people belonged to Norwood, and only left there when Norwood became a wilderness of villadom, and their old haunts were desecrated by the incursion of Cockney residents. She once showed me an old tattered and much thumbed Tarot pack, of the ordinary Italian design, and told me that these were the cards she used among her own people, but never for Georgios. She also gave me the principles of interpretation, not under any seal of secrecy, but with a general request that it should not be published, and this, needless to say, I have honourably observed. I may, however, state that it was a thoroughly logical and complete system, the four suits representing the four elements, and the four temperaments, and being judged according to their position. Thus Wands representing fire and the sanguine temperament, a Wand card occurring in a bad position would indicate danger from rash and hasty action, anger, or quarrelling; the same card in a good position would show noble and generous action, courage, energy, and the like. Curiously enough the numbers of the pips were interpreted on a system very much akin to the Pythagorean system of numbers, especially in regard to the occult meaning of odd and even numbers. Mrs. Lee laid particular stress on the arrangement of the pips on the cards, pointing out its similarity to the arrangement of spots on dice and dominoes. (The connection of this with the Pythagorean system is obvious.)[19] In the light of this explanation the appropriateness of the serpent in the design of the Two of Pentacles is manifest.[20]

Whether Mrs. Lee's explanations were common to the gipsy tribes, or merely a system of her own, I cannot say. She seemed to regard it as very private, and only shown to me as a special mark of favour.

The last time I saw Mrs. Lee was some twenty years ago at Yetholm, when the son of the late Queen Esther was crowned Gipsy King. Mrs. Lee was very contemptuous of the Yetholm gipsies—"Tinker trash," she said, "not a hundred words of Romani among the lot." This, however, may well have been the prejudice of a different tribe.

I was interested to find that what she told me of the Tarot was well known to another friend of mine, the late Mrs. Florence Farr Emery,[21] who herself claimed Romani descent, and had a great store of strange learning. She it was who first pointed out to me the correspondence of the interpretations of the pip cards with the Pythagorean system, greatly to my delight, for the meanings usually ascribed to the cards had seemed merely empiric, and founded on no system, as indeed are the meanings ascribed to cards by the ordinary type of fortune-teller to-day. More doubtful were Mrs. Emery's suggestions of Egyptian correspondences. She was a diligent student of Egyptology, though perhaps not quite as much of an authority as her friends claimed, and with natural enthusiasm was apt to see ancient Egypt everywhere.

Another unexpected gleam of light came to me from a friend of the late Charles Godfrey Leland,[22] who told me that Leland had some special knowledge of a peculiar system of gipsy cartomancy, which for reasons known to himself he was not at liberty to divulge, and of a special pack of cards used by them. The friend who told me this had never seen the cards, but from the evidence of the Tarot pack shown me by Mrs. Lee it seems more than likely that these were in fact the Tarot cards, and that the interpretation thereof had been communicated as a secret to Leland. So then there appears to be a probability, in spite of the scepticism of the folk-lorists, that the connection of the Tarot with the gipsies may have a solid foundation in fact, and on this also we must await further evidence.

Meanwhile a guess may be hazarded that, although the cards arrived in Europe before the gipsies, they may yet have a common origin. Both the tribe and the cards arrived roughly about the same time, from an utterly unknown and mysterious source; and though the cards arrived first, there is no evidence to show that they did not come from the same origin. This will be a problem for future investigators, and a problem that I would humbly suggest is to be solved, not by negations, but rather by careful and open-minded examination of all the minutest traces of evidence available. It may be perfectly true to say there is no evidence of the Egyptian origin either of the cards or the people. But like other negations it takes us no farther. It may be right to deprecate the hasty dogmatism and superstition of those who proclaim loudly, on the very slenderest authority, that the secrets of the Universe have been laid bare, and the key to universal knowledge is in the hands of some certain mystic writer or teacher, who poses as a divinely inspired final authority and revealer of mysteries. There be many such nowadays, specially of the discredited German brand.[23] But in this deprecation we should beware of falling into the opposite error, and because there is no proof, rashly assume that there is no evidence.

It is by the patient examination of minute, almost invisible, and nearly obliterated traces, that true scientific investigation triumphs at length. There are traces, faint and infinitesimal it is true, of an Egyptian origin both of the gipsies and of the Tarot cards;[24] and until some clearer indications of another origin are discovered it is wisdom to preserve these, and make the most of them, examine them with minutest care and search for others, meantime not neglecting any other clues pointing in any other direction. Above all, the careful examination of the designs of the cards, from the very earliest that can be discovered, with all their variants, must be an essential part of the inquiry. No good end can be served by redrawing the cards, however skilfully or artistically it is done. They will remain nothing but an evidence of the taste, and skill, and opinions of the artist, or his inspirer. But anyone who can in any way contribute to a reproduction of the original designs as they were, not as he thinks they ought to be, will do a real service to the study of the Tarot. Even the well-known and accepted symbols on the best of the current packs, well-drawn and coloured, and well printed to replace the crude and poor examples which are the best we can get now, would be a boon to Tarot students, and would demand neither archaeological nor mystic learning.

In common with many Tarot students I welcomed Mr. Waite's little manual, and found therein as I expected, and as one always expects from his work, the results of careful research, set forth in graceful and elegant diction, an invaluable summary for those who have not the time or the patience, perhaps, not the opportunity, to study the original works, of which he gives an excellent bibliography. But after all it carries one very little farther. *En passant*[25] I was rather surprised that he should have taken the Swords of the Tarot as the prototypes of Clubs. So learned and accurate a writer must have had some authority for this statement, but none is given, and the obvious idea that in Italian swords is *spadi*, and the form of the pips in modern cards suggest a conventionalized drawing of the Roman broad sword, is not so much as alluded to. The original symbology as I have said remains unknown, and is open to any conjecture, but it must be said that the form of the Club pip is singularly unlike a bludgeon or quarter staff. But if we take the suit of *Denarii*,[26] or Pentacles, to represent earth forces, and suggest that money or coins might symbolize material powers, and that the clover or trefoil leaf, as a product of the earth, might also symbolize the earth forces, it might be as good symbology as the derivation of bludgeons from swords. In any case it seems to be generally assumed the Cups are the prototypes of Hearts, and Sceptres of Diamonds, and if Swords or *Spadi* become Spades, there is only left the correspondence of Pentacles with modern Clubs.

There are then three ways in which we may regard the Tarot cards. Firstly the most obvious, as implements of a game of chance or skill, and this is only historically interesting. Secondly as a book of hieroglyphics, revealing, if properly interpreted, some great mystic truths. It may be some cosmogony, or history of evolution, either of the universe, or the human soul. And thirdly as a means of divination. Clearly the second of these depends entirely on our having the correct order of the cards; and as to this at present no light comes from antiquity, and modern authorities differ, as we have seen. The third, or divinatory use, depends on the chance laying down of the cards, the order in which they turn up after certain prescribed shufflings and cuttings by the querent. Mr. Waite inclines to the belief that the series of 22 Atus, or Trumps, were solely referred to the second of the above ways of regarding the cards; and the 56 pip cards, which he calls the Lesser Arcana, were for no other use than for divination or fortune-telling. This may be correct. Certainly there are examples of the Atus alone without the pip cards, and there are packs of pip cards sold now in Italy for the playing of Tarochi with no Atus. Yet there are early examples in Mr. Clulow's collection of packs containing both, and clearly related. One form at least of the game[27] is played with both, the Atus have a very special power justifying their name of trumps; and certainly also the system of divination shown to me by Mrs. Lee made use of both. I can only say that after examining all the evidence—that cited by Mr. Waite as well as some others—I have myself come to a different conclusion, but I consider the point still open to investigation.

As to divination or fortune-telling, there are many ways of laying out the cards; I have myself been shown over a dozen, and I am persuaded there are many more, some of them peculiar to individual diviners. The first method described by Mr. Waite[28] has long been familiar to me. It was sometimes used among others by Mrs. Florence Farr Emery, but the divinatory meanings were entirely different. Rightly or wrongly they were logically formed by the combination of the general meaning of the suit with the mystic properties of numbers, which Mr. Waite apparently disregards.[29] This divinatory meaning is broadly borne out by the old symbolic designs. The theory, therefore, is that the Tarot was in its origin a symbolic book, whose meaning can now only be remotely guessed at; that the original designers worked upon the fourfold division of all created things, whereof well-known examples are the four beasts of Ezekiel's vision, and of the Apocalypse, the four cherubim, the four archangels, the four letters of tetragrammaton, and many others; to which they added the mystic virtues of numbers, and upon each page of the book they placed a symbolic design still further to elucidate it. Each page on this theory would in fact form a chapter in the book, describing the good and evil influences operating from the spiritual on the material world. By the theory of divination the process of shuffling and cutting the cards according to the prescribed method would indicate the influences operating on the querent. We may perhaps compare the symbolic designs to the vignettes illustrating chapters in the Egyptian *Book of the Dead*.

If this theory is in any way correct it is obvious that it is of supreme importance to preserve by all means the ancient symbolic designs, and if possible to restore them to the state in which the original designers intended to set them forth.[30] Archaeological research is continually bringing to light new and unexpected discoveries, and it may well be that any day some fresh evidence may be forthcoming on the forms of the Tarot, before the earliest that are now known, evidence that perhaps will without doubt connect these mysterious cards with one or other of the great races of antiquity and the great systems of philosophy or prove the fallacy of this idea. I trust that Mr. Waite may some day find time to tell us from whence he derived his interpretations, and the designs illustrating them.[31]

Taking as an example the Two of Pentacles, of which I have spoken before, Pentacles represent the earth forces—the material influences ruling our mortal life—and two according to the Pythagoreans is the number of divided councils, of Good and Evil, the first number to separate itself from the divine unity, hence associated with the dual nature of the serpent, or the two serpents, the serpent of the temptation, and the brazen serpent of healing lifted up by Moses in the wilderness, which was a type of Christ. Appropriately then in the old designs is the Two of Pentacles illustrated by the serpent coiled in the symbol of infinity. The interpretation may be true or false, I claim no special inspiration for it. It is merely a suggestion. But from whence comes Mr. Waite's dancing man?[32] If he belongs to any of the old forms of the Tarot, or is in any way connected with the original designers, he is worthy of serious consideration. But one would like to know his origin and credentials. And the same remark applies to the other designs.

I am aware that my contribution is exceedingly small, but in tracing a path so obscure the faintest gleam of light may be of great value. I wholly agree with Mr. Waite in deprecating the attitude of those who assume a mighty air of mystery, and hint that an they would they could tell much. This is not the attitude of the real occult student. Those who know the secret tradition (supposing there is one) should either set forth their knowledge, if they may, and are not restrained by any pledges or honourable understanding,[33] or should be silent; and those who have any interpretation to give should give their authority, or if the source be their own intuition or clairvoyance, should frankly say so. If all commentators would follow these simple rules of scientific investigation, we might be nearer to solving the two mysteries of the origin of the Tarot cards, and the origin of the gipsies, and either proving or disproving their alleged connection.

Notes to Part Four

1. J. W. Brodie-Innes, "The Tarot Cards," in *The Occult Review* vol. XXIX, no. 2 (February 1919): p. 95.

2. Darcy Küntz, *The Complete Golden Dawn Cipher Manuscript* (Edmonds, WA: Holmes Publishing Group, 1996), p. 76.

3. *The Occult Review* (March 1919): p. 161.

4. A. E. Waite, *The Hidden Church of the Holy Graal* (London: Rebman, 1909), p. 603.

5. In Scottish criminal court cases, there are three possible verdicts: guilty, not guilty, and not proven. Both the "not guilty" and the "not proven" verdicts result in acquittal.

6. See the biographical note on George Clulow.

7. An older French name for the Magician.

8. The Female Pope, sometimes called Pope Joan. A medieval legend asserts that one of the popes was a woman disguised as a man. Her gender was exposed when she gave birth to a child while presiding over a public ceremony. In the modern Tarot, this trump is known as the High Priestess.

9. The Pope. In most modern Tarot decks, this trump is called the Hierophant.

10. A wig-maker.

11. *The Forty-Five* is an excerpt by Philip Henry Stanhope, the 5th Earl Stanhope, who bore the title Viscount Mahon, from his seven-volume *History of England*, which was published between 1836–1853. *The Forty-Five* was published as a separate work in London by John Murray in 1851 and republished in a new edition in 1869. It concerns the events surrounding the Jacobite uprising of 1745. The quotation referred to is as follows:

    "At Princess Palestrina's he [Prince Charles] asked me if I understood the game of tarrochi, which they were about to play at. I answered in the negative; upon which, taking the pack in his hands, he desired to know if I had ever seen such odd cards. I replied that they were very odd indeed. He then displaying them said, here is every thing in the world to be found in these cards—the sun, moon, the stars; and here, says he (throwing me a card), is the Pope; here is the Devil; and, added he, there is but one of the trio wanting, and you know who that should be! I was so amazed, so astonished, though he spoke this last in a laughing, good-humoured manner, that I did not know which way to look; and as to a reply, I made none."

    See Lord Mahon, *The Forty-Five: Being the Narrative of the Insurrection of 1745, Extracted from Lord Mahon's History of England* (London: John Murray, 1869), p. 141.

    The source of the passage quoted by Stanhope (Lord Mahon) is *Letters from Italy* by Lady Miller (Anna Riggs Miller), vol. 2 (London: E. and C. Dilly, 1776), p. 198.

12. Éliphas Lévi linked the Tarot trumps to the Hebrew letters in his *Rituel de la Haute Magie*, which was published at Paris in the year 1855. "We have said that the twenty-two keys of the Tarot are the twenty-two letters of the primitive kabbalistic alphabet." Lévi, *Transcendental Magic*, p. 386. This connection between the Tarot trumps and the Hebrew letters was derived by Lévi from Court de Gébelin's *Monde Primitif*. Lévi placed the card of the Fool in second-to-last place, on the Hebrew letter *Shin*—see *Transcendental Magic*, p. 392.

13. The reference here is to the trump the Magician, the posture of whose body resembles the shape of the Hebrew letter *Aleph*, to which it was linked by Éliphas Lévi and other occultists. The figures on the other trumps do not resemble the other Hebrew letters to any significant degree, so this correspondence is more fanciful than actual.

14. The Fool was variously placed at the beginning of the series of trumps, at its end, and in second-to-last place by different French occultists. S. L. MacGregor Mathers put the Fool of his new Golden Dawn Tarot at the beginning, upon the consideration that zero precedes the number one (but note that in his booklet *The Tarot*, published in 1888, he placed the Fool in its traditional second-to-last position). In traditional Tarot decks, the Fool is not zero, but is unnumbered, which makes the assignment of zero to the Fool an innovation that is both bold and questionable. By placing the Fool at the beginning of the trumps, the numbers on the trumps were displaced from the number positions of the Hebrew letters by one place, with the exception of the final trump, the World, which received the final Hebrew letter, *Tau*. Thus, the Fool (0) received the first letter, *Aleph*, which has a value of one; the Magician (I) received the second letter, *Beth*, which has a value of two; the High Priestess (II) received the third letter, *Gimel*, which has a value of three; and so on. This arrangement was embraced and justified by Aleister Crowley, and it has become the standard in modern Western occultism. It detracts somewhat from the mystique of the Fool, which, having no number in the traditional Tarots, can be placed anywhere.

15. That is to say, prior to the outbreak of the French Revolution in 1789.

16. This is the title of the book by the Spanish-born French occultist Gérard Encausse (1865–1916), who went by the pseudonym Papus: *Le Tarot des Bohémiens* (*The Tarot of the Bohemians*) (Paris: Georges Carré, 1889). First English edition translated by A. P. Morton (London: Chapman and Hall, 1892). Ronald Decker and Michael Dummett have called this English title a mistranslation in chapter 7 of their book *A History of the Occult Tarot*, saying that *Bohémiens* should be translated *Gypsies* and hence the English version of the title should be *The Tarot of the Gypsies*. However, it was common to refer to the Gypsies as Bohemians in England from at least as early as the seventeenth century, as a glance at the word *Bohemian* in the *Oxford English Dictionary* will confirm, so Morton's choice of an English title was not

inappropriate. Papus briefly became a member of the Golden Dawn in 1895, when he joined the Ahathoor Temple in Paris. See his biographical note.

17. The reference is to Waite's *The Pictorial Key to the Tarot*: "It remained for Romain Merlin, in 1869, to point out what should have been obvious, namely, that cards of some kind were known in Europe prior to the arrival of the Gipsies in or about 1417." *The Pictorial Key*, p. 54. Romain Merlin (1793–1876) wrote *Origine des Cartes à Jouer: Recherches Nouvelles sur les Naibis, les Tarots et sur les Autres Espèces de Cartes*, published by the author in Paris in 1869. See Waite's note in *The Pictorial Key*, p. 327.

18. Jean Alexandre Vaillant (1804–1886), who wrote *Les Rômes: Histoire Vraie des Vrais Bohémiens* (*The Rom: The True History of the Real Gypsies*), published in 1857. See Waite's note on this work in his *Pictorial Key*, p. 324.

19. This may be a reference to the tetractys of Pythagoras, a pattern of ten dots arranged in four rows to form a triangle.

20. In Pythagorean numerology, the duad is associated with man and woman, and with their union in marriage. Perhaps Brodie-Innes is referring to Adam and Eve united in sexual union by the wiles of the Serpent.

21. See the biographical note on Florence Farr.

22. See the biographical note on Charles Godfrey Leland.

23. Brodie-Innes's essay was written one year after the end of the First World War. During the war, the Germans had been ceaselessly demonized as baby-killers and monsters by English wartime propaganda, resulting in widespread resentment against them by the English people. It's possible that he had in mind here the German occult current that gave rise to the Hermetic Order of the Golden Dawn. For years, members of the Golden Dawn believed that their Order had been authorized by a German adept named Fraulein Anna Sprengler. A scandal ensued when this was proven to be a fiction put forth by W. Wynn Westcott.

24. There are faint similarities between Egyptian symbolism and Tarot symbolism, which is inevitable given the universal nature of symbolism, but there is no indication of any kind pointing to an Egyptian origin for the Tarot cards. Also, the theory that the Romanies originated in Egypt has long been rejected by scholars.

25. In passing.

26. Coins.

27. We know this today as the French game of Tarot, which uses a full deck of 78 cards.

28. The very popular Celtic Cross spread, which Waite referred to as "an ancient Celtic method of divination." See his *Pictorial Key*, pp. 299–305.

29. The veiled allusion here is to the ten emanations on the Tree of Life in the mystical Kabbalah, which formed a key part of the magic system of the Golden Dawn. When Brodie-Innes speaks of the "mystical properties of numbers," he is referring

more to the Kabbalistic meaning of the emanations, known as Sephiroth, than to the mystical meanings of Pythagoras—although, of course, the two overlap.

30. The fallacy in the thinking of Brodie-Innes is his assumption that the earlier designs of the Tarot must always be more meaningful. Just the opposite is true: they are less meaningful, at least in some instances. The symbolism of the Tarot evolved over a span of centuries, and the depth of occult meaning increased during this period.

    In the early centuries of the Tarot's existence, the increase in symbolic significance was unconscious and collective, the result of the social currents in which the Tarot evolved. For example, we see the very simple symbolism on the elegant paintings of the fifteenth-century Visconti-Sforza Tarot evolve into the more complex symbolism on the cruder designs of the eighteenth-century Tarot of Marseilles. During the nineteenth and twentieth centuries, individual occultists began to modify and enhance the symbolism in conscious, deliberate ways. As a result of this tendency, the current pinnacle of occult Tarot symbolism was reached in 1944 with the Book of Thoth Tarot deck, designed by Aleister Crowley and painted by Lady Frieda Harris. The Thoth Tarot, which was based on the Tarot of the Golden Dawn, has not yet been surpassed in its subtlety and complexity of meaning, although it undoubtedly will be at some future date.

    The inevitable pitfall of this tendency to add symbolism to the Tarot is the proliferation of decks with vapid, chaotic, or inappropriate symbols, and it is perhaps these sorts of Tarot decks that Brodie-Innes had foremost in mind when he voiced his warning. For every Tarot designed by a knowledgeable occultist working in the Western tradition, there are a hundred with pretty pictures of monkeys or butterflies or flowers or circus performers. These will be neglected and will soon fall by the wayside, but the symbolically meaningful occult Tarots will be valued and will endure.

31. This was written tongue-in-cheek. Brodie-Innes knew full well that Waite's Tarot designs were heavily influenced by the interpretations used by the Golden Dawn, which both he and Waite, as Golden Dawn initiates, were sworn never to reveal.

32. The Two of Pentacles in the Rider-Waite Tarot depicts a man dancing on one foot with a ball in each hand. The balls are connected by a lemniscate, the symbol of infinity. In the background the sea rolls with huge waves, tossing two sailing ships. The dancer wears an overtly phallic hat on his head. None of this symbolism, other than the lemniscate suggested by the S-shaped scroll on the Marseilles card, has any origin in traditional Tarots.

33. Both Brodie-Innes and Waite were bound by oaths of secrecy not to reveal the occult teachings of the Golden Dawn.

PART FIVE

The Isiac Tablet of
Cardinal Bembo (extract)
by
W. WYNN WESTCOTT

INTRODUCTION
TO PART FIVE

The following text was extracted from the latter portion of the monograph *Tabula Bembina sive Mensa Isiaca: The Isiac Tablet of Cardinal Bembo: Its History and Occult Significance*. The author is William Wynn Westcott, one of the three founding members of the Hermetic Order of the Golden Dawn. No date is given on the title page, but the monograph was published in 1887. No publisher is given, but it appears from other publications advertised in the back of the monograph that it was published by Robert H. Fryar (1845–1909) of Bath.[1]

Below Westcott's name on the title page appear the honorary appellations "Hon. Magus Soc. Ros. in Ang." (Honorable Magus Societas Rosicruciana in Anglia) and "Hon. Member Hermetic Soc." (Honorable Member Hermetic Society). The Rosicrucian Society of England was founded in 1867. Three of its members, Westcott, William Robert Woodman, and Samuel Liddell MacGregor Mathers, would go on to found another Rosicrucian society, the Hermetic Order of the Golden Dawn, in 1887. The Hermetic Society was founded in 1885 by Anna Kingsford and Edward Maitland, former members of Blavatsky's Theosophical Society. Both Mathers and Westcott belonged to it.

The reason I have not reproduced the entire text of the monograph is because the majority of it has nothing to do with the Tarot. It was the fantasy of Court de Gébelin that the Tarot originated in Egypt. This fantasy captured the imagination of later French occultists, chief among them Éliphas Lévi, and they elaborated it in their writings. From Lévi, Papus, Christian, and other French writers, it made its way across the Channel to the English occultists. Aleister Crowley probably titled his Tarot the Book of Thoth in reference to Lévi's use of this term for the Tarot, which is mentioned by Westcott in the following extract.

As fascinating as the Egyptian figures on the tablet are, they are not figures relating to the Tarot trumps. However, Westcott's remarks on Éliphas Lévi and his comments about the Tarot are of interest, in view of his connection with the Golden Dawn and his knowledge of occultism and the Kabbalah. It should be noted that Westcott wrote about the Tablet of Cardinal Bembo a year before the Isis-Urania Temple of the Golden Dawn was established in London. It's unlikely that the Golden Dawn Tarot created by Mathers and his wife, Möina, influenced his remarks in the monograph, since the deck probably had yet to be painted—the exact date of its creation is unknown. It is, however, likely that Westcott's views about the Tarot influenced Mathers.

The Bembine Tablet, also known as the Isiac Tablet, is a large bronze tablet enameled on its surface and inlaid with silver. Westcott states near the beginning of his monograph that it is approximately fifty inches wide and thirty inches tall. It is covered with images of Egyptian deities and Egyptian hieroglyphics. The figure of a seated Egyptian goddess occupies the center of the tablet, and it is perhaps for this reason that the tablet is referred to as the Isiac Tablet. It became known to the modern world in 1527, when it was purchased in Rome from a locksmith by the antiquarian Cardinal Pietro Bembo (1470–1547), following the Sack of Rome by the mutinous army of the Holy Roman Emperor Charles V. It is believed to have been crafted in the first century CE in Rome, where there was an active cult of Isis.

The tablet has been an object of fascination for occultists for centuries. Athenasius Kircher wrote about it in his 1652 work *Oedipus Aegyptiacus*.[2] Sir Thomas Browne referred to it in his 1658 essay "The Garden of Cyrus."[3] Manly P. Hall claimed in the eighth chapter of his *Secret Teachings of All Ages* that the classicist and translator of Greek texts Thomas Taylor believed the tablet had been present in a secret chamber beneath the Sphinx when the philosopher Plato was initiated into the Egyptian mysteries. He quoted the following from "a manuscript by Thomas Taylor" that he did not name:

> Plato was initiated into the "Greater Mysteries" at the age of 49. The initiation took place in one of the subterranean halls of the Great Pyramid in Egypt. The Isiac Table formed the altar, before which the Divine Plato stood and received that which was always his, but which the ceremony of the Mysteries enkindled and brought from its dormant state. With this ascent, after three days in the Great Hall, he was received by

the Hierophant of the Pyramid (the Hierophant was seen only by those who had passed the three days, the three degrees, the three dimensions) and given verbally the Highest Esoteric Teachings, each accompanied with Its appropriate Symbol. After a further three months' sojourn in the halls of the Pyramid, the Initiate Plato was sent out into the world to do the work of the Great Order, as Pythagoras and Orpheus had been before him.[4]

You will recognize the secret chamber under the Sphinx so dear to the hearts of the French occultists of the late eighteenth and nineteenth centuries. Comte de Mellet mentioned it in his essay, and it figured prominently in the writing of other occultists who wrote about the Tarot, such as Paul Christian (Jean-Baptiste Pitois), Edouard Schuré, and C. C. Zain (Elbert Benjamin).

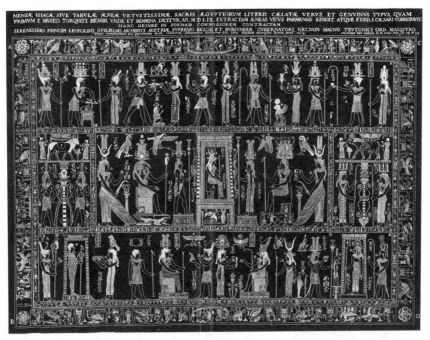

Bembine Tablet from *Oedipus Aegyptiacus* by Athanasius Kircher, 1654

THE ISIAC TABLET
OF CARDINAL BEMBO

by

W. WYNN WESTCOTT

(extract, pp. 17–19)

In the *Histoire de la Magie*, Lévi wrote: "The most curious, and at the same time the most complete key to the Tarot, or modern version of the famous Book of Thoth, is found in the Isiac Tablet of Cardinal Bembo, which has been represented by Kircher in his work on Egypt: this learned Jesuit has divined, without being able to establish complete proof, that this Tablet contained a key in hieroglyphics to the sacred alphabet. It presents to us three groups of designs, above the twelve celestial mansions, and below the twelve laborious periods of the year, and in its central portion the twenty-one sacred signs, which correspond to the letters of the Hebrew alphabet. In the middle of the central portion is seated the Image of the Pantomorphous IYNX,[5] an emblem of Universal Existence, corresponding to the Hebrew letter Jod or I. Around the central Iynx are placed the Ophionian, or Serpentine triad; these three forms refer to the Three Mother Letters, A, M, and S of the Hebrew and Egyptian Alphabets. On the right side of the Iynx are placed the Ibimorphous and Serapean triads, and on the left those of Nephta, and of Hecate; symbols respectively of:

The Active	and	the Passive.
The Volatile	and	the Fixed.
The Fecundating Fire	and	the Generative Water.

Each pair of triads in conjunction with the Iynx form a Septenary, the centre itself contains a Septenary. Thus the three Septenaries present us with the absolute number of the Three Worlds, and the complete number of Primitive

Letters; to which is added a complementary sign, just as to the nine numerals is added a Zero. The ten numerals added to the twenty-two ancient letters form the Thirty-two Ways or Paths of Kabbalistic doctrine."[6]

This is all that Eliphas Lévi writes directly about our Tablet; but he adds a diagram, or plan of the whole Table,[7] except the Limbus or Border, and this diagram tells a more occult tale to the attentive student, it presents an even more esoteric view of the matter, which he has not thought fit to explain in words. Doubtless he considered that to the wise the diagram would speak sufficiently plain, and to the profane no explanation could carry instruction; hence I feel much hesitation in lifting the veil he has thought fit to leave over the subject; but at the request of the Editor of the series of Bath Occult Reprints,[8] I proceed to give a glimpse within the Veil of the Saitic Isis.[9]

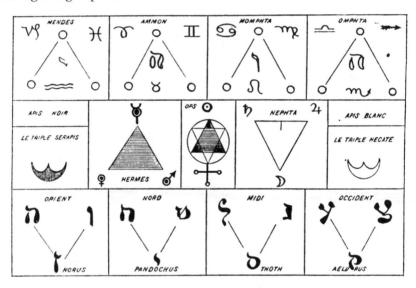

From Levi's *History of Magic.*

The Diagram of Éliphas Lévi

The diagram of Lévi, by which he explains the mystery of the Tablet, shows the Upper Region divided into the four seasons of the year, each with three signs of the Zodiac, and he has added the four-lettered sacred name, the Tetragrammaton, assigning *Jod* to Aquarius, that is Canopus, *He* to Taurus, that is Apis, *Vau* to Leo, that is Momphta, and *He* final to Typhon. Note the Cherubic parallel—Man, Bull. Lion, and Eagle. The fourth form is found either as

Scorpion or Eagle depending upon the Occult good or evil intention: in the Demotic Zodiac, the Snake replaces the Scorpion.[10]

The Lower Region he ascribes to the twelve *simple* Hebrew letters, associating them with the four quarters of the horizon, compare the *Sepher Yetzirah*, cap. v., sec. 1.

The Central Region he ascribes to the Solar powers and the Planetary. In the middle we see above, the Sun, marked Ops, and below it is a Solomon's Seal, above a cross; a double triangle Hexapla, one light and one dark triangle superposed, the whole forming a sort of complex symbol of Venus. To the Ibimorphos he gives the three dark planets, Venus, Mercury, and Mars placed around a dark triangle erect, denoting Fire. To the Nephthæan triad he gives three light planets, Saturn, Luna, and Jupiter, around a light inverted triangle which denotes Water. There is a necessary connection between water, female power, passive principle, Binah, and Sephirotic Mother, and Bride. (See the *Kabbalah* by S.L.M. Mathers.)[11] Note the ancient signs for the planets were all composed of a Cross, Solar Disc and Crescent: Venus is a cross below a Sun disc, Mercury, a disc with a crescent above and cross below, Saturn is a Cross whose lowest point touches the apex of the crescent, Jupiter is a Crescent whose lowest point touches the left hand end of a cross: all these are deep mysteries.[12] Note that Lévi in his original plate transposed Serapis and Hecate, but not the Apis noir and Apis blanc, perhaps because of the head of Bes being associated by him with Hecate. Note that having referred the 12 simple letters to the lower, the 7 double must correspond to the central region of the planets, and then the great triad A.M.S.[13] the mother letters representing Air, Water, and Fire remain to be pictured, around S the Central Iynx, or *Yod*, by the Ophionian Triad the two Serpents and the Leonine Sphinx. Lévi's word OPS in the centre is the Latin Ops, Terra, genius of the Earth; and the Greek Ops, Rhea, or Kubele (Cybele) often drawn as a goddess seated in a chariot drawn by lions, she is crowned with turrets, and holds a Key; see frontispiece to "Asclepios," Bath Occult Reprint.[14]

The Apis Bull was the image of the Sun, on earth, and Serapis was the Solar Bull deified after death; Serapis is a shortened form of Osiri-apis.

The Isiac Tablet, writes Lévi, is a Key to the ancient Book of Thoth, which has survived to some extent the lapse of centuries and is pictured to us in the still comparatively ancient set of Tarocchi cards. To him the Book of Thoth was a resumé of the esoteric learning of the Egyptians, after the decadence of their civilization, this lore became crystallized in an hieroglyphic form as the Tarot; this Tarot having become partially or entirely forgotten or misunderstood, its pictured symbols fell into the hands of the sham diviners, and of the providers of the public amusement by games of cards. The modern Tarot, or Tarocchi pack of cards consists of 78 cards, of which 22 form a special group of trumps, of pictorial design: the remaining 56 are composed of four suits of 10 numerals and four court cards, King, Queen, Knight, and Knave or Valet; the suits are Swords (Militaryism), Cups (Sacerdocy), Clubs or Wands (Agriculture), and Shekels or Coins (Commerce), answering respectively to our Spades, Hearts, Clubs and Diamonds. Our purpose is with the 22 trumps, these form the special characteristic of the pack and are the lineal descendants of the Hieroglyphics of the Tarot. These 22 correspond to the letters of the Hebrew and other sacred alphabets, which fall naturally into three classes of a Trio of mothers, a Heptad of doubles, and a Duodecad of simple letters.[15] They are also considered as a triad of Heptads and one apart, a system of Initiation and an Uninitiate. These Tarots are named:[16]

1. The Magus.

2. The Hierophantess, Pope Joan.

3. The Queen, or Empress, Juno.

4. The King, Jupiter.

5. The Hierophant, Pope.

6. Marriage, the Lovers.

7. The Conqueror in a Chariot, Osiris.

8. Justice, with Sword & Balance.

9. The Hermit, Philosopher, Sage.

10. The Wheel of Fate.

11. Fortitude, Power.

12. The Hanged Man, Judas, Prometheus, the Adept.

13. Death.

14. Temperance.

15. The Devil, Baphomet.

16. House of Plutus, Babel.

17. The Dog Star, Blazing Star.

18. The Moon.

19. The Sun.

20. The Last Judgment.

21. The World, the Crown, Kether with the Cherubim.

0. The Uninitiate, The Fool, Le Mat.

These are the Names of the Tarots, I now add some hints of their significance:

1. *Aleph.* Man, Unique God.

2. *Beth.* Woman, Sanctuary.

3. *Ghimel.* Isis, Urania, Nature.

4. *Daleth.* The Cubic Stone.

5. *He.* Religion, Inspiration.

6. *Vau.* The Two Ways, Trial.

7. *Zain.* Victory.

8. *Cheth.* Equilibrium, Themis.

9. *Teth.* Wisdom, The Veiled Lamp.

10. *Yod.* Key of Occultism, Virility.

21. *Shin.* Sensitive life, Animals.

11. *Kaph.* Triple Chain.

12. *Lamed.* the Great Work, Crux.

13. *Mem.* Death, Renewal.

11. *Nun.* The Seasons, Climate, Mutation.

15. *Samech.* Evil Magic, Sabbat.

16. *Oin.* The Lightning, Failure.

17. *Pe.* Canopus, Sirius, Astrology.

18. *Tzaddi.* Magnetism, Light.

19. *Soph.* The Stone, Gold.

20. *Resh.* Vegetables, Medicine.

0. *Tau.* The Microcosm, Pan.

Certain other cards of the Tarot Pack have also borne special Names: The 3 of Coins was Osiris; the 3 of Cups, Isis; the 2 of Cups, Apis; the 9 of Coins, Hermes; the 1 of Wands, the Serpent, Apophis; the 1 of Coins, the Sun, Apollo.

It is necessary to see and study a set of the most ancient Tarots to appreciate the essentially Egyptian character of their symbolism.[17]

The dogmas of the *Sepher Yetzirah* also form a perfect Tarot. The Three Mothers, which are: 1. *Aleph*, Air, the Firmament, the Holy Spirit. The Human Respiration, the Chest. 13. *Mem*, Water, the Earth, the Belly, the Womb. 21. *Shin*, Fire, the Heavens of Stars and Suns, the Brain, the Head. These are represented by the Centre of the Isiac Tablet. The seven doubles which correspond to the planets, and the median part of the Isiac Tablet: 2, *Beth*, Luna, Nature; 3, *Ghimel*, Mars, Force; 4, *Daleth*, Sun, Fertility; 11, *Kaph*, Venus, Generation; 17, *Pe*, Mercury, Wisdom; 20, *Resh*, Saturn, Peace; 22, or 0, *Tau*, Jupiter, Beauty, and the Twelve Single, corresponding to the Zodiacal signs, and the Upper Region of the Isiac Tablet:

5. *He.* Aries. Voice.

7. *Zain.* Gemini. Motion.

6. *Vau.* Taurus. Mind.

8. *Cheth.* Cancer. Sight.

9. *Teth*. Leo. Hearing.   10. *Yod*. Virgo. Work. Duty.

12. *Lamed*. Libra. Sexual desire.   14. *Nun*. Scorpio. Smell.

15. *Samech*. Sagittarius. Sleep.   16. *Oin*. Capricornus. Fury.

18. *Tzaddi*. Aquarius. Taste.   19. *Soph*. Pisces. Mirth.

I can strongly recommend a study of the *Sepher Yetzirah*, or *Book of Formation*, as one of the most ancient philosophic schemes of Theosophy known to us. It is far older than the Kabbalistic *Zohar*.[18]

The Symbolism of the Tarot scheme is further continued into the 56 cards of the Four Suits: these suits are associated with many most important quaternaries: and first with the letters of the Sacred Name we call Jehovah or Yehveh, IHUH; next with four cherubic figures Lion, Man, Eagle and Bull; then to the Four Elementary States, Fire, Air, Water and Earth; further with the mystical letters of the inscription of the Cross, INRI; with the letters of the Hebrew word TORA the Law; with the occult significance of the ROTA or Wheel of the learned Postel:[19] and lastly with sexual design and its emblems, Creator, Phallus, Masculine, Aaron's Rod; Great Mother, Yoni, Cteis, Female, Womb; thirdly with the Lingam, Conjunction, or with the Sun; and lastly Female, Circle, Shekel, Pantacle, Vesica Piscis, Image of the World, Malkuth, Kingdom.

Club or Wand,—I, *Yod*, Male, Phallus, Lion head, Fire. Mind.

Heart or Cup,—H, *He*, Female, Yoni, Human head, Air.[20] Soul.

Spade or Sword,—U, *Vau*, Male, Lingam, Eagle head, Water. Spirit.

Diamond or Coin,—H. *He*, Female, Vesica Piscis, Bull head, Earth. Body.

The four suits are named in France, Trefles, Piques, Cœurs and Carreaux.

Then lastly the four sets of ten numeral cards, represent the Ten Sephiroth multiplied by the letters of the Tetragrammaton, or in the four Worlds of Aziluth, Briah, Yetzirah and Assiah: thus the four Aces become the fourfold Kether, the four Twos the fourfold Chocmah, and so on to the four Tens which typify Malkuth.

From a study of these analogies and correspondences, and the symbolic associations, it will be obvious how a system of divination arose, because each card of the whole series of 78 had a meaning direct or symbolical; for example the 7 of Cups (Hearts) would mean the Netzah of *He* or the Victory of the Woman, and the 3 of Clubs the Binah of *Yod* the Understanding of the Creator.

Another curious mystery may be casually mentioned here: How comes it that some of the Court Cards are invariably drawn with the faces in profile and others of full front faces; the profile are the King of Diamonds or Coins the left, the Knave of Hearts, Cups the left, and the Knave of Spades, Swords the right profile. Number 4 of the Tarots, the King, is a profile—we trench here upon one of the most hidden dogmas of the Kabbalah,[21] for Macroprosopus is always designed as a Right Profile, while Microprosopus[22] is drawn of full face, he is the *Vau* of the Tetragrammaton. The figure of the Hindoo Addha Nari[23] is usually drawn holding in the two hands the four emblems of the Tarot pack, wand and cup in the right hand, sword and circle in the left—but enough of the Tarot.

In conclusion, I cannot refrain from quoting the words of Hermes Trismegistus, to be found in his *Dialogue of Asclepios* (see "Bath Occult Reprint"):

"O Ægypte, Ægypte, religionum tuarum supererunt
fabulæ, eæque incredibiles posteris tuis."

"O Egypt, Egypt, there will remain of thy religions,
only vague legends which posterity will refuse to believe."

QUOD SCIS, NESCIS.[24]

Notes to Part Five

1. For more information on Robert Fryar, refer to Sydney T. Chapman's essay "A Victorian Occultist and Publisher: Robert H. Fryar of Bath," published by the Widcombe Press in *The Road: A Journal of History, Myth and Legend* no. 4 (June 2011): pp. 2–11.

2. Kircher's examination of the Isiac Tablet is to be found in the third volume of *Oedipus Aegyptiacus* (Rome, 1654), pp. 79–160.

3. Sir Thomas Browne, *The Garden of Cyrus* (1658; repr., London: no publisher, 1736), p. 34.

4. Manly P. Hall, *The Secret Teachings of All Ages* (San Francisco, CA: H. S. Crocker, 1928), p. 57.

5. Pantomorphic Iÿnx is the seated female figure in the center of the Isiac Tablet. Lévi reproduced her as a full-page plate in the French edition of his *Histoire de la Magie* (plate following page 76). The text on the plate below this image reads "Pantomorphic Iÿnx. Twenty-first Key of the early Egyptian Tarot."

Iÿnx was a nymph of Greek mythology who was turned into a bird of the same name (*iynx torquilla*) by the goddess Hera. The bird was sacred to Aphrodite and was sometimes brought down to earth by the goddess to assist unfortunate or unrequited lovers. The actual bird of this name was used by sorcerers to make love magic. "The method of using the Iÿnx upon these desperately amorous and magical occasions seems to have varied considerably. Some are of opinion that the practitioners of amatory witchcraft bound the bird by its wings and legs to a wheel after the fashion of Ixion, whirling it round as they called on the name of the recusant loved one, and as they chanted or murmured their spells." *Fraser's Magazine* vol. 57, no. 339 (March 1858), pp. 347–348. Pindar called this four-spoked wheel *tetracnamon*.

A. E. Waite remarked: "Mr. G. R. S. Mead tells us that *Iynx* in its root-meaning, according to Proclus, signifies the 'power of transmission' which is said in the Chaldaean Oracles 'to sustain the fountains.' Mr. Mead thinks that the *Iyinges* were reproduced (a) as Living Spheres and (b) as Winged Globes. He thinks, also, that (a) the Mind on the plane of reality put forth (b) the one *Iyinx*, (c) after this three *Iyinges*, called paternal and ineffable, and finally (d) there may have been hosts of subordinate *Iyinges*. They were 'free intelligences.' It seems to follow that the *Iynx* was not 'an emblem of universal being,' but a product of the Eternal Mind." See Waite's translation of *History of Magic* by Lévi, p. 82, note 1.

6. A loose translation from Lévi's *Histoire de la Magie* (1860), pp. 81–82. The passage occurs in A. E. Waite's translation of the work, *The History of Magic*, rev. ed., 1969, coincidentally on the same page numbers, pp. 81–82.

7. See Lévi, *The History of Magic*, p. 83.

8. Robert H. Fryar.

9. Saitic Isis was the Isis of Sais, a town in Egypt where a temple was erected for her worship. Within this temple was a seated statue of veiled Isis that bore the inscription "I am all that has been, that is, or shall be; no mortal man yet has raised my veil." This statue was mentioned by Plutarch in his essay "On Isis and Osiris," where he identified the goddess with the Greek goddess Athena. The statue may actually have been the Egyptian goddess Neith, who was worshipped at Sais. The veil that appears over the face of the seated figure on the trump, the High Priestess, in some Tarot decks is a reference to Saitic Isis.

10. The span of days covered by the zodiac sign Scorpio (October 23–November 21) is approximately equivalent to that of the Egyptian zodiac sign of Wadget (October 28–November 26). Wadget is a cobra goddess, and the symbol of this sign is an uprearing cobra. In conjunction with the solar disk, it forms the uraeus, the emblem of royalty in the crown of the rulers of Lower Egypt.

11. *The Kabbalah Unveiled* by S. L. MacGregor Mathers, published in London in 1887. It is a partial translation of the *Kabbalah Denudata* of Knorr von Rosenroth. Mathers

wrote an extensive introduction in which he explained the basics of the practical Kabbalah.

12. On the symbolism of the astrological glyphs of the seven planets of traditional astrology, see *The Rationale of Astrology* by Alfred H. Barley, who wrote: "The symbols of 'the five planets' are all derived from the parent symbols accorded to the Sun, Moon, and Earth, namely, circle, half-circle or crescent, and cross. Now these three symbols relate to the Spirit [circle] or life principle, Soul [crescent] or plastic or fluid formative principle, and Body [cross] or concrete, focalising form or matter principle." *The Rationale of Astrology*, pp. 20–21.

The planetary glyphs are composed of these three basic symbols in different combinations. This is somewhat obscured by the practice of showing the glyph of Mars with an arrow rather than a cross, but the arrow is a distortion of the cross. Thus, Venus is circle over cross; Mars is cross over circle; Jupiter is crescent over cross; Saturn is cross over crescent; and Mercury is crescent over circle over cross. The circle of the Sun represents a celestial kind of elemental Fire, the crescent of the Moon a kind of celestial Water, and the cross of Earth a celestial kind of elemental Earth. The symbol that is uppermost is dominant, while the lower symbol provides the foundation or base.

The natural order is circle (Fire) over crescent (Water) over cross (Earth). When the order of these symbols is natural, as in Venus (circle of solar Fire above earthy cross), the result is a harmonious and free expression of their combined energies; but when the order is inverted, as in Mars (cross of Earth above circle of solar Fire), the expression of their combined energies is repressed or hindered. In the case of Mars, this results in a fiery release of force, like a contained explosion that bursts forth. In the case of Saturn, this inversion of the natural order results in coldness and the suppression of emotion, coupled with resentment and brooding. Thus, Venus and Jupiter are harmonious, Mars and Saturn are repressed, and Mercury is somewhat of both, since the crescent and circle in its glyph are not in their natural order but the circle and cross are. This makes Mercury capricious and unpredictable.

13. The three Hebrew mother letters are *Aleph*, *Mem*, and *Shin*. See Westcott's *Sepher Yetzirah*, pp. 20–21. They are called the mothers because they are "the Foundation of all the other sounds and letters"—*Sepher Yetzirah*, p. 20.

14. This plate occurs in *The Virgin of the World of Hermes Mercurius Trismegistus*, translated into English by Anna Kingsford and Edward Maitland. "Asclepios on Initiation" is the second part of this four-part work. See Kingsford and Maitland, *The Virgin of the World* (London: George Redway, 1885), p. 43, which is unnumbered. This work was printed by Robert H. Fryar as one of his Bath Occult Reprints. It was bound under the same cover with *The Divine Pymander*—see Westcott, *The Isiac Tablet of Cardinal Bembo*, p. 20, where it is advertised. The plate shows a

crowned woman seated on a cubic seat atop an open chariot with four wheels that is drawn by two male lions. In her left hand she holds out a key, and in her right hand she cradles a scepter. Her crown has the appearance of a castle turret and her skirts are covered in a pattern of flowers. She and both lions look to their left sides—the side to which she extends the key.

15. In *Sepher Yetzirah* the 22 letters of Hebrew are divided into three mothers (that give birth to the rest), seven doubles (so-called because their sounding is of two kinds), and twelve simples (their sounding is singular). The mothers are associated with the three elements Air, Water, and Fire; the seven doubles with the planets of traditional astrology; and the twelve simples with the signs of the zodiac.

16. Notice that Westcott adopts the name for the Tower given to it by Court de Gébelin, the House of Plutus. (De Gébelin called it the Castle of Plutus.)

17. The more ancient the Tarot packs, the more European their symbolism. They do take on a classical aspect, which descends from Greece and Rome. For example, the Tarocchi of Mantegna, which dates to about 1470, shows figures in flowing white robes of the kind depicted in the sculpture of ancient Greece. Some of the cards show the Muses, others the liberal arts—see Kaplan, *The Encyclopedia of Tarot*, vol. 1, pp. 37–38. I find no unique Egyptian symbolism in the early Tarots.

18. No one really knows the date of *Sepher Yetzirah*. It is generally agreed among scholars of the Kabbalah that it is the earliest surviving Kabbalistic text. Gershom Scholem wrote that the book contains "no linguistic form which may not be ascribed to second- or third-century Hebrew"—Scholem, *Kabbalah*, p. 26. He stated that the earliest actual reference to the text occurs in the sixth century (Ibid., p. 28). By contrast, the *Zohar* is quite a recent production. Most of it was written between 1280 and 1286 in Guadalajara, a town to the northeast of Madrid, by Moses de Leon (Ibid., p. 57).

19. If you write the letters *T-O-R-A* at the cardinal points of a circle, you can read them as *TORA* (law), or if you reverse the direction and start with *R*, you can read them as *ROTA* (wheel). If you start at the *O*, you can read them as *ORAT* (word), or you can start with the *T* and go the other way to get *TARO* (way, as the word is sometimes interpreted). This was held to be of great mystical significance by occultists—see Lévi's *Transcendental Magic*, p. 56. Variations on this "wheel of Postel" are to be found all over the place. A. E. Waite incorporated it into his Tarot trump the Wheel—see *The Pictorial Tarot*, pp. 108–109. Papus used it as the frontispiece for his *Tarot of the Bohemians*. His is a variation on a diagram of Postel's Key that appears on page 125 of the 1646 edition of William (Guillaume) Postel's *Key to Things Kept Secret from the Foundation of the World* (*Absconditorum à Constitutione Mundi Clavis*), which incorporated the wheel of four letters in its head. This diagram was not created by Postel, but by his editor, Abraham von Frankenberg, who added it as a

visual aid to Postel's obscure text—see Decker, Depaulis, and Dummett, *A Wicked Pack of Cards*, pp. 173–174.

20. Westcott has the elements Air and Water inverted from their usual Golden Dawn associations in this list—see Regardie, *The Golden Dawn*, 6th ed., pp. 542–543. In the Golden Dawn system, Air is linked with Swords and Water with Cups. He has stacked the elements in their natural order—Fire, Air, Water, and Earth. Fire is lightest and rises above Air; Water falls below; Earth is always at the bottom. But this arrangement does not accord well with the letters of Tetragrammaton, where the best assignment is Yod—Fire, *first He*—Water, *Vau*—Air, *second He*—Earth.

21. As was observed in part three of the present work, the direction in which the court figures face is of utmost importance to the Golden Dawn method of Tarot divination, called the Opening of the Key.

22. Macroprosopus refers here to the first Sephirah (first emanation of creation), which is called Kether (the Crown). In the Kabbalah, Kether is identified with the Macroprosopus (Vast Countenance) of God, also called *Arikh Anpin* (the Long Face). It is the highest, most exalted, and most mysterious aspect of God. It is often illustrated as the right profile of a bearded male face. In the book of the *Zohar* known as the *Greater Holy Assembly*, it is written of the Macroprosopus, "There is no left in that Ancient Concealed One, but all is right." (See Mathers, *The Kabbalah Unveiled*, p. 121.) The sense of this is that there is no evil in Kether, only good—the left side of the body represents evil, and the right side good. The Microprosopus (Lesser Countenance), also known as *Zauir Anpin* (the Short Face), is associated in a narrow sense with the sixth emanation, called Tiphareth (Beauty), which occupies the center of the Tree of Life. In a larger sense, the Microprosopus encompasses the six middle Sephiroth on the Tree: Tiphareth and the five Sephiroth that surround it (Chesed, Geburah, Netzach, Hod, and Yesod). The Messiah, or Anointed One, has his seat in Tiphareth.

23. Illustrations of the Hindu deity Addha Nari, or Ardhanarishvara ("the Lord who is half-woman"), are to be found with two arms, three arms, four arms, and eight arms. The hands hold a wide variety of objects. The right side of the figure is usually male, and the left side female, to represent the duality of male and female in divinity. Westcott appears to have had in mind an illustration showing the deity with two arms, but I have not been able to identify it. A four-armed version of the figure appears in Éliphas Lévi's *Dogme et Rituel*, vol. 1, the plate following p. 364 in the 2nd edition of 1861. It is reproduced in Waite's translation of the work, *Transcendental Magic*, on p. 162. Similar illustrations of this deity are to be found on p. 120 and p. 142 of *Qabbalah* by Isaac Myer, first published in Philadelphia in 1888. See also Edward Moor's *The Hindu Pantheon*, which was published in London in 1810. Myer's double illustration of Addha Nari on p. 142 is copied directly from the upper half of plate 24 in Moor's book—Myer refers to Moor's work in his

description of the illustration. Myer's other illustration of this being is taken from the lower half of plate 7 in Moor's book. Lévi's illustration of the deity is copied from the left side of Moor's illustration on plate 24.

24. Latin for "What you know, you do not know." The Roman dramatist Terence wrote this in his second-century comedy *Eunuchus* (*The Eunuch*). See Drysdall, *Collected Works of Erasmus: Adages* (Toronto: University of Toronto Press, 2005), p. 124, where this saying is examined at length. It was one of Westcott's magical Latin mottos. In a letter to Theodor Reuss, dated August 26, 1902, he translated it as "even what you know—you don't really know." See Edith Starr Miller, *Occult Theocrasy*, chap. 87, p. 511. A photographic reproduction of the letter appears in the back of her book.

PART SIX
"The Great Symbols of the Tarot"
by
A. E. WAITE

INTRODUCTION
TO PART SIX

Arthur Edward Waite (1857–1942) contributed three essays on the Tarot to the English periodical *The Occult Review*. The first, in the December 1909 issue, titled "The Tarot: A Wheel of Fortune," was intended primarily to promote his own Tarot, recently created in concert with the artist Pamela Colman Smith. There are numerous reproductions of the Rider-Waite cards in the essay. The second, in the March 1919 issue, titled "The Tarot and Secret Tradition," was written mainly to refute comments directed at Waite by Brodie-Innes in the February 1919 issue. (The Brodie-Innes essay is reproduced in part four of the present work.) The final essay, "The Great Symbols of the Tarot," published in the February 1926 issue of *The Occult Review*, is a more substantial and more interesting effort.

Waite traces the history of the Tarot from the cards associated with King Charles VI of France to his own Tarot drawn by Pamela Colman Smith. He devotes considerable attention to Court de Gébelin, and his remarks on this pioneer of the occult Tarot show a certain tolerant condescension, but he rejects Court de Gébelin's view that the Tarot is of Egyptian origin. His criticisms of Éliphas Lévi are more numerous and more acerbic. He dismisses Lévi as one of the "French occult dreamers" and disapproves of Lévi's efforts to add Egyptian elements to the cards. Paul Christian and Oswald Wirth are condemned for the same reason.

The "great symbols" referred to in the title of the essay are the 22 picture cards, which are usually called the Tarot trumps. Waite was afflicted with the same shortcoming that troubles so many authorities on the occult Tarot—he placed all importance on the trumps and dismissed the number cards and court cards as insignificant. Paul Christian suffered from this affliction, as did

Éliphas Lévi, Papus, and Wirth. Throughout its history, the Lesser Arcana has been treated with indifference or contempt. It would be too much to hope that Waite might resist this trend, and he did not.

His remarks on the Popess, or High Priestess, are quite interesting. Waite was convinced that this trump was symbolically out of place, a throwback to a pre-Christian age that represented some pagan goddess, perhaps "a vestige of the old Astarte cultus" in northern Italy. He refers to Leland for support for this notion, presumably to Leland's 1899 book *Aradia, or the Gospel of the Witches*, although he does not mention it by name. In the course of making this association, he dismisses the commonly held belief that this trump refers to the medieval legend of Pope Joan, the female pope who was said to have been exposed as a woman when she gave birth while presiding over a public ceremony.

Waite goes on to reject a number of assumptions commonly held by occultists about the Tarot: that the trumps correspond to the 22 Hebrew letters, that the suits correspond to the four Hebrew letters of Tetragrammaton, and that the trumps may be linked to the 22 channels on the Tree of the Sephiroth. He mocks Lévi's belief that the Page of the court cards represents a child, and finds time to ridicule a poem written by Lévi concerning the assignment of the number cards to the ten Sephiroth of the Kabbalah. Indeed, almost everything in this essay is negative. Waite contributes very little that is innovative, apart from his opinion that the Popess is the remnant of some hypothetical Astarte cult.

In closing, Waite writes, "We have to recognize, in a word, that there is no canon of authority in the interpretation of Tarot symbolism." It does not seem to have occurred to him that the canon of authority in the interpretation of Tarot symbolism that he was searching for is contained in the works of Court de Gébelin, the Comte de Mellet, Paul Christian, Éliphas Lévi, Papus, Oswald Wirth, S. L. MacGregor Mathers, W. Wynn Westcott, P. D. Ouspensky, Paul Foster Case, Aleister Crowley, and indeed, A. E. Waite himself. The canon of authority has been evolving for the past two centuries in Europe and the United States, and it will continue to evolve. It is an occult authority, and is not limited merely by the constraints of history. The material realities of the Tarot are important, but even more important are its occult realities, because it is a living and evolving occult instrument.

In spite of their prevailing negative tone, Waite's opinions have value due to his central role in Tarot development. The Rider-Waite Tarot drawn by Pamela Colman Smith, which is sometimes referred to as the Rider-Waite-Smith Tarot or the Waite-Smith Tarot, is the most popular and the most widely used Tarot pack in the world, not only in its original form but in the multiplicity of variant forms it has spawned over the more than a century of its existence. It is not the most authoritative Tarot, nor is it the most symbolically meaning-ful Tarot, but it is by far the most popular due to Waite's brilliant decision to put individual pictures on all the suit number cards.[1] The Rider-Waite Tarot is the Tarot by which all other Tarot decks are measured, and it is Waite's most valuable contribution to Western occultism. Its existence makes Waite's views about the Tarot significant.

"THE GREAT SYMBOLS
OF THE TAROT"

by

A. E. WAITE

(The Occult Review, February 1926, pp. 83–91)

O n the hypothesis that there is or may be a deeper meaning in the chief
Tarot symbols than attaches thereto on the surface, it becomes necessary
to establish certain preliminary points as an initial clearance of issues, and I will
premise in the first place that by chief symbols I mean those only which I have
been in the habit of denominating Trumps Major in other writings on the subject. First among the preliminary points there is the simple fact that we know
nothing certainly concerning the origin of Tarot cards. As usual, however,
in matters belonging to occult arts and so-called science, the place of knowledge has been occupied by uncritical reveries and invention which is not less
fraudulent because the fraud may be frequently unconscious. When the artist
Gringonneur,[2] in or about the year 1393, is affirmed to have produced a set
of picture-cards for the amusement of King Charles VI of France, it has been
affirmed that some of their designs were identical with Tarot Trumps Major.
The evidence is the fact of certain beautiful and antique card-specimens—in
all about twenty-six—which are scattered through different Continental museums and were attributed in the past to Gringonneur. They are now held to
be of Italian origin, more or less in the early years of the fifteenth century, and
there are no extant examples prior to that period. But to establish this point on
expert authority at its value is not to fix the origin of Tarot cards in respect of
date or place. It is idle, I mean, to affirm that Venetian, Bolognese and Florentine vestiges of sets allocated to 1400–1418 are the first that were ever designed.
In view, however, of the generations of nonsense which we have heard testifying

on the subject, it must be said that it is equally idle and more mischievous to affirm that they are not. When, towards the close of the eighteenth century, Court de Gebelin first drew attention, as a man of learning and an antiquary, to the fact of Tarot cards, he produced sketches of the Trumps Major in the eighth volume of *Le Monde Primitif*. In the form that he had met with they were not priceless works of art like those in the Bibliothèque Nationale, but rough, primitive and barbarous, or precisely of that kind which might be expected to circulate in country places, among lower classes of players and gamblers, or among gipsies for purposes of fortune-telling. Supposing that they had been designed and invented originally about the period mentioned, nearly four centuries had elapsed, which were more than ample time for them to get into general circulation throughout the countries in which they were traced by Court de Gebelin—namely, Southern France, Spain, Italy and Germany. If the Trumps Major were originally distinct from the minor emblems, there was also full opportunity for them to be joined together. But alternatively the designs, perhaps even in several styles, may have been old already in the year 1400—I am speaking of the Trumps Major—in which case they were married much later to the fifteenth century prototypes of our modern playing-cards. It will be seen that the field is open, but that no one is entitled in reason to maintain either view unless evidence should be found to warrant it in the designs themselves, apart from the real or presumptive age of the oldest extant copies.

Having done something in this summary manner to define the historical position, the next point is to estimate the validity of those speculations to which I have referred already. It is not possible on this occasion, nor do I find that it would serve a purpose, to do more than recapitulate my own previous decisions, reached as the result of researches made prior to 1910. The first and most favoured hypothesis concerning Tarot cards is that they are of Egyptian origin, and it was put forward by him who to all intents and purposes may be called their discoverer, namely, Court de Gebelin. It has been set aside long since by authorities apart from predispositions and ulterior purposes in view. De Gebelin was an Egyptologist of his day, when Egyptology was in its cradle, if indeed it can be said to have been born, and that which he did was to excogitate impressions and formulate them in terms of certitude. They have not been borne out, and their doom from the standpoint of sane scholarship may be said to have been sealed when they fell into the hands of French occult dreamers and were espoused zealously by them. The most salient and amazing elaborations were those of Eliphas Lévi in 1856 and onward.[3] The designs were for him not only Egyptian in the sense of the earliest dynasties, but referable to the mythical Hermes and to the prediluvian wisdom of Enoch. They formed otherwise the traditional Book of Adam which was brought to him in Paradise by an angel, was removed from him at the Fall, but was restored subsequently in response to his earnest supplications.[4] Eliphas Lévi did more, however, than theorize on the subject. He gave pictorial illustrations of the cards restored to their proper primeval forms, in which they appeared as pseudo-Egyptian designs, the work of an amateur hand.[5] The same practice prevailed after Lévi had ceased to publish. It was developed further by Christian, while long after him, under the auspices of Oswald Wirth and others, the Trumps Major appear in all the panoply of imitative Delta art.[6] These things are to all intents and purposes of dishonest device, but very characteristic unfortunately after their own manner, for the marriage of speculative occultism and intellectual sincerity has hardly ever been made in France and seldom enough elsewhere.

These are the preliminary points which are placed here for consideration—as I have said, to clear the issues. In the complete absence of all evidence on the subject, we must be content to carry an open mind as to where the Tarot originated, remembering that the earliest designs with which we are acquainted do not connote antiquity, unless possibly in one case,[7] and unless the early fifteenth century may be regarded as old enough in the absence of a *parti-pris*.[8] The statement obtains also respecting cards of any kind, including the Baldini emblems,[9] which are neither Tarots nor counters for divination, or games of chance.

I satisfied myself some years ago, and do not stand alone, that the Trumps Major existed originally independently of the other arcana and that they were combined for gambling purposes at a date which it is possible to fix roughly. I am concerned only on the present occasion with what may be called the Great Symbols. They are twenty-two in number, and there is no doubt that some of them correspond to estates and types. The Emperor and Empress, the Pope and Juggler belong obviously to this order, but if we put them back speculatively even to medieval times we cannot account in this manner for the so-called Pope Joan or High Priestess. She must be allocated to another sequence of conditions, another scheme of human community at large. It is to be noted

that though Venetian, Florentine and French packs differ somewhat clearly, between narrow limits of course, Pope Joan has never been termed the Abbess
in any, nor can I recall that she has been so depicted that such a denomination
could apply and thus include the design among ecclesiastical estates in Chris-
tendom. She comes, therefore, as I have intimated, from another region and
another order of things. This is the one Tarot Trump Major which suggests a
derivation from antiquity, not however in the sense of Court de Gebelin, who
referred it to Isis, but to an obscure perpetuation of pagan faith and rite in Italy
which the inquiries of Leland[10] seem to have established as a matter of fact. In
this case, and at the value of his researches, on which I have commented elsewhere, Pope Joan represents not improbably a vestige of the old Astarte cultus.
I do not pretend to be satisfied with the explanation, but it may be accepted
tentatively perhaps and does not necessarily carry the question of antiquity behind mediaeval times. In the midst of all the obscurity, one only point emerges
in all certainty: whatever the card may have stood for originally, it was not the
mythical female pope, an ascription which arose as a leap in the dark of ignorance on the part of people—whether in France or Italy—who knew the Pope
Joan legend but had never heard of Astarte and much less of Isis. I should regard it as a rather old leap.[11]

I have spoken of classification under types, estates or classes, but it obtains
only in respect of a few designs, seeing that the majority of the Trumps Major are occasionally allegorical and in several cases can be understood only as
belonging to a world of symbols, while a few are doctrinal in character—in
the sense of crude Christian doctrine. The Resurrection card and the Devil belong to this last class. Death, on the other hand, is a very simple allegorical
picture-emblem, like the Lovers, Justice and Strength. The symbolical cards,
which must be so termed because certainly they do not correspond to the admitted notions of allegory, are the Hanged Man, Chariot, the so-called card of
Temperance, the Tower, the Star, the Sun and Moon, and that which passes under several names, one of which is the World. The Wheel of Fortune is seemingly of composite character, partaking of both allegory and symbolism, while
the Fool is very difficult to class. On the surface he may be referable to that es-
tate which inhabits the low-life deeps—the mendicant and vagabond type. He
suggests the Italian *lazzaroni*,[12] except that he carries a wallet, as if he were on his
way through the world. He recalls, therefore, the indescribable rabble which

followed the armies in crusading and later times. He is the antithesis of the Juggler, who flourishes at the expense of others by following a knavish trade, or who profits alternatively by the lower kind of skill.

When Court de Gebelin described the Trumps Major in connection with the rest of the Tarot pack, he gave an account of their use in games of hazard, but he had heard also of their divinatory value and was at some pains to ascertain the process by which they were adapted to this purpose, in which way he is our first authority for the traditional meanings of the cards as counters in the telling of fortune. He represents in this manner another landmark in the obscure history of the subject. It is to be assumed that his knowledge was confined to the practice in France, and there are no means of knowing whether Spain, Italy and Germany followed other methods at that time. I believe that Alliette or Eteilla varied the divinatory meanings on the threshold of the nineteenth century in accordance with his own predilections, as he altered the Trumps Major themselves in respect of their arrangement and changed the original names in certain cases. In the year 1856, as we have seen, Eliphas Lévi began to issue his occult revelations, based largely on the Trumps Major, developing their philosophical meanings in a most elaborate manner. They are at times exceedingly suggestive and always curious, but it must be understood that in occult matters he depended solely on personal intuitions and invention. There was a time, over twenty years since, when I was led to think otherwise, in view of evidence which has proved worthless on further and fuller investigation. Lévi said on his own part that he owed his "initiation" only to God and his personal researches, but some of his French admirers have not hesitated, this notwithstanding, to affirm his direct connection with Masonic Rites and Orders.[13] The question does not signify, for initiations of this kind would not have communicated occult knowledge. It follows that his Tarot system—if such it can be called—is at best a work of ingenuity but often a medley of notions, and it owes, so far as can be ascertained, nothing whatever to the past which extends behind Court de Gebelin. The point is not without importance, because he speaks with an accent of great authority and certitude. When P. Christian went still further in *L'Homme Rouge des Tuileries*[14] and in his *Histoire de la Magie*, the same criticism applies, as there is no need to say that it does in the laboured excogitations of Papus, Stanislas de Guaita and others of the French school.

Now, there are twenty-two Trumps Major arranged more or less in a sequence but subject to certain variations as the packs differ respecting time and place of origin. There are also twenty-two letters of the Hebrew alphabet, and it occurred to Eliphas Lévi that it was desirable to effect a marriage between the letters and cards.[15] It seems impossible to make a combination of this kind, however arbitrary, and not find some accidents in its favour, and there is better authority in Kabalism than Eliphas Lévi ever produced in writing to connect the Hebrew letter *Beth* with the so-called Pope Joan or Sovereign Priestess of the Tarot.[16] But he was concerned very little with any root in analogy, or he might have redistributed the Trumps Major, seeing that their sequence is—as I have said—subject to variation in different sets and that there seems no particular reason to suppose that any arrangement of the past had a conscious purpose in view. In this manner he might have found some curious points by taking the old Yetziratic classification of the Hebrew letters[17] and placing those cards against them which corresponded to their conventional allocations. It was sufficient, however, for his purpose that there are twenty-two letters and twenty-two palmary symbols, and if he remembered, he cared nothing apparently for the fact that the numerical significance of Hebrew letters belies his artificial combination after the letter *Yod*. We can say if we choose that the eleventh Trump is that which is called Strength, though it depends on the arrangement adopted in the particular pack; but the letter *Caph* is not eleven in the alphabet, for it corresponds to the number 20. Death is the thirteenth card and seems placed well in the Tarot sequence because thirteen is the number of mortality; but the letter *Nun* is 40 and has no such fatal connection. The folly of the whole comparison is best illustrated by the card which is called the Fool and is not numbered in the series, the cipher Nought[18] being usually placed against it. In Lévi's arrangement it corresponds to the letter *Shin*, the number of which is 300. But wherever it is placed in the series the correspondence between Trumps Major and the Hebrew alphabet is *ipso facto*[19] destroyed.

It is to be noticed further that Lévi allocated meanings to each letter individually of the Hebrew alphabet, but they are his own irresponsible invention, except in two or three very obvious cases—e.g., that *Beth*, the second letter, corresponds to the duad, *Ghimel* to the triad, and *Daleth* to the tetrad. It may be interesting to note that his number 15, which answers to the Tarot symbol of the Devil, is explained to be so-called occult science,[20] an eloquent tribute to his own fantastic claims in respect of the subject which he followed. As an explanation unawares it is otherwise of some value, for there is of course no ordered occult science, though there are certain forms of practice which bring into operation those psychic powers of which we know darkly in the way of their manifestation only, and it is a matter of experience that they are more likely to open the abyss rather than the path to heaven.

Lévi's instituted connection between Tarot cards and the Hebrew alphabet has proved convincing to later occultism in France and elsewhere. He is also the originator of another scheme which creates a correspondence of an equally artificial kind between the four suits, namely, Clubs, Cups, Swords and Pantacles, which make up the Lesser Arcana of the Tarot, and the Ten Sephiroth of Kabalistic theosophy. Because of the number four it was inevitable that in a mind like his they should be referred to the four letters of the sacred Tetragram—*Jod, He, Vau, He*—which are commonly pronounced Jehovah. It is the uttermost fantasy as usual, as exhibited by his attempted identification of *Jod* with Clubs, while Cups and Pantacles or Deniers are both coerced into correspondence with the letter *He*.[21] As regards the constituent cards of the four suits, even his ingenuity failed to discover a ground of comparison between the Sephiroth and the court-cards, so he offers the following couplet as a commentary on the King, Queen, Knight and Knave or Squire:

The married pair, the youth, the child, the race:
Thy path by these to unity retrace.[22]

But this comes to nothing, for the Knight is not necessarily a youth, nor does the ancient or modern Jack correspond to the idea of a child. Had Lévi understood Sephirotic Kabalism better, again he could have done better by affirming—as it would have been easy for him—that the French *damoiseau*[23] had replaced a primitive *damoiselle*, the Squire court-card being really feminine. He could then have allocated correctly as follows: the King to *Chokmah*, the Queen to *Binah*, the Knight to the six lower Sephiroth from *Chesed* to *Yesod* inclusive, governed by the semi-*Sephira Daath*, and the *Damoiselle* to *Malkuth*.[24] He would have found also in this manner a complete correspondence between these Trumps Minor and the four letters of the Tetragram. Finally, he would have established the operation of the sacred Name in the four Kabalistic worlds and would have exhibited the distinctions and analogies between Shekinah in transcendence and the Shekinah manifested in life and time. But Lévi was the magus of a world of fancy and not of a world of knowledge.

He found his opportunity, however, with the so-called pips, points or numbered cards, for he had the clear and talismanic fact that there are ten numbered cards in each suit, while the Sephiroth are also ten. But because there is no other correspondence in the nature of things he did badly enough in the development and produced the following nonsense rhymes, which are borrowed from the literal translation that I have made elsewhere.[25]

> Four signs present the Name of every name.
>
> Four brilliant beams adorn His crown of flame.
>
> Four rivers ever from His wisdom flow.
>
> Four proofs of His intelligence we know.
>
> Four benefactions from His mercy come.
>
> Four times four sins avenged His justice sum.
>
> Four rays unclouded make His beauty known.
>
> Four times His conquest shall in song be shown.
>
> Four times He triumphs on the timeless plane.
>
> Foundations four His great white throne maintain.
>
> One fourfold kingdom owns His endless sway,
>
> As from His crown there streams a fourfold ray.[26]

In this manner the four Aces correspond to Kether because it is the first Sephira in the mystery of coming forth from Ain Soph Aour, the Limitless Light; the four twos to Chokmah, four threes to Binah and so forward till the denary is completed. But what is to be understood by the four proofs of divine understanding, the four divine benefactions and the sixteen sins which are avenged by Geburah or Justice we know as little as of the reason for believing that the divine victories shall be celebrated only four times in song, or how in the philosophy of things it is possible to triumph four times on a plane where no time exists. If Eliphas Lévi could have furnished the omitted explanations, it is certain that Zoharic Kabalism knows nothing about them.[27]

At the back of all these reveries is the well-known fact that the ten Sephiroth are inter-connected in the Kabalistic Tree of Life by means of twenty-two paths, to which the Hebrew letters are attributed, *Kether* communicating with *Chokmah* by the Path of *Aleph*, with *Binah* by that of *Beth*, and so downward. A diagram showing these allocations was published by Athanasius Kircher in *Oedipus Aegyptiacus*.[28] The allocation of the Tarot Trumps Major to the paths of the Tree of Life is obviously the next step, and attempts have been made in this direction by blundering symbolists, but they have forgotten that in the mystical Tree the Sephiroth are also paths, making thirty-two Paths of Wisdom, from which it follows that in the logic of things there ought to be thirty-two Trumps.[29]

The study of the Tarot has been pursued since the days of Lévi in France, England and America, the developments being sometimes along lines established by him and sometimes the result of an independent departure. Speaking generally, he has been followed more or less. I have shown that his allocations are for the most part without any roots in the real things of analogy, while as to later students of the subject all that they have to offer is ingenuities of their own excogitation. We have to recognize, in a word, that there is no canon of authority in the interpretation of Tarot symbolism. The field is open therefore: it is indeed so open that any one of my readers is free to produce an entirely new explanation, making no appeal to past speculations: but the adventure will be at his and her own risk and peril as to whether they can make it work and thus produce a harmony of interpretation throughout. The sentence to be pronounced on previous attempts is either that they do not work, because of their false analogies, or that the scheme of evolved significance is of no real consequence. There is an explanation of the Trumps Major which obtains throughout the whole series and belongs to the highest order of spiritual truth: it is not occult but mystical; it is not of public communication and belongs to its own sanctuary. I can say only concerning it that some of the symbols have suffered a pregnant change.[30] Here is the only answer to the question whether there is a deeper meaning in the Trumps Major than is found on their surface.

And this leads up to my final point. If anyone feels drawn in these days to the consideration of Tarot symbolism they will do well to select the Trumps Major produced under my supervision by Miss Pamela Coleman Smith.[31] I am at liberty to mention these as I have no interest in their sale. If they seek to place upon each individually the highest meaning that may dawn upon them in a mood of reflection, then to combine the messages, modifying their formulation until the whole series moves together in harmony, the result may be something of living value to themselves and therefore true for them.

It should be understood in conclusion that I have been dealing with pictured images; but the way of the mystics ultimately leaves behind it the figured representations of the mind, for it is behind the kaleidoscope of external things that the still light shines in and from within the mind, in that state of pure being which is the life of the soul in God.

Notes to Part Six

1. Prior to the Rider-Waite Tarot, the only Tarot with pictures on the number cards of the suits was the Sola Busca Tarot, a pack of 78 hand-colored engravings from Venice or Ferrara dating from the late fifteenth century. For black-and-white examples of this pack, refer to Kaplan, *The Encyclopedia of Tarot*, vol. 1, pp. 126–127, where, unfortunately, no number cards are shown.

   It is evident that the Sola Busca Tarot was the inspiration for Waite's number cards. Both decks bear a picture on each number card, along with a multiple of the suit symbol that is worked into the picture. Compare the Six of Pentacles in the Sola Busca Tarot with the Eight of Pentacles in the Rider-Waite Tarot—both show essentially the same subject, a metal worker with a hammer, bent over his work. Compare the Three of Swords in both decks, where three swords pierce a large heart. Compare the Ten of Swords in the Sola Busca Tarot with the Ten of Wands in the Rider-Waite Tarot—both show a man walking away with head bowed, carrying an awkward and heavy bundle in his arms, in one case a bundle of swords, and in the other a bundle of staves. The connection is obvious.

2. Jacquemin Gringonneur. See his biographical note.

3. The two parts of Lévi's *Dogme et Rituel de la Haute Magie* were first published in their combined edition in 1856.

4. On this matter, Lévi wrote, "The personage Enoch, author of the primeval sacred book, is in effect identical with Thoth among the Egyptians, Cadmus among the Phoenicians and Palamedes among the Greeks." *Transcendental Magic*, p. 396. Papus wrote, "Yes; the game of cards called the Tarot, which the Gypsies possess, is the Bible of Bibles. It is the book of Thoth Hermes Trismegistus, the book of Adam, the book of the primitive Revelation of ancient civilizations." *The Tarot of the Bohemians*, p. 9.

5. It is characteristic of Waite's critical attitude toward his fellow occultists that he tried to diminish the artistry of Éliphas Lévi by calling his drawings the "work of an amateur hand." To the contrary, Lévi's drawings are brilliant compositions expertly executed, and some of them have attained the status of occult icons, the most obvious example being Lévi's drawing of Baphomet, which in a slightly altered form—the female breasts were removed—has become the god of modern Satanists. See *Transcendental Magic*, p. 186.

6. "Delta art" refers to the Nile Delta of Lower Egypt; Egyptian art. Waite appears to have had in mind the Egyptian Tarot designs of René Falconnier and Otto Wegener that appear in *Lames Hermétiques du Tarot Divinatoire*, published in Paris in 1896, or one of the derivative Egyptianized Tarot sets.

7. The exception Waite refers to is the *La Papesse*, the Popess or Female Pope, called in modern Tarot decks the High Priestess. Waite expands on his reasoning about this trump later in his essay.

8. *Parti-pris* is French for "decision taken" and signifies in modern English a bias or prejudice of opinion.

9. Baccio Baldini (c. 1436–1487) was a Florentine goldsmith and engraver credited with highly symbolic engravings on classical subjects. A number of them bear a general but nonspecific resemblance to the Tarot trumps. Baldini was incorrectly credited with creating the Tarocchi of Mantegna, which dates from around 1470. The Tarocchi of Mantegna is not a Tarot, but a set of fifty emblematic cards. This card set was sometimes referred to as *Carte di Baldini*, on the presumption that Baldini was its artist. See Kaplan, *The Encyclopedia of Tarot*, vol. 1, p. 35.

10. Leland wrote in his preface to *Aradia, or the Gospel of the Witches*, "Witchcraft is known to its votaries as *la vecchia religone*, or the old religion, of which Diana is the Goddess and her daughter Aradia (or Herodias) the female Messiah." *Aradia*, p. viii.

11. I see no reason to suppose that the female figure who bears the title *La Papesse* in older French Tarot decks is anything other than a female pope, as the title explicitly states, and the reasonable conclusion is that it is a reference to the legend of Pope Joan, which was immensely popular in medieval times. However, Gertrude Moakley set forth the theory that the figure on the card is intended to represent the Umiliati nun Maifreda da Pirovano, the cousin to Matteo Visconti, ancestor to Bianca Maria Visconti.

    Maifreda was a follower of the holy woman and miracle worker Princess Blazena Vilemina, daughter of King Premysl Ottokar I of Bohemia. The princess, called Guglielma of Bohemia, gained the reputation of a holy woman and miracle worker soon after her arrival at Milan in the 1260s. She gathered around her a sect of Christians referring to themselves as the Gugliemites until her death in 1281. Maifreda received a vision that Guglielma was an incarnation of the Holy Spirit—Guglielma was said to have been born on the Pentecost and to have carried the holy stigmata. Maifreda predicted that Guglielma would rise up from the dead like Christ.

    Maifreda declared herself "the new Peter," which is to say, the new pope, and began to act as a priest, consecrating hosts over the grave of Guglielma. She presided over Easter Mass in 1300, and then over a mass on the Pentacost in the expectation that the holy princess would rise from her tomb. When nothing happened, the Inquisition, which had been watching Maifreda since 1284, took her into custody, interrogated her, put her on trial, and had her burned at the stake. See Gertrude Moakley,

The Tarot Cards Painted by Bonifacio Bembo for the Visconti-Sforza Family (New York: New York Public Library, 1966), pp. 72–73. See also Sharla Hutchison and Rebecca A. Brown, *Monsters and Monstrosity from the Fin de Siècle to the Millennium* (Jefferson, NC: McFarland & Co., 2015) p. 102.

12. The *lazzironi* were the poorest class of the Kingdom of Naples. They lived in the streets and subsisted by begging, performing small services, and petty crime. They were prone to form mobs and be easily swayed by political rhetoric. Because of their large numbers, their political support was important to rulers and revolutionaries during the eighteenth and nineteenth centuries.

13. According to R. A. Gilbert, Éliphas Lévi became a Freemason on March 14, 1861, when he was initiated into the Lodge Rose du Parfait Silence under the Grand Orient of France—see Gilbert's preface to the 2000 Weiser edition of Lévi's *The Mysteries of the Qabalah*, p. 10. Lévi was dropped from the rolls or resigned on August 21, 1861, having been a Freemason for only a little over five months.

14. *The Red Man of the Tuileries (L'Homme Rouge des Tuileries)*, self-published in Paris in 1863, presents Paul Christian's unique and idiosyncratic system of astrology. Part of it (pp. 86–116) includes a description of the Tarot cards. Christian Egyptianized their symbolism and changed the names of the trumps from those used in the Marseilles Tarot. The red man of the title refers to a Benedictine monk, Dom Bonaventure Guyon, who according to Christian came dressed in a red cloak to converse with the Emperor Napoleon at the Palais des Tuileries, a royal palace with extensive gardens in Paris. (It was burned down by rioters in 1871.) The second half of the book is presented by Christian as a manuscript written by this Guyon. It contains Christian's system of astrology.

15. Connecting the Hebrew letters with the trumps occurred to Lévi because it was suggested in both the essay of Court de Gébelin and that of the Comte de Mellet.

16. In *Sepher Yetzirah, Beth* is one of the double letters associated with the seven planets of traditional astrology. The way in which the planets are to be assigned to the letters is not perfectly explicit in this ancient Kabbalistic text, but the Golden Dawn assigned the Moon to Beth. Waite is intimating that the High Priestess of the Tarot belongs with Beth because of this link between Beth and the Moon.

17. In the Kabbalistic text *Sepher Yetzirah*, the 22 Hebrew letters are divided into three groups—three mothers, seven doubles, and 12 singles or simples. These groups are associated respectively in this text with the three active elements (Fire, Air, Water), the seven planets of traditional astrology, and the twelve signs of the zodiac. In assigning the Tarot trumps to the Hebrew letters, S. L. MacGregor Mathers and W. Wynn Westcott followed the cipher manuscript obtained by Westcott that formed the foundation for the Golden Dawn system of magic. The division of the Hebrew letters into these three groups in the cipher manuscript is the same as the

division in *Sepher Yetzirah*—see Küntz, *The Complete Golden Dawn Cipher Manuscript*, pp. 117 and 124. The origin of the cipher manuscript is unknown, although various guesses have been made as to its author. This manuscript was responsible for Mathers's inversion of the places of Justice and Strength in the sequence of the trumps, an inversion that Waite followed in his own Rider Tarot.

18. The zero.

19. *Ipso facto* is Latin for "by the fact itself."

20. Lévi referred to his version of Baphomet as the "sphinx of the occult sciences." See *Transcendental Magic*, p. 309.

21. This is the arrangement of the suits on Tetragrammaton adopted by Aleister Crowley for his Thoth Tarot: Yod–Wands, first He–Cups, Vau–Swords, second He–Pentacles.

22. Lévi, *Transcendental Magic*, p. 103.

23. The French term *damoiseau* refers to a young nobleman who has not yet been made into a knight. Waite makes this same point in his *Pictorial Key to the Tarot*, p. 32.

24. This is the Golden Dawn arrangement of the court cards on the Tree of the Sephiroth.

25. Waite's English translation of Lévi's *Dogme et Rituel*. See *Transcendental Magic*, pp. 101–102.

26. This poem refers to the ten successive stages of emanation from the godhead that brought about the creation of the universe from non-being, according to the doctrine of the Jewish Kabbalah. The "Name of every name" is Tetragrammaton. The first Sephirah is called Kether (Crown); the second is Chokmah (Wisdom); third is Binah (Understanding); fourth is Chesed (Mercy); fifth is Geburah (Strength), also called Din (Judgment, or Severity); sixth is Tiphareth (Beauty); seventh is Netzach (Victory); eighth is Hod (Splendor); ninth is Yesod (Foundation); and tenth is Malkuth (Kingdom).

   Lévi's repetition of the number *four* refers to the four worlds of the Kabbalah, each of which contains the ten Sephiroth, and which extend downward one from another. The highest realm of Atziluth (World of Archetypes) gives rise to Briah (World of Creation), which in turn yields Yetzirah (World of Formation), which produces Assiah (World of Action). See Regardie, *The Golden Dawn*, 6th ed., p. 63.

27. The *Sepher Zohar* (*Book of Splendor*) is the primary text of the system of Jewish mysticism known as the Kabbalah. It is actually a collection of texts presented in the form of dialogues between learned Jewish rabbis concerning the mystical interpretation of the Torah.

28. Kircher's diagram of the Tree of the Sephiroth was used by Mathers when he applied the Tarot trumps to the 22 channels that connect the ten Sephiroth together. It became an essential part of the Golden Dawn teachings on the Kabbalah and

the Tarot. Its structure does not agree with the Tree of the Kabbalist Isaac Luria, which I regard as the correct structure. The main difference is that Kircher's Tree has three channels extending up from the lowest sphere, Malkuth, whereas Luria's Tree has only one channel extending upward. Luria draws crossing channels between Chokmah-Geburah and Binah-Chesed. These channels do not exist on the Tree of Kircher, and as a consequence the position of the quasi-eleventh-Sephirah, Daath, is never defined on Kircher's Tree.

29. "In thirty-two mysterious Paths of Wisdom did Jah, the Jehovah of hosts, the God of Israel, the living Elohim, the King of ages, the merciful and gracious God, the Exalted One, the Dweller in eternity, most high and holy—engrave his name by the three Sepharim—Numbers, Letters, and Sounds." Westcott, *Sepher Yetzirah*, p. 15.

The ten Sephiroth are indeed considered to be paths in *Sepher Yetzirah*, and when added to the 22 connecting channels, the total number of paths is 32. However, it must be pointed out that the paths of the Sephiroth themselves, and the paths connecting the Sephiroth together, are obviously not the same. It was the practice of the Golden Dawn to place the Tarot trumps on the 22 connecting channels, and the number cards of the Lesser Arcana on the 10 paths of the Sephiroth, four cards for each Sephirah to represent the four worlds of the Kabbalah.

30. Waite's use of the term *pregnant* here is interesting, because the figure of the Female Pope, or Popess, is often said to be pregnant; and indeed, in the older traditional Tarots she looks pregnant. It is possible that Waite connected her pregnancy with a significant birth in legend or prophecy. He was obsessed with the legend of the Holy Grail, and may have linked the child to be born of the Popess with the Grail in his own imaginings.

31. Waite misspelled the artist's name. It should be Colman, not Coleman.

PART SEVEN

"An Analysis of Tarot Cards"
by
MANLY P. HALL

INTRODUCTION
TO PART SEVEN

The following essay on the Tarot was extracted from Manly Palmer Hall's remarkable book *The Secret Teachings of All Ages: An Encyclopedic Outline of Masonic, Hermetic, Qabbalistic, and Rosicrucian Symbolical Philosophy*, which was privately published in 1928 in San Francisco. The printer was H. S. Crocker Company, Inc.

The original edition is a lavish and somewhat quirky work—Hall numbered his pages with Roman numerals, and did not number his chapters at all. The greatest value of the work lies in its many detailed esoteric engravings, but the text itself is not without its interest. Hall was widely studied in esoteric matters, and although he did not originate anything new, he codified and summarized existing esoteric lore in a way that made it accessible to his readers.

It may be regretted that Hall was not more precise in his references. He usually gives only the name of the book to which he refers, or only the name of the author, and sometimes not even that. In the notes at the end of this part of the present work, I have done my best to rectify this vagueness—I will not call it laziness because it may have been deliberate. Hall may have wished his readers to do the extra work required to track down his references, as I have done for this essay. If so, it is doubtful that any will thank him for it.

Hall's essay on the Tarot, which constitutes one of the chapters in his great book *The Secret Teachings of All Ages*, shows the influence of Court de Gébelin, Lévi, Christian, Papus, Wirth, Waite, Ouspensky, Case, and other leading authorities on the Tarot. His understanding of Tarot is very much in the Western occult tradition of the nineteenth and early twentieth centuries. He gathered snippets of Tarot lore from this and that author and sewed them together into a workmanlike garment that is worth reading due to the enormous influence his teachings exerted on a certain segment of the Western esoteric tradition. His followers were strongly influenced by the Spiritualism movement, Theosophy, and Freemasonry, and it was for them that Hall wrote his book.

Hall focuses his description of the Tarot trumps in this essay on two Tarot packs: that of Oswald Wirth and the Egyptian Tarot originated by René Falconnier and Maurice Otto Wegener. *The Secret Teachings of All Ages* was illustrated by the artist J. Augustus Knapp (1853–1938). Hall would later collaborate with Knapp to produce his own interpretation of the Tarot. This deck was published in 1929 and is known as the Knapp Tarot, the Hall-Knapp Tarot, or the Revised New Art Tarot.[1] The trumps were inspired by those of Oswald Wirth but contain symbolic variations. The rod in the hand of the Magician is a caduceus, for example. The suit cards take after the Egyptian designs as they appear in *Practical Astrology* by the Comte C. de Saint-Germain, but the patterns of the suit emblems are different.

The only significant innovation of the Hall-Knapp Tarot is the inclusion on all the cards except the Fool of small shields that bear graphic symbols. For example, the shield on 10. The Wheel bears the Pythagorean arrangement of ten dots called the tetractys. The shield on 21. The World bears a circle with a cross inside it, the symbol of Earth. The World is not numbered 21 in the Knapp deck, however—is bears the double Arabic number 21 and 22, to allow users of the deck to conveniently place 0. The Fool either in its traditional second-to-last spot between trumps 20. Judgment and 22. The World, or at the end of the trumps, with the World assuming number 21. The Fool bears the Hebrew letter *Shin*, which is the second-to-last Hebrew letter, suggesting that its position was presumed by Hall to be second to last in the sequence of trumps.

The fact that Hall took the time and effort to collaborate with Knapp on a new version of the Tarot shows that his interest in the Tarot was more than casual. He recognized its central position in modern Western occultism. However, his placement of the Fool in the second-to-last position in the trump sequence is telling. It suggests that he was largely unfamiliar with the Golden Dawn teachings on the Tarot, although he must have acquired some of those teachings secondhand through his reading of Paul Foster Case. He followed the traditional placement of the Fool used by Éliphas Lévi and A. E. Waite.[2]

"AN ANALYSIS OF TAROT CARDS"

by

MANLY P. HALL

(*The Secret Teachings of All Ages*, pp. 129–132)

Opinions of authorities differ widely concerning the origin of playing cards, the purpose for which they were intended, and the time of their introduction into Europe. In his *Researches into the History of Playing Cards*, Samuel Weller Singer advances the opinion that cards reached Southern Europe from India by way of Arabia.[3] It is probable that the Tarot cards were part of the magical and philosophical lore secured by the Knights Templars from the Saracens or one of the mystical sects then flourishing in Syria. Returning to Europe, the Templars, to avoid persecution, concealed the arcane meaning of the symbols by introducing the leaves of their magical book ostensibly as a device for amusement and gambling. In support of this contention, Mrs. John King Van Rensselaer states:

> That cards were brought by the home-returning warriors, who imported many of the newly acquired customs and habits of the Orient to their own countries, seems to be a well-established fact; and it does not contradict the statement made by some writers who declared that the gypsies—who about that time began to wander over Europe—brought with them and introduced cards, which they used, as they do at the present day, for divining the future. (See *The Devil's Picture Books*.)[4]

Through the Gypsies the Tarot cards may be traced back to the religious symbolism of the ancient Egyptians. In his remarkable work, *The Gypsies*, Samuel Roberts presents ample proof of their Egyptian origin. In one place he writes: "When Gypsies originally arrived in England is very uncertain.

They are first noticed in our laws, by several statutes against them in the reign of Henry VIII.; in which they are described as 'an outlandish people, calling themselves Egyptians,—who do not profess any craft or trade, but go about in great numbers,...'"[5] A curious legend relates that after the destruction of the Serapeum in Alexandria, the large body of attendant priests banded themselves together to preserve the secrets of the rites of Serapis. Their descendants (Gypsies) carrying with them the most precious of the volumes saved from the burning library—the Book of Enoch, or Thoth (the Tarot)—became wanderers upon the face of the earth, remaining a people apart with an ancient language and a birthright of magic and mystery.

Court de Gébelin believed the word Tarot itself to be derived from two Egyptian words, *Tar*, meaning "road," and *Ro*, meaning "royal." Thus the Tarot constitutes the royal road to wisdom. (See *Le Monde Primitif.*) In his *History of Magic*, P. Christian, the mouthpiece of a certain French secret society,[6] presents a fantastic account of a purported initiation into the Egyptian Mysteries wherein the 22 major Tarots assume the proportions of trestleboards of immense size and line a great gallery.[7] Stopping before each card in turn, the initiator described its symbolism to the candidate. Edouard Schuré, whose source of information was similar to that of Christian's, hints at the same ceremony in his chapter on initiation into the Hermetic Mysteries. (See *The Great Initiates.*)[8] While the Egyptians may well have employed the Tarot cards in their rituals, these French mystics present no evidence other than their own assertions to support this theory. The validity also of the so-called Egyptian Tarots[9] now in circulation has never been satisfactorily established. The drawings are not only quite modern but the symbolism itself savors of French rather than Egyptian influence.

The Tarot is undoubtedly a vital element in Rosicrucian symbolism, possibly the very book of universal knowledge which the members of the order claimed to possess. The Rota Mundi[10] is a term frequently occurring in the early manifestoes of the Fraternity of the Rose Cross. The word Rota by a rearrangement of its letters becomes Taro, the ancient name of these mysterious cards. W. F. C. Wigston has discovered evidence that Sir Francis Bacon employed the Tarot symbolism in his ciphers. The numbers 21, 56, and 78, which are all directly related to the divisions of the Tarot deck, are frequently involved in Bacon's cryptograms. In the great Shakespearian Folio of 1623 the

Christian name of Lord Bacon appears 21 times on page 56 of the Histories. (See *The Columbus of Literature.*)[11]

Many symbols appearing upon the Tarot cards have definite Masonic interest. The Pythagorean numerologist will also find an important relationship to exist between the numbers on the cards and the designs accompanying the numbers.[12] The Qabbalist will be immediately impressed by the significant sequence of the cards, and the alchemist will discover certain emblems meaningless save to one versed in the divine chemistry of transmutation and regeneration. As the Greeks placed the letters of their alphabet—with their corresponding numbers—upon the various parts of the body of their humanly represented Logos, so the Tarot cards have an analogy not only in the parts and members of the universe but also in the divisions of the human body.[13] They are in fact the key to the magical constitution of man.

The Tarot cards must be considered (1) as separate and complete hieroglyphs, each representing a distinct principle, law, power, or element in Nature; (2) in relation to each other as the effect of one agent operating upon another; and (3) as vowels and consonants of a philosophic alphabet. The laws governing all phenomena are represented by the symbols upon the Tarot cards, whose numerical values are equal to the numerical equivalents of the phenomena. As every structure consists of certain elemental parts, so the Tarot cards represent the components of the structure of philosophy. Irrespective of the science or philosophy with which the student is working, the Tarot cards can be identified with the essential constituents of his subject, each card thus being related to a specific part according to mathematical and philosophical laws. "An imprisoned person," writes Eliphas Levi, "with no other book than the Tarot, if he knew how to use it, could in a few years acquire universal knowledge, and would be able to speak on all subjects with unequalled learning and inexhaustible eloquence." (See *Transcendental Magic.*)[14]

The diverse opinions of eminent authorities on the Tarot symbolism are quite irreconcilable. The conclusions of the scholarly Court de Gébelin and the bizarre Grand Etteila—the first authorities on the subject—not only are at radical variance but both are equally discredited by Levi, whose arrangement of the Tarot trumps was rejected in turn by Arthur Edward Waite and Paul Case as being an effort to mislead students. The followers of Levi—especially Papus, Christian, Westcott, and Schuré—are regarded by the "reformed Tarotists" as honest but benighted individuals who wandered in darkness for lack of Pamela Coleman Smith's new deck of Tarot cards with revisions by Mr. Waite.

Most writers on the Tarot (Mr. Waite a notable exception) have proceeded upon the hypothesis that the 22 major trumps represent the letters of the Hebrew alphabet. This supposition is based upon nothing more substantial than the coincidence that both consist of 22 parts. That Postel, St. Martin, and Levi all wrote books divided into sections corresponding to the major Tarots is an interesting sidelight on the subject.[15] The major trump cards portray incidents from the Book of Revelation; and the Apocalypse of St. John is also divided into 22 chapters. Assuming the Qabbalah to hold the solution to the Tarot riddle, seekers have often ignored other possible lines of research. The task, however, of discovering the proper relationship sustained by the Tarot trumps to the letters of the Hebrew alphabet and the Paths of Wisdom thus far has not met with any great measure of success. The major trumps of the Tarot and the 22 letters of the Hebrew alphabet cannot be synchronized without first fixing the correct place of the unnumbered, or zero, card—*Le Mat*, the Fool. Levi places this card between the 20th and 21st Tarots, assigning to it the Hebrew letter *Shin* (ש). The same order is followed by Papus, Christian, and Waite, the last, however, declaring this arrangement to be incorrect. Westcott makes the zero card the 22nd of the Tarot major trumps. On the other hand, both Court de Gébelin and Paul Case place the unnumbered card before the first numbered card of the major trumps, for if the natural order of the numbers (according to either the Pythagorean or Qabbalistic system) be adhered to, the zero card must naturally precede the number 1.

This does not dispose of the problem, however, for efforts to assign a Hebrew letter to each Tarot trump in sequence produce an effect far from convincing. Mr. Waite, who reedited the Tarot, expresses himself thus: "I am not to be included among those who are satisfied that there is a valid correspondence between Hebrew letters and Tarot Trump symbols." (See introduction to *The Book of Formation* by Knut Stenring.)[16] The real explanation may be that the major Tarots no longer are in the same sequence as when they formed the leaves of Hermes' sacred book, for the Egyptians—or even their Arabian successors—could have purposely confused the cards so that their secrets might be better preserved.[17] Mr. Case has developed a system which, while superior to most, depends largely upon two debatable points, namely, the accuracy of

Mr. Waite's revised Tarot and the justification for assigning the first letter of the Hebrew alphabet to the unnumbered, or zero, card. Since *Aleph* (the first Hebrew letter) has the numerical value of 1, its assignment to the zero card is equivalent to the statement that zero is equal to the letter *Aleph* and therefore synonymous with the number 1.[18]

With rare insight, Court de Gébelin assigned the zero card to AIN SOPH, the Unknowable First Cause. As the central panel of the Bembine Table represents the Creative Power surrounded by seven triads of manifesting divinities, so may the zero card represent that Eternal Power of which the 21 surrounding or manifesting aspects are but limited expressions. If the 21 major trumps be considered as limited forms existing in the abstract substance of the zero card, it then becomes their common denominator. Which letter, then, of the Hebrew alphabet is the origin of all the remaining letters? The answer is apparent: *Yod*.[19] In the presence of so many speculations, one more may not offend. The zero card—*Le Mat*, the Fool—has been likened to the material universe because the mortal sphere is the world of unreality. The lower universe, like the mortal body of man, is but a garment, a motley costume, well likened to cap and bells. Beneath the garments of the fool is the divine substance, however, of which the jester is but a shadow; this world is a Mardi Gras—a pageantry of divine sparks masked in the garb of fools. Was not this zero card (the Fool) placed in the Tarot deck to deceive all who could not pierce the veil of illusion?

The Tarot cards were entrusted by the illumined hierophants of the Mysteries into the keeping of the foolish and the ignorant, thus becoming playthings—in many instances even instruments of vice. Man's evil habits therefore actually became the unconscious perpetuators of his philosophical precepts. "We must admire the wisdom of the Initiates," writes Papus, "who utilized vice and made it produce more beneficial results than virtue."[20] Does not this act of the ancient priests itself afford proof that the entire mystery of the Tarot is wrapped up in the symbolism of its zero card? If knowledge was thus entrusted to fools, should it not be sought for in this card?

If *Le Mat* be placed before the first card of the Tarot deck and the others laid out in a horizontal line in sequence from left to right, it will be found that the Fool is walking toward the other trumps as though about to pass through the various cards.[21] Like the spiritually hoodwinked and bound neophyte,[22] *Le Mat* is about to enter upon the supreme adventure—that of passage through the gates of the Divine Wisdom. If the zero card be considered as extraneous to the major trumps, this destroys the numerical analogy between these cards and the Hebrew letters by leaving one letter without a Tarot correspondent. In this event it will be necessary to assign the missing letter to a hypothetical Tarot card called the elements, assumed to have been broken up to form the 56 cards of the minor trumps. It is possible that each of the major trumps may be subject to a similar division.

The first numbered major trump is called *Le Bateleur*, the juggler, and according to Court de Gébelin, indicates the entire fabric of creation to be but a dream, existence a juggling of divine elements, and life a perpetual game of hazard. The seeming miracles of Nature are but feats of cosmic legerdemain. Man is like the little ball in the hands of the juggler, who waves his wand and, presto! the ball vanishes. The world looking on does not realize that the vanished article is still cleverly concealed by the juggler in the hollow of his hand. This is also the Adept whom Omar Khayyám calls "the master of the show."[23] His message is that the wise direct the phenomena of Nature and are never deceived thereby.

The magician stands behind a table on which are spread out a number of objects, prominent among them a cup—the Holy Grail and the cup placed by Joseph in Benjamin's sack;[24] a coin—the tribute money and the wages of a Master Builder, and a sword, that of Goliath and also the mystic blade of the philosopher which divides the false from the true. The magician's hat is in the form of the cosmic lemniscate, signifying the first motion of creation. His right hand points to the earth, his left holds aloft the rod of Jacob[25] and also the staff that budded[26]—the human spine crowned with the globe of creative intelligence. In the pseudo-Egyptian Tarot the magician wears an uræus or golden band around his forehead, the table before him is in the form of a perfect cube, and his girdle is the serpent of eternity devouring its own tail.

The second numbered major trump is called *La Papesse*, the Female Pope, and has been associated with a curious legend of the only woman who ever sat in the pontifical chair. Pope Joan is supposed to have accomplished this by masquerading in male attire, and was stoned to death when her subterfuge was discovered. This card portrays a seated woman crowned with a tiara surmounted by a lunar crescent. In her lap is the Tora, or book of the Law (usually partly closed), and in her left hand are the keys to the secret doctrine, one gold and the other silver. Behind her rise two pillars (Jachin and Boaz) with a multicolored veil stretched between. Her throne stands upon a checker-board floor. A figure called Juno is occasionally substituted for *La Papesse*. like the female hierophant of the Mysteries of Cybele, this symbolic figure personifies the Shekinah, or Divine Wisdom. In the pseudo-Egyptian Tarot the priestess is veiled, a reminder that the full countenance of truth is not revealed to uninitiated man. A veil also covers one-half of her book, thus intimating that but one-half of the mystery of being can be comprehended.

The third numbered major trump is called *L'Impératrice*, the Empress, and has been likened to the "woman clothed with the sun" described in the Apocalypse.[27] On this card appears the winged figure of a woman seated upon a throne, supporting with her right hand a shield emblazoned with a phoenix and holding in her left a scepter surmounted by an orb or trifoliate flower. Beneath her left foot is sometimes shown the crescent. Either the Empress is crowned or her head is surrounded by a diadem of stars; sometimes both. She is called *Generation*, and represents the threefold spiritual world out of which proceeds the fourfold material world. To the graduate of the College of the Mysteries she is the *Alma Mater* out of whose body the initiate has been "born again." In the pseudo-Egyptian Tarot the Empress is shown seated upon a cube filled with eyes and a bird is balanced upon the forefinger of her left hand. The upper part of her body is surrounded by a radiant golden nimbus. Being emblematic of the power from which emanates the entire tangible universe, *L'Impératrice* is frequently symbolized as pregnant.

The fourth numbered major trump is called *L'Empereur*, the Emperor, and by its numerical value is directly associated with the great Deity revered by the Pythagoreans under the form of the tetrad. His symbols declare the Emperor to be the Demiurgus, the Great King of the inferior world. The Emperor is dressed in armor and his throne is a cube stone, upon which a phoenix is also clearly visible. The king has his legs crossed in a most significant manner and carries either a scepter surmounted by an orb or a scepter in his right hand and an orb in his left. The orb itself is evidence that he is supreme ruler of the world. Upon his right and left breasts respectively appear the symbols of the sun and moon, which in symbolism are referred to as the eyes of the Great King. The position of the body and legs forms the symbol of sulphur, the sign of the ancient alchemical monarch. In the pseudo-Egyptian Tarot the figure is in profile. He wears a Masonic apron and the skirt forms a right-angled triangle. Upon his head is the Crown of the North[28] and his forehead is adorned with the coiled uræus.

The fifth numbered major trump is called *Le Pape*, the Pope, and represents the high priest of a pagan or Christian Mystery school. In this card the hierophant wears the tiara and carries in his left hand the triple cross surmounting the globe of the world.[29] His right hand, bearing upon its back the stigmata, makes "the ecclesiastic sign of esotericism,"[30] and before him kneel two suppliants or acolytes. The back of the papal throne is in the form of a celestial and a terrestrial column.[31] This card signifies the initiate or master of the mystery of life and according to the Pythagoreans, the spiritual physician. The illusionary universe in the form of the two figures (polarity) kneels before the throne upon which sits the initiate who has elevated his consciousness to the plane of spiritual understanding and reality. In the pseudo-Egyptian Tarot the Master wears the uræus. A white and a black figure—life and death, light and darkness, good and evil—kneel before him. The initiate's mastery over unreality is indicated by the tiara and the triple cross, emblems of rulership over the three worlds which have issued from the Unknowable First Cause.

The sixth numbered major trump is called *L'Amoureux*, the Lovers. There are two distinct forms of this Tarot. One shows a marriage ceremony in which a priest is uniting a youth and a maiden (Adam and Eve?) in holy wedlock. Sometimes a winged figure above transfixes the lovers with his dart. The second form of the card portrays a youth with a female figure on either side. One of these figures wears a golden crown and is winged, while the other is attired in the flowing robes of the bacchante and on her head is a wreath of vine leaves. The maidens represent the twofold soul of man (spiritual and animal), the first his guardian angel and the second his ever-present demon. The youth stands at the beginning of mature life, "the Parting of the Ways," where he must choose between virtue and vice, the eternal and the temporal. Above, in a halo of light, is the genius of Fate (his star), mistaken for Cupid by the uninformed. If youth chooses unwisely, the arrow of blindfolded Fate will transfix him. In the pseudo-Egyptian Tarot the arrow of the genius points directly to the figure of vice, thereby signifying that the end of her path is destruction. This card reminds man that the price of free will—or, more correctly, the power of choice—is responsibility.

The seventh numbered major trump is called *Le Chariot*, the Chariot, and portrays a victorious warrior crowned and riding in a chariot drawn by black and white sphinxes or horses. The starry canopy of the chariot is upheld by four columns. This card signifies the Exalted One who rides in the chariot of creation. The vehicle of the solar energy being numbered seven reveals the arcane truth that the seven planets are the chariots of the solar power which rides victorious in their midst. The four columns supporting the canopy represent the four Mighty Ones who uphold the worlds represented by the starstrewn drapery.[32] The figure carries the scepter of the solar energy and its shoulders are ornamented with lunar crescents—the Urim and Thummim. The sphinxes drawing the chariot resent the secret and unknown power by which the victorious ruler is moved continuously through the various parts of his universe. In certain Tarot decks the victor signifies the regenerated man, for the body of the chariot is a cubic stone.[33] The man in armor is not standing in the chariot but is rising out of the cube,[34] thus typifying the ascension of the 3 out of the 4— the turning upward of the flap of the Master Mason's apron.[35] In the pseudo-Egyptian Tarot the warrior carries the curved sword of Luna, is bearded to signify maturity, and wears the collar of the planetary orbits. His scepter (emblematic of the threefold universe) is crowned with a square upon which is a circle surmounted by a triangle.

The eighth numbered major trump is called *La Justice*, Justice, and portrays a seated figure upon a throne, the back of which rises in the form of two columns. Justice is crowned and carries in her right hand a sword and in her left a pair of scales. This card is a reminder of the judgment of the soul in the hall of Osiris. It teaches that only balanced forces can endure and that eternal justice destroys with the sword that which is unbalanced. Sometimes justice is depicted with a braid of her own hair twisted around her neck in a manner resembling a hangman's knot.[36] This may subtly imply that man is the cause of his own undoing, his actions (symbolized by his hair) being the instrument of his annihilation. In the pseudo-Egyptian Tarot the figure of Justice is raised upon a dais of three steps, for justice can be fully administered only by such as have been elevated to the third degree. Justice is blindfolded, that the visible shall in no way influence its decision. (For reasons he considers beyond his readers' intelligence, Mr. Waite reversed the eighth and eleventh major trumps.)[37]

The ninth numbered major trump is called *L'Hermite*, the Hermit, and portrays an aged man, robed in a monkish habit and cowl, leaning on a staff. This card was popularly supposed to represent Diogenes in his quest for an honest man. In his right hand the recluse carries a lamp which he partly conceals within the folds of his cape. The hermit thereby personifies the secret organizations which for uncounted centuries have carefully concealed the light of the Ancient Wisdom from the profane. The staff of the hermit is knowledge, which is man's main and only enduring support. Sometimes the mystic rod is divided by knobs into seven sections, a subtle reference to the mystery of the seven sacred centers along the human spine.[38] In the pseudo-Egyptian Tarot the hermit shields the lamp behind a rectangular cape to emphasize the philosophic truth that wisdom, if exposed to the fury of ignorance, would be destroyed like the tiny flame of a lamp unprotected from the storm. Man's bodies form a cloak through which his divine nature is faintly visible like the flame of the partly covered lantern. Through renunciation—the Hermetic life—man attains depth of character and tranquility of spirit.

The tenth numbered major trump is called *La Roue de Fortune*, the Wheel of Fortune, and portrays a mysterious wheel with eight spokes—the familiar Buddhist symbol of the Cycle of Necessity. To its rim cling Anubis and Typhon—the principles of good and evil. Above sits the immobile Sphinx, carrying the sword of Justice and signifying the perfect equilibrium of Universal Wisdom.[39] Anubis is shown rising and Typhon descending; but when Typhon reaches the bottom, evil ascends again, and when Anubis reaches the top good wanes once more. The Wheel of Fortune represents the lower universe as a whole with Divine Wisdom (the Sphinx) as the eternal arbiter between good and evil. In India, the chakra, or wheel, is associated with the life centers either of a world or of an individual. In the pseudo-Egyptian Tarot the Sphinx is armed with a javelin, and Typhon is being thrown from the wheel. The vertical columns, supporting the wheel and so placed that but one is visible, represent the axis of the world with the inscrutable Sphinx upon its northern pole. Sometimes the wheel with its supports is in a boat upon the water.[40] The water is the Ocean of Illusion, which is the sole foundation of the Cycle of Necessity.

The eleventh numbered major trump is called *La Force*, Strength, and portrays a girl wearing a hat in the form of a lemniscate, with her hands upon the mouth of an apparently ferocious lion. Considerable controversy exists as to whether the maid is closing or opening the lion's mouth. Most writers declare her to be closing the jaws of the beast, but a critical inspection conveys the opposite impression. The young woman symbolizes spiritual strength and the lion either the animal world which the girl is mastering or the Secret Wisdom over which she is mistress. The lion also signifies the summer solstice and the girl, Virgo, for when the sun enters this constellation, the Virgin robs the lion of his strength. King Solomon's throne was ornamented with lions and he himself was likened to the king of beasts with the key of wisdom between its teeth. In this sense, the girl may be opening the lion's mouth to find the key contained therein for courage is a prerequisite to the attainment of knowledge. In the pseudo-Egyptian Tarot the symbolism is the same except that the maiden is represented as a priestess wearing an elaborate crown in the form of a bird surmounted by serpents and an ibis.

The twelfth numbered major trump is called *Le Pendu*, the Hanged Man, and portrays a young man hanging by his left leg from a horizontal beam, the latter supported by two tree trunks from each of which six branches have been removed. The right leg of the youth is crossed in back of the left and his arms are folded behind his back in such a way as to form a cross surmounting a downward pointing triangle. The figure thus forms an inverted symbol of sulphur and, according to Levi, signifies the accomplishment of the *magnum opus*.[41] In some decks the figure carries under each arm a money bag from which coins are escaping. Popular tradition associates this card with Judas Iscariot, who is said to have gone forth and hanged himself, the money bags representing the payment he received for his crime.

Levi likens the hanged man to Prometheus, the Eternal Sufferer, further declaring that the upturned feet signify the spiritualization of the lower nature. It is also possible that the inverted figure denotes the loss of the spiritual faculties, for the head is below the level of the body. The stumps of the twelve branches are the signs of the zodiac divided into two groups—positive and negative. The picture therefore depicts polarity temporarily triumphant over the spiritual principle of equilibrium. To attain the heights of philosophy, therefore, man must reverse (or invert) the order of his life. He then loses his sense of personal possession because he renounces the rule of gold in favor of the golden rule. In the pseudo-Egyptian Tarot the hanged man is suspended between two palm trees and signifies the Sun God who dies perennially for his world.

The thirteenth numbered major trump is called *La Mort*, Death, and portrays a reaping skeleton with a great scythe cutting off the heads, hands, and feet rising out of the earth about it.[42] In the course of its labors the skeleton has apparently cut off one of its own feet. Not all Tarot decks show this peculiarity, but this point well emphasizes the philosophic truth that unbalance and destructiveness are synonymous. The skeleton is the proper emblem of the first and supreme Deity because it is the foundation of the body, as the Absolute is the foundation of creation. The reaping skeleton physically signifies death but philosophically that irresistible impulse in Nature which causes every being to be ultimately absorbed into the divine condition in which it existed before the illusionary universe had been manifested. The blade of the scythe is the moon with its crystallizing power. The field in which death reaps is the universe, and the card discloses that all things growing out of the earth shall be cut down and return to earth again.

Kings, queens, courtesans, and knaves are alike to Death, the master of the visible and apparent parts of all creatures. In some Tarot decks death is symbolized as a figure in armor mounted on a white horse which tramples under foot old and young alike. In the pseudo-Egyptian Tarot a rainbow is seen behind the figure of death, thus signifying that the mortality of the body of itself achieves the immortality of the spirit. Death, though it destroys form, can never destroy life, which continually renews itself. This card is the symbol of the constant renovation of the universe—disintegration that reintegration may follow upon a higher level of expression.

The fourteenth numbered major trump is called *La Temperance*, Temperance, and portrays an angelic figure with the sun upon her forehead. She carries two urns, one empty and the other full, and continually pours the contents of the upper into the lower. In some Tarot decks the flowing water takes the form of the symbol of Aquarius. Not one drop, however, of the living water is lost in this endless transference between the superior vessel and the inferior. When the lower urn is filled the vases are reversed, thus signifying that life pours first from the invisible into the visible, then from the visible back into the invisible. The spirit controlling this flow is an emissary of the great

Jehovah, Demiurgus of the world. The sun, or light cluster, upon the woman's forehead controls the flow of water, which, being drawn upward into the air by the solar rays, descends upon the earth as rain, to be drawn up and fall again *ad infinitum*. Herein is also shown the passage of the human life forces back and forth between positive and negative poles of the creative system. In the pseudo-Egyptian Tarot the symbolism is the same, except that the winged figure is male instead of female. It is surrounded by a solar nimbus and pours water from a golden urn into a silver one, typifying the descent of celestial forces into the sublunary spheres.

The fifteenth numbered major trump is called *Le Diable*, the Devil, and portrays a creature resembling Pan with the horns of a ram or deer, the arms and body of a man, and the legs and feet of a goat or dragon. The figure stands upon a cubic stone, to a ring in the front of which are chained two satyrs. For a scepter this so-called demon carries a lighted torch or candle. The entire figure is symbolic of the magic powers of the astral light, or universal mirror, in which the divine forces are reflected in an inverted, or infernal, state. The demon is winged like a bat, showing that it pertains to the nocturnal, or shadow inferior sphere. The animal natures of man, in the form of a male and a female elemental, are chained to its footstool. The torch is the false light which guides unillumined souls to their own undoing. In the pseudo-Egyptian Tarot appears Typhon—a winged creature composed of a hog, a man, a bat, a crocodile, and a hippopotamus—standing in the midst of its own destructiveness and holding aloft the firebrand of the incendiary. Typhon is created by man's own misdeeds, which, turning upon their maker, destroy him.

The sixteenth numbered major trump is called *Le Feu du Ciel*, the Fire of Heaven, and portrays a tower the battlements of which, in the form of a crown, are being destroyed by a bolt of lightning *issuing from the sun*. The crown, being considerably smaller than the tower which it surmounts, possibly indicates that its destruction resulted from its insufficiency. The lightning bolt sometimes takes the form of the zodiacal sign of Scorpio, and the tower may be considered a phallic emblem. Two figures are failing from the tower, one in front and the other behind. This Tarot card is popularly associated with the traditional fall of man. The divine nature of humanity is depicted as a tower. When his crown is destroyed, man falls into the lower world and takes upon himself the illusion of materiality. Here also is a key to the mystery of sex. The

tower is supposedly filled with gold coins which, showering out in great numbers from the rent made by the lightning bolt, suggest potential powers. In the
pseudo-Egyptian Tarot the tower is a pyramid, its apex shattered by a lightning
bolt. Here is a reference to the missing capstone of the Universal House.[43] In
support of Levi's contention that this card is connected with the Hebrew letter
Ayin, the failing figure in the foreground is similar in general appearance to the
sixteenth letter of the Hebrew alphabet.[44]

The seventeenth numbered major trump is called *Les Etoiles*, the Stars,[45] and
portrays a young girl kneeling with one foot in water and the other on land,
her body somewhat suggesting the swastika. She has two urns, the contents of
which she pours upon the land and sea. Above the girl's head are eight stars, one
of which is exceptionally large and bright. Count de Gébelin considers the great
star to be Sothis or Sirius; the other seven are the sacred planets of the ancients.
He believes the female figure to be Isis in the act of causing the inundations of
the Nile which accompanied the rising of the Dog Star.[46] The unclothed figure of
Isis may well signify that Nature does not receive her garment of verdure until
the rising of the Nile waters releases the germinal life of plants and flowers. The
bush and bird (or butterfly) signify the growth and resurrection which accompany the rising of the waters. In the pseudo-Egyptian Tarot the great star contains a diamond composed of a black and white triangle, and the flowering bush
is a tall plant with a trifoliate head upon which a butterfly alights. Here Isis is in
the form of an upright triangle and the vases have become shallow cups. The
elements of water and earth under her feet represent the opposites of Nature
sharing impartially in the divine abundance.

The eighteenth numbered major trump is called *La Lune*, the Moon, and
portrays Luna rising between two towers—one light and the other dark. A dog
and a wolf are baying at the rising moon,[47] and in the foreground is a pool of
water from which emerges a crawfish. Between the towers a path winds, van-
ishing in the extreme background. Court de Gébelin sees in this card another
reference to the rising of the Nile and states on the authority of Pausanius that
the Egyptians believed the inundations of the Nile to result from the tears of
the moon goddess which, falling into the river, swelled its flow.[48] These tears
are seen dropping from the lunar face. Court de Gébelin also relates the towers
to the Pillars of Hercules, beyond which, according to the Egyptians, the luminaries never passed. He notes also that the Egyptians represented the tropics as

dogs who as faithful doorkeepers prevented the sun and moon from penetrating too near the poles. The crab or crawfish signifies the retrograde motion of the moon.

This card also refers to the path of wisdom. Man in his quest of reality emerges from the pool of illusion. After mastering the guardians of the gates of wisdom he passes between the fortresses of science and theology and follows the winding path leading to spiritual liberation. His way is faintly lighted by human reason (the moon), which is but a reflection of divine wisdom. In the pseudo-Egyptian Tarot the towers are pyramids, the dogs are black and white respectively, and the moon is partly obscured by clouds. The entire scene suggests the dreary and desolate place in which the Mystery dramas of the Lesser Rites were enacted.[49]

The nineteenth numbered major trump is called *Le Soleil*, the Sun, and portrays two children—probably Gemini, the Twins—standing together in a garden surrounded by a magic ring of flowers. One of these children should be shown as male and the other female. Behind them is a brick wall apparently enclosing the garden. Above the wall the sun is rising, its rays alternately straight and curved. Thirteen teardrops are falling from the solar face. Levi, seeing in the two children Faith and Reason, which must coexist as long as the temporal universe endures, writes: "Human equilibrium requires two feet, the worlds gravitate by means of two forces, generation needs two sexes. Such is the meaning of the arcanum of Solomon, represented by the two pillars of the temple, Jakin and Bohas." (See *Transcendental Magic*.)[50] The sun of Truth is shining into the garden of the world over which these two children, as personifications of eternal powers reside. The harmony of the world depends upon the coordination of two qualities symbolized throughout the ages as the mind and the heart. In the pseudo-Egyptian Tarot the children give place to a youth and a maiden. Above them in a solar nimbus is the phallic emblem of generation—a line piercing a circle. Gemini is ruled by Mercury and the two children personify the serpents entwined around the caduceus.

The twentieth numbered major trump is called *Le Jugement*, the Judgment, and portrays three figures rising apparently from their tombs, though but one coffin is visible. Above them in a blaze of glory is a winged figure (presumably the Angel Gabriel) blowing a trumpet. This Tarot represents the liberation of man's threefold spiritual nature from the sepulcher of his material constitution.

Since but one-third of the spirit actually enters the physical body, the other two-thirds constituting the Hermetic *anthropos* or *overman*, only one of the three figures is actually rising from the tomb.[51] Court de Gébelin believes that the coffin may have been an afterthought of the card makers and that the scene actually represents creation rather than resurrection. In philosophy these two words are practically synonymous. The blast of the trumpet represents the Creative Word, by the intoning of which man is liberated from his terrestrial limitations. In the pseudo-Egyptian Tarot it is evident that the three figures signify the parts of a single being, for three mummies are shown emerging from one mummy case.

The twenty-first numbered major trump is called *Le Monde*, the World, and portrays a female figure draped with a scarf which the wind blows into the form of the Hebrew letter *Kaph*. Her extended hands—each of which holds a wand—and her left leg, which crosses behind the right, cause the figure to assume the form of the alchemical symbol of sulphur. The central figure is surrounded by a wreath in the form of a *vesica piscis* which Levi likens to the Qabbalistic crown *Kether*. The Cherubim of Ezekiel's vision occupy the corners of the card. This Tarot is called the Microcosm and the Macrocosm because in it are summed up every agency contributing to the structure of creation. The figure in the form of the emblem of sulphur represents the divine fire and the heart of the Great Mystery. The wreath is Nature, which surrounds the fiery center. The Cherubim represent the elements, worlds, forces, and planes issuing out of the divine fiery center of life. The wreath signifies the crown of the initiate which is given to those who master the four guardians and enter into the presence of unveiled Truth. In the pseudo-Egyptian Tarot the Cherubim surround a wreath composed of twelve trifoliate flowers—the decanates of the zodiac. A human figure kneels below this wreath, playing upon a harp of three strings, for the spirit must create harmony in the triple constitution of its inferior nature before it can gain for itself the solar crown of immortality.

The four suits of the minor trumps are considered as analogous to the four elements, the four corners of creation, and the four worlds of Qabbalism. The key to the lesser Tarots is presumably the *Tetragrammaton*, or the four-letter name of Jehovah, IHVH. The four suits of the minor trumps represent also the major divisions of society: *cups* are the priesthood, *swords* the military, *coins* the tradesmen, and *rods* the farming class. From the standpoint of what Court de Gébelin calls "political geography," cups represent the northern countries, swords the Orient, coins the Occident, and rods the southern countries. The ten pip cards of each suit represent the nations composing each of these grand divisions. The *kings* are their governments, the *queens* their religions, the *knights* their histories and national characteristics, and the *pages* their arts and sciences. Elaborate treatises have been written concerning the use of the Tarot cards in divination, but as this practice is contrary to the primary purpose of the Tarot no profit can result from its discussion.[52]

Many interesting examples of early playing cards are found in the museums of Europe, and there are also noteworthy specimens in the cabinets of various private collectors. A few hand-painted decks exist which are extremely artistic. These depict various important personages contemporary with the artists. In some instances, the court cards are portraitures of the reigning monarch and his family. In England engraved cards became popular, and in the British Museum are also to be seen some extremely quaint stenciled cards. Heraldic devices were employed; and Chatto, in his *Origin and History of Playing Cards*, reproduces four heraldic cards in which the arms of Pope Clement IX adorn the king of clubs.[53] There have been philosophical decks with emblems chosen from Greek and Roman mythology, also educational decks ornamented with maps or pictorial representations of famous historic places and incidents. Many rare examples of playing-cards have been found bound into the covers of early books.[54] In Japan there are card games the successful playing of which requires familiarity with nearly all the literary masterpieces of that nation. In India there are circular decks depicting episodes from Oriental myths. There are also cards which in one sense of the word are not cards, for the designs are on wood, ivory, and even metal. There are comic cards caricaturing disliked persons and places, and there are cards commemorating various human achievements. During the American Civil War a patriotic deck was circulated in which stars, eagles, anchors, and American flags were substituted for the suits and the court cards were famous generals.

Modern playing cards are the minor trumps of the Tarot, from each suit of which the *page*, or *valet*, has been eliminated, leaving 13 cards. Even in its abridged form, however, the modern deck is of profound symbolic importance, for its arrangement is apparently in accord with the divisions of the year. The two colors, red and black, represent the two grand divisions of the year— that during which the sun is north of the equator and that during which it is south of the equator. The four suits represent the seasons, the ages of the ancient Greeks, and the *Yugas* of the Hindus. The twelve court cards are the signs of the zodiac arranged in triads of a Father, a Power, and a Mind according to the upper section of the Bembine Table.[55] The ten pip cards of each suit represent the Sephirothic trees existing in each of the four worlds (the suits). The 13 cards of each suit are the 13 lunar months in each year, and the 52 cards of the deck are the 52 weeks in the year. Counting the number of pips and reckoning the jacks, queens, and kings as 11, 12, and 13 respectively, the sum for the 52 cards is 364. If the joker be considered as one point, the result is 365, or the number of days in the year. Milton Pottenger believed that the United States of America was laid out according to the conventional deck of playing cards, and that the government will ultimately consist of 52 States administered by a 53rd undenominated division, the District of Columbia.[56]

The court cards contain a number of important Masonic symbols. Nine are full face and three are profile. Here is the broken "Wheel of the Law," signifying the nine months of the prenatal epoch and the three degrees of spiritual unfoldment necessary to produce the perfect man. The four armed kings are the Egyptian Ammonian Architects who gouged out the universe with knives. They are also the cardinal signs of the zodiac. The four queens, carrying eight-petaled flowers symbolic of the Christ, are the fixed signs of the zodiac. The four jacks, two of whom bear acacia sprigs—the jack of hearts in his hand, the jack of clubs in his hat—are the four common signs of the zodiac. It should be noted also that the court cards of the spade suit will not look upon the pip in the corner of the card but face away from it as though fearing this emblem of death. The Grand Master of the Order of the Cards is the king of clubs, who carries the orb as emblematic of his dignity.

In its symbolism chess is the most significant of all games. It has been called "the royal game"—the pastime of kings. Like the Tarot cards, the chessmen represent the elements of life and philosophy. The game was played in India and China long before its introduction into Europe. East Indian princes were wont to sit on the balconies of their palaces and play chess with living men standing upon a checkerboard pavement of black and white marble in the courtyard below. It is popularly believed that the Egyptian Pharaohs played chess, but an examination of their sculpture and illuminations has led to the conclusion that the Egyptian game was a form of draughts. In China, chessmen are often carved to represent warring dynasties, as the Manchu and the Ming. The chessboard consists of 64 squares alternately black and white and symbolizes the floor of the House of the Mysteries. Upon this field of existence or thought move a number of strangely carved figures, each according to fixed law. The white king is Ormuzd; the black king, Ahriman; and upon the plains of Cosmos the great war between Light and Darkness is fought through all the ages. Of the philosophical constitution of man, the kings represent the spirit; the queens the mind; the bishops the emotions; the knights the vitality; the castles, or rooks, the physical body. The pieces upon the kings' side are positive; those upon the queens' side, negative. The pawns are the sensory impulses and perceptive faculties—the eight parts of the soul. The white king and his suite symbolize the Self and its vehicles; the black king and his retinue, the not-self—the false Ego and its legion. The game of chess thus sets forth the eternal struggle of each part of man's compound nature against the shadow of itself. The nature of each of the chessmen is revealed by the way in which it moves; geometry is the key to their interpretation. For example: The castle (the body) moves on the square; the bishop (the emotions) moves on the slant; the king, being the spirit, cannot be captured, but loses the battle when so surrounded that it cannot escape.

Notes to Part Seven

1. Ronald Decker and Michael Dummett, *A History of the Occult Tarot*, 2013 e-book edition, p. 302.

2. Aleister Crowley wrote concerning the placement by traditional writers on the Tarot of the Fool in the second-to-last position, "To make it quite clear to initiates that they did not understand the meaning of the card called The Fool, they put him down between the cards XX and XXI, for what reason it baffles the human imagination to conceive." Aleister Crowley, *The Book of Thoth*, p. 39.

3. Singer wrote: "From hence it may be fairly supposed, that the game of Cards, like the game of Chess, travelled from India to the Arabians; particularly as it seems that the Gipsies were originally Indians, driven from their country; and as they traversed the north of Asia and Africa before they reached Europe, introduced the game of Cards into those countries, from whence it passed over to Europe long before them." Samuel Weller Singer, *Researches into the History of Playing Cards*, p. 17.

4. Hall omits a piece of this quotation, which should read: "That cards were brought from the East to Europe about the time of the Crusades, and probably by the home-returning warriors, who imported many of the newly acquired customs and

habits of the Orient into their own countries, seems to be a well established fact; and it does not contradict the statement made by some writers, who declare that the gypsies—who about that time began to wander over Europe—brought with them and introduced cards, which they used, as they do at the present day, for divining the future." Mrs. John King van Rensselaer, *The Devil's Picture-Books*, pp. 11–12.

5. "When the Gypsies originally arrived in England is very uncertain. They are first noticed in our laws, by several statutes against them in the reign of Henry VIII.; in which they are described as 'an outlandish people, calling themselves Egyptians; who do not profess any craft or trade, but go about in great numbers, from place to place, using insidious and underhand means to impose on his Majesty's subjects, making them believe that they understand the art of foretelling men and women their good and evil fortune, by looking into their hands, whereby they defraud people of their money.' It then proceeds to lay a penalty of forty pounds on any one importing any such Egyptian." Samuel Roberts, *The Gypsies*, p. 27.

6. It is not clear which secret society Hall had in mind. Christian is not strongly associated with any particular occult organization. Ross Nichols hinted in his biographical note "Paul Christian: A Memoir" at a connection with the Martinists, writing, "There may be a link with the Saint-Martin group," but this appears to have been only speculation, and Christian could scarcely be called a spokesman for the Martinists. Paul Christian, *The History and Practice of Magic*, p. xii.

7. "At the twenty-second step is a grill of bronze, through which the postulate is able to see a long gallery, supported by caryatides sculpted in the shape of twenty-four sphinxes. In the spaces between the sphinxes the walls are covered with frescoes representing mysterious personages and symbols. These twenty-two pictures face each other in pairs, and are illuminated by eleven tripods of bronze arranged in a line down the middle of the gallery." Paul Christian, *Histoire de la Magie*, bk. 2, chap. 2, p. 112. See also the abridged English translation of Christian's work *The History and Practice of Magic*, pp. 93–94.

8. "At last the candidate found himself in front of some bronze rails opening into an extensive gallery supported by immense caryatids. At intervals along the walls could be seen two rows of symbolic frescoes. There were eleven of these on each side, dimly lit by crystal lamps which the lovely caryatids held aloft in their hands....The twenty-two symbols represented the first twenty-two arcana and constituted the alphabet of occult science, i.e., the absolute principles and universal keys which, when applied by the will, become the source and origin of all wisdom and power. These principles were fixed in the memory by their correspondence with the letters of the sacred tongue and with the numbers attached to these letters." Edouard Schuré, *The Great Initiates*, pp. 179–180.

It appears that Schuré lifted this description whole from Paul Christian's *Histoire de la Magie*. Christian's book was published in Paris in 1870, and Schuré's book in 1889.

9. There were two main versions of the Egyptian Tarot current in Manly P. Hall's day. One was the trumps created by René Falconnier in his *Lames Hermétiques du Tarot Divinatoire* (1896), which were drawn by the artist Maurice Otto Wegener based on the descriptions of the trumps in Paul Christian's *Histoire de la Magie* (1870). These trumps appeared in *Practical Astrology*, published in 1901 by the Comte C. de Saint-Germain (Edgar de Valcourt-Vermont). Saint-Germain added to the trumps of Falconnier a set of suit cards to make up a complete Tarot.

   The other Egyptian Tarot was created by C. C. Zain (Elbert Benjamine), the founder of the Brotherhood of Light (which later became the Church of Light). In 1918 Zain wrote a series of twelve lessons on the Tarot based on the Tarot images in Saint-Germain's *Practical Astrology*. He also published a black-and-white Tarot pack to go along with his lessons that was derived directly from Saint-Germain's book. The Tarot lessons were gathered together and published as *The Sacred Tarot* in 1927. Zain revised his Tarot lessons and had the Tarot images that illustrated the pamphlets redrawn by the artist Gloria Beresford, who was a member of his group, in 1935–1936. These pamphlets were bound together into a new edition of *The Sacred Tarot* in 1936. For this new edition, Zain included one of his older lessons on the Kabbalah at the beginning of his book. See Decker and Dummett, *A History of the Occult Tarot*, chap. 14.

   The Zain Egyptian Tarot trumps resemble the Falconnier Egyptian trumps but are not identical to them. The differences are stylistic and superficial rather than symbolically meaningful. The suit cards of the Zain Tarot resemble the suit cards in Saint-Germain's *Practical Astrology*, but the geometric patterns of the suit symbols on the number cards differ.

10. Literally translated from the Latin, *rota mundi* means "wheel of the world." It can also be translated as "wheel of fortune."

11. The reference is to the section (pp. 178–183) in chapter 10 of Wigston's book *The Columbus of Literature* that is titled "The Tarot of the Bohemians." In it, Wigston discusses the ROTA wheel referred to by Hall, which was of such great importance to Lévi and other French occultists of the nineteenth century. Wigston wrote, "There is very little doubt this Tarot was used in some way as a secret cipher" (p. 180). He referred to John Dee's Enochian tables of numbers and letters in this context, but gave no link of any kind between the Tarot and Dee's Enochian tables. Elsewhere he declared, "It seems there is very little doubt the Rosicrucians were in possession of the real Tarot" (p. 178), but again he gave no evidence of any kind to support his statement.

Wigston's book is the kind that made Aleister Crowley shake his head in disgust. It is an example of what happens when an occultist begins to apply numerology and the techniques of the practical Kabbalah to every rock and stone in the field. By finding esoteric connections between everything, he in effect finds nothing.

12. This point was previously raised by Brodie-Innes in part four of this work, and was echoed by A. E. Waite in part six, with reference to remarks concerning Pythagorean numerology conveyed to them by Florence Farr. By "the designs accompanying the numbers," Hall probably means the geometric arrangement of the pips on the number cards.

13. In the Jewish esoteric system known as the Kabbalah, the ten emanations by which God created the universe are placed on the various parts of the body of heavenly Adam, called Adam Kadmon, the first man who existed in gigantic spirit form prior to the making of the Adam of flesh and blood who was cast out of Eden. In Western occultism, the cards of the Tarot are applied to these ten emanations and the pathways that link them together into what is generally called the Tree of Life. In this way, the Tarot cards can be associated with various parts of the human body. See also *Sepher Yetzirah*, chaps. 4 and 5, where the Hebrew letters assigned to the planets and the zodiac signs are linked with various parts of the human body. Tarot trumps may be placed on these parts of the body through their connection with these letters.

14. This very famous line from Éliphas Lévi occurs in Waite's English translation of Lévi's *Dogme et Rituel*, retitled *Transcendental Magic*, on p. 394. It can be found in the original French in volume 2 of *Dogme et Rituel de la Haute Magie*, p. 356. Lévi's statement is, of course, absurd, but it is typical of the hyperbole of his writing style.

15. Both volumes of Lévi's *Dogme et Rituel de la Haute Magie* are divided into 22 chapters.

16. "It may be well to add that I am not to be included among those who are satisfied that there is a valid correspondence between Hebrew letters and Tarot Trump symbols." A. E. Waite in his introduction to Stenring, *The Book of Formation*, pp. 15–16.

17. The whole point of a deck of cards is that they are not bound together, but are separate unbound leaves that may be mixed and reordered. This is not an oversight or a weakness—it is the strength of the Tarot, symbolized by the Fool, which in traditional packs bore no number at all, and therefore was free to move where he wished.

18. The occult formula $0 = 1$ may be regarded as the key to the occult Tarot, where the numbers of the trumps in Roman numerals are displaced by one place from the number values of the Hebrew letters. The trump 0. The Fool receives the first Hebrew letter, *Aleph*, with a value of one; I. The Magician receives the second Hebrew letter, *Beth*, with a value of two; II. The High Priestess receives *Gimel*, the third Hebrew letter, with a value of three; and so on. The first Sephirah, Kether

(the Crown of Creation), is both 1 and yet 0. It exists, being the first manifest thing, and yet does not exist, in that it is the coming forth into being from nothingness, not being itself. Kether is a portal between the *Ain Soph* and the universe, but like the present moment, which has no duration, Kether has no dimension of its own. The formula expresses the contrast between the number 2 in Pythagorean numerology, where it is regarded as female, a symbol of marriage, and the number 2 in the Kabbalah, where the second Sephirah, Chokmah, is the first created thing, singular in nature and wholly male in its expression. Aleister Crowley put forth the occult formula $0 = 2$ as the key to the Tarot. He wrote, "This is the true Magical Doctrine of Thelema: Zero equals Two." *The Book of Thoth*, p. 4. But I would suggest that the formula $0 = 1$ is a more fundamental description of the Latin-Hebrew duality of the occult Tarot.

19. In the Kabbalah, *Yod* is said to have given rise to all the other Hebrew letters, because its simple shape begins or ends all of them. The Yod is in all of them, just as God is in every thing.

20. Papus, *The Tarot of the Bohemians*, p. 9. In the original 1889 French edition, *Le Tarot des Bohémiens*, p. 14.

21. This is true for the Fool in the Egyptian Tarot, the Wirth Tarot, and in the Marseilles Tarot, but not in the Rider-Waite pack, where the Fool faces the opposite way.

22. It is common in Freemasonry and other secret societies to blindfold and symbolically bind the wrists of the candidate for initiation. Once the candidate has been accepted, his hands are freed and his blindfold removed.

23. Quatrain LXVIII from Edward FitzGerald, *Rubaiyat of Omar Khayyám*, 4th ed., p. 42:

> "We are no other than a moving row
> Of Magic Shadow-shapes that come and go
> Round with this Sun-illumin'd Lantern held
> In Midnight by the Master of the Show."

24. Genesis 44.

25. Genesis 30:37.

26. Numbers 17:8–10.

27. Revelation 12:1.

28. Ancient Egypt was divided into two kingdoms, one in the north (Lower Egypt) and the other in the south (Upper Egypt). The "Upper" and "Lower" pertained to the River Nile, which flowed from its headwaters at a higher elevation in the south northward into the Mediterranean, at sea level. The ruler of each kingdom had his own distinctive crown. The white crown of the Upper Kingdom symbolized the goddess Hedjet, and the red crown of the Lower Kingdom represented the goddess Wadjet. When the kingdoms were merged into one under a single ruler, the crowns were also merged.

29. This statement that the triple cross surmounts a globe of the world is factually inaccurate for most of the Tarot packs I have consulted. There is no trace of a globe beneath the cross on the Tarot of Marseilles, or in the Court de Gébelin trump, or in most of the traditional Tarots based on the older French design. Waite does not mention a globe in his description of this trump in his *Pictorial Key* (see p. 88 of that work), nor does Lévi mention such a globe in his description of the trump in his *Dogme et Rituel* (refer to p. 387 of *Transcendental Magic*). There is a small ball below the cross on the trump in the Rochias Fils Tarot, a Swiss pack of the late eighteenth century (see Kaplan, *The Encyclopedia of Tarot*, vol. 1, p. 153), and Oswald Wirth has placed the same small ball below the triple cross on his version of the Pope (see Kaplan, vol. 1, p. 286), but it would be an exaggeration to characterize this tiny ball as a globe of the world. Such a globe does indeed appear below the simple cross on the scepters held by the Emperor and the Empress in many older Tarots, but not on the trump of the Pope.

30. The quotation is a reference to A. E. Waite, who in his *Pictorial Key to the Tarot* wrote concerning this trump: "In his left hand he holds a sceptre terminating in the triple cross, and with his right hand he gives the well known ecclesiastical sign which is called that of esotericism, distinguishing between the manifest and concealed part of the doctrine." Waite, *The Pictorial Key to the Tarot*, p. 88.

31. The "celestial and terrestrial" columns are features of lodge furnishings in Freemasonry. They are known as the Wardens' Columns and are inspired by the columns Jachin and Boaz of the Bible (First Kings 7:21). The celestial column, Jachin, is associated with the Senior Warden and the Moon; and the terrestrial column, Boaz, with the Junior Warden and the Sun.

32. In Egyptian mythology the sky was held up by four gods at the corners of the world, who supported the starry heavens on their staffs. They were sometimes represented as four pillars. As above, so below. The poet William Blake wrote, "Four Mighty Ones are in every Man." See "The Four Zoas," Night I, line 9, in Blake, *The Complete Writings* (London: Oxford University Press, 1974), p. 264.

33. The body of the chariot is cubic in the Waite Tarot and the Wirth Tarot. Lévi explicitly calls it "cubic" in his description of it in *Dogme et Rituel* (see *Transcendental Magic*, p. 388). Papus also calls it "cubic" (*The Tarot of the Bohemians*, p. 135). Paul Christian refers to it as "square in shape" (*The History and Practice of Magic*, p. 101). In none of these sources is it referred to as a cubic stone, which seems a bizarre conception for this trump—if the chariot is made of stone, it cannot be moved, hence it is not a chariot, merely a stone in the shape of a chariot. Paul Foster Case does describe the chariot as "of gray stone" (see Case, *The Tarot*, p. 97), and one of Case's earlier works on the Tarot may be the source for Hall's description. The cube is, of course, a symbol for matter. The charioteer rides upon a cubic chariot

to signify his dominance over the material realm. In most older Tarots, the chariot is roughly cubic in shape, but there is no indication that it is made of stone.

34. There is nothing in most traditional Tarot versions of the Chariot to suggest that the charioteer is only a torso extending upward from a solid cubic block, except perhaps bad artwork on the part of the artists who drew the card.

35. The symbolic apron worn by Freemasons typically has a square shape with a triangular flap that hangs down from the top. When the flap is raised, it defines a triangle above a square. Until the mid-eighteenth century, it was sometimes the custom for Freemasons to wear the apron with the flap raised and held up by means of a button. Some interpreters of the Tarot, such as Paul Foster Case, see a triangle above a square in the general structure of the Chariot trump. Case wrote: "Lines drawn from the Charioteer's hands to his crown, and from hand to hand, form the upright triangle of Fire. This rests on the square face of the Chariot, so that the complete figure is a triangle surmounting a square. It symbolizes the number Seven (3 plus 4) and also the union of Spirit and Matter." Case, *An Introduction to the Study of the Tarot*, chap. 7, in *Azoth*, vol. 4, no. 4 (April 1919), p. 220.

36. I do not find a braid of hair around the neck of Justice in the Tarots that I have examined. However, the figure is sometimes depicted with a braided necklace or collar.

37. The inversion of Justice and Strength in the sequence of the trumps was done by Waite based on the Golden Dawn association of the Hebrew letters to the trumps. In the Golden Dawn system, each Hebrew letter is linked either with one of the three active elements (Fire, Air, Water), one of the seven planets of traditional astrology, or one of the twelve signs of the zodiac. Both Justice and Strength are associated with Hebrew letters corresponding with zodiac signs. In the traditional sequence of trumps, with Justice numbered VIII and placed ninth in the sequence, the Hebrew letter falling on it is the ninth Hebrew letter, *Teth*, which is linked with the sign of Leo, the Lion. With Strength in its traditional place and numbered XI, the twelfth Hebrew letter falls on it, *Lamed*, which is linked with the sign Libra, the Scales.

This seemingly obvious inversion, which S. L. MacGregor Mathers made in the sequence of trumps in the Golden Dawn Tarot, is indicated in the cipher manuscript that was the foundation for the Golden Dawn system of magic. See Küntz, *The Complete Golden Dawn Cipher Manuscript*, p. 117. A. E. Waite did the same in his Rider Tarot, without ever bothering to explain to his readers why. Waite's arrogance in this matter is insufferable, but is typical of this man. He wrote concerning the trump Strength: "For reasons which satisfy myself, this card has been interchanged with that of Justice, which is usually numbered eight. As the variation carries nothing with it which will signify to the reader, there is no cause for explanation." Waite, *The Pictorial Key to the Tarot*, p. 100. On the matter of this inversion of the places of these two trumps, see Crowley, *The Book of Thoth*, p. 9.

38. Oswald Wirth, in his version of the Hermit, divided his staff, but he divided it into eight parts, not seven. On the Wirth trump, it resembles a length of bamboo. The shape of his staff in the Tarot of Marseilles, and particularly in the design of Court de Gébelin, is serpentine, which seems to me to be a more meaningful symbol, as the serpent represents both wisdom and deathlessness.

39. Éliphas Lévi identified the three demonic creatures on the Wheel of Fortune as Hermanubis, Typhon, and the Sphinx—see *Transcendental Magic*, p. 390. These identifications appear completely fanciful, without any basis in the actual symbolism of traditional Tarots.

40. Balancing the Wheel of Fortune in a little banana-shaped boat was an innovation of Éliphas Lévi. See the illustration in his *Key of the Mysteries*, p. 85. Oswald Wirth imitated Lévi's design in his own Tarot. See the illustration on the left in Papus, *The Tarot of the Bohemians*, p. 145.

41. *Magnum opus* is Latin for "great work," the ultimate goal of alchemy, which was understood either in a material sense as the manufacture of gold, or sometimes the making of the elixir of eternal life; or in a spiritual sense as the refining and purging from the soul of all gross associations, thereby perfecting it. Éliphas Lévi wrote about this trump, "The man's arms and head constitute a triangle, and his entire hieroglyphical shape is that of a reversed triangle surmounted by a cross, an alchemical symbol known to all adepts and representing the accomplishment of the Great Work." Lévi, *Transcendental Magic*, p. 286.

42. The human hands, feet, and heads rising up from the earth to be cut off by the sweeping scythe of the Grim Reaper is a clear expression of the biblical saying "All flesh is grass" (Isaiah 40:6).

43. It is believed that originally the Great Pyramid of Egypt was capped with a stone sheathed in pure gold, so that it reflected the sunlight with blazing brilliance as the sun moved across the heavens. However, since before the time of Christ, there has been no capstone on the Great Pyramid. It is unknown when, how, or why it was removed, or who removed it, but the general assumption is that the gold sheathing was stolen. The pyramid presently has a flat top some thirty feet or so across. This flat-topped pyramid is commemorated on the US dollar bill.

44. "One of the personages in his fall reproduces perfectly the letter *Ayin*." Lévi, *Transcendental Magic*, p. 391.

45. This trump is usually titled *L'Etoile* (the Star), singular, in older Tarots. However in a nineteenth-century version of the Tarot of Etteilla, it is indeed plural, *Les Étoiles*. See Kaplan, vol. 1, p. 143, second card top row. The plural form also appears in the Lando Tarot, circa 1760—see Kaplan, *The Encyclopedia of Tarot*, p. 150. It would be difficult to say whether the title for this trump should be singular or plural. One could make an argument for the singular form based on the large star that often,

but not always, appears above the figure's head; but one could equally well argue for the plural based on the undeniable fact that there are always many stars above her head, and indeed in the night sky.

46. Every year without fail, the Nile River overflowed its banks and flooded the land on either side with river silt, which was black and incredibly rich in minerals and nutrients. This flooding took place at the time of year when the star Sirius, called the Dog Star, rose in the night sky, and it made Egypt the most fertile farming land in all of the ancient world.

47. In most older Tarots, it is quite obvious that both beasts on the trump of the Moon are dogs, not a dog and a wolf. Nor are the towers usually light and dark, but more commonly both are similar in shading.

48. "They say, that the Egyptians celebrate the festival of Isis in that part of the year in which she bewails Osiris; that then the Nile begins to ascend; and that the vulgar of the natives say, that the tears of Isis cause the Nile to increase and irrigate the fields." Ed S. Taylor, *Description of Greece, by Pausanias*, vol. 3, p. 174.

49. The Mystery schools of Egypt and Greece had Lesser Rites and Greater Rites. Anyone might be admitted to the lesser, but the greater were reserved for a select few who proved themselves worthy.

50. Lévi, *Transcendental Magic*, p. 166.

51. "According to the Mystery teachings, not all the spiritual nature of man incarnates in matter. The spirit of man is diagrammatically shown as an equilateral triangle with one point downward. This lower point, which is one-third of the spiritual nature but in comparison to the dignity of the other two is much less than a third, descends into the illusion of material existence for a brief space of time. That which never clothes itself in the sheath of matter is the Hermetic *Anthropos*—the Overman—analogous to the Cyclops or guardian *dæmon* of the Greeks, the *angel* of Jakob Böhme, and the Oversoul of Emerson, 'that Unity, that Oversoul, within which every man's particular being is contained and made one with all other.'" Hall, *The Secret Teachings of All Ages*, chap. 14, p. 76.

52. The higher purpose of the esoteric Tarot is the Great Work, the perfection of the soul. By comparison, fortune-telling appears to be a trivial use for the Tarot, and for this reason some occultists hold divination with the Tarot to be a debasement of it.

53. William Andrew Chatto, *Facts and Speculations on the Origin and History of Playing Cards*, the plate following p. 152.

54. Book binders used whatever scraps of paper they could find to make into book board for the covers of their books. Not only playing cards but also leaves from rare manuscripts are sometimes found glued into the boards of older books.

55. That is, the Isiac Tablet.

56. "We started with thirteen states corresponding to the thirteen cards in each suit. We have grown to forty-five (with three knocking at the door): There will be fifty-two before the perfect fulfillment of the law, before the object of the birth of the United States will be fully realized and known." Milton Alberto Pottenger, *Symbolism*, p. 148. In a box on the title page of this most unusual work by Pottenger is the following text: "The Pack of Playing Cards, or Book of Fifty-two, an Ancient Masonic Bible; Each Card a Symbol of Universal Law. The United States a Masonic Nation, whose Duty and History are Read in these Ancient Sacred Symbols."

PART EIGHT

English Method of Fortune-Telling
with Playing Cards
by
VARIOUS AUTHORS

INTRODUCTION
TO PART EIGHT

M y readers may be asking themselves why, in a book of Tarot source texts, have I included essays on divination by ordinary playing cards? I have done so because it is impossible to gain a full comprehension of the occult meanings of the suit cards of the Tarot and their use in divination without an understanding of the similar occult meanings and use of playing cards.

It seems likely that divination with playing cards preceded divination with Tarot cards by many decades. There is no way to prove this since the beginnings of card divination are lost to history, but playing cards in Europe predate Tarot cards by almost a century. Cards are first mentioned in an Italian manuscript by Pipozzo di Sandro, the original of which was dated 1299. (The only surviving copy of the manuscript is from the fifteenth century, and some authorities doubt that cards were ever mentioned in the original text.) Tarot cards, on the other hand, cannot be dated earlier than 1392, when Jacquemin Gringonneur was hired to paint three packs for the amusement of King Charles VI of France (and it is very possible that their origin is decades later than this, since these may have been packs of common playing cards—the cards are not described in the account book of Charles Poupart, treasurer to Charles VI, where Poupart recorded their purchase).

The earliest book explicitly describing divination by cards is *Le Sorti* by Francesco Marcolini, published in Venice in 1540, and no Tarot trumps are mentioned, only suit cards. William Chatto dated fortune-telling by playing cards as early as 1483–1498 based on a reproduction of a painting supposedly made during the reign of Charles VIII.[1]

Since playing cards are so much older than Tarot cards, it is not unreasonable to speculate that divination by playing cards is also older than divination with the Tarot. If this is true, then the occult use of playing cards greatly pre-dates the occult use of the Tarot. This cannot be proved one way or the other, but it is worth noting that the suit cards of the Tarot, which are treated so slightingly by so many writers on the occult Tarot, may in fact embody the esoteric foundation of the Tarot, whereas the trumps, which are given such primacy and importance, may only be later additions to the suit cards.

In any case, while researching the English Method of divination by common playing cards described in the following essays, I was able to trace this method back to 1784, and it is undoubtedly decades older, at the very least. It was associated with the Romanies who at the time lived in Norwood, England, but this association may be apocryphal.[2] Card divination with common playing cards by laying the cards out in rows is mentioned in a one-act farce that was published in London in 1730 called *Jack the Gyant-Killer*, but the description of the layout is very brief. Rows of nine are not explicitly mentioned, and there is no way to know if the anonymous author of the play was describing the English Method. One of the cards is said by the author to lie "oblique"—this detail of reading the cards does not appear in any description of the English Method I have seen.[3]

The essay "The Folklore of Playing Cards," in which the English Method was described at length, appeared in the first volume of Robert Chambers's *Book of Days*, published in 1863. It had an enormous influence later on the divinatory interpretation of the suit cards of the Tarot, in particular on the occultist Arthur Edward Waite. The meanings for the cards in Waite's 1889 work *A Handbook of Cartomancy* (written under the pseudonym Grand Orient), which was republished in a fourth edition in 1909 with the title *A Manual of Cartomancy*, are lifted directly from the *Book of Days*, and many meanings for the suit cards in his 1910 *Key to the Tarot*, republished in 1911 with illustrations as the *The Pictorial Key to the Tarot*, are based at least in part on the folk interpretations in this essay.[4]

The Tarot cards known as the Rider-Waite Tarot that were designed by Waite and described in his *Pictorial Key* greatly influenced the divinatory interpretations of the Tarot by other occultists. Indeed, it would not be an exaggeration to call this deck of Waite's, which was drawn by the artist Pamela Colman Smith, the most influential Tarot of the past two centuries. Countless other Tarot decks have been based on it. Because Waite was such a well-recognized and well-respected occultist, his meanings for the cards carried an authority that they perhaps do not deserve on their own merits.

The method described in the following essays uses the full deck of 52 ordinary playing cards. Many fortune-tellers of the eighteenth and nineteenth centuries, such as Etteilla (1738–1791), Mademoiselle Le Normand (1772–1843), and Sepharial (real name Walter Gorn Old, 1864–1929), made use of a reduced deck of playing cards. Etteilla, who also divined with the full Tarot, used a deck of 32 cards, discarding the number cards from 2 to 6 in each suit, when he divined with common playing cards. Sepharial used the same 32-card reduced deck, as did Le Normand,[5] although she may have sometimes used a deck of 36 cards by adding the deuces to the 32 cards of Etteilla.[6]

The full deck of 52 cards yields a much richer meaning, but it increases the degree of complexity and makes for a larger and more awkward card layout, which are perhaps reasons why fortune-tellers reduced the number of cards. In the case of Mademoiselle Le Normand, a reduced deck of 36 cards would have allowed her to lay out the cards in four rows of nine cards each.

Nine was considered a highly significant number in card divination, as you will notice in these essays. The number nine held great mystical significance for the Celts, Druids, and Vikings. It is a highly spiritual number, consisting as it does of three groups of three—the number three is the number of the Trinity and is the most sacred of all numbers.

Nine is also the last numeral in the decimal series before the introduction of the zero shifts the numbers to a higher order, where they repeat. For this reason, it was regarded as a number of transition, a kind of doorway between worlds that linked one with the other. To reach the higher plane, you must pass through nine. Those familiar with the Kabbalah will at once see the connection here with Yesod, the ninth emanation that links the higher spheres with the lower sphere of the four elements. Nine is the number of the Moon, and the Moon is the gateway to the heavenly spheres.

The layout of the cards described in these essays uses rows of nine cards each, but since 52 cards are used, the final row of the card spread contains only seven cards. Meanings are interpreted in sets of nine cards, or "octaves," as the anonymous author of the Chambers's essay terms them. He wrote, "Every card, something like the octaves in music, is *en rapport* with the ninth card from it."⁷ Pairs of cards nine places apart in the layout are considered occultly connected.

A peculiarity of this English Method of fortune-telling by cards is the large number of negative or unfortunate meanings attached to the cards. Usually in fortune-telling, the number of unfortunate interpretations is minimized. The reason for this is practical. No one wants to hear bad news. Negative readings are depressing and tend to put off those seeking card readings. Professional card readers downplay the unhappy interpretations of the cards and try to put the best possible spin on unpromising revelations. For example, when a card indicates death, it is often euphemized as "a change" or "a transition."

In the method given in Chambers's *Book of Days* essay, all of the Spades are unfortunate, seven of the Clubs could be classed as unfavorable, two of the Hearts are unfavorable, and four of the Diamonds are unfortunate. This adds up to 26 bad cards out of 52. Some of the remaining cards, while they cannot be classed as overtly bad, are not overtly good cards, either. They are equivocal.

Overall, this is an astonishingly negative interpretation of the cards, and it is to be wondered how anyone could give readings to the public using these card meanings without radically softening them. A young woman of the nineteenth century for whom the cards were read without amelioration would probably run from the room in tears. But professional card readers were adept at putting the best face on readings and softening the harsher meanings of the cards.

The meanings for the cards given in these essays are the folk meanings. The author of the Chambers essay referred to this method of cartomancy as "folk-lore." These meanings are not based on any coherent esoteric system. They do not derive from the Kabbalah or from the elemental associations for the suit cards of the Tarot that were used in the card divination developed in the Hermetic Order of the Golden Dawn. There is a certain attraction in their simplicity. They refer to the common events of everyday life and to the common personality traits of average human beings.

The phrase "a card of caution" occurs frequently in the lists of card meanings. By this is meant a card that is given by the Fates to the person receiving the reading as a warning of present or future danger. It is not necessarily a card of disaster, but rather a card of possible misfortune if the warning is unheeded and the wrong actions are taken.

It may be useful to list again the popularly accepted correspondences between the suits of common playing cards and the suits of the Tarot, as a quick reference for the essays that follow.

Wands (Fire) = Clubs
Cups (Water) = Hearts
Swords (Air) = Spades
Pentacles (Earth) = Diamonds

One rationale for this common arrangement is that both Wands and Clubs are pieces of wood, which can be burned with Fire—the Ace of Wands in early Tarot decks is actually depicted as a knobbed wooden club. Cups, which are shaped like the womb, are receptacles that hold Water, the element of the emotions, and the Heart that pumps liquid blood is regarded as the organ of emotion in the human body. Both Swords and Spades are pointed steel instruments that cut through the Air and pierce physical obstacles. Diamonds are a form of wealth, and Pentacles, also called Coins in some Tarot decks, represent monetary value, or more abstractly, the materialism of elemental Earth.

INTRODUCTION TO "THE ART OF FORTUNE-TELLING BY CARDS"

from Breslaw's Last Legacy

reslaw's Last Legacy; or, The Magical Companion is an odd little book that
B was first published at London in 1784. The second corrected edition was
brought forth in the same year, and it is from this that I have extracted the present essay on divination by playing cards, which constitutes the seventh chapter
of the work. It was wildly popular. In the forty years following its initial publication, sixteen editions appeared.[8] The compiler of the work describes himself
as "the editor," and in the text he refers to Breslaw in the third person, so it
seems that Phillip Breslaw was not the author, or at least not the sole author.
Breslaw was a stage magician who performed in London during the latter half
of the eighteenth century—see his biographical note.

The book is a chaotic collection of bits and pieces that appear to have only
one purpose in common: the amusement of the reader. The editor wrote in
his preface, "The design of it is, to amuse, instruct, and promote innocent diversions; to relieve, and give new vigour to the mind."[9] The book can scarcely
claim to have a coherent design of any kind. Subject matter ranges from how
to construct a hydrogen balloon to the meaning of the signs of the zodiac, simple sleight-of-hand parlor tricks, mathematical magic, card tricks, the interpretation of dreams, palmistry, moleosophy, riddles, conundrums, dinner toasts,
songs, amusing stories, and similar diversions.

Hidden in the midst of this flotsam and jetsam of the Georgian era mind
is a highly compressed description of the method of fortune-telling with a full
deck of 52 common playing cards, which was commonly known as the *English
Method*. This brief essay from the editor of *Breslaw's Last Legacy* shows that card
divination by laying out a full deck in rows of nine was in common practice

in England at the same time that Court de Gébelin composed his speculative essay on the Tarot, and the essays that follow it demonstrate that it remained virtually unchanged in form from the eighteenth to the twentieth century. I have no doubt that it is still being used today.

It is unfortunate that, in the chaotic jumble of card meanings presented by the author, a number of cards have been omitted. No meanings are given for the Two and Six of Clubs; the Two, Six, and Seven of Hearts; and the Two, Four, Six, and Seven of Diamonds. Only the meanings for the suit of Spades are complete.

Readers should not despair over the missing card meanings. The English Method of fortune-telling by cards is described at greater length in the essays that follow, where meanings for all the cards are supplied. Also, do not be too concerned about the very brief, almost cryptic description of the method that is given here, because it is described much more clearly in the subsequent essays.

This essay appeared in the August 1791 issue of *The Conjuror's Magazine*, where it is quoted directly from *Breslaw's Last Legacy* and attributed to Breslaw.[10] The editor of the magazine, Henry Lemoine, managed to omit the meaning for the Nine of Clubs, an easy error to make given the chaotic arrangement of the card meanings in *Breslaw's*.

Paragraph breaks and capitalization have been added in the present work to make the text a little easier to read, and archaic spelling has been modernized, but otherwise the text is unchanged.

In the following table, I have organized the jumble of meanings for the number cards into four suit lists, for quick reference. The meanings for the court cards appear in the text. Several of the same numbered cards occuring together in a divination have a special meaning, as indicated in the table.

	Clubs	Hearts	Spades	Diamonds
Ace	a letter	your house	death, spite, or quarrelling	a ring
Two			a false friend	
Three	fighting	a kiss	tears	speaking with a friend
Four	a strange bed	a marriage bed	a sick bed	
Five	a bundle	a present	a surprise	a settlement
Six			a child	
Seven	a prison		a removal	
Eight	confusion	new clothes	a road way	new clothes
Nine	merry-making	feasting	a disappointment	business
Ten	going by water	some place of amusement	sickness	a journey
Multiples	drink	love	vexation	money

I.

"THE ART OF FORTUNE-TELLING BY CARDS"

by

PHILLIP BRESLAW

(*Breslaw's Last Legacy*, 1784, chap. 7, pp. 102–104)

Take a pack of cards, and making yourself which Queen you please, lay them out on a table, nine of a row, and wherever you find yourself placed, count nine cards every way, making yourself one,[11] and then you will see what card you tell to, and whatever that is, will happen to you.

If the two red Tens are by you, it is a sign of marriage, the Ace of Diamonds is a ring; the Ace of Hearts is your house, the Ace of Clubs is a letter, the Ace of Spades is death, spite or quarrelling (for that is the worst card in the pack); the Ten of Diamonds is a journey, the Three of Hearts is a kiss, the Three of Spades is tears, the Ten of Spades is sickness, the Nine of Spades a disappointment; the Nine of Clubs a merry-making; the Nine of Hearts feasting; the Ten of Clubs going by water; the Ten of Hearts, some place of amusement, the Five of Hearts a present, the Five of Clubs a bundle, the Six of Spades a child, the Seven of Spades a removal, the Three of Clubs fighting; the Eight of Clubs confusion; the Eight of Spades a road way; the Four of Clubs a strange bed; the Nine of Diamonds business; the Five of Diamonds a settlement; the Five of Spades a surprise; the two red Eights new clothes; the Three of Diamonds speaking with a friend; the Four of Spades a sick bed; the Seven of Clubs a prison; the Two of Spades a false friend; the Four of Hearts a marriage bed; when several Diamonds come together, it is a sign of money; several Hearts, love; several Clubs, drink; and several Spades, vexation.

If a married woman lays the cards, she must make her husband the King of the same suit she is Queen of; but if a single woman tries it, she may make her sweetheart what King she likes; the Knaves of the same suit are the men's thoughts; so that you may know what they are thinking of by telling nine cards from where they are placed, making them one; and if any one chooses to try if she shall have her wish, let her shuffle the cards well (as she must likewise when she tells her fortune) wishing all the time for some one thing: she must then cut them once, and minding what card she cuts, shuffle them again, and then deal them out into three parcels, which done, look over every parcel, and if the card you cut comes next yourself, or next the Ace of Hearts, you will have your wish; but if the Nine of Spades is next, you will not, for that is a disappointment; however, you may try it three times.[12]

This method of telling fortunes is innocent, and much better than for a young woman to tell her secrets to a fortune-teller, who can inform her no better, if she pays a shilling for the intelligence.

INTRODUCTION TO "THE ART OF FORTUNE-TELLING BY CARDS"

from The Universal Dream Book

*T*he *Universal Dream Book* was typical of fortune-telling chapbooks produced by the score during the late eighteenth and early nineteenth centuries. They were generally inexpensive productions on cheap paper and cheaply bound, with astonishingly poor copyediting. The present edition is not an exception to these general characteristics. There is no date of publication indicated in the book, but Google Books dates it to 1816. It was printed and sold by J. Bailey in Chancery Lane, London. It was part of a wildly popular genre. Charles Mackay, the author of *Popular Delusions*, estimated that this book and another similar chapbook on fortune-telling (*The Norwood Gypsy*) went through "upwards of fifty editions" in London printings over a span of the same number of years.[13]

The book is a rambling collection of dream interpretations and methods of fortune-telling by such things as moles, palms, and tea leaves. It even included a recipe for something called a "dumb cake" for divining the identity of a future husband. The cake takes its name from the necessity of those preparing the cake not to speak while so engaged. It is not a cake you would wish to eat, since the flour is moistened not with milk or water but with the urine of the woman seeking the divination. In the midst of all this is a brief chapter on divination by playing cards using the English Method of 52 cards laid out in rows of nine.

The anonymous author purported to have discovered the manuscript lying in the leaf mold beneath a hollow tree in Norwood, England. He wrote in his preface to the work:

As the Editor of this Work was taking a morning's walk near Mother Bridget's Cave, in Norwood, (a well-known place not many miles from

London) just at the foot of a hollow tree he kicked a small bundle of rags,...whereupon he took out his knife and cut the weeds off, and having taken the rags away, he found a bundle of paper, containing in manuscript the substance of this book, wrote in a very crabbed hand, seemingly that of a woman. It was inscribed "to the curious" and intitled "Mother Bridget's last Legacy, &c." and bequeathed to "her dear and well-beloved son, or child of chance." The man who should be so fortunate as to find it.[14]

Mother Bridget was an actual person. She was the niece of Margaret Finch, who was reputed to be the "Queen of Gypsies" living in Norwood. Margaret died in 1740 and Bridget took her crown and lived in a hut on Norwood common until her death on August 4, 1768. She was renowned for her fortune-telling abilities, and over her career managed to accumulate what at the time was a sizable fortune for a commoner, estimated to have been between 200 and 1,000 pounds.[15] Despite the number of fortune-telling books attributed to her name, there is no reason to believe that she ever wrote a book, or indeed that she even knew how to write.

The description of the method of fortune-telling by cards in the book is very brief and not very clear. It appears to have been lifted from *Breslaw's Last Legacy*—or at any rate, the two descriptions had the same source. Both essays have the same title. However, the list of meanings given for the individual cards is uncommonly detailed and completely different from that given in the *Breslaw's* essay. There is also considerable divergence in card meanings between *The Universal Dream Book* and the essays that follow. The meanings supplied by the apocryphal Mother Bridget are interesting on this account, and in my opinion justify the inclusion of this essay.

The Six of Spades was inadvertently omitted from the list of card meanings by the author. I have indicated its omission in the list with square brackets.

II.
"THE ART OF FORTUNE-TELLING BY CARDS"

by

MOTHER BRIDGET

(*The Universal Dream Book*, c. 1816, pp. 49–53)

Take a pack of cards, and making yourself which Queen you please, lay them out on the table, nine in a row, and wherever you find yourself placed count nine cards every way, making yourself one, and then you will see what card you tell to, and whatever that is, it will happen to you.

If a married woman lays the cards, she must make her husband the King she likes.[16] The Knaves of the same suit are the men's thoughts, so that you may know of what they are thinking by telling nine cards from where they are placed, making them one. Any one choosing to try if she shall have her wish, let her shuffle the cards well, as she must likewise when she tells her fortune, wishing all the time for some one thing; she must then cut them once, and minding what card she cuts, shuffle them again, and then deal them out into three parcels. When this is done, look over every parcel, and if the card you cut comes next yourself, or next the Ace of Hearts, you will have your wish; but if the Nine of Spades is next, you will not, for that is a disappointment. However you may try it three times.

Ace of Clubs promises great wealth, much prosperity in life, and tranquility of mind.

King of Clubs announces a man who is humane, upright, affectionate, and faithful in all his engagements; happy himself, and striving to make all happy who are connected with him.

Queen of Clubs shows a tender, mild, and a somewhat amorous disposition, one who will probably yield her maiden person to a generous lover before the matrimonial knot be tied, but they will be happy, love each other, and be married.

Knave of Clubs shows a generous, sincere friend, who will exert himself warmly for your interest and welfare.

Ten of Clubs denotes great riches from an unexpected quarter, but it also threatens that you will at the same time lose a dear friend.

Nine of Clubs shows that you will displease some of your friends by too steady adherence to your own way of thinking.

Eight of Clubs shows the party to be covetous, and exceeding fond of money; that he will obtain it, but that it will rather prove a torment than a comfort to him, as he will not make a proper use of it.

Seven of Clubs promises the most brilliant fortune, and complete happiness that this world can afford; but beware of the opposite sex, from whom alone you can experience misfortune.

Six of Clubs shows that you will engage in a very lucrative partnership, and that your children will do well.

Five of Clubs shows you will be married to a person who will better your circumstances.

Four of Clubs denotes inconstancy for the sake of money, and change of object.

Trey of Clubs shows that you will be three times married, and each time to a wealthy person.

Deuce of Clubs shows that there will be some unfortunate opposition to your favourite inclination, which will much disturb you.

Ace of Diamonds signifies a letter.

King of Diamonds shows a man of a fiery temper, preserving his anger long, seeking for opportunities of revenge, and obstinate in his resolution.

Queen of Diamonds signifies that the woman shall be fond of company, a coquette, and not over virtuous.

Knave of Diamonds, however nearly related, will look more after his own interest than yours; he will be tenacious of his own opinion, and fly off if contradicted.

Ten of Diamonds promises a country husband or wife, with great wealth, and many children, the card next to it will tell the number of children; it also signifies a purse of gold.

Nine of Diamonds declares that the person will be of a roving disposition, never contented with his lot.

Eight of Diamonds shows that the person in youth will be an enemy to marriage, and so run the risk of dying unmarried; but if such person do marry, it will be late in life, and with one whose disposition is so ill-suited to their own that it will be the cause of great unhappiness.

Seven of Diamonds denotes that you will be troubled by the infidelity of your conjugal partner, or lover, and loss of property.

Six of Diamonds marks an early marriage and premature widowhood, but that the second marriage will probably be more unfortunate.

Five of Diamonds shows that you will have good children, who will endeavour to make your life easy.

Four of Diamonds notes incontinence[17] in the person to whom you will be married, and great vexation to yourself, through the greatest part of your life.

Trey of Diamonds denotes that you will be engaged in quarrels, lawsuits, and domestic disagreements; your partner for life will be a vixen, and fail in the performance of her nuptial duties, and make you unhappy.

Deuce of Diamonds denotes that your heart will be engaged in love at an early period; that your friends will not approve your choice; and that if you marry without their consent they will hardly forgive you.

Ace of Hearts signifies feasting and pleasure; if the Ace is attended by Spades, it foretells quarrelling; if by Hearts, it shows affection and friendship; if by Diamonds, you will hear of some absent friend; if by Clubs, it denotes merry-making.

King of Hearts shows a man of a good-natured disposition, rather hasty and passionate, rash in his undertakings, and very amorous.

Queen of Hearts denotes a woman of a fair complexion, faithful and affectionate.

Knave of Hearts is a person of no particular sex, but always the dearest friend or nearest relation of the consulting party. You must pay great attention to the cards that stand next to the Knave, as from them alone you can judge whether the person it represents will favour your inclination or not.

Ten of Hearts shows good-nature and many children; it is a corrective of the bad tidings of the cards that may stand next to it; and if neighbouring cards are of good import, it ascertains and confirms their value.

Nine of Hearts promises wealth, grandeur, and high esteem; if cards that are unfavourable stand near it, you must look for disappointments and a reverse; if favourable cards follow these at a small distance, expect to retrieve your losses, whether of peace or of goods.

Eight of Hearts is a sign of drinking and feasting.

Seven of Hearts shows the person to be fickle, and of an unfaithful disposition, addicted to vice, and incontinent, and subject to the mean art of recrimination to excuse themselves, although without foundation.

Six of Hearts shows a generous, open, and credulous disposition, easily imposed upon, and ever the dupe of flatterers, but the good-natured friend of the distressed; if this card come before your King or Queen you will be the dupe, if after, you will have the better.

Five of Hearts shows a wavering and unsteady disposition, never attached to one object, and free from any violent passion or attachment.

Four of Hearts shows that the person will not be married until very late in life, and that this will proceed from too great a delicacy in making a choice.

Trey of Hearts shows that your own imprudence will greatly contribute to your experiencing the ill will of others.

Deuce of Hearts shows that extraordinary success and good fortune will attend this person; though if unfavourable cards attend, this will be a long time delayed.

Ace of Spades totally relates to the affairs of love, without specifying whether lawful or unlawful; it also signifies death, when the card is upside down.

King of Spades shows a man ambitious and successful at court, or with some great man, who will have it in his power to advance him, but let him beware of a reverse.

Queen of Spades shows a person that will be corrupted by the great of both sexes; if she is handsome, great attempts will be made on her virtue.

Knave of Spades shows a person who, although he has your welfare at heart, will be too indolent to pursue it with zeal, unless you take frequent opportunities of rousing his attention.

Ten of Spades is a card of bad import; it will, in a great measure, counteract the good effects of the cards near you.

Nine of Spades is the worst card in the whole pack; it portends dangerous sickness, a total loss of fortune, cruel calamities, and endless dissentions in your family.

Eight of Spades shows that you will experience strong opposition from your friends, or whom you imagine to be such; if this card comes close to you, abandon your enterprise, and pursue another plan.

Seven of Spades shows the loss of a valuable friend, whose death will plunge you into very great distress.

[*Six of Spades...*]

Five of Spades will give very little interpretation of your success; it promises you good luck in the choice of a companion for life; that you will meet with one very fond of you, and immoderately attached to the joys of Hymen;[18] but shows temper rather sullen.

Four of Spades shows speedy sickness, and that your friends will injure your fortune.

Trey of Spades shows that you will be unfortunate in marriage, that your partner will be inconstant, and that you will be made unhappy.

Deuce of Spades always signifies a coffin, but who it is for must depend entirely on the cards that are near it.

INTRODUCTION TO
"THE FOLKLORE OF PLAYING CARDS"

from Chambers's *Book of Days*

The following essay, "The Folklore of Playing Cards," appeared on pages 281–284 in the first volume of Chambers's *Book of Days*, an enormous compendium of historical and literary anecdotes, bits of folklore, short biographies, and brief essays of general interest arranged on the days of the year with which they were associated. Volume 1 was published at Edinburgh and London in 1863, and volume 2 came out the following year. The essay describes in great detail the method of fortune-telling with ordinary playing cards that was in vogue in the middle of the nineteenth century in England, called the English Method, and it was written by someone with firsthand knowledge of the subject.

This essay is often presumed to have been written by Robert Chambers (1802–1871), but this is incorrect based on the content of the essay itself. Chambers is described as the editor of the *Book of Days* on its title page, not as its author, and the work lacks a list of contributors. Undoubtedly Robert Chambers did write much of the material in this great work, but there is no reason to think he wrote this essay on fortune-telling by cards, and good reason to think he did not. The anonymous author of the essay described his own early life in the following terms:

Many years ago the exigencies of a military life, and the ravages of a pestilential epidemic, caused the writer, then a puny but not very young child, to be left for many months in charge of a private soldier's wife, at an out-station in a distant land. The poor woman, though childless herself, proved worthy of the confidence that was placed in her. She was too ignorant to teach her charge to read, yet she taught him the only accomplishment she possessed—the art of "cutting cards," as she termed it; the word cartomancy, in all probability, she had never heard.[19]

Elsewhere in the essay, the author makes passing reference to the "Australian diggings"—presumably a reference to Australian gold or diamond mining. This suggests that the "out-station in a distant land" referred to by the author of the essay may have been in Australia.

None of these details matches the early life of Robert Chambers, who moved from Peebles, in Scotland, where he was born, to Edinburgh in 1813, where he eventually became a bookseller in partnership with his brother William.

The terms *Trey* and *Deuce* are used for the number cards Three and Two, as was customary for the period. The court card commonly known as the Jack is here called the *Knave*.

There are a few period details in the essay that will give a modern reader pause. The author makes disparaging reference to "a negro cymbal-player" to emphasize that the King of Diamonds indicates merely a man in uniform—it is the uniform that is important, not the nature of the man wearing it. Also note that in the example given of a card reading, the person seeking the reading is referred to as "a young lady." The gender is significant here—the implication of our author is that fortune-telling by cards is a trivial pursuit suitable mainly for women and beneath the dignity of men. The Knave of Spades is described as "A lawyer. A person to be shunned." The humor may be unintentional.

III.
"THE FOLKLORE OF PLAYING CARDS"
edited by

ROBERT CHAMBERS

(*The Book of Days*, 1863, vol. 1, pp. 281–284)

The long disputed questions respecting the period of the invention of play-ing-cards, and whether they were first used for purposes of divination or gambling, do not fall within the prescribed limits of this paper. Its object is simply to disclose—probably for the first time in print—the method or system of divination by playing-cards, constantly employed and implicitly depended upon, by many thousands of our fellow-countrymen and women at the present day. The smallest village in England contains at least one "card-cutter," a per-son who pretends to presage future events by studying the accidental combina-tions of a pack of cards. In London, the name of these fortune-tellers is legion, some of greater, some of lesser repute and pretensions: some willing to draw the curtains of destiny for a sixpence, others unapproachable except by a previ-ously paid fee of from one to three guineas. And it must not be supposed that all of those persons are deliberate cheats: the majority of them "believe in the cards" as firmly as the silly simpletons who employ and pay them. Moreover, besides those who make their livelihood by "card-cutting," there are numbers of others, who, possessing a smattering of the art, daily refer to the paste-board oracles, to learn their fate and guide their conduct. And when a ticklish point arises, one of those crones will consult another, and then, if the two can-not pierce the mysterious combination, they will call in a professed mistress of the art, to throw a gleam of light on the darkness of the future. In short, there are very few individuals among the lower classes in England who do not know something respecting the cards in their divinatory aspect, even if it be no more than to distinguish the lucky from the unlucky ones: and it is quite common to hear a person's complexion described as being of a Heart, or Club colour. For these reasons, the writer—for the first time as he believes—has applied the well-known term folklore to this system of divination by playing cards, so extensively known and so continually practised in the British dominions.

The Archduke of Austria Consulting a Fortune-Teller

The art of cartomancy, or divination by playing-cards, dates from an early period of their obscure history. In the museum of Nantes there is a painting, said to be by Van Eyck,[20] representing Philippe le Bon, Archduke of Austria, and subsequently King of Spain, consulting a fortune-teller by cards. This picture, of which a transcript is here given, cannot be of a later date than the fifteenth century. When the art was introduced into England is unknown: probably, however, the earliest printed notice of it in this country is the following curious story, extracted from *Rowland's Judicial Astrology Condemned*: "Cuffe, an excellent Grecian, and secretary to the Earl of Essex, was told, twenty years before his death, that he should come to an untimely end, at which Cuffe laughed, and in a scornful manner intreated the soothsayer to shew him in what manner he should come to his end, who condescended to him, and calling for cards, intreated Cuffe to draw out of the pack any three which pleased him. He did so, and drew three knaves, and laid them on the table by the wizard's direction, who then told him, if he desired to see the sum of his bad fortune, to take up those cards. Cuffe, as he was prescribed, took up the first card, and looking on it, he saw the portraiture of himself cap-à-pie,[21] having men encompassing him with bills and halberds. Then he took up the second, and there he saw the judge that sat upon him; and taking up the last card, he saw Tyburn, the place of his execution, and the hangman, at which he laughed heartily. But many years after, being condemned, he remembered and declared this prediction."[22]

The earliest work on cartomancy was written or compiled by one Francesco Marcolini,[23] and printed at Venice in 1540. There are many modern French, Italian, and German works on the subject: but, as far as the writer's knowledge extends, there is not an English one. The system of cartomancy, as laid down in those works, is very different from that used in England, both as regards the individual interpretations of the cards, and the general method of reading or deciphering their combinations. The English system, however, is used in all British settlements over the globe, and has no doubt been carried thither by soldiers' wives, who, as is well known to the initiated, have ever been considered peculiarly skilful practitioners of the art. Indeed, it is to a soldier's wife that this present exposition of the art is to be attributed. Many years ago the exigencies of a military life, and the ravages of a pestilential epidemic, caused the writer, then a puny but not very young child, to be left for many months in charge of a private soldier's wife, at an out-station in a distant land. The poor woman, though childless herself, proved worthy of the confidence that was placed in her. She was too ignorant to teach her charge to read, yet she taught him the only accomplishment she possessed—the art of "cutting cards," as she termed it: the word cartomancy, in all probability, she had never heard. And though it has not fallen to the writer's lot to practice the art professionally, yet he has not forgotten it, as the following interpretations of the cards will testify.

DIAMONDS

King. A man of very fair complexion; quick to anger, but soon appeased.

Queen. A very fair woman, fond of gaiety, and a coquette.

Knave. A selfish and deceitful relative: fair and false.

Ten. Money. Success in honourable business.

Nine. A roving disposition, combined with honourable and successful adventure in foreign lands.

Eight. A happy prudent marriage, though rather late in life.

Seven. Satire. Scandal. Unpleasant business matters.

Six. Marriage early in life, succeeded by widow-hood.

Five. Unexpected news, generally of a good kind.

Four. An unfaithful friend. A secret betrayed.

Trey. Domestic troubles, quarrels and unhappiness.

Deuce. A clandestine engagement. A card of caution.

Ace. A wedding ring. An offer of marriage.

HEARTS

King. A fair, but not very fair, complexioned man: good natured, but rather obstinate, and, when angered, not easily appeased.

Queen. A woman of the same complexion as the King; faithful, prudent, and affectionate.

Knave. An unselfish relative. A sincere friend.

Ten. Health and happiness, with many children.

Nine. Wealth. High position in society. The wish-card.

Eight. Fine clothes. Pleasure. Mixing in good society. Going to balls, theatres, etc.

Seven. Many good friends.

Six. Honourable courtship.

Five. A present.

Four. Domestic troubles caused by jealousy.

Trey. Poverty, shame and sorrow, caused by imprudence. A card of caution.

Deuce. Success in life, position in society, and a happy marriage, attained by virtuous discretion.

Ace. The house of the person consulting the decrees of fate.

SPADES

King. A man of very dark complexion, ambitious and unscrupulous.

Queen. A very dark-complexioned woman, of malicious disposition. A widow.

Knave. A lawyer. A person to be shunned.

Ten. Disgrace: crime: imprisonment. Death on the scaffold. A card of caution.

Nine. Grief: ruin: sickness: death.

Eight. Great danger from imprudence. A card of caution.

Seven. Unexpected poverty caused by the death of a relative. A lean sorrow.[24]

Six. A child. To the unmarried a card of caution.

Five. Great danger from giving way to bad temper. A card of caution.

Four. Sickness.

Trey. A journey by land. Tears.

Deuce. A removal.

Ace. Death; malice; a duel; a general misfortune.

CLUBS

King. A dark-complexioned man, though not so dark as the King of Spades: upright, true, and affectionate.

Queen. A woman of the same complexion, agreeable, genteel, and witty.

Knave. A sincere, but rather hasty-tempered friend.

Ten. Unexpected wealth, through the death of a relative. A fat sorrow.[25]

Nine. Danger caused by drunkenness. A card of caution.

Eight. Danger from covetousness. A card of caution.

Seven. A prison. Danger arising from the opposite sex. A card of caution.

Six. Competence by hard-working industry.

Five. A happy, though not wealthy marriage.

Four. Danger of misfortunes caused by inconstancy, or capricious temper. A card of caution.

Trey. Quarrels. Or in reference to time may signify three years, three months, three weeks, or three days. It also denotes that a person will be married more than once.

Deuce. Vexation, disappointment.

Ace. A letter.

The foregoing is merely the alphabet of the art: the letters, as it were, of the sentences formed by the various combinations of the cards. A general idea only can be given here of the manner in which those prophetic sentences are formed. The person who desires to explore the hidden mysteries of fate is represented, if a male by the King, if a female by the Queen, of the suit which

accords with his or her complexion. If a married woman consults the cards, the
King of her own suit, or complexion, represents her husband: but with single
women, the lover, either in *esse* or *posse*,[26] is represented by his own colour:
and all cards, when representing persons, lose their own normal significations.
There are exceptions, however, to these general rules. A man, no matter what
his complexion, if he wear uniform, even if he be the negro cymbal-player in a
regimental band, can be represented by the King of Diamonds: note, the dress
of policemen and volunteers is not considered as uniform. On the other hand,
a widow, even if she be an albiness, can be represented only by the Queen of
Spades.

The Ace of Hearts always denoting the house of the person consulting the
decrees of fate, some general rules are applicable to it. Thus the Ace of Clubs
signifying a letter, its position, either before or after the Ace of Hearts, shows
whether the letter is to be sent to or from the house. The Ace of Diamonds,
when close to the Ace of Hearts, foretells a wedding in the house: but the Ace
of Spades betokens sickness and death.

The Knaves represent the thoughts of their respective Kings and Queens,
and consequently the thoughts of the persons whom those Kings and Queens
represent, in accordance with their complexions. For instance, a young lady
of a rather but not decidedly dark complexion, represented by the Queen of
Clubs, when consulting the cards, may be shocked to find her fair lover (the
King of Diamonds) flirting with a wealthy widow (the Queen of Spades, attended by the Ten of Diamonds), but will be reassured by finding his thoughts
(the Knave of Diamonds) in combination with a letter (Ace of Clubs), a wedding ring (Ace of Diamonds), and her house (the Ace of Hearts): clearly signifying that, though he is actually flirting with the rich widow, he is, nevertheless,
thinking of sending a letter, with an offer of marriage, to the young lady herself. And look, where are her own thoughts, represented by the Knave of Clubs:
they are far away with the old lover, that dark man (King of Spades) who, as is
plainly shown by his being attended by the Nine of Diamonds, is prospering
at the Australian diggings or elsewhere. Let us shuffle the cards once more,
and see if the dark man, at the distant diggings, ever thinks of his old flame,
the Club-complexioned young lady in England. No! he does not. Here are his
thoughts (the Knave of Spades) directed to this fair, but rather gay and coquettish woman (the Queen of Diamonds): they are separated but by a few Hearts,

one of them, the Sixth (honourable courtship), shewing the excellent understanding that exists between them. Count, now, from the Six of Hearts to the ninth card from it, and lo! it is a wedding ring (the Ace of Diamonds): they will be married before the expiration of a twelvemonth.

The general mode of manipulating the cards, when fortune-telling, is very simple. The person, who is desirous to know the future, after shuffling the cards *ad libitum*,[27] cuts the pack into three parts. The seer, then, taking up these parts, lays the cards out, one by one, face upwards, upon the table, sometimes in a circular form,[28] but oftener in rows consisting of nine cards in each row. Nine is the mystical number. Every nine consecutive cards form a separate combination, complete in itself: yet, like a word in a sentence, no more than a fractional part of the grand scroll of fate. Again, every card, something like the octaves in music, is *en rapport* with the ninth card from it: and these ninth cards form other complete combinations of nines, yet parts of the general whole. The Nine of Hearts is termed the "wish-card." After the general fortune has been told, a separate and different manipulation is performed, to learn if the pryer into futurity will obtain a particular wish; and, from the position of the wish-card in the pack, the required answer is deduced.

In conclusion, a few words must be said on the professional fortune-tellers. That they are, generally speaking, wilful impostors is perhaps true.

Yet, paradoxical though it may appear, the writer feels bound to assert that those "card-cutters" whose practice lies among the lowest classes of society, really do a great deal of good. Few know what the lowest classes in our large towns suffer when assailed by mental affliction. They are, in most instances, utterly destitute of the consolations of religion, and incapable of sustained thought. Accustomed to live from hand to mouth, their whole existence is bound up in the present, and they have no idea of the healing effects of time. Their ill-regulated passions brook no self-denial, and a predominant element of self rules their confused minds. They know of no future, they think no other human being ever suffered as they do. As they term it themselves, "they are up-set." They perceive no resource, no other remedy than a leap from the nearest bridge, or a dose of arsenic from the first chemist's shop. Haply some friend or neighbour, one who has already suffered and been relieved, takes the wretched creature to a fortune-teller. The seeress at once perceives that her client is in distress, and, shrewdly guessing the cause, pretends that she sees it all in the cards. Having thus asserted her superior intelligence, she affords her sympathy and consolation, and points to hope and a happy future: blessed hope! though in the form of a greasy playing card. The sufferer, if not cured, is relieved. The lacerated wounds, if not healed, are at least dressed: and, in all probability, a suicide or a murder is prevented. Scenes of this character occur every day in the meaner parts of London.

Unlike the witches of the olden time, the fortune-tellers are generally esteemed and respected in the districts in which they live and practise. And, besides that which has already been stated, it will not be difficult to discover sufficient reasons for this respect and esteem. The most ignorant and depraved have ever a lurking respect for morality and virtue; and the fortune-tellers are shrewd enough to know and act upon this feeling. They always take care to point out what they term "the cards of caution," and impressively warn their clients from falling into the dangers those cards foreshadow, but do not positively foretell, for the dangers may be avoided by prudence and circumspection. By referring to the preceding significations of the cards, it will be seen that there are cards of caution against dangers arising from drunkenness, covetousness, inconstancy, caprice, evil temper, illicit love, clandestine engagements, etc. Consequently the fortune-tellers are the moralists, as well as the consolers of the lower classes. They supply a want that society either cannot or will not do. If the great gulf which exists between rich and poor cannot be filled up, it would be well to try if, by any process of moral engineering, it could be bridged over.

INTRODUCTION TO "FORTUNE-TELLING WITH COMMON PLAYING CARDS"

from The History of Playing Cards

The anonymous essay published by Chambers in 1863 appears in a somewhat restructured format in a work titled *The History of Playing Cards*, which was published in London in 1865.[29] The title page of the work states that it was edited by the late Reverend Ed. S. Taylor. In his preface to the book, the publisher, John Camden Hotten, revealed why Taylor is described as the editor rather than the author:

> Five years ago I purchased from an eminent French publisher some tasteful wood-engravings, illustrative of the History of Playing Cards. These, with the small work in which they originally appeared, were placed in the hands of the late Rev. Ed. S. Taylor, of Ormesby St. Margaret, Great Yarmouth, as material for a History of Playing Cards, English and Foreign, which he had offered to undertake for me.[30]

Taylor was of ill health and died while working on the latter section of the book. It appears that Taylor, the publisher Hotten, or someone Hotten hired to finish the editing of the work lifted the essay on fortune-telling out of Chambers's *Book of Days* and rearranged the material, without however adding very much interest or value, and without ever explicitly stating the source. Although the editor of *The History of Playing Cards* did quote from the *Book of Days* essay at the end of his plagiarism, he nowhere admitted that the material he was providing on fortune-telling was wholly derived from the *Book of Days*.

Such boldness in literary theft was by no means uncommon during the nine-teenth century.

Because the essay in Taylor's book is quite brief, I have added the portion that concerns the method of fortune-telling by cards after the *Book of Days* essay for purposes of comparison, and because its variant point of view may help readers comprehend the method of divination it describes. It was extracted from the body of Taylor's text—the title that heads it is my own. I have not bothered to reproduce the rest of the material plagiarized by Taylor. Suffice it to say that almost the entire Chambers essay is reproduced in pieces.

An error was made in typesetting the work on page 474, where what should have been the top line on the page was inadvertently placed at the bottom of the page. I have corrected this error. I have also added additional paragraph breaks, since the original paragraphs are excessively long.

You will notice that the meanings for some of the cards have been changed in subtle ways that go beyond mere rearranging of words. For example, the Nine of Diamonds is said in the Chambers essay to indicate "honourable and successful adventure in foreign lands." Taylor has omitted the word "honour-able" from this part of the description. In the Chambers essay for the Six of Clubs, the words "Competence by hard-working industry" are changed by Taylor to "Competence by honourable industry"—"honourable industry" and "hard-working industry" are two different things. There are other examples that you may discover for yourself by comparing the two essays.

Our author did add one useful bit of information to the Chambers essay: the manner of using the wish card, or Nine of Hearts. For some reason, this was omitted from the Chambers essay, although the wish card was mentioned there. For this material alone, the Taylor essay is worth reading, since the use of the wish card is a necessary component of English fortune-telling with a full deck of common playing cards.

IV.
"FORTUNE TELLING WITH COMMON PLAYING CARDS"

edited by

REV. ED S. TAYLOR

(*The History of Playing Cards*, 1865, pp. 471–479)

The mode of fortune-telling used by the English "card-cutters," as they are familiarly termed, has now to be described.

A man of very fair complexion is represented by the King of Diamonds; a woman by the Queen of the same suit. Persons of less fair complexion, according to sex, by the King and Queen of Hearts. A man and woman of very dark complexion, by the King and Queen of Spades; while those not quite so dark are represented by Clubs.

If a married woman consults the cards, the King of her own colour represents her husband, whether he be fair or dark, and *vice versa* if the cards be consulted by a married man. Lovers, whether in *esse* or *posse*, are always represented by cards of their peculiar colours; and all cards when representing persons, lose their normal significations.

There are exceptions, however, to all general rules. A widow, no matter how fair she may be, can be represented only by the Queen of Spades; while a man wearing uniform, even if a negro cymbal-player in a regimental band, may be represented by the King of Diamonds—the dress of a police man is not considered as uniform.

The Ace of Hearts denotes the house of the person consulting the decrees of fate. The Ace of Clubs, a letter. The Ace of Diamonds, a wedding ring. The Ace of Spades, sickness and death.

The Knave of Diamonds is a selfish and deceitful friend. The Knave of Hearts, an unselfish sincere friend. The Knave of Spades is a lawyer, a person to be avoided. The Knave of Clubs is a sincere friend, but of very touchy temper. In all instances, however, the Knaves signify the thoughts of their respective Kings and Queens; and, consequently, the thoughts of the persons whom those Kings and Queens represent, in accordance with their complexion; and when doing so, lose their normal signification.

Generally speaking, Diamonds and Hearts are more fortunate than Spades and Clubs. Several Diamonds coming together, signify the receipt of money; several Hearts denote love. A concourse of Clubs foretells drunkenness and debauchery, with their consequent ill-health; and a number of Spades together, indicate disappointment, with its accompanying vexation.

The Kings and Queens, besides representing persons, according to colour, have private significations of their own, that may be of interest to the physiognomist. Thus, the King of Diamonds is quick to anger, but easily appeased; while the Queen is fond of gaiety, and of rather a coquettish disposition. The King of Hearts is slow to anger, but when put in a passion, is appeased with great difficulty; he is good-natured, but particularly obstinate; his Queen, however, is a model of sincere affection, devotion, and prudence. The King of Spades is so ambitious, that in matters of either love or business, he is much less scrupulous than he ought to be; while his Queen, is a person not to be provoked with impunity, never forgetting an injury, and having a considerable spice of malice in her composition. The King and Queen of Clubs are everything that can be desired; he is honourable, true, and affectionate; she is agreeable, genteel, and witty.

The interpretations of the minor cards are as follows:

DIAMONDS

Ten. Wealth. Honourable success in business.

Nine. A roving disposition, combined with successful adventure in foreign lands.

Eight. A happy marriage, though perhaps late in life.

Seven. Satire. Scandal.

Six. Early marriage, succeeded by widowhood.

Five. Unexpected, though generally good, news.

Four. An unfaithful friend. A secret betrayed.

Trey. Domestic quarrels, trouble, unhappiness.

Deuce. A clandestine engagement. A card of caution.

HEARTS

Ten. Health and happiness, with many children.

Nine. Wealth, and good position in society.

Eight. Fine clothes. Mixing in good society. Invitations to balls, theatres, parties.

Seven. Good friends.

Six. Honourable courtship.

Five. A present.

Four. Domestic troubles caused by jealousy.

Trey. Poverty, shame, and sorrow, the result of imprudence. A card of caution.

Deuce. Success in life, and a happy marriage attained by virtuous discretion.

SPADES

Ten. Disgrace, crime, imprisonment. Death on the scaffold. A card of caution.

Nine. Grief, ruin, sickness, death.

Eight. Great danger from imprudence. A card of caution.

Seven. Unexpected poverty, through the death of a relative.

Six. A child. To the unmarried, a card of caution.

Five. Great danger from giving way to bad temper. A card of caution.

Four. Sickness.

Trey. Tears. A journey by land.

Deuce. A removal.

CLUBS

Ten. Unexpected wealth, through the death of a relative.

Nine. Danger through drunkenness. A card of caution.

Eight. Danger from covetousness. A card of caution.

Seven. A prison. Danger from the opposite sex. A card of caution.

Six. Competence by honourable industry.

Five. A happy, though not wealthy marriage.

Four. Misfortunes through caprice or inconstancy. A card of caution.

Trey. Quarrels. It also has a reference to time, signifying three years, three months, three weeks, or three days; and denotes that a person will be married more than once.

Deuce. Disappointment, vexation.

The general mode of operating is simple enough. The person consulting fortune, after shuffling the cards, cuts them into three parts. The seeress, then, taking up the parts,[31] lays them out one by one, face upwards, on the table, in rows, nine in each row, save the last.

Nine, in fact, is the mystical number. Every ninth card bearing a portentous import, while each nine consecutive cards forms a separate combination, complete in itself; yet like a word in a sentence, no more than a fractional part of the grand scroll of fate. Moreover, every card, something like the octaves in music, has a peculiar bearing on the ninth card from it, and these ninth cards form in themselves peculiar combinations of nines, though parts of the general whole.

After the cards are thus laid out, then comes the reading of this strange book, which we may attempt to describe from a fanciful disposition of the cards in our mind's eye, be it remembered.

The young lady, who is examining the future, being fair, but not too fair, is, as the card-cutters express it, of a Heart colour, and represented by the Queen of Hearts. Sad to say her fair lover (the King of Diamonds) is found flirting with a widow (the Queen of Spades) rich in this world's goods, being accompanied with the Ten of Diamonds. But, her lover's thoughts (the Knave of Diamonds) are directed towards her house (the Ace of Hearts); a letter (the Ace of Spades) and a wedding ring (the Ace of Diamonds) are in close combination; evidently signifying that though the lover is actually flirting with the widow, he is thinking of sending a letter with an offer of marriage to the young lady herself.

There is a legacy (Ten of Clubs) in store, for the seeker after fortune; but a lawyer (the Knave of Spades) stands between her and it, who will cause some vexation (the Deuce of Clubs) and disappointment. A sincere friend (the Knave of Hearts) will assist to put matters right. The unfaithful friend (the Four of Diamonds) will find both satire and scandal (Seven of Diamonds) helpless to injure our interesting Queen of Hearts. A present (Five of Hearts) will soon be received by her, honourable courtship (Six of Hearts) will lead her to a happy marriage (Deuce of Hearts), the reward of her virtuous discretion; health and happiness, and troops of children (Ten of Hearts) will be her enviable lot.

Do this young lady's thoughts, represented by the Knave of Hearts, ever stray far from home? Yes, look, there they are far away with the old, hot-tempered, dark-complexioned lover (King of Spades) who, as is plainly shown by his being accompanied by the Ten of Diamonds, is prosperously engaged at the Australian diggings, or elsewhere. Does he ever think of his old flame, the Heart-complexioned young lady now consulting the cards in England? No. His thoughts (the Knave of Spades) are fixed on that very fair but rather gay and coquettish lady, (the Queen of Diamonds): they are only divided by a few good Hearts, one of them (the Six) representing honourable courtship. Count now from that Six of Hearts to the ninth card from it, and lo! it is a wedding-ring (the Ace of Diamonds)—they will be married in less than a year.

The Nine of Hearts is known as "the wish card," for there is always a secret something, an aspiration of some kind or another, lying in the lowest depth of the human heart, that even general good fortune, health and happiness, can not gratify. So, after the fortune has been told, as we have described, *secundem artem*,[32] the grand question arises, will this particular wish be gratified? To solve this important problem, the cards are well shuffled, and cut, the cut card being particularly remembered.

The pack is again well shuffled, and cut into three heaps, each of which are taken up and examined separately. If the wish card, the Nine of Hearts, be found in any of these heaps near the representative card of the person, whose fortune is being told, the wish will be gratified, sooner or later, according to the relative positions of the cards. If the Nine of Spades, Deuce of Clubs, or other very unlucky card be in the same heap, the gratification of the wish, according to the number of the unlucky cards is doubtful, or will be greatly delayed. But, mark, if the card first out[33] be in the same heap, the evil effect of the opposing unlucky cards, will be greatly, if not entirely, modified.[34]

Card-cutting, as practised among the lower classes in England, not only foretells the certain future, but also warns against dangers that may be avoided. In an able article on this subject, in that valuable compilation, Chambers' *Book of Days*, the author says:

Unlike the witches of the olden time, the fortune-tellers are generally esteemed and respected in the districts in which they live and practice. And it will not be difficult to discover sufficient reasons for this respect and esteem. The most ignorant and depraved have ever a lurking respect for morality and virtue; and the fortune-tellers are shrewd enough to know and act upon this feeling. They always take care to point out what they term "the cards of caution," and impressively warn their clients from falling into the dangers those cards foreshadow, but do not positively foretell, for the dangers may be avoided by prudence and circumspection. By referring to the preceding significations of the cards, it will be seen that there are cards of caution arising from drunkenness, covetousness, inconstancy, caprice, evil temper, illicit love, clandestine engagements.[35]

Consequently, the "card-cutters" really exercise a considerable effect of a most beneficial kind, on the moral conduct of the poorer and more ignorant classes dwelling in the crowded unhealthy houses of our large towns and cities.

INTRODUCTION TO "THE ENGLISH METHOD OF FORTUNE-TELLING BY CARDS"

from A Manual of Cartomancy

One of the more prominent members of the Hermetic Order of the Golden Dawn, Arthur Edward Waite, wrote a book titled *A Handbook of Cartomancy, Fortune-Telling, and Occult Divination* (London: George Redway, 1889). It proved very popular, going through five editions by 1912. It was renamed in its fourth edition of 1909 *A Manual of Cartomancy, Fortune-Telling, and Occult Divination*, the title by which it is generally known today. The subject matter was more frivolous than Waite's usual weightier occult topics, such as alchemy, Kabbalah, and Freemasonry, and perhaps for this reason Waite chose to adopt the pseudonym Grand Orient for this book.[36]

The title of the book is a bit misleading, since cartomancy makes up only a small part of it. It does, however, contain the English Method of fortune-telling with a full pack of ordinary playing cards that we are examining in this part of the present work. The divinatory meanings are derived almost directly from Chambers's *Book of Days*, but as was the case with Taylor and *The History of Playing Cards*, Waite reproduces the material without giving any credit to the Chambers publication.

I have provided the full text of Waite's version, drawn from the fourth edition of his book, to give yet another take on this interesting and influential English Method of card divination.

In general, Waite adhered to the meanings given in the *Book of Days* essay, but a scattering of them he discarded to introduce in their places completely different interpretations. For example, the meaning for the Six of Spades in the

Book of Days is "A child. To the unmarried a card of caution." Waite threw this meaning away and replaced it with "Wealth through industry."

Waite's meaning for the Six of Spades is completely out of keeping with the rest of the suit. In the Chambers essay, the implication is not explicit, but neither is it difficult to gather: a child is a danger to an unmarried woman because it would be a bastard born out of wedlock. Perhaps Waite's Victorian prudery would not allow him to keep this meaning for the card.

In other cases, Waite merely modified the meaning of a card in the *Book of Days*. For example, for the Three of Spades, Waite gave "A journey." In itself, this has no baneful connotation. But the original meaning in the Chambers essay is "A journey by land. Tears." This indicates that the journey will not be a happy one. It also provides important information about the nature of the journey—that it will be over land, not by sea.

Waite modified a number of meanings for the cards in ways that seem arbitrary. For example, in the Chambers essay, the meaning for the Ten of Diamonds is "Money. Success in honourable business." Waite in his *Manual of Cartomancy* gives for this card simply "Money."

Some of the folk meanings for playing cards were carried over by Waite to the suit cards of the Tarot. The Tarot suit of Pentacles, Disks, or Coins is equivalent to the suit of Diamonds in common playing cards. In his *Pictorial Key to the Tarot*, Waite gave for the upright meaning of the Ten of Pentacles "Gain, riches; family matters, archives, extraction, the abode of a family."[37] Waite has expanded the meaning for this Tarot card, but he heads it with the basic meaning given in the *Book of Days* essay.

By the way, the rest of Waite's upright meaning for the Ten of Diamonds in his *Pictorial Key* is derived from the Tarot essay of S. L. MacGregor Mather, which was published in 1888 as *The Tarot*. Mathers gave as the upright meaning for this card "house, dwelling, habitation, family."[38]

Waite added a section to his *Pictorial Key to the Tarot* that at first glance appears unnecessary. He titled it "Some Additional Meanings of the Lesser Arcana." It was to a significant degree drawn from Mathers's booklet *The Tarot*. For example, Waite gave as the upright meaning for the Nine of Swords "An ecclesiastic, a priest; generally a card of bad omen." Mathers gave the upright meaning "An ecclesiastic, a priest, conscience, probity, good faith, integrity." Waite gave as the reversed meaning "Good ground for suspicion against a doubtful person." Mathers's reversed meaning for this card is "Wise distrust, suspicion, fear, doubt, shady character."

As you can see by a comparison of the two works, the folk meanings for playing cards from the Chambers essay and the divinatory meanings for the suit cards of the Tarot given by Mathers in his *Tarot* essay come together in the primary meanings provided by Waite for the suit cards of his own Rider Tarot in his *Pictorial Key to the Tarot*.

V.

"THE ENGLISH METHOD
OF FORTUNE-TELLING BY CARDS"

by

GRAND ORIENT (A. E. WAITE)

(*A Handbook of Cartomancy*, 4th ed., 1909, pp. 111–118)

In fortune-telling by cards—as in all games at which they are employed—the Ace ranks highest in value. Then comes the King, followed by the Queen, Knave, Ten, Nine, Eight and Seven, with the other numbers in their order.

The comparative value of the different suits is as follows: first on the list stand Clubs, as they mostly portend happiness, and, no matter how numerous or how accompanied, they are rarely or never of bad augury. Next come Hearts, which usually signify joy, liberality, or good temper. Diamonds, on the contrary, denote delay, quarrels and annoyance, while Spades, the worst of all, signify grief, sickness and loss of money.

I am, of course, speaking generally, as, in many cases, the position of cards changes their signification entirely, their individual and relative meaning being often widely different. Thus, for example, the King of Hearts, the Nine of Hearts and the Nine of Clubs signify respectively a liberal man, joy, and success in love; but change their position by placing the King between the two nines, and you would read that a man, then rich and happy, would be ere long consigned to a prison.

I will, in the first place, give a complete list of the cards, together with their precise significance, and then briefly describe the manner of their arrangement by English seers, with a view to the successful disclosure of their mystic oracles.

Ace of Clubs.—Wealth, happiness and peace of mind.

King of Clubs.—A dark man, upright, faithful and affectionate in disposition.

Queen of Clubs.—A dark woman, gentle and pleasing.

Knave of Clubs.—A sincere but hasty friend. Also a dark man's thoughts.

Ten of Clubs.—Unexpected riches, and loss of a dear friend.

Nine of Clubs.—Disobedience to friends' wishes.

Eight of Clubs.—A covetous man. It also warns against speculations.

Seven of Clubs.—Promises good fortune and happiness, but bids a person beware of the opposite sex.

Six of Clubs.—Predicts a lucrative business.

Five of Clubs.—A prudent marriage.

Four of Clubs.—Cautiousness against inconstancy or change of object for the sake of money.

Three of Clubs.—Shows that a person will be more than once married.

Two of Clubs.—A disappointment.

Ace of Diamonds.—A letter—but from whom and what about must be judged by the neighbouring cards.

King of Diamonds.—A fair man, hot tempered, obstinate and revengeful.

Queen of Diamonds.—A fair woman, fond of company and a coquette.

Knave of Diamonds.—A near relation who considers only his own interests. Also a fair person's thoughts.

Ten of Diamonds.—Money.

Nine of Diamonds.—Shows that a person is fond of roving.

Eight of Diamonds.—A marriage late in life.

Seven of Diamonds.—Satire, evil speaking.

Six of Diamonds.—Early marriage and widowhood.

Five of Diamonds.—Unexpected news.

Four of Diamonds.—Trouble arising from unfaithful friends; also a betrayed secret.

Three of Diamonds.—Quarrels, law-suits and domestic disagreements.

Two of Diamonds.—An engagement against the wishes of friends.

Ace of Hearts.—The house. If attended by Spades, it foretells quarrelling—if by Hearts, affection and friendship—if by Diamonds, money and distant friends—if by Clubs, feasting and merrymaking.

King of Hearts.—A fair man, of good-natured disposition, but hasty and rash.

Queen of Hearts.— A fair woman, faithful, prudent and affectionate.

Knave of Hearts.—The dearest friend of the consulting party. Also a fair person's thoughts.

Ten of Hearts.—Is prophetic of happiness and many children; is corrective of the bad tidings of cards next to it, and confirms their good tidings.

Nine of Hearts.—Wealth and high esteem. Also the wish card.

Eight of Hearts.—Pleasure, company.

Seven of Hearts.—A fickle and false friend, against whom be on your guard.

Six of Hearts.—A generous but credulous person.

Five of Hearts.—Troubles caused by unfounded jealousy.

Four of Hearts.—A person not easily won.

Three of Hearts.—Sorrow caused by a person's own imprudence.

Two of Hearts.—Great success, but equal care and attention needed to secure it.

Ace of Spades.—Great misfortune, spite.

King of Spades.—A dark, ambitious man.

Queen of Spades.—A malicious, dark woman, generally a widow.

Knave of Spades.—An indolent, envious person; a dark man's thoughts.

Ten of Spades.—Grief, imprisonment.

Nine of Spades.—A card of very bad import, foretelling sickness and misfortune.

Eight of Spades.—Warns a person to be cautious in his undertakings.

Seven of Spades.—Loss of a friend, attended with much trouble.

Six of Spades.—Wealth through industry.

Five of Spades.—Shows that a bad temper requires correcting.

Four of Spades.—Sickness.

Three of Spades.—A journey.

Two of Spades.—A removal.

The court cards of Hearts and Diamonds usually represent persons of fair complexion—Clubs and Spades the opposite.[39]

Any picture-card between two others of equal value, as two Tens, two Aces, etc., denotes that the person represented by that card runs the risk of imprisonment.

Signification of Different Cards of the same Denomination[40]

Four Aces coming together, or following each other, announce danger, failure in business and sometimes imprisonment. If one or more of them be reversed, the danger will be lessened, but that is all.

Three Aces coming in the same manner, signify good tidings; if reversed, folly.

Two Aces.—A plot; if reversed, it will not succeed.

Four Kings.—Honours, preferment, good appointments. Reversed, the good things will be of less value, but will arrive earlier.

Three Kings.—A consultation on important business, the result of which will be highly satisfactory; if reversed, success will be doubtful.[41]

Two Kings.—A partnership in business; if reversed, a dissolution of the same. Sometimes this only denotes friendly projects.

Four Queens.—Company, society; one or more reversed denotes that the entertainment will not go off well.

Three Queens.—Friendly calls; reversed—chattering and scandal, or deceit.

Two Queens.—A meeting between friends; reversed—poverty, and troubles in which one will involve the other.

Four Knaves.—A noisy party, mostly young people; reversed—a drinking bout.

Three Knaves.—False friends; reversed—a quarrel with some low person.

Two Knaves.—Evil intentions; reversed—danger.

Four Tens.—Great success in projected enterprises; reversed—the success will not be so brilliant, but still it will be sure.

Three Tens.—Improper conduct; reversed—failure.

Two Tens.—Change of trade or profession; reversed—denotes that the prospect is only a distant one.

Four Nines.—A great surprise; reversed—a public dinner.

Three Nines.—Joy, fortune, health; reversed—wealth lost by imprudence.

Two Nines.—A little gain; reversed—trifling losses at cards.

Four Eights.—A short journey; reversed—the return of a friend or relative.

Three Eights.—Thoughts of marriage; reversed—folly, flirtation.

Two Eights.—A brief love-dream; reversed—small pleasures and trifling pains.

Four Sevens.—Intrigues among servants or low people, threats, snares and disputes; reversed—that their malice will be impotent to harm, for the punishment will fall on themselves.

Three Sevens.—Sickness, premature old age; reversed—slight and brief indispo-
sition.

Two Sevens.—Levity; reversed—regret.

N.B.—In order to know whether the Ace, Ten, Nine, Eight and Seven of
Diamonds are reversed, it is better to make a small pencil-mark on each to
show which is the top of the card.

It requires no great effort to commit these significations to memory, but it
must be remembered that they are only as the alphabet is to the printed book;
a little attention and practice, however, will soon enable the learner to form
these mystic letters into words, and words into phrases—in other language, to
assemble the cards together, and then read the events, past and to come, which
their symbols pretend to reveal.

Having given the signification of the various cards, I will now proceed
to describe the manner of their employment. After having well shuffled, cut
them three times, and lay them out in rows of nine cards each. Select any King
or Queen you please to represent yourself,[42] and wherever you find that card
placed, count nine cards every way, reckoning it as one;[43] and every ninth card
will prove the prophetic one. Before beginning to count, study well the disposition of the cards, according to their individual and relative signification.
If a married woman consult the cards, she must make her husband the King
of the same suit of which she is Queen; but if a single woman, she may make
any favourite male friend King of whatever suit she pleases.[44] As the Knaves of
the various suits denote the thoughts of the persons represented by the picture
cards of a corresponding colour, they should also be counted from.

To Tell Whether You Will Get Your Wish

To try whether you will get your wish, shuffle the cards well, all the time keeping your thoughts fixed upon whatever wish you may have formed. Cut them once, and remark what card you cut; shuffle them again, and deal out into three parcels. Examine each of these in turn, and if you find the card you turned up[45] next to either the one representing yourself, the Ace of Hearts, or the Nine of Hearts, you will get your wish.[46] If it be in the same parcel with any of these, without being next them, there is a chance of your wish coming to pass at some more distant period; but if the Nine of Spades should make its appearance,[47] you may count on disappointment.

INTRODUCTION TO
"SOME ENGLISH METHODS
OF TELLING"

from Card Fortune Telling

This essay is extracted from chapter 4 of a book by Charles Platt titled *Card Fortune Telling: A Lucid Treatise Dealing with All the Popular and More Abstruse Methods*. It was published at London by W. Foulsham & Co. and is undated, but it appears to be from around 1920. Concerning the author, almost no information exists other than the assertion that he was born in 1865.[48] He was the author of other books, among them a book on palmistry, another on chess and draughts, and one on pop psychology. Unfortunately for his posthumous celebrity, he is not the most prominent man of his period to bear his name.

I've included this material from Platt because it illuminates the method of divination by nines that was mentioned so casually in the Chambers essay and glossed over by both Taylor and Waite. This method may be profitably applied to divinations using the Tarot.

VI.
"SOME ENGLISH METHODS OF TELLING"

by

CHARLES PLATT

(*Card Fortune Telling*, c. 1920, pp. 53–61)

Although Madame Lenormand's method is wide-spread and popular, there are many other fascinating ways for dealing the cards. To make a change, we now give a method which can be followed with the full pack.

Of the different suits, Clubs stand generally for happiness and rarely are of bad omen. Next come Hearts, which are not so deep in their significance and show joy, liberality, good temper. Diamonds denote delay, quarrels, annoyances; while Spades are the fateful suit, and signify grief, misfortune, illness, death. It is important to pick up the cards quite haphazard, as those which are reversed in the pack have quite a different significance. Such cards as the Ace, Ten, Nine, Eight, etc., of Diamonds should have a small pencil mark to show the top.

Shuffle the pack well, cut the cards three times, and lay them out in rows of nine cards each. Select a King or Queen to represent the person who is consulting you—Hearts representing blonde types; Diamonds the ordinary fair people;[49] Clubs the brunettes, and Spades the very dark ones. Some well-known users of the cards allow their consultant to choose any King or Queen to represent themselves—this, of course, must be done before the cards are touched. If preferred, the pack can be cut, and the exposed card would indicate the suit to be used.

Having dealt your cards in the above way, look for the type card and count nine every way, reckoning the type card as number one. The cards thus indicated will be the prophetic ones. In the case of a married woman, the King of the same suit of which she is the Queen would represent her husband, and should be counted from in a similar way, as the marriage partner's influence is naturally of great importance. In the case of a married man, the reverse applies, the Queen of his own suit representing his wife.

The Jack of the type suit shows the thoughts of the person, and they also should be counted from.

The meaning to be attached to the various prophetic cards is as follows:

THE CLUB SUIT

Ace.—Peace of mind, happiness, a success card.

King.—The influence in your life of a dark man, upright, faithful and affectionate.

Queen.—A brunette, gentle and pleasing.

Jack.—The thought of the King for the questioner. In the case of any court card, you should count nine in every direction from it for the prophetic cards for your guidance.

Ten.—Unexpected good.

Nine.—Disobedience to the wishes of friends.

Eight.—A warning against speculation.

Seven.—Good fortune and happiness if you are careful in your dealings with someone of the opposite sex.

Six.—Business success.

Five.—A prudent marriage.

Four.—Be careful of changes in your plans or mode of life.

Three.—Indicates a second marriage.

Two.—A disappointment, but not a serious one, unless other prophetic cards are bad.

Take notice of all the prophetic cards before making any conclusions from them.

THE HEART SUIT

Ace.—This indicates your home, and if Spade cards touch it quarrelling is foretold. If other Hearts are next to it they foretell friendships and true affection. If Diamonds, money and distant friends—and if Clubs, feasting and merry making.

King.—A fair man, good-natured but rash.

Queen.—A fair woman.

Jack.—This covers the thoughts of the dearest person of the one who consults the cards.

Ten.—Refers to children. It also softens the bad tidings of the cards near it and increases the good.

Nine.—Money and position. Also, where the cards are consulted about one single question or wish, the Nine of Hearts is the key card upon which all depends.

Eight.—Pleasure, companions.

Seven.—A false friend.

Six.—A generous person.

Five.—Troubles caused by jealousy.

Four.—A person near you, not easily convinced.

Three.—Sorrow caused by your own indiscretion.

Two.—Success, but it will need care.

THE DIAMOND SUIT

Ace.—A letter. You must look at the surrounding cards to judge the result.

King and Queen.—A fair man or woman.

Jack.—Thoughts as before.

Ten.—Money.

Nine.—Travel.

Eight.—A late marriage.

Seven.—Unpleasant rumours, scandal.

Six.—Early marriage and possible widowhood.

Five.—Unexpected news.

Four.—Trouble through friends, a secret betrayed.

Three.—Quarrels and legal troubles.

Two.—An engagement, but against the wishes of friends.

THE SPADE SUIT

Ace.—Great Misfortune. Death when the card is reversed.

King, Queen and Jack.—Dark people and their thoughts.[50]

Ten.—Grief and trouble.

Nine.—Sickness and misfortune, a most unlucky card.

Eight.—A warning to be careful.

Seven.—Loss of a friend, much trouble.

Six.—Money through hard work.[51]

Five.—A bad temper that causes trouble.

Four.—Sickness.

Three.—A journey.

Two.—A removal.

Be careful to notice if two or more cards of the same value come together.[52]

Two Aces.—Trickery.

Three Aces.—Good news.

Four Aces.—Danger and failure.

Two Kings.—A business partnership or the joining with a friend in some enterprise.

Three Kings.—Important business, generally successful.

Four Kings.—Rewards, dignities, public honours.

Two Queens.—A meeting with a friend.

Three Queens.—Visits.

Four Queens.—An entertainment of some sort.

Two Jacks.—Evil intentions.

Three Jacks.—False friends.

Four Jacks.—A noisy party, drinking.

Two Tens.—Change of profession or business.

Three Tens.—Indiscreet conduct.

Four Tens.—Great and certain success.

Two Nines.—A small gain.

Three Nines.—Good health and fortune.

Four Nines.—A great surprise.

Two Eights.—A brief love dream.

Three Eights.—Contemplation of marriage.

Four Eights.—A short journey.

Two Sevens.—Indiscretion.

Three Sevens.—Sickness and failure of strength.

Four Sevens.—Trouble from servants or employees.

Should any of these cards be reversed, it greatly lessens the strength of the combination—thus, it would increase an evil influence, but would lessen or destroy a good one, and merely show that such a happy possibility had been lost.[53]

We stated that the cards carrying most meaning were the ninth cards in every direction, and we will make this quite clear by an illustration. Let us suppose that the fifty-two cards are arranged in rows of nine as follows:

7C	7S	KS	AD	AH	JC	4H	8H	JS
2D	3D	2H	6H	KD	5C	2C	5S	3H
5H	6D	4C	QC	5D	3S	KH	4D	10S
9S	QS	8D	6C	AS	QD	KC	JH	6S
9H	10D	8C	7D	AC	9C	9D	JD	10H
10C	8S	QH	7H	4S	3C	2S		

A fifty-two card method.

If the King of Hearts represents the person who consults the cards, we shall find this key card in the third row; it is indicated as KH. We can now count nine to the right, reckoning the key card as one. Our third card, however, finishes the row, so we have four routes open to us: (1) to turn upwards and keep to the outer cards, in which case the ninth card would be the Ace of Hearts which we know to represent the home, and as no Spade card adjoins it, all should go well. (2) We can turn downwards and keep to the outer cards, in which case we reach the Seven of Hearts, indicating a false friend, and touching this card are a fair woman, a warning against speculation, unpleasant rumours, a success card (Ace of Clubs), an illness—the presence of the Ace of Clubs just saving us from a very ugly series of disasters. (3) We can turn upwards, and continue along the second row, in which case we reach the Six of Hearts, a generous person, which is surrounded by a brunette woman, a warning of care in changing plans, a note of success if care is taken, a dark man, a letter, a fair man, and unexpected news—other people are far too much mixed up in the life and plans of the enquirer and great care is necessary. (4) We can turn downwards and proceed along the fourth row and thus reach the Six of Clubs, business success, which is surrounded by unpleasant rumours, warning against speculation, a late marriage, a warning against change of plans, a brunette woman, unexpected news, a fatality, and a success card (Ace of Clubs)—a most unpleasant mixture, just saved from disaster by the Ace of Clubs!

The key card itself, the King of Hearts, is surrounded by a dark man, a fair woman, a journey, a prudent marriage, a slight disappointment, temper, trouble with friends, the thoughts of someone—so it seems reasonable to assume that a marriage, rather late in life, probably with a woman as fair as or fairer than himself (the Queens of Hearts, Clubs, and Diamonds are all among the cards to which we have referred, but the only Jack, for thoughts, is that of Hearts), and a fresh home, made after a journey, will see our subject through his troubles, but that bad temper and quarrelling will certainly be one result.

It is a recognised rule in "telling the cards" (as it is called) that they should only be consulted again after an interval of nine days on behalf of any one person. But it is quite a frequent practice to mix the pack thoroughly, re-shuffle and cut and deal as before for a second and a third time at one sitting, carefully noting all the cards that come into view each time, and thus averaging the result of the three attempts.

It would, however, be wiser to vary the counting of the nines instead—thus, for a second attempt, you could count to the left instead of to the right; or you could count upwards or downwards from the King of Hearts. All four ways would lead to a different series of cards, and thus a greater degree of accuracy would certainly be attained.

Let us examine the results very briefly—thus, by counting to the right, as already worked out in detail, the cards that we come in contact with are: Hearts—Ace, Two, Six, Seven, Jack, Queen. Clubs—Ace, Two, Four, Five, Six, Eight, Jack, Queen, King. Diamonds—Ace, Four, Five, Seven, Eight, Queen, King. Spades—Ace, Three, Four, Five, King.

The following simple table shows at a glance the results of all four methods:

HEART SUIT.
Right Count: 2, 6, 7, J, Q, A.
Left Count: 2, 5, 9.
Up Count: 2, 3, 4, 5, 6, 8, J.
Down Count: 3, 7, 9, J, Q.

CLUB SUIT.
Right Count: 2, 4, 5, 6, 8, J, Q, K, A.
Left Count: 4, 7, 8, 10.

Up Count: 2, 4, 5, 7, J.
Down Count: 3, 8, 9, 10, J, A.

DIAMOND SUIT.
Right Count: 4, 5, 7, 8, Q, K, A.
Left Count: 2, 3, 6, 8, 10.
Up Count: 2, 3, 4, 6, A.
Down Count: 4, 7, 9, 10, J, Q.

SPADE SUIT.
Right Count: 3, 4. 5, K, A.
Left Count: 7, 8, 9, Q, K.
Up Count: 5, 6, 7, 10, K.
Down Count: 2, 4, 5, 6, 8, 9, 10, Q.

The cards surrounding the Heart King are included in the right count in the above Table. It will be noticed that by following this full method of using the cards that four key cards are reached twice over—they obviously are the most important. They are the Three of Diamonds, showing quarrels and legal troubles; the Nine of Hearts, showing money and position; the Seven of Hearts representing a false friend ; and the Ten of Spades indicating grief and trouble. This confirms our previous reading that the enquirer will have much trouble and difficulty, but will eventually win his way through.

In the above Table it will also be noticed that certain cards appear once only—they are of little importance to the enquirer. Those that appear twice are seldom worth considering, but the really important are those that appear three or four times—the latter being very rare, of course. There are seven cards, however, that appear three times in the present experiment and we quote them in full.

HEART SUIT.
Two.—Success, but it will need care.
Jack.—Thoughts—this card appears next the Heart King.

CLUB SUIT.
Four.—Be careful of changes in plans.
Eight.—A warning against speculation.

DIAMOND SUIT.

Four.—Trouble through friends—this card also appears next the Heart King.

SPADE SUIT.

Five.—Temper and quarrelling—this also touches the enquirer's personal card.

King.—Obviously the dangerous friend.

In this way also we get a startling confirmation of our prediction, which is taken from actual experience and has proved correct.

The method of card divination that we have just described is known as the English—not because it originated over here, but to distinguish it from the many continental methods where only thirty-two cards are used.

Notes to Part Eight

1. William Andrew Chatto, *Facts and Speculations on the Origin and History of Playing Cards*, p. 116.

2. See Mother Bridget, *The Universal Dream Book* (1816), in which the English Method is described. In the preface of this work, the anonymous editor claimed to have found a manuscript titled "Mother Bridget's Last Legacy" near the cave of the celebrated Romani fortune-teller Mother Bridget. It is far more likely that the editor was the author and that the book has no connection of any kind with Mother Bridget.

3. Anonymous, *Jack the Gyant-Killer*, pp. 14–15.

4. Mary K. Greer makes this point in her blog, *Mary K. Greer's Tarot Blog*, in a post from April 1, 2008, called "Origins of Cartomancy (Playing Card Divination)," under the subheading "1863—Chambers's Book of Days," https://marykgreer.com/2008/04/01/origins-of-divination-with-playing-cards/.

5. "She clearly always used a piquet pack, i.e. a 32-card pack." Decker, Depaulis, and Dummett, *A Wicked Pack of Cards*, p. 124.

6. The method associated with Mademoiselle Le Normand by C. Thorpe uses 36 cards arranged in four rows of nine. "Lenormand's method employs 36 cards—the four deuces or twos are added to the usual [Piquet] pack, and the cards are laid out, in four rows of nine each." See Thorpe, *Card Fortune Telling*, pp. 41–53.

7. Robert Chambers, *The Book of Days: A Miscellany of Popular Antiquities*, vol. 1 (London & Edinburgh: W. & R. Chambers, 1863), p. 284.

8. Owen Davies, *Popular Magic: Cunning-folk in English History* (2003; repr., London: Hambledon Continuum, 2007), p. 47.

9. Phillip Breslaw, *Breslaw's Last Legacy; or, The Magical Companion*, 2nd ed. (London: printed for T. Moore, 1784), p. vii.

10. *The Conjuror's Magazine, or, Magical and Physiognomical Mirror* (August 1791), pp. 17–18. London: printed for W. Locke.

11. By "making yourself one," the author means that you begin your count of nine by counting "one" on the Queen, then "two" on the card beside it, and so on up to "nine." The assumption is that the person doing the reading is a woman and is thus represented in the card layout by one of the Queens. A man laying out the cards would "make himself" one of the Kings. The count of nine from the court card representing the querent is extended both to the right and to the left, and also upward and downward in the card layout, to arrive at a number of cards that are interpreted according to their meanings. It is described at greater length and much more lucidly in the last essay in part eight, "Some English Methods of Telling" by Charles Platt.

12. The method for determining whether a wish will come true is described at greater length in the fourth essay in part eight, "Fortune Telling with Common Playing Cards" by Ed. S. Taylor. There the card that confirms the fulfillment of the wish is the Nine of Hearts, not the Ace of Hearts, as it is in the Breslaw essay. The Nine of Hearts is known as the "wish card" for this reason. It also has its own independent meaning when encountered elsewhere in the layout, which Breslaw gives as "feasting," but which in Taylor is "wealth, and good position in society."

13. Owen Davies, *Witchcraft, Magic and Culture, 1736–1953* (Manchester and New York: Manchester University Press, 1999), p. 133. See Charles Mackey, *Memoirs of Extraordinary Popular Delusions*, vol. 2, p. 301, the footnote.

14. Mother Bridget, *The Universal Dream Book*, p. 2.

15. Owen Davies, *Witchcraft, Magic and Culture, 1736–1953*, pp. 134–135.

16. If you compare this text with the same place in the essay from *Breslaw's Last Legacy*, you will see that the author in his haste to copy has dropped out a necessary block of words and in this way managed to destroy the meaning. The text should read, "She must make her husband the King of the same suit she is Queen of; but if a single woman tries it, she may make her sweetheart what King she likes."

17. Here, "incontinence" is used to signify a lack of restraint or self-control, not a weak bladder.

18. Which is to say, someone fond of lovemaking.

19. Robert Chambers, *The Book of Days*, vol. 1, p. 282.

20. The original painting upon which this engraving was based was by Lucas van Leyden, not by van Eyck. The engraving appeared in the French periodical *Le Magasin Pittoresque* in volume X, the October 1842 issue, p. 324. This error was first noticed by Detleff Hoffmann in the 1970s. In 1980 Michael Dummett included the information in his *Game of Tarot* (p. 94). There is dispute as to whether the woman

is performing cartomancy or playing a card game in the original painting by van Leyden. The French text under the *Le Magasin Pittoresque* engraving reads in part, "Museum of Nantes—Philippe-le-Bon consults a card reader, by Van Eyck," but in the text under the Chambers engraving, this has become the "Archduke of Austria consulting a fortune teller."

21. An English expression derived from an Old French term that literally means "from head to foot." It signified a man armed for battle from head to toe, or fully armed.

22. From William Rowland's *Judicial Astrology Judicially Condemned* (London: 1652). This sad tale of Henry Cuffe was earlier related by John Melton in his *Astrologaster; or, The Figure-Caster* (1620). Fred Gettings in *The Book of Tarot* (London: Triune Books, 1973), pp. 9–10, makes the assumption that the three cards drawn by Cuffe, which the author of the Chambers essay calls "knaves," were actually Tarot trumps; specifically, the Devil, Justice, and the Hanged Man. This seems to me very unlikely, since the Tarot was not widely used for purposes of cartomancy in the sixteenth century—Cuffe was hanged at Tyburn in 1601, twenty years after this fateful card reading, which must have taken place around 1580.

23. Francesco Marcolini (1500–1559) was an Italian printer and writer. The work referred to is *Le sorti di Francesco Marcolino da Forli intitolate Giardino di pensieri allo illustrissimo signore hercole Estense duca di Ferrara*, published in 1540.

24. It was a proverbial expression in Victorian England that "a lean sorrow is worse than a fat sorrow." By this was meant that sorrow is always harder to endure on an empty stomach—that is to say, when there is no money to buy food.

25. See note 24, above.

26. The term "in *esse*" means something that exists; "in *posse*" means something in potential that does not have actual existence. Our anonymous author appears to be distinguishing between lovers who have (*esse*) or have not yet (*posse*) found each other; that is to say, between lovers actual and lovers potential.

27. The Latin term *ad libitum* means "at one's pleasure" or, in this instance, "as much as is desired."

28. Sepharial, who used a reduced deck of 32 cards, divined with them by laying out 12 cards in a circle counterclockwise on the houses of the zodiac, beginning with Aries on the left. He then laid cards 13, 14, 15, and 16 clockwise in the center of the circle so that these four cards defined a cross, and placed card 17 in the center of this cross. Cards 18–29 were dealt just outside the circle of the zodiac counterclockwise, as before, beginning with Aries, so that each house ended up with two cards. The final three cards left over are "what goes out of the life." This method, which he called the Wheel of Fortune, is described and illustrated in his book *A Manual of Occultism*, part 2, chap. 4. In the same chapter, he also used a method which he called the Star, in which a card representing the consultant is placed in

the center of the table. From the remaining deck, successive cards are dealt above the consultant card below it; above the card above it, below the card below it; to its left, to its right; to the left of the card on the left, to the right of the card on the right; in the upper-left corner, the upper-right corner, and the lower-left corner, the lower-right corner. The 13th card from the pack is dealt on top of the consultant card. He called this last card the "court of final appeal." If a good card, it gives a favorable outcome, especially if it is a Heart. Both these "circular" methods would work using a full deck of 52 cards. See Sepharial, *A Manual of Occultism* (London: William Rider & Son, 1914), pp. 240–244.

29. Rev. Ed. S. Taylor, *The History of Playing Cards* (London: John Camden Hotten, 1865).

30. Ibid., pp. 471–478.

31. The person doing the reading recombines the three packets in the reverse order to which they were cut by the querent, then deals them out.

32. A Latin term meaning "in accordance with the standard practice of the profession."

33. By "card first out," I take our author to mean the card that was revealed by the initial cut of the cards, before the pack was reshuffled and divided into three piles.

34. It is curious to note that the description given by Taylor of the use of the wish card, the Nine of Hearts, is much more detailed and useful than the remarks concerning it provided in the Chambers essay. Taylor must have relied on an external source of information for this point, which leads one to wonder if the essay published by Chambers was the original and complete version of the essay.

35. Quoted from Chambers's *Book of Days*, vol. 1 (the entry for February 21), p. 284.

36. The *Grand Orient* is the name of a Grand Lodge of Freemasons in France. It is the largest and oldest order of Freemasonry in continental Europe, having been created in 1728.

37. Arthur Edward Waite, *The Pictorial Key to the Tarot* (1910; repr., New York: Samuel Weiser, 1980), p. 262.

38. S. L. MacGregor Mathers, *The Tarot* (1888; repr., New York: Samuel Weiser, n.d., p. 21.

39. Waite does not distinguish between the complexions of the court cards in the suits of Diamonds and Hearts, calling both "fair." Similarly, he makes no distinction in complexions of the court cards in the suits of Spades and Clubs, calling both "dark." A finer gradation in complexion was provided by the Chambers essay. Diamonds are "very fair," Hearts are "fair," Clubs are "dark," and Spades are "very dark." All of these descriptions from the nineteenth century should be understood to have originally applied to white Europeans. "Very dark" would be a man or woman with olive skin, black hair, and dark eyes. "Very fair" would be a man or woman with pale, translucent skin, blond hair, and gray or blue eyes.

40. Notice that the multiples of the same cards stop at seven. From this, it is obvious that Waite derived his meanings for the quadruplicates, triplicities, and pairs from a text on card divination that uses the truncated deck of 32 cards.

41. The three Kings and their meaning were omitted from Waite's list of multiples by some oversight during publication of the 4th edition of *A Manual of Cartomancy*. It appears to me that Waite must also have placed the meaning for the missing three Kings on the four Kings. I have shifted Waite's meaning for the four Kings back to the three Kings, and have inserted on the four Kings the meaning that appears in P. R. S. Foli's *Fortune-Telling by Cards* (New York: R. P. Fenno & Co., 1915), p. 30. By the way, this same error occurs in the 1891 edition published by George Redway. How the book could have gone through so many editions without this error being corrected is a mystery only Grand Orient could have answered.

42. This contradicts instructions in the previous essays, where the court card that represents the querent is selected on the basis of complexion. Although, on this matter, see the Platt essay in part eight, "Some English Methods of Telling," where several options are given for the selection of the card that signifies the querent.

43. By "reckoning it as one," Waite meant that you start counting on the court card that represents the querent, by counting it as "one," and then continue on to the ninth card.

44. The cards chosen to represent the querent, the spouse, or the lover should be selected and agreed upon before beginning the divination.

45. The card revealed by the cut of the cards. When Waite uses the term *turned up*, he means that the deck of cards is cut, and the upper section held in the hand of the person who does the cutting is inverted to reveal the card on its bottom. That is the card "turned up."

46. Notice that Waite gives two wish cards, the usual Nine of Hearts and also the Ace of Hearts that we previously encountered in the first essay in part eight, "The "Art of Fortune-Telling by Cards" from *Breslaw's Last Legacy*.

47. If the Nine of Spades should be in the same packet of cards that contains the card representing the querent, the result will be disappointment.

48. Platt's date of birth is given as 1865 at the link for his book *Card Fortune Telling* on Internet Archive, archive.org/details/cardfortunetelli00plat/page/n6.

49. Here it appears that Hearts denote the fairest complexion, and Diamonds one that is less fair. This is opposite to the designation of these two red suits in the previous essays.

50. Platt has used a kind of shorthand here—he means that the King of Spades stands for a dark man, the Queen for a dark woman, and the Jack for their thoughts.

51. It appears that Platt drew on Waite's *A Manual of Cartomancy* as one of his sources. He reproduced Waite's odd meaning for the Six of Spades.

52. Again the multiples stop with the Sevens, as they must when a reduced deck of only 32 cards is used, the Sixes, Fives, Fours, Treys, and Deuces being discarded. Platt's meanings for the multiples are the same upright meanings given by Waite, with only slightly different wording. It is interesting to note that Platt's meaning for three Kings is Waite's upright meaning for four Kings, but in different words. Platt's meanings for the multiples of the Kings agree with those of P. R. S. Foli, which leads me to suspect that Waite not only omitted the three Kings but also placed the meaning for the three Kings on the four Kings. I have corrected these errors in the Waite essay.

53. Platt is indicating here that a reversal does not reverse the meaning of a card, but always intensifies difficulties. It is usual in modern Tarot divination to interpret a reversed card as weaker in its influence—thus a good card reversed is read as less good, and a bad card reversed as less bad. Following Platt's direction, a good card reversed would be less good, but a bad card reversed would be even worse.

BIOGRAPHICAL NOTES

Alliette, Jean-Baptiste (1738–1791). Pen name: Etteilla, often misspelled Eteilla or Etteila. He was born in Paris of working-class parents, and took up his father's profession of seed merchant. At some point he transitioned from selling seeds to making wigs, which at the time was a lucrative and necessary profession since all the nobility of France wore powdered wigs. As a sideline he began to tell fortunes with common playing cards. This soon overshadowed his wig-making. In 1770 he wrote a book on how to tell fortunes with playing cards. He premiered his professional name, *Etteilla*, which is *Alliette* spelled backward, in the title of this book: *Etteilla, ou Manière de Se Récréer avec un Jeu de Cartes (Etteilla, or a Way to Entertain Yourself with a Deck of Cards).*

Reading Court de Gébelin's essay on the Tarot in 1781 turned his interest to these more ornamental cards, and in 1785 Alliette produced his own work titled *Manière de Se Récréer avec le Jeu de Cartes Nommées Tarots (How to Entertain Yourself with the Pack of Cards Called Tarots).* He created his own Tarot designs, which differ greatly from the traditional designs, and included a special card he called the *Etteilla*, after himself. (One cannot doubt his gift for self-promotion, whatever his talents as a card reader may have been.)

Alliette holds the distinction of being the first known occultist to use the Tarot for the purpose of divination in a professional capacity. Although his version of the Tarot is still being published today, his modifications have not stood up well over time and are not considered to have any serious value by most modern occultists.

Benjamine, Elbert (1882–1951). Pen name: C. C. Zain. His birth name was Benjamin Parker Williams, but he changed it to Elbert Benjamine when he became serious about the study of occultism to avoid embarrassing his relatives. His father was a physician and a deacon in the Church of Christ in Adel, Iowa. A fascination with hypnotism as a teenager led to the study of astrology. He became interested in the occult in a more general sense after reading *The Light of Egypt* by the spirit medium Thomas H. Burgoyne. This led him to the Hermetic Brotherhood of Luxor, which Burgoyne had helped to found. Burgoyne was dead, but a branch of the Outer Circle of the HBL existed in Denver. Benjamine was induced to join the Brotherhood in 1910 after being psychically contacted by the Interior Circle of spiritual beings that presided over it. The spirits informed him that they wanted him to receive and record their future teachings.

Benjamine moved to Los Angeles in 1915 and created the Brotherhood of Light, the members of which met in secret. He began to write up a series of lessons in occultism transmitted to him by the spirits of the Interior Circle of the Hermetic Brotherhood of Luxor. For these lessons, which numbered 210, he used the pen name C. C. Zain. He chose the name *Zain* for numerological reasons. In 1918 the Brotherhood of Light went public and published a set of black-and-white Tarot cards derived from *Practical Astrology* by the Comte C. de Saint-Germain (Edgar de Valcourt-Vermont), whose 1901 trump designs were copies of the 1896 Falconnier designs drawn by Maurice Otto Wegener. Zain gave two lectures on his teachings every week in a rented classroom in downtown Los Angeles, and conducted a mail order occult correspondence course from his house in the hills.

The Sacred Tarot, published in 1927, was compiled from Hermetic Brotherhood of Light lessons numbered 22 to 33. These had been separately published in 1918. In 1932 the elected officials of Los Angeles County planned to ban astrology, which was being abused by confidence artists. To avoid this ban, Benjamine reorganized the Brotherhood of Light into the Church of Light. As a church it was immune to local political meddling under the US Constitution. In 1936 Benjamine published a new edition of *The Sacred Tarot*, with the black-and-white card images redrawn by the artist Gloria Beresford, who was a member of his church. Lesson number 48, on the Kabbalah, was added to the front of the book, which was otherwise unchanged.

Benjamine died of a brain aneurysm in 1951, but the Church of Light continues to exist, relocated in 2005 to Albuquerque, New Mexico, and still issues its correspondence courses through the mail, assigning various certificates to members who pass examinations and qualify for higher grades.

Blavatsky, Helena Petrovna, née Helena Petrovna von Hahn (1831–1891). She was more commonly known as Madame Blavatsky, or by her initials as H. P. Blavatsky. She was born into a noble Russian family in the town of Yekaterinoslav, in what is now Ukraine. Even in childhood she was strongly mediumistic and claimed to be able to see things others could not. At age seventeen she married the government official Nikifor Vladimirovich Blavatsky, a man in his forties, but the marriage did not last. She left him and spent the next decade traveling the world, studying different systems of esoteric belief, including, by her own account, those of Tibet. In 1871 she attempted to establish a Spiritualism society in Egypt, but was quickly exposed as a fraud.

In 1873 Blavatsky went to New York, where she met Henry Steel Olcott and William Quan Judge. The three established the Theosophical Society in 1875. Her first major piece of writing, *Isis Unveiled*, was published in 1877, and the following year she became an American citizen. She took up residence in India in 1879, where she found a more welcoming environment for her Theosophical teachings. In 1888 and 1889 she published the two volumes of her second great work, *The Secret Doctrine*, through her own publishing house, the Theosophical Publishing Company.

Much of the influence of Theosophy around the world was due to the large number of essays and books published by the Society, both in its various magazines, such as *Lucifer* and *The Theosophist*, and through its book publishing company. These included not only Theosophical writings but also esoteric writings by non-Theosophists. Due to the explosion of Spiritualism, the late nineteenth century was a pregnant time for all manner of esoteric speculations on both sides of the Atlantic, and many occultists who would go on to form their own fraternities got their beginnings in Theosophical doctrine.

All her life, Blavatsky had used trickery to lend her mediumship more importance, and in 1884 she was finally exposed by a married couple, Emma and Alexis Coulomb, who had known her since her early fraudulent mediumship days in Cairo in 1871. The Coulombs worked for the Society but came to believe that Blavatsky was treating them poorly and not paying them enough. They tried to blackmail her, and when she failed to pay and threw them out, they did a public exposé on Blavatsky that led to an official inquiry. The results were published in the Hodgson Report, the main finding of which was that Blavatsky had committed fraud in her claimed communications with spiritual entities. Although the Theosophical Society continued to grow and Blavatsky would go on from the inquiry to bring forth *The Secret Doctrine*, her reputation as a spiritual leader never fully recovered from this investigation.

Boissard, Jean Jacques (1528–1602). Boissard was a French antiquary and Latin poet who was born in Besançon, France, and studied in Louvain. He gathered together a collection of Roman statues, monuments, and other antiquities, and wrote a number of beautifully illustrated works, among them *Romanae urbis topographia et antiquitates* (1597–1602), which contains many fine engravings of the pieces in his collection, views of ancient Rome, Roman buildings and Roman monuments. He is not to be confused with his kinsman Robert Boissard (1570–1603), an engraver born in Valence, France, whose engravings appear in some of Jean Jacques Boissard's works.

Breslaw, Phillip (1726–1803). Breslaw was a German-born Jew who became renowned for his mind-reading act. He was the first stage magician to do mind-reading, and was also noted for his card tricks. He gained a reputation first by performing in Ireland, then at age thirty-three he moved to England, where he took up residence in London. His career spanned more than four decades. It is unlikely that very much, if anything, in *Breslaw's Last Legacy* was actually written by Phillip Breslaw.

Brodie-Innes, John William (1848–1923). Brodie-Innes was an Edinburgh lawyer who joined the Hermetic Order of the Golden Dawn in 1890, taking the Latin occult motto *Sub Spe* (Under Hope). He became a prominent member of its Amon-Ra Temple in Edinburgh and eventually served as one of the human Chiefs of the Order. (There were nominally three human Chiefs and three spiritual Chiefs. The original three human Chiefs were the three founders of the Order: S. L. MacGregor Mathers, W. Wynn Westcott, and William Robert Woodman.)

Case, Paul Foster (1884–1954). Born in Farpoint, New York, the son of a librarian and deacon of a Congregationalist church, Case was taught music by his mother and began to play organ in his father's church at an early age. He went on to become an accomplished violinist and orchestra conductor. A series of lucid dreams in childhood sparked his interest in the occult. In 1900 he began to study the Tarot. Over the following decade, he took up the practice of yoga postures and yoga breathing. In 1907 he began to correspond by mail with the esoteric writer William W. Atkinson, one of the conjectured authors of *The Kybalion* who may have cowritten this work with Case. (The authors of the work are anonymous.) He published *The Secret Doctrine of the Tarot* as a series of articles in the occult periodical *The Word* in 1916. Case was invited to join the Thoth-Hermes Lodge in Chicago of the Alpha et Omega, an offshoot of the Golden Dawn, in 1918, by Michael James Whitty, the editor of the periodical *Azoth*. He quickly rose to the rank of Praemonstrator, but in 1921 he was asked to resign from the A. O. by Moïna Mathers, who objected to Case's teachings concerning sexual symbolism. The following year, Case began to issue a series of correspondence courses on magic and the Tarot, and in 1923 he formed the School of Ageless Wisdom, the precursor to the Builders of the Adytum, an esoteric order that continues to exist today. Most of Case's teachings are direct offshoots of the Golden Dawn teachings and concern the Tarot, the Kabbalah, and Hermetic philosophy.

Clulow, George (1835–1919). Clulow and Brodie-Innes were fellow members of the Sette of Odd Volumes, an English dining club for bibliophiles founded in 1878. Clulow served as its seventh president in 1886, and Brodie-Innes was the club's master of the rolls. Clulow was a maker of playing cards who amassed a vast card collection. The collection was acquired by the Vanderbilt Libraries in 2017. Clulow wrote *The Origin and Manufacture of Playing Cards*, a slender booklet published in 1889 based on a speech he gave on May 8 of that year before the Society of Arts in London. In it, he repeated the common belief of the time that cards had been introduced into Europe by the Romanies.

Collins, Mabel (1851–1927). She was an English Theosophist born in St. Peters Port, Guernsey, the author of the nonfiction self-help book *Light on the Path* (1885) and forty-five other books with Theosophical trappings. She was a spirit medium who conducted séances. In 1881 she read Blavatsky's book *Isis Unveiled*, and in 1884 had several meetings with Blavatsky in London. Blavatsky convinced her to abandon mediumship as dangerous and came to live in Collins's cottage in Norwood, where the two founded the Theosophical periodical *Lucifer*, which Collins edited from 1887 to 1889. *Light on the Path*, which became an immediate bestseller, was claimed by C. W. Leadbeater and Annie Besant to have been dictated to Collins by the Master Hilarion, one of Blavatsky's Mahatmas, or enlightened spirit teachers. Between 1885 and 1975, the book was issued eighteen times in English editions.

Constant, Alphonse Louis (1810–1875). Pen name: Éliphas Lévi. Lévi was the most prominent French occultist of the nineteenth century. His influence on modern magic has been enormous through his numerous writings and through the authority he exerted over other French and English occultists of his period. Born in Paris, the son of a shoemaker, he studied to enter the Roman Catholic priesthood, but became romantically entangled with a women in 1836 and was never ordained. He began to publish radical political tracts, advocating what he described as "neo-Catholic communism," and was thrown into prison for it. Disillusionment with politics caused him to turn his attentions to occultism. His great work, *Dogme et Rituel de la Haute Magie,* was published in two separate parts in 1854 (*Dogme*) and 1855 (*Rituel*), then combined in a two-volume set in 1856. A. E. Waite translated it into English in 1896 under the title *Transcendental Magic.* Each volume has 22 chapters to match the 22 Tarot trumps. In it, Lévi expressed his views about the Tarot trumps and gave descriptions of the cards. His drawing of Baphomet in this work presently forms the idol of modern American Satanists in a slightly modified form–the Satanists removed the female breasts.

Diogenes of Sinope (412–323 BCE). Also called Diogenes the Cynic, he was a Cynic philosopher famed throughout the ancient world for his original sayings and doings. He had a complete disregard for common customs. Diogenes lived on the streets and took shelter when it rained in an old clay pot that was turned on its side, an image that appears in some older Tarot packs—see the trump the Sun in the D'Este cards, a fifteenth-century deck (Kaplan, *The Encyclopedia of Tarot,* vol. 1, p. 118). His only possession was a wooden bowl, but one day he saw a boy using his hand to cup water to his mouth to drink, so he smashed his bowl in disgust as an unnecessary burden. He is said to have urinated on those he disliked and defecated at theaters during performances, and to have masturbated whenever he chose in full view of passersby. Diogenes is most famous for carrying a lamp around in broad daylight. When asked what he was doing, he replied that he was "looking for a man." This is usually interpreted to mean that he was looking for an honest man, but he may have been seeking a man with whom to have sex.

Encausse, Gérard Anaclet Vincent (1865–1916). Pen name: Papus. He was born in Spain but was transported to France at the age of four when his father, a chemist, took up residence in Paris. For a short while in 1884–1885, he was a member of Madame Blavatsky's Theosophical Society, but he disliked its emphasis on Eastern mysticism, and left it to study the magic of the West. In 1888 (the year the first temple of the Hermetic Order of the Golden Dawn was established in London), he cofounded in Paris the Kabbalistic Order of the Rose-Croix. After the Golden Dawn opened a temple in Paris, Encausse became a member. In 1894 he received the degree of Doctor of Medicine from the University of Paris and opened his own clinic, which became prosperous. He was closely connected with influential French occultists Oswald Wirth and Stanislas de Guaita. His primary writing on the Tarot is *Clef Absolue des Sciences Occultes: Le Tarot des Bohémiens, le plus ancien livre du monde* (Paris: Carré, 1889). This is usually known in English as *The Tarot of the Bohemians*.

Farr, Florence (1860–1917). Farr was a prominent member of the Golden Dawn for many years. As a young woman, she tried her hand at teaching but did not like it, and turned to the theater. She became a professional actress on the London stage. In 1884 she married Edward Emery, a fellow actor, but they did not get along and she soon separated from him, although they were not divorced until 1895. She continued to use his name for the rest of her life. She was initiated into the Golden Dawn through her lover, the poet W. B. Yeats, in 1890, taking as her occult motto the Latin phrase *Sapientia Sapienti Dono Data* (Wisdom Is Given to the Wise as a Gift), and became active in the Order's management. She led the Sphere Group, a subgroup of occultists within the Golden Dawn who met regularly to scry the astral planes and ascend through the Tarot trumps up the pathways on the Tree of Life.

An emancipated woman for her time, Farr cared nothing for social propriety. George Bernard Shaw remarked in 1894 that she had amassed a list of fourteen lovers. He was in a position to know, being one of them. Even though she was magnetically attractive to men, sex bored her and left her indifferent. Her passions were ritual magic and the study of ancient Egypt. She was the author of *Egyptian Magic*, a collection of bits and pieces of occult Egyptian lore that was first published in W. Wynn Westcott's *Collectanea Hermetica*, the series of 1896. It was republished in book form in 1982 by the Aquarian Press of Wellingborough, Northamptonshire. In her final years, Farr returned to her original career, when she became the principal of a girl's school in Ceylon (present-day Sri Lanka), where she died.

Gichtel, Johann Georg (1638–1710). Gichtel studied theology in Strasbourg and entered the profession of legal advocate, but abandoned it to teach a mystical form of Christianity. His criticism of Lutheranism, in particular of the Lutheran teaching of justification by faith alone, led to his banishment from Germany in 1665. After wandering stateless for two years, he settled in the Netherlands in 1667, but again aroused the ire of the local authorities and was forced to move. He took up residence in Amsterdam the following year, where he became an enthusiastic advocate for the mystical teachings of Jakob Böhme. He published Böhme's works in Amsterdam in two volumes, and attracted around himself a group of followers who called themselves Gichtelians. Gichtel's letters were collected and published under the title *Theosophia Practica* in 1701, then in an expanded form in 1708.

Gringonneur, Jacquemin (fl. 1380). Also referred to as Jean Gringonneur, he was a painter attached to the court of King Charles VI. Almost nothing is known about him, except that he was commissioned in 1392 to paint three packs of cards for the French king to distract and amuse him during his period of insanity. For a long time these were assumed to have been Tarot cards, but there is no evidence for this—they may have been decks of playing cards, or emblematic cards such as the Mantegna deck. The surviving cards that had been associated with Gringonneur are now known to be of northern Italian origin, and they probably date from the early fifteenth century. For this work, he was paid 56 Parisian sols. (A *sol* was a gold coin of the period.) He may also have painted the portrait of one of Charles VI's counselors, Juvenal des Ursins, but this is uncertain.

Guaita, Stanislas de (1861–1897). De Guaita was born in Moselle, a region in eastern France, of a noble Italian family. After attending school in Nancy and studying chemistry, he moved to Paris and took up the occupation of poet and occultist. Since he had some family money, he soon attracted around him a circle of young artists and writers interested in the occult. Inspired by the ideals of the Rosicrucians, he founded the Cabalistic Order of the Rosicrucian in 1888 with the assistance of the novelist and Martinist Joséphin Péladan and the occultist Gérard Encausse (who took the name *Papus*). The Order provided members with a course of training in the Kabbalah, conducted examinations of their knowledge, and conferred upon them various degrees. In his book *La Clef de la Magie Noire* (*The Key to Black Magic*), in which he examines the Tarot trumps, De Guaita originated the drawing of the goat's head inside an inverted pentagram that later became as infamous a symbol of Satanism as Lévi's drawing of Baphomet.

Hall, Manly Palmer (1901–1990). Hall was born in Ontario, Canada. His mother was a member of the Rosicrucian Fellowship, and it was perhaps through her interest that Hall became attracted to esotericism. In 1919 Hall moved to Los Angeles, California, to live with her, after being separated from her for many years. He became a preacher of the Church of the People, an alternative church in Los Angeles, and in 1923 was elected its permanent pastor. He began to give lectures on occult and spiritual topics and to produce books.

Hall was supported in these endeavors by Caroline Lloyd, a member of a wealthy California oil family. She and her daughter became devout followers of Hall. It's difficult to look at this phase of Hall's life and see him as anything other than the leader of a cult. His photographs from that era reveal a charismatic and dominating personality.

In 1928 Hall used some of the Lloyd oil money to publish the enormously expensive *The Secret Teachings of All Ages*, which is reputed to have cost $150,000—a king's ransom at the time. Copies of the book sold for seventy-five dollars. The book was offered to interested buyers by subscription prior to its printing, and in this way the cost was made manageable.

In 1934 Hall founded the Philosophical Research Society in Los Angeles, which he intended to serve for the study of all things metaphysical, esoteric, and occult. Thanks to the money from the Lloyd family, he was able to publish and travel as freely as he wished without being inconvenienced by the necessity to work for a living. Caroline Lloyd died in 1946 and left him a house and a sizable income in her will.

A large portion of Hall's energies throughout his life were devoted to his involvement with esoteric Freemasonry, an interest he shared with the founders of the Hermetic Order of the Golden Dawn and many other occultists of his period. In 1973 he achieved the 33rd degree of Masonry, the highest possible degree, conferred upon him by the Supreme Council of the Scottish Rite. He died in Los Angeles at age 89.

Heraclitus of Ephesus (c. 535–c. 475 BCE). Heraclitus was an early Greek philosopher who suffered from severe depression. He was known as "the Weeping Philosopher." He was a misanthrope who avoided human company and had a dim view of human nature. To avoid other people, he would wander alone in the mountains, surviving on a diet of grass and wild herbs.

Jones, Charles Stansfeld (1886–1950). Pen name: Frater Achad. Born in London, Jones resided in British Columbia, Canada, for most of his life. As a young man, he became an accountant, but was strongly drawn to Western magic. He studied Aleister Crowley's periodical, *The Equinox,* and in this way came to learn of Crowley's occult order, the Argentum Astrum, which he joined in 1909. Jones also became a member of the Ordo Templi Orientis, through Crowley's influence, in 1915. For a time, Crowley looked upon Jones as his "magickal child." Jones had some mediumistic ability and worked with the Ouija board under Crowley's general guidance. His 1923 book *Crystal Vision Through Crystal Gazing* involves the technique of scrying into a crystal globe, but he is best remembered for his 1922 book *Q. B. L., or The Bride's Reception,* in which he proposed an inverted arrangement of the Tarot trumps on the channels of the Tree of the Sephiroth. Crowley strongly rejected this arrangement, and in the end rejected Jones as well. In 1936 he expelled Jones from the O.T.O. Even so, Jones continued to refer to himself as the Past Grand Master of the O.T.O. for the United States of America.

Kircher, Athanasius (1602–1680). The youngest of nine children, Kircher was born in the village of Geisa, near Fulda, Germany. He went to school in a Jesuit college in Fulda from age twelve to sixteen, and outside of school was tutored in Hebrew by a Jewish rabbi. He became a novitiate of the Jesuits in Paderborn, Germany, in 1618, and studied philosophy and theology. For a number of years, he worked as a teacher, teaching mathematics and languages such as Hebrew and Syriac. In 1628 he was made a Jesuit priest and became a professor of ethics and mathematics at the University of Würzburg in Germany. For a brief while he taught at the University of Avignon in France, but in 1634 he settled in Rome, and made this city his base of operations for the remainder of his life.

Kircher was one of the outstanding geniuses of his age, with an interest in all the arts and sciences, but he was particularly fascinated by ancient Egypt, and was intent on deciphering the Egyptian hieroglyphics. This he failed to do, but *Oedipus Aegyptiacus*, his great work published in three volumes in Rome in consecutive years from 1652–1654, is filled with the lore of Egypt, along with many other topics such as magic squares, talismans, numerology, astrology, geomancy, and other obscure studies. To read it fully, one would need to be very well schooled indeed, since parts of it are written in Greek, Hebrew, Arabic, and even Chinese, in addition to Latin. The diagram of the Kabbalistic Tree of the Sephiroth in the second volume of this work was adopted by the Hermetic Order of the Golden Dawn as the centerpiece of their system of magic.

Knapp, J. Augustus (1853–1938). Knapp was born in Ohio and studied art at the McMicken School of Design in Cincinnati. He worked as a commercial artist in various capacities, which included designing cards, calendars, posters, and playbills, and he contributed art to *McGuffey's Readers*, the standard reading textbooks for schools. He was a member of the Theosophical Society and attended Spiritualist séances as a young man, although his interest in these activities waned later in his life. He was also a Freemason. Knapp met Manly P. Hall in 1923 and began to do illustrations for his books on Masonry. For Hall's *The Secret Teachings of All Ages* (1928), Knapp painted forty-six watercolor plates. Knapp and Hall later collaborated to produce the Revised New Art Tarot, an occult Tarot that is more generally known as the Hall-Knapp Tarot, or simply as the Knapp Tarot.

Leland, Charles Godfrey (1824–1903). Leland was an American folklorist and the author of *Aradia, or The Gospel of the Witches* (1899), which concerns the lore of Italian witchcraft. He is also remembered for *The English Gipsies* (1873), *The Gypsies* (1882), and *Gypsy Sorcery and Fortune Telling* (1891).

Linote, Mademoiselle (d. circa 1780). Almost nothing is known about her. She was an artist and close personal friend of Court de Gébelin who taught herself how to engrave in order to illustrate his *Monde Primitif*. She did illustrations for volumes 1 and 4, as well as the Tarot trumps and Aces that appear in plates at the end of volume 8.

Lully, Raymond (c. 1232–c. 1315). He was also known as Raymond Lull and Raymundus Lullius. He was born to a wealthy Catalonian family in Palma, on the Spanish island of Majorca, in what was then the Kingdom of Majorca. Lully received the best possible education and soon excelled at mathematics and philosophy. He became the tutor to James II of Aragon and the household administrator to the future James II of Majorca, who was related to his wife, but in 1263 a series of visions convinced him that he was intended by God to devote his life to the conversion of the Muslims to Christianity. He left his wife and wealth and became a Franciscan. In 1314 he traveled to Tunis, in North Africa, where he was stoned by a mob of Muslims. Badly injured, he was taken back to Majorca, where he died in Palma the following year.

Lully is best known for a system of categorization of information by means of complex tables, which he referred to as his *Art.* He wrote several books describing it, the main one being his *Ars Magna (Great Art)* in 1305. The Art was intended by Lully to help Christian missionaries respond to questions and challenges by Muslims concerning Christian theological doctrine. A question could be entered into the tables and an answer derived from them automatically. In this sense, the Art was somewhat similar to the functioning of a computer.

Mathers, Moïna (1865–1928). Née Mina Bergson. Moïna Mathers was born in Geneva, Switzerland. Her father, a Polish Jew, was a musician and composer of operas. Her oldest brother, Henri Bergson, achieved fame as a philosopher and went on to win the Nobel Prize. In 1867 her family moved to Paris, and in 1873 they took up residence in London. Moïna enrolled at the Slade School of Fine Art in London at age fifteen on a scholarship. In 1882 at Slade she met Annie Horniman, later to become a prominent member of the Hermetic Order of the Golden Dawn and its financial backer.

Moïna was a talented artist who practiced copying classical art pieces in the British Museum. While engaged in this work in 1887, she was noticed by her future husband, Samuel Liddell Mathers, who was in the British Museum doing research on occult manuscripts. Mathers was so struck by Moïna that he resolved on the spot to marry her, but she remarked at the time in a joking way to her friend Annie Horniman that Mathers was a man she definitely did not intend to marry. She became the first person initiated into the Golden Dawn in 1888, but was not married to Mathers until 1890. Mathers changed her name from *Mina* to *Moïna* because it sounded more Celtic to his ears, and she kept the name change for the remainder of her life.

There was a popular rumor, circulated by Aleister Crowley, that Mathers used his occult powers as a magician to enthrall Moïna into a kind of spell or trance, like some Rosicrucian Svengali. True or not, they remained faithful to each other until his death, even though their union was never sexual—both abhorred the grossness of physical sex. After his death in 1918, Moïna went on to head the descendant organization of the Golden Dawn, the Alpha et Omega, until her own death.

Moïna was highly psychic and mediumistic. She and Mathers worked together closely to receive the teaching curriculum of the Golden Dawn from the Secret Chiefs, the three spiritual beings who were the esoteric leaders of the Order. Moïna used her artistic talents to design and paint the Golden Dawn Tarot, after the instructions of the Secret Chiefs conveyed through Mathers, and it became the model for the occult Tarot used by Golden Dawn members. The Thoth Tarot of Aleister Crowley is based on the original Tarot pack painted by Moïna Mathers, which appears to have been lost (or is hidden in some private collection).

Mathers, Samuel Liddell "MacGregor" (1854–1918). Mathers was born in Hackney, London. His father died when he was a boy. He attended Bedford School and worked as a clerk in Bournemouth, Dorsetshire. In 1877 he became a Freemason, an activity that was to dominate his adult life, and achieved the rank of Master Mason the following year. In 1882 he became a member of the Societas Rosicruciana in Anglia, a Masonic order devoted to esoteric studies, where he met William Robert Woodman and William Wynn Westcott. After the death of his mother in 1885, Mathers moved to London. In 1887 he founded the Rosicrucian society known as the Hermetic Order of the Golden Dawn, along with Westcott and Woodman.

In some regards, Mathers's life parallels that of A. E. Waite. The fathers of both men died when they were young. They both took jobs as clerks, but their real interest lay in occult studies. They were drawn to Freemasonry and spent a great deal of time doing research in the Reading Room at the British Museum.

They both became published writers, although Waite's output far exceeded that of Mathers.

While studying in the British Museum, Mathers met Mina Bergson, the sister of Henri Bergson. She was at the museum practicing her painting skills. Mathers married her in 1890. It was a good partnership. She enthusiastically embraced his obsession with magic and the spirit world, and assisted him in receiving from spirits known as the Secret Chiefs the teachings that would constitute the Golden Dawn system of magic. Mathers was a strange, otherworldly figure. William Butler Yeats called him "eccentric." He spent much of his time talking to invisible spirits. According to Aleister Crowley, Mathers would sit playing chess with them. This was probably Enochian Chess, a form of chess Mathers received from the Secret Chiefs. He was preoccupied with his lineage and believed himself descended from Scottish kings, although there is no evidence to support it. He added *MacGregor* to his name on this account. According to Dion Fortune, Mathers died of the Spanish influenza, which was ravaging England in 1918, following the end of the First World War.

Nietzsche, Friedrich (1844–1900). A German philosopher, Nietzsche was the son of a Lutheran pastor. He was a brilliant scholar, the youngest man ever to hold the Chair of Classical Philology at the University of Basil, at age twenty-four. His unorthodox views about Christianity, and his statement "God is dead," expressed in his flamboyant writings, made him unemployable at universities. He is responsible for popularizing the concepts of the *Übermensch* (Overman, sometimes translated as Superman), the death of God, and the idea of an eternal return, in which the universe repeats itself over and over. He grew despondent and morose, became a drug addict in 1882, and in 1889 finally went insane. At the time, he was diagnosed with syphilis, although this diagnosis has been disputed. For the remainder of his life, he was cared for by his mother and sister. Among his works are *Human, All Too Human* (1878), *Thus Spake Zarathustra* (1883), and *Beyond Good and Evil* (1886).

Old, Walter Gorn (1864–1929). Pen name: Sepharial. Old studied medicine as a young man, but began to write an astrology page in a newspaper in 1886 when his interest turned to more esoteric subjects. The following year he was admitted to the Theosophical Society and began to give lectures at the London and Birmingham Theosophical lodges. He soon penetrated the inner circle of the

Theosophical movement in England. When Madame Blavatsky died, Old was sitting beside her bed, holding her hand. Astrology, numerology, and writing about occultism became his profession as well as his passion. He wrote numerous books, most of them on astrological subjects or numerology. He was a friend to noted astrologers Alan Leo and Alfred H. Barley.

Ouspenskii, Pyotr Demianovich (1878–1947). Anglicized name: Peter D. Ouspensky. This Russian mystic and esoteric philosopher was born in Kharkiv, in the northeastern part of what is today Ukraine. He was expelled from school at age sixteen for painting graffiti on a wall, but only two years later had managed to get an editorial job at the Moscow daily newspaper, *The Morning.* In 1907 he developed an interest in Theosophy, the system of esoteric spiritualism developed by the Russian Helena Petrovna Blavatsky.

Ouspensky was a mathematician and was fascinated by the concept of higher dimensions. In 1909 he wrote *The Fourth Dimension,* which was influenced by the ideas of the British mathematician Charles Howard Hinton (1853–1907). This was followed by his finest work, *Tertium Organum,* published in 1912, in which he questioned the very nature of reality. He traveled to Adyar, India, in 1913 to study with the Theosophists, but was forced to return to Russia at the outbreak of the First World War the following year.

In 1915 while in Moscow, Ouspensky met George Evanovich Gurdjieff (1866–1949), a charismatic Armenian mystical philosopher who taught something called "the Method" or "the Work," by which his students attempted to fully awaken their consciousness. Ouspensky decided to break with Gurdjieff in 1918, but continued to work with him on an irregular basis until 1924, when he made a formal announcement in London that he intended to pursue his esoteric work independently. Even so, he taught and practiced elements of the Method he had acquired as Gurdjieff's student for many years thereafter.

The background of the Bolshevik Revolution probably played a significant part in destroying the harmony that had existed between the two men. Ouspensky hated the communists. Both he and Gurdjieff became exiles from Russia. Ouspensky settled in London after the end of the First World War. Gurdjieff was prohibited from living in England by order of the British government, and took up residence in France.

After the two men were forcibly separated in this way, Gurdjieff's influence over Ouspensky declined. Eventually Ouspensky found the courage to declare publicly that he was no longer a follower of the Russian mystic.

Ouspensky was never explicit as to why he felt the need to separate himself from Gurdjieff, but remarks he made in the final chapter of his book *In Search of the Miraculous* suggest that he had grown disillusioned with the personal behavior of his guru. One explanation he gave was that Gurdjieff had begun to teach in a more religious and monastic way, and that even though Ouspensky did not see anything wrong with the religious way of enlightenment, it was not his way.

Pearson, Sir Cyril Arthur (1866–1921). Pen name: Professor P. R. S. Foli. Born in the village of Wookey, in Somerset, Pearson became an English baronet, a newspaper owner, and a publisher. His first job was writing for the magazine *Tit-Bits.* In 1890 he started his own publishing business with the periodical *Pearson's Weekly,* which was enormously successful. He went on to found the *Daily Express,* and in 1898 he purchased the *Morning Herald* and founded the *Royal Magazine.* His interests were wide-ranging. He authored a number of books on the occult, among them *Handwriting as an Index to Character* (1902), *Fortune Telling by Cards* (1915), and *Pearson's Dream Book* (1933).

Pitois, Jean-Baptiste (1811–1877). Pen name: Paul Christian. Very little is known with certainty about Pitois's life. He was born in Remirement, a town in the northeastern part of France. He was born out of wedlock, which at the time was a serious social stigma. In 1828 he entered the monastery of La Trappe, intending to become a Trappist monk, but left a year later without taking his vows. After studying at the Academy in Strasbourg, he wandered around for a time campaigning for various liberal causes. In 1836 he worked as a staff writer for *Revue Germanique* in Paris, and two years later as the editor of *L'Eclair.* In 1839 he became the editor of the *Gazette des Salons.* A friend who was the chief librarian for the Bibliothèque de l'Arsenal got Pitois a job as the librarian for the Ministry of Public Instruction, a good, solid government job with a reliable income stream.

Pitois began to publish articles and books on a wide variety of topics under the pen name Paul Christian, which he assumed for his private life as well. It is not known for certain when or how his interest in the occult began, but Christian himself asserted in an autobiographical text that he became interested in astrology after reading the 1582 book *Des Jugemens Astronomiques sur les Nativitez* (*Astronomical Judgments Based on Birthdates*) by Auger Ferrier, which was one of the books in the library where he worked. There is a rumor that around 1852 he became a neighbor of Éliphas Lévi and began to study magic under his guidance. Whether this is true or not, Christian was strongly influenced by Lévi's occult writings, particularly those on the Tarot. In his own work, he integrated the Tarot with astrology.

In 1863 Christian published his first significant book on magic, *L'Homme Rouge des Tuileries* (*The Red Man of Tuileries*), which is concerned with prophetic astrology, numerology, and the Tarot. His greatest work, *Histoire de la Magie* (*History of Magic*), published in 1870, carried on these themes. It is heavily weighted toward astrology. In it, Christian gave his famous account of initiation into the Egyptian Mysteries, during which the initiate is shown the trumps of the Tarot on large tablets in a gallery beneath the Sphinx. Christian claimed to have derived this account from *On the Mysteries* by Iamblichus, but this colorful passage is wholly his own invention, and no trace of it can be found in the work of Iamblichus or anywhere else.

Plotinus (204–270). Plotinus was a Greek philosopher born in Egypt. In Alexandria, he studied under Ammonius Saccas. He established his own school of philosophy in Rome in 244, and is regarded as the founder of Neoplatonism. His most famous student was Porphyry, who gathered and arranged his master's writings into a collection of six books, each containing nine treatises. This is known as the *Enneads* (Greek: "groups of nine").

Pogosskaia, Madame Aleksandra Loginova (1848–1921). Anglicized to Alexandra Pogosky or Pogossky. The usual form of her name that appears in print is A. L. Pogosky, but she was more familiarly known as Madame Pogosky, a Russian artist, writer, and Theosophist. In 1888 she heard William Morris give a lecture on tapestry weaving at the First Arts and Crafts Exhibition in London. This affected her profoundly and moved her to dedicate the rest of her life to reviving cottage industries in Russia. The following year, at the Second Arts and Crafts Exhibition in London, Madame Pogosky exhibited her own work, a burnt-wood stool, and gave demonstrations in the burnt-wood technique at the Ladies Industrial Exhibition in Belfast in 1891. In 1902 she established a dye-house near

St. Petersburg that dyed threads to be used in weaving with natural vegetable dyes that had not been used in Russian for a century (see Pogosky, *Fellowship In Work*, pp. 88–89). She was a contributor to various Theosophical periodicals, and in 1912 had two articles on craftwork published in the December issue of *The Path: A Theosophical Monthly*. A year later, Madame Pogosky translated P. D. Ouspensky's *Symboly Tarot* from Russian into English under the title *The Symbolism of the Tarot*. With the help of her eldest daughter, she maintained for many years (from at least 1906 to 1916) Russian Peasant Industries, a business located at 41 Old Bond Street, London, that exhibited and sold Russian peasant arts and crafts. In 1918 she published *Revival of Village Industries in Russia* in London through the Theosophical Publishing House.

Regardie, Israel (1907–1985). He was born Israel Regardie in London to a Jewish Orthodox family that emigrated to Washington, D.C. in 1921. While enrolled in an art school in Philadelphia, Regardie became interested in Theosophy. He read one of Aleister Crowley's books and was impressed enough to write to him. The two began a correspondence, and in 1928 Crowley offered Regardie a job as his personal secretary in Paris. Regardie lied to his father, saying he was studying art in Paris, since the practice of ritual magic was not in accord with traditional Jewish values. The family discovered his deception, and his sister complained to the French authorities and managed to get Crowley and his entourage expelled from France in March of 1929. When Regardie rejoined Crowley in Britain, Crowley informed him that he could no longer afford to pay his salary, so the two men parted company.

In 1932 Regardie published two very influential books, *A Garden of Pomegranates* and *The Tree of Life*, which included some of the Golden Dawn system of magic he had learned while working for Crowley. Two years later, Regardie joined the Stella Matutina, an offshoot of the original Golden Dawn. He rose rapidly through the grades, but was not happy with the attitude of his fellow members and soon left. In 1936 he published an exposé of the Stella Matutina in a book titled *My Rosicrucian Adventure*, in which he characterized its leadership as incompetent. He returned to the United States the following year, carrying with him the teaching documents he had acquired while a member of the Order. These, along with documents he had gathered as Crowley's secretary, became the substance of his great work, *The Golden Dawn*, which was published in four volumes between 1937 and 1940. This laid bare the entire corpus of Golden

Dawn magic in a systematic way for the first time, although Crowley had earlier published much of these teachings in his periodical, *The Equinox*.

This publication angered members of the Golden Dawn offshoot groups, who still looked upon the Golden Dawn teaching documents as secret material. Regardie was attacked in print by them, and also by his former employer, Crowley. For many years, Regardie turned his back on occultism and pursued the practice of psychotherapy. In 1970 he wrote a biography of Crowley titled *The Eye in the Triangle*. During this period he published a number of slender books on ritual magic based on Golden Dawn practices, such as *The One Year Manual* (1969) and *How to Make and Use Talismans* (1972). These elevated his name recognition among New Age occultists. In 1978 he worked with the artist Robert Wang to recreate a version of the original Golden Dawn Tarot. He became more actively involved in a revival of the Golden Dawn in the US during the last years of his life. In 1981 he retired to Sedona, Arizona, where he died.

Saint-Martin, Louis Claude de (1743–1803). Saint-Martin was a French philosopher who studied esotericism under Martinez de Pasqually (1727–1774), a French freemason who founded the Masonic *l'Ordre de Chevaliers Macons Élus Coëns de l'Univers (the Order of Knight-Masons Elect Priests of the Universe)* in 1761. This is regarded as the beginning of the esoteric religious movement known as Martinism. Saint-Martin joined this order in 1768 and worked as secretary for de Pasqually from 1768 to 1771, when he left to teach his own brand of mystical philosophy. Saint-Martin became disenchanted with the Kabbalistic rituals of the Order. He was an ardent admirer of the mystic Jakob Böhme (1575–1624) and came to believe that the way to union with God was through contemplation, not ritual. Under the pseudonym *The Unknown Philosopher,* Saint-Martin wrote books and translated works by Böhme from the German. His teaching inspired Gérard Encausse (Papus) in 1884 to form, in company with other French occultists, the *Ordre Martiniste (Martinist Order)*. A. E. Waite wrote a book in 1922 about Martinism titled *Saint-Martin: The French Mystic and the Story of Modern Martinism*.

Schuré, Edouard (1841–1929). Schuré was a French philosopher born in Strasbourg, a French town on the German border. He was the son of a doctor. His father died when he was fourteen. He received a law degree from the University of Strasbourg but never went into the legal profession. Instead, he became a writer and began to turn out plays, poetry, novels, and literary criticism. He enjoyed a friendship with Richard Wagner, and in 1873 he came to know Friedrich Nietzsche through their common admiration for Wagner's music. In 1884 he met Madame Blavatsky, leader of the Theosophical Society, and his interests became more focused on the occult, particularly on the teachings of Fabre d'Olivet. His 1889 book, *Les Grands Initiés* (*The Great Initiates*), which describes the path followed by a number of great spiritual leaders, enjoyed enormous success and was hailed in some quarters as a masterpiece. Schuré met Rudolf Steiner in 1906. Steiner would go on to found the Anthroposophical Society, of which Schuré became a member. Schuré has become a somewhat controversial figure in modern times due to his views concerning the superiority of the Aryan race, expressed in his 1912 book, *From Sphinx to Christ*.

Smith, Pamela Colman (1878–1951). This artist was born in Pimlico, London, but moved with her parents to Jamaica in 1889. In 1893, at the tender age of fifteen, she went to live in Brooklyn, New York, where she studied art at the Pratt Institute. Her mother died in 1896, and Smith was forced to leave the university in 1897 without obtaining her degree. She became a commercial illustrator. When her father died in 1899, she returned to London and continued to make her living with commercial art and theatrical design. She traveled with the Lyceum Theatre Group, doing stage painting and costumes. In 1901 she established her own art studio, where she held a weekly open house for painters, actors, and writers. The poet William Butler Yeats introduced her to the Hermetic Order of the Golden Dawn in 1901, where she met Arthur Edward Waite. She published a literary periodical, *The Green Sheaf*, in 1903, but it failed in just over a year. Meanwhile, she continued to make her way with various commercial projects, such as book illustration work for Bram Stoker, the actress Ellen Terry, and Yeats. In 1907 her paintings were successfully exhibited in New York, and again in 1908 and 1909.

Her interpretations of the Tarot designs of the occultist A. E. Waite were published by William Rider & Son as a deck of Tarot cards in November of 1909. Over the past century in its various incarnations, it has become by far the most popular Tarot that has ever existed. Smith completed this project in only six months, between April and October, working from Waite's textual descriptions. The original designs were black-and-white line drawings, to which colors were later added during the printing process. Her original illustrations have unfortunately been lost.

Waite, Arthur Edward (1857–1942). Waite was born in Brooklyn, New York. His father died at an early age, and he was taken by his mother back to her native England. He attended school in London, then took a job as a clerk, but he had a scholarly disposition by nature. He began to spend his spare time studying in the Reading Room of the British Museum. The death of his sister in 1874 had sparked his interest in Spiritualism, which was then enjoying an explosion of interest throughout Europe and the United States. His research led him into all aspects of Western occultism.

Waite began to write on esoteric subjects and soon became the most prolific occult writer in England. A veritable river of books, novels, translations, reviews, poems, and articles flowed from his pen, all of them on esoteric topics. In 1891 he joined the Hermetic Order of the Golden Dawn, in 1901 he became a Freemason, and the following year he joined the *Societas Rosicruciana in Anglia*, an esoteric Masonic order to which all three founders of the Golden Dawn had also belonged. Waite formed his own offshoot of the Golden Dawn in 1903, and when the Golden Dawn disbanded in 1914, he went on to establish his own original occult order, the Fellowship of the Rosy Cross.

By inclination, Waite was a mystic and an academic, not a practitioner of magic. This put him at odds with some members of the Golden Dawn, who felt he was trying to turn the Order into a religion rather than a school of the Hermetic arts, as Mathers intended it to be. One of them, Aleister Crowley, made Waite into his foil and nicknamed him "Dead Waite." He mocked Waite for his writing style, which is convoluted and obtuse to an unnecessary degree. It was natural that Waite and Crowley should butt heads, since both wanted to run the Golden Dawn. Crowley outlived Waite by only five years. Waite was killed in a German bombing raid during the London Blitz of World War Two.

Westcott, William Wynn (1848–1925). Westcott was born in Leamington, Warwickshire, in central England. When he was ten, he lost both his parents and was adopted by an uncle, a medical doctor. Westcott took up the study of medicine and graduated from the University College in London with a bachelor's degree in medicine. For a time he practiced medicine with his uncle in Soberest, but in 1880 he obtained the position of coroner in London, where he presided over inquests. He was already a Freemason by this time, having joined the Masonic Lodge in Crewkerne in 1875, under the tutelage of Dr. W. R. Woodman. Westcott became a member of the Societas Rosicruciana in Anglia, to which Woodman also belonged, and there he met S. L. MacGregor Mathers. The three men would go on to found the Hermetic Order of the Golden Dawn in 1887 and establish the Isis-Urania Temple in London the following year. Westcott was also a member of the Theosophical Society, which he joined in 1889.

In 1886 Westcott made a set of drawings in ink of the Tarot trumps, all of which are extant except for the trump, the Devil. It's unknown if this sketch was lost from the set or if he never drew it in the first place, although the former seems more likely. The drawings are based on the trump descriptions in Éliphas Lévi's *Transcendental Magic*. Westcott also made copies of the court cards from the original Tarot of Moïna Mathers. These were provided by Anthony Fuller to Darcy Küntz, who published them in a slender booklet of thirty-six pages in 2001 with the title *Golden Dawn Court Cards: As Drawn by Moina Mathers*.

Westcott's most important esoteric publications are his translation of *Sepher Yetzirah* (1887), which had a strong influence on the role of the Tarot in the Golden Dawn system of magic, and his edition of the *Chaldaean Oracles of Zoroaster* (1895), the language of which figured prominently in Golden Dawn grade rituals. Both works appeared as part of his *Collectanea Hermetica*, a series of Hermetic publications that he edited and contributed to from 1893 to 1896.

Wigston, William Francis Chalmers (c. 1845–1927). Wigston was the author of *The Columbus of Literature* (1892), *Bacon, Shakespeare, and the Rosicrucians* (1888), *A New Study of Shakespeare* (1884), and other works examining the Hermetic symbolism in Shakespeare's plays and the conjectured link between Shakespeare and Francis Bacon.

Wirth, Joseph Paul Oswald (1860–1943). Born in Brienz, Switzerland, Wirth was a Freemason, artist, hypnotist, and occultist. His father was a painter, his mother a devout Roman Catholic. Wirth helped his father with painting until the death of his mother in 1878 forced him to become an accountant. He went to work in London the following year in this profession, but hated it and spent as much time as possible in Paris. He became a Freemason in 1884 and quickly rose to the rank of Master Mason. In 1887 he received an invitation to meet with the nobleman Stanislas de Guaita, who had become infamous as an occultist in the French press. The two quickly became close friends, and de Guaita hired Wirth as his secretary. Under de Guaita's guidance, Wirth designed a set of Tarot trumps based on the Tarot writings of French occultists such as Éliphas Lévi. After de Guaita's death from a drug overdose in 1897, Wirth became a librarian but continued his occult studies and writings on such subjects as Freemasonry and the Tarot. A limited edition of 350 packs of his Tarot was printed in 1889. In 1927, Wirth's book *Le Tarot des Imagiers du Moyan Age* was published in Paris. It was translated into English by Richard Gardner and Diana Faber and published as *The Tarot of the Magicians* (York Beach, Maine: Weiser, 1985).

Woodman, Dr. William Robert (1828–1891). Surprisingly little is known about Woodman's early life. He was born in England, where he studied to become a medical doctor, earning his medical degree in 1851. Woodman volunteered to serve as physician to English soldiers fighting the forces of Napoleon III, who seized power in France that same year, and after obtaining release from this service, he settled in Stoke Newington, where he set up his own practice and also served as local police surgeon. In 1871 he retired to Exeter on property he had inherited, but he moved to London in 1887, where he lived the few remaining years of his life.

Woodman was a prominent Freemason and a keen student of the Egyptian Mysteries, the Jewish Kabbalah, and the esoteric teachings of the Neoplatonists. In 1867 he was admitted to the Societas Rosicruciana in Anglia, a Masonic order devoted to esoteric lore, to which Samuel L. MacGregor Mathers and W. Wynn Westcott would later also belong. (Westcott joined in 1880 and Mathers in 1882.) In 1878 Woodman became Supreme Magus of the S.R.I.A, which prospered greatly under his leadership. In a letter opened after his death, he named Westcott as his successor to head the S.R.I.A.

Woodman, Westcott, and Mathers united in 1887 to form a new Rosicrucian order called the Hermetic Order of the Golden Dawn. The three men became its human Chiefs in counterpoint to its three corresponding spiritual Chiefs, with whom Mathers established psychic contact. Woodman was given the honorary grade of Exempt Adept. When the Isis-Urania Temple was established in 1888 in London, Woodman assumed the title of Imperator. He died before the Second Order was formed, and for this reason had little involvement in the evolution or teachings of the Golden Dawn.

BIBLIOGRAPHY

Achad, Frater [Charles Stansfeld Jones]. *Q. B. L. or The Bride's Reception*. 1922. Reprint, New York: Samuel Weiser, 1972.

Anonymous. *The Astrologer and Oracle of Destiny: A Repository of the Wonderful In Nature and the Curious In Art*. Vol. 1. London: published at the Office, 11, Wellington Street North, Strand, 1845.

Anonymous. *Jack the Gyant-Killer: A Comi-Tragical Farce of One Act*. London: Printed for J. Roberts, near the Oxford-Arms in Warwick-Lane, M.DCC.XXX, 1730.

Anonymous. *Règles du Jeu de Tarots (Rules of the Game of Tarot)*. Pamphlet published in Besançon in 1862.

Anonymous. *The Standard Hoyle: A Complete Guide and Reliable Authority Upon All Games of Chance or Skill Now Played in the United States*. New York: Excelsior Publishing House, 1847.

Barley, Alfred H. *The Rationale of Astrology*. 1905. Reprint, London: 9 Lyncroft Gardens, West Hampstead, n.d.

Baughan, Rosa. *The Influence of the Stars: A Book of Old World Lore*. London: Kegan Paul, Trench, Trübner & Co., 1891.

Bellows, Henry Adams, trans. *The Poetic Edda*. New York: The American-Scandinavian Foundation, 1923.

Blake, William. *The Complete Writings*. Edited by Geoffrey Keynes. Corrected paperback edition. London: Oxford University Press, 1974.

Blavatsky, Helena. "The Hexagon with the Central Point, or the Seventh Key." In *Collected Writings*, vol. 14. Compiled by Boris de Zirkoff. Wheaton, IL: Theosophical Publishing House, 2009.

Breslaw, Phillip. *Breslaw's Last Legacy; or, The Magical Companion.* 2nd ed. London: Printed for T. Moore, 1784.

Bridget, Mother. *The Universal Dream Book, Containing an Interpretation of All Manner of Dreams, Alphabetically Arranged, to Which Is Added, the Art of Fortune-Telling by Cards, or Tea and Coffee Cups.* London: J. Bailey, n.d.

Brodie-Innes, J. W. "The Tarot Cards." In *The Occult Review*, vol. XXIX, no. 2 (Feb. 1919): 90–98. London: Rider and Co.

Browne, Sir Thomas. *The Garden of Cyrus.* 1658. Reprint, London: no publisher, 1736.

Burgoyne, Thomas H. *The Light of Egypt.* Two volumes. San Francisco, CA: The Religio-Philosophical Publishing House, 1889.

Case, Paul Foster. *An Introduction to the Study of the Tarot.* Published in twelve successive chapters in *Azoth: The Occult Magazine of America*, from vol. 3, no. 4 (Oct. 1918) to vol. 5, no. 3 (Sept. 1919).

————. *The Tarot: A Key to the Wisdom of the Ages.* Richmond, VA: Macoy, 1947.

Chambers, Robert, ed. *The Book of Days: A Miscellany of Popular Antiquities.* Vol. 1. London and Edinburgh: W. & R. Chambers, 1863.

Chapman, Sydney T. "A Victorian Occultist and Publisher: Robert H. Fryar of Bath." Essay published by the Widcombe Press in *The Road: A Journal of History, Myth and Legend* no. 4 (June 2011).

Chatto, William Andrew. *Facts and Speculations on the Origin and History of Playing Cards.* London: John Russell Smith, 1848.

Christian, Paul [Jean-Baptiste Pitois]. *Histoire de la Magie, du Monde Surnaturel et de la Fatalité a travers les Temps et les Peuples.* Paris: Furne, Jouvet et Cie, 1870.

————. *The History and Practice of Magic.* 1870. Abridged edition of Christian's *Histoire de la Magie.* Edited by Ross Nichols. New York: Citadel Press, 1963.

————. *L'Homme Rouge des Tuileries.* Paris: self-published, 1863.

Clement, of Alexandria, Saint. *Stromata.* Bk. 5, chap. 7. Translated by William Wilson. From *Ante-Nicene Christian Library.* Vol. 2. Edited by Alexander Roberts and James Donaldson. Edinburgh: T. & T. Clark, 1869.

Clulow, George. *The Origin and Manufacture of Playing Cards.* London: Chiswick Press, 1889.

Court de Gébelin, Antoine. *Monde Primitif, Analysé et Comparé avec le Monde Moderne.* Nine volumes (unfinished). Paris: privately published, 1773–1782.

Crowley, Aleister. *The Book of Thoth.* 1944. Reprint, New York: Samuel Weiser, 1974.

Davies, Owen. *Popular Magic: Cunning-Folk in English History.* 2003. Reprint, London: Hambledon Continuum, 2007

———. *Witchcraft, Magic and Culture, 1736–1953.* Manchester and New York: Manchester University Press, 1999.

Decker, Ronald, and Michael Dummett. *A History of the Occult Tarot, 1870–1970.* 2002. Reprint, London and New York: Duckworth Overlook, 2013. e-book.

Decker, Ronald, Thierry Depaulis, and Michael Dummett. *A Wicked Pack of Cards.* New York: St. Martin's Press, 1996.

Drysdall, Denis, trans. *Collected Works of Erasmus: Adages.* Edited by John N. Grant. Toronto: University of Toronto Press, 2005.

Du Bois, Louis. *De Mlle Le Normand, et de Ses Deux Biographies, Récemment Publiées.* Paris: Chez France, 1843.

Dummett, Michael. *The Game of Tarot: From Ferrara to Salt Lake City.* London: Duckworth, 1980.

———. "Origins of Tarot." Letter in *The New York Review of Books* (May 14, 1981).

———. *Twelve Tarot Games.* London: Duckworth, 1980.

Elson, Louis C. *Curiosities of Music: A Collection of Facts Not Generally Known, Regarding the Music of Ancient and Savage Nations.* Boston, MA: Oliver Ditson, 1880.

Etteilla [Jean-Baptiste Alliette]. *Etteilla, ou la Seule Manière de Tirer les Cartes: Revue, Corrigée, et Augmentée par l'Auteur; Sur Son Premier Manuscrit.* Amsterdam: Chez Lesclapart, Libraire, Quai de Gèvres, 1773.

Falconnier, René. *Les XXII Lames Hermétiques du Tarot Divinatoire, Exactement Reconstituées d'après les Textes Sacrés et Selon la Tradition des Mages de l'Ancienne Égypte.* Drawings by Maurice Otto Wegener. Paris: Librairie de l'Art Indépendant, 1896.

Farley, Helen. *A Cultural History of the Tarot: From Entertainment to Esotericism.* London: I. B. Tauris, 2009.

Farr, Florence. *Egyptian Magic.* 1896. Wellingborough, Northamptonshire: Aquarian Press, 1982.

FitzGerald, Edward, trans. *Rubaiyat of Omar Khayyám.* 4th edition. 1859. San Francisco, CA: Dodge Book and Stationery Co., 1896.

Foli, P. R. S. *Fortune-Telling by Cards.* 1915. New York: R. P. Fenno & Co., n.d.

Gettings, Fred. *The Book of Tarot.* London: Triune Books, 1973.

Hall, Manly P. *The Secret Teachings of All Ages.* San Francisco, CA: H. S. Crocker, 1928.

Herodotus. *The History.* Translated by George Rawlinson. Four volumes. London: John Murray, 1858–1860.

Hutchison, Sharla, and Rebecca A. Brown, eds. *Monsters and Monstrosity from the Fin de Siècle to the Millennium: New Essays.* Jefferson, NC: McFarland & Co., 2015.

Josephus, Flavius. *The Complete Works of Flavius Josephus.* Translated by William Whiston. London: T. Nelson and Sons, 1860.

Kaplan, Stuart R. *The Encyclopedia of Tarot.* Three volumes. Stamford, CT: U.S. Games Systems, 1978–1990.

Kingsford, Anna, and Edward Maitland, eds. and trans. *The Virgin of the World of Hermes Mercurius Trismegistus.* London: George Redway, 1885.

Kircher, Athanasius. *Oedipus Aegyptiacus.* Three volumes. Rome: Ex Typographia Vitalis Mascardi, 1652–1654.

Küntz, Darcy. *The Complete Golden Dawn Cipher Manuscript.* Edmonds, WA: Holmes Publishing Group, 1996.

Le Normand, Madame [pseud.]. *The Oracle of Human Destiny: or, The Unerring Foreteller of Future Events, and Accurate Interpreter of Mystical Signs & Influences; Through the Medium of Common Cards.* 2nd ed. 1825. London: Printed for C. S. Arnold, 1826.

Leland, Charles Godfrey. *Aradia, or The Gospel of the Witches.* London: David Nutt, 1899.

Lévi, Éliphas [Alphonse Louis Constant]. *Dogme et Rituel de la Haute Magie.* 1854. Reprint, Paris: Germer Baillière, 1861.

———. *The Great Secret.* Wellingborough, Northamptonshire: Thorsons, 1975.

————. *Histoire de la Magie, avec une Exposition Claire et Précise de Ses Procédés, de Ses Rites et de Ses Mystères*. Paris: Germer Baillière, 1860.

————. *The History of Magic, Including a Clear and Precise Exposition of Its Procedure, Its Rites and Its Mysteries*. French: 1860; English: 1913. Translated into English by A. E. Waite. Revised edition. London: Rider & Co., 1969.

————. *The Key of the Mysteries*. Translation by Aleister Crowley of Lévi's work *La Clef des Grands Mystères* (Paris: 1861). First published in English in *The Equinox*, vol. 1, no. 10 (1913). London: Rider & Co., 1959.

————. *The Mysteries of the Qabalah, or, The Occult Agreement of the Two Testaments*. Preface by R. A. Gilbert. York Beach, ME: Samuel Weiser, 2000.

————. *Transcendental Magic*. A. E. Waite's English translation of *Dogme et Ritual de la Haute Magie*. London: Rider & Co., 1896.

Mackey, Charles. *Memoirs of Extraordinary Popular Delusions*. 1841. Two volumes bound as one. Philadelphia, PA: Lindsay & Blakiston, 1850.

Mahon, Lord [Philip Henry Stanhope]. *The Forty-Five: Being the Narrative of the Insurrection of 1745, Extracted from Lord Mahon's History of England*. London: John Murray, 1869.

Mathers, S. L. MacGregor. *The Kabbalah Unveiled*. 1887. Reprint, London: Routledge & Kegan Paul, 1962.

————. *The Tarot: Its Occult Signification, Use In Fortune-Telling, and Method of Play, Etc.* 1888. Reprint, New York: Samuel Weiser, n.d.

Melton, John, Sir. *Astrologaster: or, The Figure-Caster*. London: Barnard Alsop, for Edward Blackmore, 1620.

Merlin, Romain. *Origine des Cartes à Jouer: Recherches Nouvelles sur les Naibis, les Tarots et sur les Autres Espèces de Cartes*. Paris: Chez L'Auteur, 1869.

Miller, Edith Starr [Lady Queenborough]. *Occult Theocrasy*. Two volumes. Privately printed in France by F. Paillart in Abbeville, 1933.

Moakley, Gertrude. *The Tarot Cards Painted by Bonifacio Bembo for the Visconti-Sforza Family: An Iconographic and Historical Study*. New York: New York Public Library, 1966.

Moor, Edward. *The Hindu Pantheon*. 1810. Reprint, Los Angeles, CA: Philosophical Research Society, 1976.

Myer, Isaac. *Qabbalah: The Philosophical Writings of Avicebron.* 1888. Reprint, New York: Samuel Weiser, 1970.

Nietzsche, Friedrich. *Thus Spake Zarathustra: A Book for All and None.* Translated by Alexander Tille. New York: Macmillan, 1896.

Oliver, George. *The Pythagorean Triangle; or, The Science of Numbers.* London: John Hogg & Co., 1875.

Ouspensky, Peter D. *A New Model of the Universe.* 1931. Reprint, New York: Vintage Books, 1971.

———. *The Symbolism of the Tarot: Philosophy of Occultism in Pictures and Numbers.* 1913. Reprint, New York: Dover, 1976.

Papus [Gérard Encausse]. *The Tarot of the Bohemians.* Translated into English by A. P. Morton. French: 1889; English: 1910. Reprint, New York: U.S. Games Systems, 1978.

Philo, of Alexandria. *The Works of Philo: Complete and Unabridged.* Trans. C. D. Yonge. 1854–1855. Reprint, Peabody, MA: Hendrickson, 1993.

Platt, Charles. *Card Fortune Telling: A Lucid Treatise Dealing with All the Popular and More Abstruse Methods.* London: W. Foulsham & Co., c. 1920.

Plotinus. *Plotinus: The Six Enneads.* Translated by Stephen MacKenna and B. S. Page. Chicago: Encyclopaedia Britannica, 1980.

Plutarch. "Of Isis and Osiris." In *Plutarch's Morals: Translated from the Greek by Several Hands, Vol. 4,* edited by William W. Goodwin, 65–139. 1874. Five volumes. Boston, MA: Little, Brown and Company, 1871–1878.

Pogosky, A. L. *Fellowship In Work.* London: C. W. Daniel, 1913.

Postello, Guilielmo [William Postel]. *Absconditorum à Constitutione Mundi Clavis.* Amsterdam: Apud Joannem Janssonium, 1646.

Pottenger, Milton Alberto. *Symbolism.* Sacramento, CA: Symbol, 1905.

Raphael [pseud.]. *The Book of Fate: Whereby All Questions May Be Answered Respecting the Present and Future.* 1886. London: W. Foulsham and Co., 1887.

Raphael [Robert Cross Smith]. *The Familiar Astrologer.* London: Printed for John Bennett, 1831.

Regardie, Israel. *The Complete Golden Dawn System of Magic.* Tempe, AZ: New Falcon, 1984.

———. *The Golden Dawn.* 4th ed. St. Paul, MN: Llewellyn Publications, 1971.

————. *The Golden Dawn*. Edited by David Godwin. 6th ed. St. Paul, MN: Llewellyn Publications, 1989.

Roberts, Samuel. *The Gypsies: Their Origin, Continuance, and Destination, as Clearly Foretold in the Prophecies of Isaiah, Jeremiah, and Ezekiel*. London: Longman, Rees, Orme, Brown, Green, and Longman, 1836.

Saint-Germain, Comte C. de [Edgar de Valcourt-Vermont]. *Practical Astrology*. 1901. Reprint, Hollywood, CA: Newcastle, 1973.

Scholem, Gershom. *Kabbalah*. Jerusalem: Keter Publishing House, 1974.

Schuré, Édouard. *The Great Initiates: Sketch of the Secret History of Religions (Les Grands Initiés: Esquisse de l'Histoire Secrète des Religions)*. Translated by Fred Rothwell. Two volumes. 1889. Reprint, London: William Rider & Son, 1920.

The Scots Magazine. MDCCLXXXV. Volume XLVII. Edinburgh: Printed by Murray and Cochrane, June 1785.

Scott, Julie. "The Cloak." Essay in *Rosicrucian Digest* vol. 92, no. 1 (2014). San Jose, CA: AMORC, 2014.

Sepharial [Walter Gorn Old]. *A Manual of Occultism*. London: William Rider & Son, 1914.

Singer, Samuel Weller. *Researches into the History of Playing Cards; with Illustrations of the Origin of Printing and Engraving on Wood*. London: Printed by T. Bensley and Son for Robert Triphook, 1816.

Smart, C., trans. *The Works of Horace, Translated Literally into English Prose*. New York: Harper & Brothers, 1863.

Spare, Austin Osman. *Two Tracts on Cartomancy*. London: Fulgur, 1997.

Stanley, Thomas. *The History of Philosophy*. London: Printed for Humphrey Moseley and Thomas Dring, 1660.

Stenring, Knut, trans. *The Book of Formation (Sepher Yetzirah) by Rabbi Akiba ben Joseph*. London: William Rider & Son, 1923.

Taylor, Ed. S., ed. *The History of Playing Cards, with Anecdotes of Their Use in Conjuring, Fortune-Telling, and Card-Sharping*. London: John Camden Hotten, 1865.

Taylor, Thomas, trans. *Description of Greece, by Pausanias*. Three volumes. London: R. Priestly, 1824.

————. *Iamblichus' Life of Pythagoras*. London: printed by A. J. Valpy, 1818.

Temkin, C. Lilian, George Rosen, Gregory Zilboorg, and Henry E. Sigerist, trans. *Four Treatises of Theophrastus Von Hohenheim, Called Paracelsus.* Baltimore, MD: Johns Hopkins University Press, 1941.

Thorpe, C. *Card Fortune Telling.* London: W. Foulsham and Co., 1972.

Thureau-Dangin, Paul. *Saint Bernardine of Siena.* London: J. M. Dent and Co., 1906.

Vaillant, Jean Alexandre. *Les Rômes: Histoire Vraie des Vrais Bohémiens.* Paris: E. Dentu, 1857.

Van Rensselaer, John King, Mrs. *The Devil's Picture-Books: A History of Playing-Cards.* New York: Dodd, Mead, and Co., 1890.

Voltaire. *Siècles de Louis XIV et Louis XV.* Five volumes. Paris: Pierre Didot, 1817.

Waite, Arthur Edward (writing as Grand Orient). *A Manual of Cartomancy, Fortune-Telling, and Occult Divination.* 4th ed. London: William Rider & Son, 1909. Originally published as *A Handbook of Cartomancy, Fortune-Telling, and Occult Divination* in 1889.

Waite, Arthur Edward. "The Great Symbols of the Tarot." In *The Occult Review* vol. XLIII, no. 2 (Feb. 1926): 83–91. London: Rider and Co.

———. *The Hidden Church of the Holy Graal: Its Legends and Symbolism.* London: Rebman, 1909.

———. *The Pictorial Key to the Tarot.* 1910. Reprint, New York: Samuel Weiser, 1980.

———. "The Tarot: A Wheel of Fortune." In *The Occult Review* vol. X, no. 6 (Dec. 1909): 307–317. London: Rider and Co.

———. "The Tarot and Secret Tradition." In *The Occult Review* vol. XXIX, no. 3 (March 1919): 157–1561. London: Rider and Co.

Westcott, William Wynn. *Golden Dawn Court Cards: As Drawn by Moina Mathers.* Edited by Darcy Küntz. London: Holmes Publishing Group, 1996.

———. *The Magical Ritual of the Sanctum Regnum Interpreted by the Tarot Trumps:Translated from the Mss. of Éliphaz Lévi and edited by W. Wynn Westcott, M. B.* London: George Redway, 1896.

———. *Sepher Yetzirah: The Book of Formation with the Fifty Gates of Intelligence and the Thirty-Two Paths of Wisdom.* 3rd ed. 1887; revised 1893. Reprint, New York: Samuel Weiser, 1980.

———. *Tabula Bembina sive Mensa Isiaca: The Isiac Tablet of Cardinal Bembo: Its History and Occult Significance*. Bath: M. H. Fryar, 1887.

Wigston, William Francis C. *The Columbus of Literature; or, Bacon's New World of Sciences*. Chicago, IL: F. J. Schulte & Co., 1892.

Willshire, William Hughes. *A Descriptive Catalogue of Playing and Other Cards in the British Museum*. London: Chiswick Press, 1876.

Wirth, Oswald. *The Tarot of the Magicians*. French: 1927. Reprint, York Beach, ME: Samuel Weiser, 1985.

Zain, C. C. [Elbert Benjamine]. *The Sacred Tarot*. Series of pamphlets bound together as a book. Los Angeles, CA: The Church of Light, 1935–1936.

INDEX

To Write to the Author

If you wish to contact the author or would like more information about this book, please write to the author in care of Llewellyn Worldwide Ltd. and we will forward your request. Both the author and the publisher appreciate hearing from you and learning of your enjoyment of this book and how it has helped you. Llewellyn Worldwide Ltd. cannot guarantee that every letter written to the author can be answered, but all will be forwarded. Please write to:

Donald Tyson
℅ Llewellyn Worldwide
2143 Wooddale Drive
Woodbury, MN 55125-2989

Please enclose a self-addressed stamped envelope for reply,
or $1.00 to cover costs. If outside the U.S.A., enclose
an international postal reply coupon.

Many of Llewellyn's authors have websites with additional
information and resources. For more information,
please visit our website at http://www.llewellyn.com.